Life
Sentences

DISCOVER THE

KEY THEMES

OF 63 BIBLE

CHARACTERS

Life Sentences

WARREN W.
WIERSBE

ZONDERVAN®

ZONDERVAN.com/
AUTHORTRACKER
follow your favorite authors

We want to hear from you. Please send your comments about this book to us in care of zreview@zondervan.com. Thank you.

Life Sentences
Copyright © 2007 by Warren W. Wiersbe

Requests for information should be addressed to:

Zondervan, *Grand Rapids, Michigan* 49530

Library of Congress Cataloging-in-Publication Data
  Wiersbe, Warren W.
    Life sentences : discover the key themes of 63 Bible characters / Warren W. Wiersbe.
      p. cm.
    Includes bibliographical references and index.
    ISBN-13: 978-0-310-27282-3
    ISBN-10: 0-310-27282-3
    1. Bible — Biography — Meditations.   I. Title.
    BS571.W54   2007
    220.9'2 — dc22   2006032086

Published in association with the literary agency of Mark Sweeney & Associates, Bonita Springs, Florida 34135

Interior design by Nancy Wilson

Printed in the United States of America

07 08 09 10 11 12 13 14 15 • 10 9 8 7 6 5 4 3 2 1

DEDICATED TO:

Michael and Terri Catt and the congregation of
the Sherwood Baptist Church
Albany, Georgia

and to

Jim and Carol Cymbala and the congregation of
the Brooklyn Tabernacle
Brooklyn, New York

For all of you, your life sentence is:

"'And [we] will give our attention to prayer
and the ministry of the word.'"
ACTS 6:4

WARREN AND BETTY WIERSBE

CONTENTS

Part Two

NEW TESTAMENT CHARACTERS

HOW I CAME TO WRITE THIS BOOK

*F*or what would you like to be remembered at the end of your life? If by faith you know Jesus Christ as your Savior and Lord, then you ought to ask your Father for a life sentence that sums up who you are and what you do for Him in this world. Reading this book should help you start thinking about your life sentence. What do I mean by life sentence?

The idea for this book came from reading sermon #1610 of Charles Haddon Spurgeon, which he delivered to his London congregation on July 24, 1881. The text was Genesis 39:2: "The LORD was with Joseph." When I began to read the sermon, Spurgeon's first statement arrested me: "Scripture frequently sums up a man's life in a single sentence."

I stopped reading, put volume 27 of *The Metropolitan Tabernacle Pulpit*[1] on the desk, and wrote on my notepad, "Do a book on Bible sentences that seem to be the keys to the lives of Bible personalities." Then I returned to reading the sermon.

Later, while rereading *The Heart of Emerson's Journals*, edited by Bliss Perry, I discovered that Ralph Waldo Emerson had been thinking along the same lines. In September 1842, the Sage of Concord wrote, "All persons are puzzles until at last we find in some word or act the key to the man, to the woman; straight way all their past words and actions lie in light before us."[2]

These chapters are only vignettes to help you get started in your own study of the personalities of the Bible. Not everybody will agree on the sentences I have chosen or the personalities I have selected. The important thing is that all of us learn from these Bible personalities and apply the Word to our own hearts. Where there is faith, let's imitate it, and where there is folly, let's avoid it, so that one day we will hear the sentence in Matthew 25:21 spoken to us by the Lord: "Well done, good and faithful servant!"

---

1. Charles Haddon Spurgeon, *The Metropolitan Tabernacle Pulpit*, vol. 27, sermon #1610 (Pasadena, Tex.: Pilgrim Publications, 1881).

2. Ralph Waldo Emerson, *The Heart of Emerson's Journals*, ed. Bliss Perry (Boston: Houghton Mifflin, 1926), 183.

This book offers a better understanding of the message of the Bible and its key characters, and what both mean to the reader personally. Truth understood and received can transform our lives.

Busy pastors and teachers will find this book to be a helpful tool. There are dozens of books of sermons and articles about Bible characters, but very few of them introduce the reader to the heart of the character's personality. In our fast-food and sound-bite society, this book presents such material in a concise and easy-to-read format.

In the appendix you will find a chart that provides two months' worth of suggested daily Bible readings for use in your personal devotions. These readings coordinate with the chapters in the book. So if you choose to use this book for personal enrichment, you have an option to follow the reading plan at the back of the book, coordinating Scripture reading with the reading of this book.

If you are involved in speaking or teaching, you may wish to use this book to obtain ideas in preparation for ministry. At the back of the book, I have included a listing of other books on biblical characters for those who wish to do further study.

Part

One

LOOKING AT THE LIVES OF

OLD TESTAMENT
CHARACTERS

AND THEIR LIFE SENTENCES

1

THE LORD GOD

[handwritten: GEN 1:1]

O LORD my God, you are very great.

PSALM 104:1

[handwritten box: IN THE BEGinning God!]

Reading this book will help you get acquainted with some personalities in the
Bible whose life experiences will help you better know God and yourself as well.
You will meet them in the order in which they appear in Scripture so you can
better follow the plot.

The Bible presents a true story with a cast of thousands and an amazing plot
that covers thousands of years. The story is so simple a child can grasp it yet so
profound that it challenges the most brilliant theologian. In the Hebrew text,
fourteen books of the Old Testament begin with "And" as if to remind us that
each book is connected with the others, like links in a living chain.

The record begins in the garden of Eden where our first parents ate the fruit
of the forbidden tree and brought sin and death into the human race. The story
climaxes in a garden city called heaven where the citizens of the city eat the fruit
of the Tree of Life that grows along the banks of the River of Life (Rev. 22:1–2).
The Bible opens with the garden of Eden and closes with the garden city of heaven.
It goes from sin and death to holiness and life. What caused the change?

Between those two gardens is the garden of Gethsemane where the Son of
God prayed "not my will, but yours be done" (Luke 22:42) and went forth courageously to die on a cross. Because Jesus died and rose again, the curse caused in the
first garden has been overcome. The last book in the English Old Testament ends
with the word *curse* (Mal. 4:6), but in the last book of the New Testament we read,
"No longer will there be any curse" (Rev. 22:3). The gift of eternal life is available
to all who put their trust in Jesus. The Bible records this remarkable story so that
you and I may read it, believe it, and experience all that God has for us.

But before we look at these selected personalities, we must begin with God.
Why? Because our quest isn't for the facts of history and biography, but for the
truths of reality and eternity, and that means we must start with God. The story
of the Bible is about God, not just the activities of people. God put the key to
Scripture at the front door: "In the beginning God" (Gen. 1:1). Apart from God,
history is a mystery, a puzzling drama with pages missing from the script and a
plot that doesn't always make sense to us. We must begin with God because He

devised the plot, wrote the script, and chose the cast. He isn't an absentee director out in the wings; He's on stage at all times whether we recognize Him or not. Nobody will miss a cue or flub a line. It will all come out just as He planned. History is His story.

This doesn't mean that human history is a puppet show, with God manipulating people against their will and then lightly tossing them aside when He is through with them. In His sovereignty, God is able to move characters and change scenery successfully, even though the cast has the freedom to choose otherwise. The drama will go on. God operates by decree, not by consensus or committee. "Our God is in heaven", wrote the psalmist, "he does whatever pleases him" (Ps. 115:3). The atheist denies this, the agnostic questions it, but the follower of Jesus Christ accepts it and rejoices in it.

Nobody knows all about God. But there are some basic truths about God's relationship to humankind that we must grasp if we are going to understand the people in this book and, as a result, better understand ourselves and what God wants us to do.

GOD THE CREATOR

The worshiping Israelite said, "Come, let us bow down in worship, let us kneel before the LORD our Maker" (Ps. 95:6). The skeptical materialist asks, "Where did God come from?" and the believing disciple asks, "Where did matter and life come from?" The materialist replies, "Pure accident" and invokes his sacred trinity of matter, time, and chance. The disciple answers, "Divine appointment," and invokes his sacred Trinity of Father, Son, and Holy Spirit. There is no way to avoid "In the beginning God" (Gen. 1:1).

God was not only at the beginning of creation and at the beginning of the Hebrew nation that taught us about God, but He is also at the beginning of each individual life. "For you created my inmost being", wrote David, "you knit me together in my mother's womb.... My frame was not hidden from you when I was made in the secret place. When I was woven together in the depths of the earth, your eyes saw my unformed body" (Ps. 139:13, 15–16). The people we meet in the Bible were all prepared and equipped by God for the special purposes He had ordained for them. This is also true of the people we meet today—and it's true of you and me!

GOD THE PROVIDER

It is significant that the Lord formed and filled the heavens and the earth before He made the first people. Just as expectant parents lovingly prepare their home for the arrival of their baby, so the Father lovingly prepared this world for us. Everything we need is here, and God wants us to use it wisely and not waste it or destroy it.

God also provided us with the abilities to understand and appreciate this immeasurable wealth, for He made us in His own image. We have bodies so we can use and enjoy the physical world, but we have spirits so we can fellowship with God and enjoy the riches of the spiritual world. We have minds to think with, wills to decide with, and hearts to love with, and God has appointed us to "have dominion" over His creation and work with Him in accomplishing His wonderful purposes. "You made him ruler over the works of your hands," said David (Ps. 8:6), and this fact utterly overwhelmed him. "Who and what are we," he asked, "that almighty God should pay any attention to us?"

The people we will meet in the Bible are of two kinds: those who trust God, obey Him, and discover that He meets every need, and those who disobey God—or even worse, rebel against Him—and rob themselves of the riches of His wisdom, power, grace, and glory. Like the Prodigal Son (Luke 15:11–24), they starve in the pigpen of their own proud self-sufficiency when they could be rejoicing and feasting at the Father's table.

That leads us to a third basic truth about God: He is Father.

GOD THE FATHER

The LORD Jehovah called Israel His "firstborn" (Ex. 4:22) and lovingly dealt with His chosen people as parents deal with their children. "As a father has compassion on his children, so the LORD has compassion on those who fear him" (Ps. 103:13). "Can a mother forget the baby at her breast and have no compassion on the child she has borne? Though she may forget, I will not forget you!" (Isa. 49:15). Like a careful parent, God took Israel by the hand and led them out of Egypt (Jer. 31:32). He led them and fed them in the wilderness, and whenever they rebelled, He chastened them the way any loving parent would discipline a disobedient child. "Know then in your heart that as a man disciplines his son, so the LORD your God disciplines you" (Deut. 8:5). The critic who calls the God of the Old Testament a bully and a tyrant hasn't taken time to read the record and see the vivid examples of God's love, kindness, generosity, and longsuffering toward His people.

It was Jesus who made the fatherhood of God visible and real, for He said, "Anyone who has seen me has seen the Father" (John 14:9). If God were a bully and a tyrant, would He become like one of us, live in our world, share our burdens and difficulties, and finally, bear our sins on the cross? Would He weep with the sorrowing, receive the children into His arms, feed the hungry, forgive the sinners, and lovingly teach the common people the saving truth about God? His earthly life and ministry can be summed up in one word: love, for God is love. Today the Holy Spirit in our hearts witnesses of the Father and assures us that we are indeed His children. Those who trust Jesus Christ have received "the Spirit of sonship," and "by him we cry, 'Abba, Father'" (Rom. 8:15; cf. Gal. 4:5–6). "Abba" is the Aramaic equivalent of our English word "Daddy," and it speaks of love and intimacy.

The will of God is the expression of the love of God for each of us. "But the plans of the LORD stand firm forever, the purposes of his heart through all generations" (Ps. 33:11). As we mature in love and faith, the Father's character and plans become clearer and clearer, we love Him more and more, and we want to serve Him better and better. While the *expression* of God's love is uncondi-tional, our *enjoyment* of His love depends on our knowing His Word and obeying it. If we have surrendered to Jesus, God is our Father, come what may; but He can't be a Father to us if we deliberately disobey Him and permit sin in our lives (2 Cor. 6:17 – 18). Just as parents rejoice over their children and delight to see them honor their name by maturing in character and conduct, so our heavenly Father rejoices over His obedient children and the honor they bring to His name.

As we get acquainted with these Bible personalities, we will see how God loved them and by His love sought to motivate them to obedience so that He might bless them more. Some deliberately rejected His love, while others rejoiced in His love and shared it with others. "He who loves me," said Jesus, "will be loved by my Father, and I too will love him and show myself to him.... My Father will love him, and we will come to him and make our home with him" (John 14:21, 23). This is one thing Paul prayed about in Ephesians 3:14 – 21, that Jesus Christ would feel at home in our hearts so we would be "rooted and established in love" and experience God's love in its fullness.

GOD THE JUDGE   God Loves Justice!

God lovingly disciplines His children when they need it and justly allows both believers and unbelievers to suffer when they disobey Him. The LORD's judgments don't come as surprises, because He sends warnings in advance, and his judgments are not unjust. "Will not the Judge of all the earth do right?" asked Abraham (Gen. 18:25), and the answer Moses gave is correct: "His works are perfect, and all his ways are just" (Deut. 32:4). God's justice is the expression of his holiness and his love. "The LORD loves righteousness and justice; the earth is full of his unfailing love" (Ps. 33:5). "For I, the LORD, love justice" (Isa. 61:8).

A righteous God doesn't violate his own nature or break his own laws. He warned our first parents not to eat of the Tree of the Knowledge of Good and Evil, for if they did, they would die (Gen. 2:17). When they disobeyed, he de-clared them guilty and handed down the sentence, "To dust you will return" (Gen. 3:19). God in his grace forgave their sin, but in his justice he didn't change the consequences. God's grace and God's government—John calls it "grace and truth" (John 1:17)—are friends and not enemies, for grace reigns through righ-teousness (Rom. 5:21).

A pastor was preaching a series of messages titled "The Sins of the Saints," and some of the church members didn't appreciate it at all. "If you want to preach about sin," they said, "preach to the unbelievers. After all, sin in the life of a Chris-tian is different from sin in the life of an unbeliever." "Yes," replied the pastor. "It's worse!"

"God doesn't permit His children to sin successfully," said Charles Spurgeon, and it was to his own people that the Lord said, "The LORD will judge his people" and "It is a dreadful thing to fall into the hands of the living God" (Deut. 32:36; Heb. 10:30–31). God gives His people many gifts and privileges, but He never gives them the privilege of sinning and getting away with it. We shall find this truth repeated many times as we meet the personalities discussed in these pages. Even forgiven sins have consequences.

The Bible record is an honest record, and God tells the truth about His children. What is written is there to warn us not to sin (1 Cor. 10:6–12) and to encourage us to keep trusting God (Rom. 15:4). Believers do sin, and they suffer for it, but this is no excuse for unbelievers to remain as they are. "And, 'If it is hard for the righteous to be saved, what will become of the ungodly and the sinner?'" (1 Peter 4:18; cf. Prov. 11:31). If the temporal consequences of sin bring grief and pain to God's own children in this life, what will be the *eternal* consequences of sin for those who reject Jesus Christ when they leave this life?

> *Let those who love the LORD hate evil.*
> PSALM 97:10

> *All who hate me love death.*
> PROVERBS 8:36

God — IN THE BEGINNING GOD. HISTORY is HIS STORY.
Bible -- to know God Better. Fourteen Books begin w AND.
Garden of Eden — Garden of Heaven.
CREATOR — prepared and equipped us for purpose.
PROVIDER -- GOD lovingly prepared the world for us.
Bodies for physical world. Spirits for spiritual world.
FATHER -- He who Loves Jesus.. Father will love him & come in to him and make their home with him. John 14:21
JUDGE -- God loves justice. Even forgiven sins have consequences. God never gives His people privilege of sinning and getting away with it.
(WE REAP WHAT WE SOW!)

selfish Prideful Ambition inflates the ego and destroys the soul.
The enemy is a liar & deceiver.

2

LUCIFER

wants to be like the Most High.

"I will make myself like the Most High."

ISAIAH 14:14

Deceiver selfish prideful ambition liar

The name Lucifer comes from a Latin word that means "light bearer." Some of the church fathers gave the name "Lucifer" to Satan, basing it on their interpretation of Isaiah 14:12: "How you have fallen from heaven, O morning star, son of the dawn!" The being we know as Satan was originally a holy angel, created by God; and in the Bible, angels are compared to stars. When God created the universe, "the morning stars sang together and all the angels shouted for joy" (Job 38:7), and Lucifer was among them. In some unexplained way, at some undefined time, the pride of this great angel led to his judgment and his fall from heaven (cf. Rev. 12:1–9). "The raw material of a devil is an angel bereft of holiness," said Spurgeon.[1]

In its primary meaning, Isaiah 14:9–23 is a "taunt song" about the king of Babylon. He boasted that he would climb up to heaven and be like God, but he ended up falling into Sheol, the realm of the dead, and being like every other dead monarch. We find a similar passage in Ezekiel 28 where God announces the fall of the prince of Tyre (see vv. 11–19). While the basic interpretation of both passages refers to actual monarchs—the king of Babylon and the prince of Tyre—behind both passages there seems to be lurking the prince of the power of the air, Satan, the Devil, the enemy of God and God's people. In the activities and falls of these two proud rulers, we have a vivid illustration of the character and work of Satan and of his final judgment.

The key sentence is Isaiah 14:14—"I will make myself like the Most High"—a statement that reveals the character of Satan.

AMBITION

Ambition can be good or bad, depending on the motive and the method. Lucifer was ambitious to dethrone the Lord and take His place, and this was wicked.

If our motive is self-promotion and selfish gain, and if our method is deceptive and harmful to others, then ambition is wrong. But if our motive is to glorify

---

1. Spurgeon, *Metropolitan Tabernacle Pulpit*, vol. 35, 302.

God and our method is to do His will and wait for His timing, then ambition is good. Galatians 5:20 mentions "selfish ambition" as one of the works of the flesh, and Philippians 2:3 admonishes us to "do nothing out of selfish ambition or vain conceit." James 3:14–16 states clearly that envy and selfish ambition create serious problems in life and have their origin in the world, the flesh, and the Devil.

But in the Lord, ambition can be a blessing. First Thessalonians 4:11 says, "Make it your ambition to lead a quiet life," and Paul confessed that it was always his ambition "to preach the gospel where Christ was not known" (Rom. 15:20) and "to please [God]" (2 Cor. 5:9). Like the man in the parable who buried his talent, to have no ambition is to be a "wicked, lazy servant" (Matt. 25:24–27), and to be like David's son Absalom and use lies and bribery to "get to the top" is to ask for the judgment of God.

Ancient monarchs saw themselves as gods and acted accordingly. Pharaoh asked, "Who is the LORD, that I should obey him and let Israel go?" (Ex. 5:2), and Nebuchadnezzar boasted, "Is not this the great Babylon I have built as the royal residence, by my mighty power and for the glory of my majesty?" (Dan. 4:30). The Lord's response was to wipe out Egypt and transform Nebuchadnezzar into a beast for seven years. After his oration, Herod Agrippa enjoyed hearing the people shout, "This is the voice of a god, not of a man" (Acts 12:22), and that act of pride led to his death.

This deification of kings helps us understand the connection between the rulers of Babylon and Tyre and the angel we call Lucifer. Angels are creatures, not creators, God's servants, not his masters; and Lucifer's desires were evil. He wanted to be like the true God who had created him, and he claimed he could do it by himself! The Hebrew verb is reflexive: "I will make myself like the Most High." The Scriptures don't fully explain all that happened, but when Lucifer rebelled, he must have made the same empty promise to other angels, for many of them followed him and were also judged and cast out (see Rev. 12:4, 9). John Milton's classic poem *Paradise Lost* is based on this event.

PRIDE

Pride feeds selfish ambition; in fact, many theologians believe that pride lies at the heart of all sin. For this reason, pride is one of the sins the Lord especially hates (Prov. 6:16–17). "Pride goes before destruction, a haughty spirit before a fall" (Prov. 16:18). Lucifer's "I will make myself like the Most High" became "You will be like God" when Lucifer tempted Eve (Gen. 3:5), and he has been using that bait successfully ever since. "You can become somebody" is a promise that appeals to the vanity of the human species.

Behavioral scientists tell us that much neurotic behavior is linked directly to pride, and that healthy and honest self-esteem is the best remedy. Both Jesus and Paul knew what it was like to live in a society that was motivated primarily by pride, for the Romans were masters of the vainglorious. "You know that the rulers of the Gentiles lord it over them," Jesus warned His disciples, "and their high officials exercise authority over them. Not so with you" (Matt. 20:25–26). Jesus practiced what He preached and willingly gave up His equality with God and became a servant and a sacrifice on a cross, the perfect example of humility (Phil. 2:1–11). What a contrast to Lucifer!

"Do not think of yourself more highly than you ought, but rather think of yourself with sober judgment" was Paul's wise counsel (Rom. 12:3). He warned the churches not to select immature believers as leaders lest they "become conceited and fall under the same judgment as the devil" (1 Tim. 3:6). Woe unto that church whose leaders believed the Devil when he whispered to them, "Now you are somebody important."

Too often, contemporary advertising and promotion encourage people to believe that status, authority, recognition, and possessions measure their self-worth. The absence of authentic national heroes and heroines makes it easy for the public to adore and almost worship high-profile people whose "fame" is manufactured by public relations experts and maintained by spin doctors. When people worship movie stars and sports idols, it's just as detestable to the Lord as if they worshiped Baal or Zeus. All idols are made by human minds and hands and are false. A "fan club mentality" (A. W. Tozer's phrase) has invaded the church, and we now seem to have more celebrities and fewer servants. If you question this assessment, take time to read some of the ads in religious publications.

What is basically wrong with pride? Pride moves a person into an unreal world, and a life based on unreality cannot be nourished or fulfilled. It's like children at the circus having cotton candy for lunch instead of eating nourishing food. Selfish ambition inflates the ego but destroys the soul. It impresses some people, but it grieves the Lord.

DECEPTION

When God wants to work in and through His children, He uses the truth of the Word of God, taught by the Spirit, because the Holy Spirit is "the Spirit of truth" (John 14:17; 15:26; 16:13). God uses truth to accomplish His work, but Satan uses lies. Satan first appears in Scripture as a serpent who deceives (Gen. 3:1–4, 13–14), and it is as a deceiver that he is described by both Jesus and Paul. Jesus called him "a murderer" and "a liar" (John 8:44), and Paul warned the Corinthian believers against the serpent's cunning deception (2 Cor. 11:3). Unless Christian soldiers are equipped with the belt of truth and the sword of God's Word, the enemy will defeat them (Eph. 6:14–17). In the book of Revelation, the deceiving serpent is also the destroying dragon (Rev. 12:9–17; 20:1–3) who will one day be imprisoned in hell (Rev. 20:10).

Basically, Satan is a counterfeiter who began his career by attempting to counterfeit God. Since his fall, he has produced a counterfeit gospel of salvation by good works (Gal. 1:6–9). He plants counterfeit Christians (Matt. 13:24–30, 36–43; see also the chapter on Cain below) who have a counterfeit righteousness (Rom. 9:30–10:4). His counterfeit ministers serve him (2 Cor. 11:13–15) in a counterfeit church (Rev. 2:9; 3:9). Ultimately Satan will unveil a counterfeit Christ—the Antichrist—whom the spiritually blind world will worship and obey (2 Thess. 2; Rev. 13). Satan has always wanted to be worshiped, and for a short time he will achieve his goal.

When Satan tempted Eve, he told her three lies. First, he suggested that God wasn't really generous to her and Adam by prohibiting them from eating of the Tree of the Knowledge of Good and Evil. Second, he denied that they would die if they ate of the tree. Third, he affirmed that instead of dying, they would become like God. (There's that old lie again!) In modern terms, Satan claimed that there are no absolute truths from God, no consequences for personal disobedience, and no limits to what people can achieve. Do as you please and enjoy life! These three lies appear today in various philosophies and religions—especially the so-called New Age movement, which is as old as Genesis 3—and have even infected the thinking of true believers who ought to know better.

When we believe a lie, Satan goes to work in our lives; when we believe the truth of God, the Holy Spirit goes to work in our lives. When we cultivate unholy ambition, we serve the world, the flesh, and the Devil, and the result is trouble; when we seek to please God only, we serve Him, and the result is blessing.

In *The Great Divorce*, C. S. Lewis writes, "There are only two kinds of people in the end: those who say to God, 'Thy will be done,' and those to whom God says, in the end, '*Thy* will be done.' All that are in Hell, choose it."[2]

And all this trouble started with Lucifer.

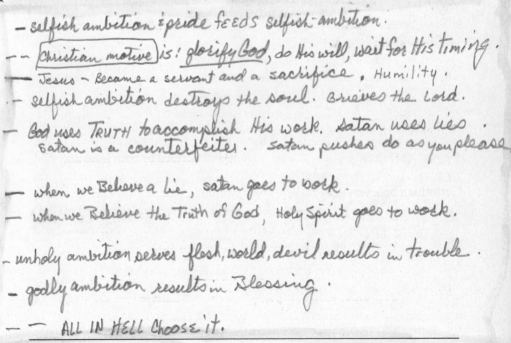

- selfish ambition + pride feeds selfish ambition.
- Christian motive is: glorify God, do His will, wait for His timing.
- Jesus - Became a servant and a sacrifice, Humility.
- selfish ambition destroys the soul. Grieves the Lord.
- God uses TRUTH to accomplish His work. satan uses lies. satan is a counterfeiter. satan pushes do as you please
- when we Believe a lie, satan goes to work.
- when we Believe the Truth of God, Holy Spirit goes to work.
- unholy ambition serves flesh, world, devil results in trouble.
- godly ambition results in Blessing.
- ALL IN HELL Choose it.

2. C. S. Lewis, *The Great Divorce* (San Francisco: HarperCollins, 2001), 75.

Handwritten notes at top:
Man created for a purpose. Man has a history, not a cycle.
We are in the image of God — we have a spiritual nature.
Relates to God.
we think, love & will.

Handwritten note:
1st Adam & last Adam brought death & life.
living BEING — Living Spirit.

3

ADAM

For as in Adam all die.

1 CORINTHIANS 15:22

Handwritten note in box:
Made in image of God... has a spiritual nature.
1st Adam   last Adam

"What a good thing Adam had," wrote Mark Twain. "When he said a good thing, he knew nobody had said it before."

But Adam doesn't say much as far as the biblical record is concerned. He sang a beautiful wedding song in Genesis 2:23, and he gave the Lord a feeble explanation and excuse in Genesis 3:10–12, and that's it. However, Adam isn't remembered for the good things he said; he's remembered primarily for a bad thing he did. He ate of the tree that God had forbidden and thus brought sin and death into the human race. Paul put it bluntly—"in Adam all die"—and then he amplified the statement in Romans 5:12–21. From Genesis 3 on, the Bible records the tragic consequences of that one sinful act and how a gracious God made it possible for us to regain the paradise from which our first parents were expelled.

When God made Adam, the first human, what did He actually make? We might understand ourselves and others better if we could answer that question accurately, and we would also better understand God's purposes for us in this world. Genesis 1:26–2:7 is our basic text as we consider the "contradictions" or "paradoxes" that we can't help seeing as we look at man.[1]

DUST AND DEITY

The name Adam is derived from a Hebrew word that means "red ground," because Adam was formed from the soil by the hand of God. In Genesis 2:7–8 the word translated "formed" carries with it the idea of "formed for a purpose, formed with intent." It is related to the Hebrew word *yoṣer*, which means "potter." God had spent six days creating the heavens and the earth and filling them with everything Adam and Eve needed to fulfill their purpose on earth. Earth was prepared for them, and they were equipped to enjoy and use it. In God's wisdom, it was a perfect match.

1. In this discussion, the word *man* is used generically and is the equivalent of "mankind" or "human beings" and includes "woman." Genesis 5:2 uses "man" in this way.

It is a great mistake to forget that the name of our first father was Adam —
"dust, earth." God "remembers that we are dust" (Ps. 103:14) and has decreed
that we will return to dust (Gen. 3:19), but we are prone to think we are made
of steel and will be here on earth forever. H. C. Leupold translates Ecclesiastes
6:10: "Whatever one may be, his name was given him long ago, and it is known
that he is man."[2] That last phrase might be translated, "he is Adam," meaning,
"he is only dust." Even if your name is famous worldwide, the name God gave
you hasn't changed. It is still "dust." One day you will die, and one day your
given name will be forgotten. I have four thick volumes in my library titled
Who Was Who. They contain the names and biographies of men and women
who once were famous but today are recognized by only a few historians. From
God's point of view, they all had the same name — Adam — "dust."

Adam's body came from the ground, but his essential life came from God
who breathed life into him and made him "a living being." One reason many
people find it difficult to define what human beings are is that humans are a
unique combination of dust and deity, with physical bodies that identify them
with the earth and a spiritual nature that identifies them with heaven. Leave
God out of the picture and Adam must be defined as a mere animal, very gifted
perhaps, but still an animal.

Naturalist Roy Chapman Andrews did just that when he defined man as "an
ape with possibilities," but he didn't tell why he had those possibilities or where
they came from. The British poet T. S. Eliot said that man was "no more than an
extremely clever, adaptable and mischievous animal," and Sigmund Freud, the
father of psychiatry, said, "Man is not a being different from the animals, nor
superior to them." Yet the American philosopher and educator Mortimer Adler
wrote a book titled The Difference of Man and the Difference It Makes, in which
he sought to determine "Is man unique, and if so, what are the implications for
humanity of this uniqueness?" Does man differ from brute animals only in de-
gree but not in kind?

In our world, lower forms of life have life cycles, while humans have histories.
You can write a book titled The Life of the Bee, because one bee's life is very much
like every other bee's life, but you can't write The Life of the Human, because
each man and woman has a personal story to tell. Yes, we are all conceived and
born in the same way, and we grow up and eventually will die, but what happens
between those events is absolutely unique. God made (formed) the livestock and
wild animals, but the record doesn't tell us that He breathed life into them as He
did with Adam (Gen. 1:24–25), nor does it tell us that they were made in the
image of God (Gen. 1:27).

Let's consider the paradox of humans having both the image of God and the
image of Adam.

---

2. H. C. Leupold, Exposition of Ecclesiastes (Grand Rapids, Mich.: Baker, n.d.), 142.

ADAM'S IMAGE AND GOD'S IMAGE

When God created Adam, He made him "in [His] own image" (Gen. 1:26–27; 5:1), but Adam's children were conceived in the image and likeness of their father (Gen. 5:3). An insightful note on Genesis 5:3 in *The NIV Study Bible* says, "As God created man in his own perfect image, so now sinful Adam has a son in his own imperfect image."

Being created in the image of God implies that we have something in our inner nature that relates us to God. Plants and animals have life from God in various degrees, and God cares for them, but there is no evidence that they relate to God as humans do. Animals and humans were both created from the earth (Gen. 2:7, 19); both were given the same food (Gen. 1:29–30) and the same mandate to reproduce (Gen. 1:22, 28); but only humans were made in God's image. That almighty God would impress his image into fragile clay is a tremendous act of grace!

Because we are created in God's image, we are *persons* and not just things. We have minds for knowing and thinking, hearts for loving and desiring, and wills for determining and deciding. Even more, God gave us "rule" or "dominion" (Gen. 1:26–28) so that we might share in God's sovereign rule over the earth. We are responsible before God to be worshipful and obedient and to glorify Him with all He has given to us. We are also responsible to treat others as made in the image of God (Gen. 9:6; James 3:9).

Before Adam fell, he cooperated with the Lord in accomplishing His will. Adam worked in the garden, named the animals, and submitted to divine surgery so that God might give him a suitable helper (Gen. 1:8–24). He and his wife fellowshiped with the Lord and enjoyed His blessings together as they did His will.

But then Adam disobeyed, and this brought about a drastic change in their relationship with the Lord. God's image was now marred so that they ran and hid from God instead of enjoying His presence (Gen. 3:1–8). That act of sin has affected all of Adam and Eve's descendants, so that in our thinking, loving, and willing, it is easier for us to go our own way instead of God's way. For a description of our sad condition, read Ephesians 4:17–19 and Romans 1:18–32.

Our problem now is that we have a divided inner nature. Only God can really satisfy us, but like our first parents, we are prone to hide from Him because we have other desires that seem much more exciting. "Thou hast made us for Thyself, and our hearts are restless until they rest in Thee," wrote Augustine, and he was right. But Adam bequeathed us a sinful nature that wants to resist God. To add to the problem, he also bequeathed each of us a body that will one day die and turn to dust. The awesome fear of death—something that animals instinctively feel but can't contemplate—has an iron grip on humankind. Death is an enemy against which we have no successful weapons (1 Cor. 15:26). We can ignore it, give it harmless names, pretend that it won't happen, and perhaps be able to postpone it when it threatens, but we can't defeat it. The last enemy will attack and win. God can heal every disease and injury, but everyone will face death.

SOVEREIGNTY AND SLAVERY

Had Adam not sinned, he and Eve would have reigned with the Lord over the old creation and exercised dominion over the sea creatures, the birds, and the land animals. When they lost their innocence, they lost their crowns, and this left them crippled sovereigns as well as slaves of sin, for the image of God in them was marred. They could still use their bodies, minds, and wills, but their understanding, desires, and motives were poisoned by sin, and they couldn't control the consequences.

That problem is with us today, and it is magnified by centuries of growth of scientific knowledge. Researchers develop insecticides that successfully kill noxious pests, but the consequences are disastrous—polluted water that may cause cancer, infected fish that pass the pollution along to humans, and destroyed vegetation that leaves precious soil prey to erosion. Almost every good thing we come up with produces one or more bad things, which means that we solve one problem and then have to solve two or three more. When we sin, we invent various ways of covering it up, and this only makes the sin worse.

We don't deliberately try to upset life or the balance of nature, but since Adam's fall, we humans are a strange mixture of creator and destroyer, sovereign and slave, and we are prone to use God's gifts in the wrong ways and for the wrong purposes. Created in God's image, we are lower than the angels but higher than the animals, but it is easier to sink to the animal level than to soar to the heavenly realms. We even use animal characteristics to describe one another: dirty as a pig, stubborn as a mule, dumb as an ox, slippery as an eel, cunning as a fox, clumsy as a bull in a china shop. If we do something commendable, people call us angels.

We transcend nature yet are a part of nature. Is there a solution to this life of paradox and contradiction?

Emphatically—yes!

THE FIRST ADAM AND THE LAST ADAM

According to Romans 5:12–21, when Adam was crowned king of the old creation, he represented the entire human race. Theologians call this his "federal headship." It's something like the bargain the Philistines made with Israel. "Choose a man to fight Goliath. If your champion wins, we become your servants; if Goliath wins, Israel becomes our servants" (see 1 Sam. 17:8–11).

Some skeptics may ask, "But is God fair in charging Adam's disobedience to the entire human race?" It's not a matter of fairness but of grace. If God did what was "fair," He'd have to condemn the whole human race and forget about salvation. Furthermore, if you and I had been in Adam's place, we would have failed just as he did. But even more, the fact that all humans were judged because of what the first Adam did in the garden made it possible for God to save sinners because of what the last Adam did on the cross. It is not a matter of law or fairness but of the bountiful grace of God. "For as in Adam all die, so in Christ all will be made alive" (1 Cor. 15:22). Adam's disobedience brought the reign of sin and death into the world, but Christ's sacrifice on the cross brought the reign of grace and the promise of glorious resurrection to all who trust Him. This is a very wise and gracious solution to a complex problem.

When we were born the first time, we were born into the old creation and "in Adam," and that made us lost sinners. When we were born again, we were born into the new creation (2 Cor. 5:17) and placed "in Christ," and that made us the children of God. "'The first man Adam became a living being,'" wrote Paul in 1 Corinthians 15:45, quoting Genesis 2:7, but then he added, "the last Adam, a life-giving spirit." Jesus Christ "gives life to whom he is pleased to give it" (John 5:21). Because of this new life in the Spirit, the marred image of God in each believer can be transformed and we can become more and more like Jesus Christ! As we meditate on the Word, pray, worship, suffer, serve, and fellowship with God's people, we "put on the new self, created to be like God in true righteousness and holiness" (Eph. 4:24; and see Col. 3:9–10; Rom. 8:29).

The first Adam was lord of the old creation, but he became a thief and with his wife was cast out of paradise. While dying on the cross, the last Adam turned to the thief on the cross next to Him and said, "I tell you the truth, today you will be with me in paradise" (Luke 23:43).

Jesus is no longer on the cross, but He is still saving sinners and receiving them into paradise. Praise God for the last Adam!

ONLY GOD CAN SATISFY US!

ADAM. RED GROUND. FORMED WITH PURPOSE.
DUST- Earth   DIETY. SPIRITUAL NATURE IDENTIFIED W Heaven.
ADAM IMAGE   GOD IMAGE -- DEATH ___ Life. Relates to God.
1 st Adam   Last Adam - living being — life-giving Spirit.

4

EVE

Adam named his wife Eve, because she would
become the mother of all the living.

GENESIS 3:20

gives of life or living — chase, mature,
conduct / to helping eternal life.

Adam's name means "earth," and this identifies him with death (Gen. 3:19),
but Eve is identified with life because her name means "life" or "living." By
giving her this name, Adam announced his faith in God's promise that the
woman would have offspring (Gen. 3:15) and therefore live. The Lord had just
announced that Adam and Eve would die because of their disobedience (Gen.
3:19), but Adam believed that gracious salvation promise and named his wife
"life." God accepted their faith, forgave their sins, and shed the blood of animals
to clothe them in acceptable garments. This is the first clear illustration of the
gospel of God's grace found in the Bible and the first mention of blood being
shed for the forgiveness of sin. Genesis 3:15 is also the first messianic promise
in Scripture.

Obviously, much is implied in Eve's name "life."

SHE WAS FORMED FROM LIFE

In his Bible commentary, Matthew Henry wrote of Genesis 2:21, "The man
was dust refined, but the woman was dust double-refined." God made Adam
out of dust and had to breathe into his nostrils to give him life, but the woman
was made from living tissue, a part of Adam's side, and there is no mention
of God's life-imparting breath. We wonder if the apostle John had this fact
in mind when he wrote about the opening of Jesus' side on the cross (John
19:31–37). "This is now bone of my bones and flesh of my flesh," sang Adam
(Gen. 2:23), and the apostle Paul saw in this a picture of Christ and His bride,
the church (Eph. 5:30–32). The first Adam went to sleep in order to get a bride,
but the last Adam died in great pain that He might have His bride.

Just as Eve partook of Adam's life, so believers share in the life of Christ.
"Whoever believes in the Son has eternal life, but whoever rejects the Son will
not see life, for God's wrath remains on him" (John 3:36). "And this is the
testimony: God has given us eternal life, and this life is in his Son" (1 John
5:11).

SHE WAS FORMED TO SHARE LIFE

Before Adam had a wife to name, he had to name the animals, and in naming them he discovered that among them there was "no suitable helper" for him (Gen. 2:19–20). The word "helper" doesn't imply that God was looking for a servant for Adam, because the text means "someone corresponding to him, in equality with him, and able to aid him." No matter how much an animal and a person may love each other, seek to understand each other, and even help each other, no pet can take the place of a normal mature human being. The word "helper" doesn't suggest lesser value or lower position. Use *partner* and you come closer to the meaning. That cynical philosopher Friedrich Nietzsche wrote that "woman was God's second blunder," but he was wrong. She was God's great gift to Adam, to humankind in general, and to the world.

When Peter said that the wife was the "weaker vessel" (KJV), he meant that the Christian husband should treat his wife as though she were a piece of fine, expensive porcelain (1 Peter 3:7). The wife and husband must assess their personal strengths and weaknesses and agree on what each one will do to make the marriage a success. Paul himself was never married, but he must have expected more from the women than from the men, for he wrote in Romans 1:26, "Even their women …," as though such sin was never to be associated with women!

Matthew Henry has an oft-quoted word about this in his note on Genesis 2:22. He asks us to note that the woman "was not made out of his head to rule over him, nor out of his feet to be trampled upon by him, but out of his side to be equal with him, under his arm to be protected, and near his heart to be beloved." In marriage, the man and woman complement each other and serve each other, and therefore grow in their need for each other and love for each other. While not everyone is supposed to marry (Matt. 19:11–12), those who marry "in the Lord" find that this loving partnership is true. They "complete" each other and are "lost" without each other.

When a man and a woman consummate their marriage, they "become one flesh," and that oneness deepens in every area of life as they live together and serve one another in the Lord. God's plan is that one man and one woman leave their parents and devote themselves to each other in the will of God in a lifetime commitment. God "created them male and female and blessed them. And when they were created, he called them 'man'" (Gen. 5:2). Whenever Adam thought about his name—dust—and the inevitability of death, he looked at Eve and thought, "Life!"

Martin Luther playfully called his wife, Catherine, "Kitty my rib" and confessed that they had a happy marriage. "The greatest treasure on earth," he said, "is a dear wife."

Knowing the Genesis account of the creation of Eve, Paul wrote that man was not created for woman, but woman for man (1 Cor. 11:9), but this statement doesn't suggest that the woman is the junior partner in marriage. Christian marriage counselor Dr. Dwight Hervey Small explains it best: "It is humbling to the woman to know that she was created for the man, but it is for her glory to know that she alone can complete him. Likewise, it is humbling to the man to know that he is incomplete without a woman, but it is to his glory that the woman was created for him."[1]

SHE WAS FORMED TO NURTURE LIFE

The consummation of marriage makes the husband and wife one, and conception makes them three—or more! Society today too often brands children as nuisances that interfere with the free life of adults. Sex, yes; children, no—and millions of times in our world each year, abortion is their method of birth control. But the Lord loves the children and considers them treasures. "Sons are a heritage from the LORD, children a reward from him" (Ps. 127:3). The womb was never designed to be a tomb, for the womb is God's "workshop" where He lovingly "weaves" each child according to His perfect plan (Ps. 139:13–16). God honored the woman by forming her to be the nurturer. She carries the unborn child next to her heart for nine months, and then nurses the little one over her heart until it's time for weaning. Her arms embrace each child, her hands labor for them, her voice teaches and encourages, her smile approves, and her eyes sometimes fill with tears. She is the nurturer.

Because Christians use masculine terms to refer to the persons in the divine Trinity, misinformed people sometimes call us "sexist" and classify the Bible as a "sexist book." But God is spirit and has no physical body, therefore He is genderless. When we speak of "the Father," we are referring to His office and activity, and not to gender. Jesus was conceived and born a baby boy because He is the last Adam, the Lord of the new creation. Like the Father, the Holy Spirit has no gender and indwells both male and female believers. (I have often wondered why some people resent having the Godhead addressed as masculine, but they never protest Satan being addressed as masculine.)

However, it is important to understand that there is a "motherhood" aspect to God's nature that must not be denied or ignored. Like a mother, *God is unchanging in His love*. He says, "Can a mother forget the baby at her breast and have no compassion on the child she has borne? Though she may forget, I will not forget you!" (Isa. 49:15). Like a mother, *God is unsparing in His comfort*. "As a mother comforts her child, so will I comfort you; and you will be comforted over Jerusalem" (Isa. 66:13). Children who are sick, injured, afraid, or brokenhearted usually call for their mother, even though they know that their father loves them and cares, because a mother's comfort is very special.

God is unsparing in His joy. "The LORD your God is with you, he is mighty to save. He will take great delight in you, he will quiet you with his love, he will rejoice over you with singing" (Zeph. 3:17). Can you imagine God joyfully

---

1. Dwight Hervey Small, *Design for Christian Marriage* (Westwood, N. J.: Revell, 1959), 32.

holding His children in His arms and singing to them? What a picture of the "motherhood" of God!

Like a mother, *God is unchanging in His purpose.* What is that purpose? To guide the child into maturity. One of the tasks God has given parents is that of helping their children mature and enter into the responsibilities, joys, and demands of adult life. "My heart is not proud, O LORD, my eyes are not haughty; I do not concern myself with great matters or things too wonderful for me. But I have stilled and quieted my soul; like a weaned child with its mother, like a weaned child is my soul within me" (Ps. 131:1–2). We don't like it when God takes away our toys and hands us tools, but that's the way life works. God has a wonderful life prepared for us, and He loves us too much to allow us to remain pampered and immature.

The father has his responsibilities in providing and protecting, and sometimes disciplining, but it is the mother who, from the child's conception, nurtures the child and lovingly leads him or her forward in growth and maturity. Both the mother and father must "continue in faith, love and holiness with propriety" (1 Tim. 2:15) if they want God to help the mother safely carry and deliver the baby. In ancient days, childbirth wasn't an easy thing, and many mothers died. In Ephesus, where Timothy was serving, many expectant mothers went to the temple of Diana and dedicated themselves and their children to the goddess, asking for her help, but Paul encouraged Christian couples to trust God to see them through.

SHE HAS HELPED TO BRING ETERNAL LIFE INTO THE WORLD

God said to Satan, "And I will put enmity between you and the woman, and between your offspring and hers; he will crush your head, and you will strike his heel" (Gen. 3:15).

This first promise of the coming of the Redeemer was God's response to Lucifer's victory over Adam and Eve. It was a declaration of war and an announcement that the ultimate victory would be God's. The Son of God would make Himself like the sons of men and come as a servant to die obediently on a cross. "The Word became flesh and made his dwelling among us" (John 1:14). "But when the time had fully come, God sent his Son, born of a woman" (Gal. 4:4).

Born of a woman!

Genesis 3:15 announced that the Redeemer would be a human being and not an angel. Genesis 12:1–3 revealed that the Redeemer would be a Jew and not a Gentile, and Genesis 49:10 that He would come from the tribe of Judah. God told David that the Savior would come from his family (2 Sam. 7), and the prophet Micah pointed to Bethlehem—"the city of David"—as the birthplace (Micah 5:2). Isaiah 7:14 promised that He would be born of a virgin, that He would come as a baby! Luke 1:26–56 tells the moving story of how Mary received the news that she was that chosen virgin.

Adam was given a body without the assistance of a man or a woman. Eve received her body from a man without a woman, but all the rest of us got our bodies the normal way—we had a mother and a father. Jesus Christ, however, received His body through a woman without the involvement of a man! He was "born of a woman" but not conceived by a man, for He was conceived by the Holy Spirit in the virgin womb of a daughter of Eve. Mary claimed no praise for herself but instead worshiped the Lord and magnified Him. After all, the angel Gabriel had said to her, "He [the Son] will be great and will be called the Son of the Most High" (Luke 1:32).

Every husband has a name for his wife whether spoken or unspoken.

Blessed is that marriage when the name he gives is "Life."

[EVE.] mother of all the living · [Life]

Eve formed from life out of Adam's side.

Eve formed to share life · God's gift to Adam.

Eve formed to nuture life.

Eve helped to bring ETERNAL Life into the world.

5

CAIN

Cain, who belonged to the evil one ...

1 JOHN 3:12

Main difference between Cain & Abel was FAITH.

Adam and Eve were evicted from the garden and forbidden to return, but when they left, they took their marriage with them. When we consider the state of marriage in western society today, it's difficult to believe that it had its beginning in paradise, but it did. God performed the first wedding when He brought Eve to Adam, who awakened to discover that he was a married man. It was love at first sight, and he was a happy man and sang a song.

Because Adam and Eve had lost their dominion, they no longer had creation submitting at their feet; but they still had the promise that a Redeemer would be born who would ultimately restore all things, a promise that is fulfilled in Christ (Heb. 2:6–9). Did Adam and Eve think that their first child was the fulfillment of that promise? If they did, they were certainly wrong, for Cain turned out to be just the opposite.

A GIFT FROM THE LORD

Even outside paradise, our first parents still had the blessing of married love and the responsibility to be fruitful and multiply. They shared their love, and God gave Eve conception. How she responded to this first experience of pregnancy isn't recorded, but surely the Lord taught her what she needed to know. In the conceiving of new life, Adam and Eve were sharing in God's creative work, and they gave Him the glory. "With the help of the LORD I have brought forth a man," said Eve, and she named her son Cain (Gen. 4:1). The name probably comes from a Hebrew word which means "gotten" or "acquired."

From the very beginning of family life, the Scriptures clearly teach that children are to be received as gifts from God, blessings and not burdens. In her sorrow and disappointment, Rachel said to her husband, "Give me children, or I'll die!" and Jacob asked her, "Am I in the place of God?" (Gen. 30:1–2). Jacob knew that while impregnation was a human act, conception is in the hands of God (Ps. 139:13–18). To reject a child is to reject a gift from God, and to abort a child is to interrupt a miracle from God. When Esau asked his brother, Jacob, about the large group of people with him, Jacob replied, "They are the children God has graciously given your servant" (Gen. 33:5). Years later, when Jacob met Joseph's two sons and asked who they were, Joseph said, "They are the sons God has given me here" (Gen. 48:9). Children are indeed a "heritage from the LORD" (Ps. 127:3).

Cain was the Lord's gift to Adam and Eve, as was his brother Abel ("vanity"). Children are God's gifts to us, and when parents raise them in "the training and instruction of the Lord" (Eph. 6:4), that's their gift to God. How strange that Cain and Abel were so different in their values, but this happens in the best of homes.

THE CHILD OF THE WICKED ONE

"Do not be like Cain, who belonged to the evil one and murdered his brother" (1 John 3:12; Gen. 4). When we considered the career of Lucifer, we learned that the Devil is a "counterfeiter" who leads people to become false children of God (1 John 3:10). In the parable of the tares (Matt. 13:24–30, 36–43), Jesus taught that the children of God, the true believers, are like seeds that God plants in different places so that they can produce fruit. But wherever God plants the true believers, the Devil plants counterfeits, and they grow together and one can hardly tell them apart. In other words, there are people in this world who pretend to be Christians and may actually think that they are, but in the last judgment they will be rejected. Here is what Jesus said about this:

> Not everyone who says to me, "Lord, Lord," will enter the kingdom of heaven, but only he who does the will of my Father who is in heaven. Many will say to me on that day, "Lord, Lord, did we not prophesy in your name, and in your name drive out demons and perform many miracles?" Then I will tell them plainly, "I never knew you. Away from me, you evildoers!"
> MATTHEW 7:21–23

God no sooner "sowed" John the Baptist by the Jordan River than along came the Pharisees and Sadducees, and John called them "a brood of vipers." Children of the Devil, the serpent! Jesus used the same language when addressing the Pharisees (Matt. 12:34; 23:33) and bluntly said, "You belong to your father, the devil" (John 8:44). Neither Jesus nor John ever used this kind of language with the publicans and prostitutes; they reserved it for the self-righteous religious crowd that rejected God's righteousness and said with Lucifer, "I will make myself like the Most High." Alas, churches are filled with these respectable counterfeit Christians who establish their own righteousness and will not submit by faith to God's righteousness as revealed in Jesus Christ (Rom. 10:1–4).

Cain and Abel were raised in the same home by the same believing parents, who taught them to honor God. Cain was a hardworking farmer who brought gifts to God's altar, yet God rejected his gifts because they were not accompanied by faith. The main difference between Cain and Abel was *faith.* Each of them brought an offering to God, but only Abel's offering was accepted by the Lord, because he exercised faith. "By faith Abel offered God a better sacrifice than Cain did" (Heb. 11:4). Cain's heart was not right with God nor with his brother. His heart was filled with envy and anger, and the Devil was just outside the door, waiting to be invited in (Gen. 4:6–7). Cain closed the door on God and his brother and opened the door to the Devil, and his anger became murder (Matt. 5:21–26). When God asked him about his brother, Cain denied knowing his whereabouts. Like his father, Satan, Cain was a liar and a murderer (John 8:44). He had a "form of godliness" (2 Tim. 3:5) but not the true righteousness that comes by faith. He was a counterfeit.

This is what the Bible calls "the way of Cain" (Jude 11). It's the way of unbelief, self-righteousness, and man-made religion. It's the way of Satan, who said, "I will make myself like the Most High!" It's the way of pride, the way that leads to eternal death. But in spite of all this, the way of Cain is the popular way, and now let's find out why.

A BUILDER OF A CITY

When Cain killed Abel, he actually attacked God, because Abel was made in the image of God. By rights, Cain should have been slain for such a wicked deed. "Whoever sheds the blood of man, by man shall his blood be shed; for in the image of God has God made man" (Gen. 9:6). Instead of taking Cain's life, God gave him a "living death" and made him a helpless wanderer on the earth. Cain never repented of his sins, although he did complain about the pain of his punishment. Death might have been a relief! To make sure Cain wasn't slain, God marked him in some special way, and Cain was forced to live with his sin and guilt (Gen. 4:10–15).

But instead of fleeing to God for mercy, Cain wandered off east of Eden where he built a city and tried to forget the past. The Lord had cursed the ground (Gen. 4:10–12), so he ceased to farm and instead built a city and became the founder of what the Bible calls "the world." In that city he sought to find substitutes for the blessings he had lost because of his sins. His descendants built cities, manufactured tools and musical instruments, and composed music. God's original plan for marriage was abandoned and violence began to take over (Gen. 4:16–24). There's nothing wrong with cities, tools, and music, *unless you leave God out of the picture*, and that's exactly what Cain's descendants did. The civilization that Cain built became so wicked and violent that the Lord finally had to wipe the earth clean with a flood (Gen. 6:1–13).

Cain was a counterfeiter, and his sons and daughters followed in his footsteps. When you compare the names of Cain's descendants (Gen. 4:16–18) with those of the godly line of Seth, who replaced Abel (Gen. 5), you see several similarities—Enoch/Enosh/Enoch (4:17; 5:6, 18); Mehujael/Mahalalel (4:18; 5:12); Methushael/Methuselah (4:18; 5:21); and Lamech/Lamech (4:18; 5:25). But Seth's line ends at Noah, the man who, with his family, saved the human race. Cain's Enoch had the same name as Seth's Enoch, but Cain's Enoch didn't walk with God and then go to heaven (Gen. 5:22–24).

Alas, the line of godless Cain and godly Seth got closer and closer, and before long they merged (Gen. 6:1–2), and Noah and his family were the only faithful people God could find on the earth. The Lord decided to wipe out the Cainite civilization and start over again with Noah's family. God wiped the earth clean, but the hearts of the inhabitants were as sinful as ever. Nimrod took up the task of restoring Cain's civilization and built Babylon (Gen. 10:8–10), a project that so defied God, He stopped their work. Throughout Scripture, Babylon represents "the world," man-made society that is without God and attempts to be a substitute for God. Babylon is contrasted with the heavenly city in Revelation 17–18; one is the filthy harlot and the other is the pure virgin bride.

All true believers in Jesus Christ have their citizenship in heaven (Luke 10:20; Phil. 3:19–20) and don't belong to the world system that so fascinates Cain's descendants (John 17:14–17). But "the sons of this world are more shrewd in their generation than the sons of light," said Jesus (Luke 16:8 NKJV)—and they are. They know how to make money and achieve what the world calls "success," but they enjoy it only "in their generation." They can't see beyond this world and never seem to take eternity into consideration. Consequently, what they live for won't bring satisfaction and won't last. Scripture bears this out:

"Fallen! Fallen is Babylon the Great!"
REVELATION 18:2

The world and its desires pass away, but the man who does the will of God lives forever.
1 JOHN 2:17

Cain - Belonged to the evil one.
The way of Cain - Jude 11 ... unbelief, self-righteous, man-made religion.
Cain was a counterfeiter.
Cain killed Abel. Cain was a builder of a city — founder of the world. — the civilization became wicked and violent. THUS: THE FLOOD!
Cain - cloaked in false righteousness of religious activity.

6

ABEL

By faith he was commended as a righteous man.

HEBREWS 11:4

ABEL - means meaningless, vanity.

The most important thing in life isn't what we think about ourselves or what others think about us, but what God thinks about us. He is the final Judge. When He examines and evaluates our motives, words, and actions, are we commended, as was Abel, or are we condemned, as was his brother Cain? "The LORD does not look at the things man looks at," God told the prophet Samuel. "Man looks at the outward appearance, but the LORD looks at the heart" (1 Sam. 16:7).

From a human point of view, both brothers were good sons, hard workers, and openly religious; but from the divine perspective, Cain's heart belonged to the Devil, while Abel's heart belonged to the Lord. Because of Abel's faith, God commended him as a righteous man. If we want God's approval, we need that kind of righteousness, but what kind of righteousness is it?

RIGHTEOUSNESS THAT COMES BY FAITH

"By faith Abel offered God a better sacrifice than Cain did. By faith he was commended as a righteous man, when God spoke well of his offerings" (Heb. 11:4). Faith is only as good as the object, and the object of Abel's faith was the Lord God. Adam and Eve had learned that they couldn't cover their sins through their own efforts of sewing together leafy garments. When God clothed them in animal skins, He taught them that the way of forgiveness is through the shedding of innocent blood (Gen. 3:7, 21). Abel learned this important lesson from his parents and followed their example by trusting what the Lord said. He was saved by faith and clothed in God's own righteousness.

The fundamental truth that God's righteousness is received by faith is found throughout the Scriptures, because this is the only way God can save sinners. "Abram believed the LORD, and he credited it to him as righteousness" (Gen. 15:6). "Blessed is he whose transgressions are forgiven, whose sins are covered," sang David after months of disobedience and deception. "Blessed is the man whose sin the LORD does not count against him and in whose spirit there is no deceit" (Ps. 32:1–2). The apostle Paul quoted Genesis 15:6 and Psalm 32:1–2 in the fourth chapter of his epistle to the Romans to help explain the marvelous doctrine of justification by faith, being once-for-all declared righteous through faith in Jesus Christ. The prophet Habakkuk condensed all of this to seven words: "The righteous will live by his faith" (Hab. 2:4), a verse that is quoted in Romans 1:17; Galatians 3:11; and Hebrews 10:37–38.

God honored Abel's faith because Abel brought the right sacrifice. Paul made that clear in Romans 5:9: "Since we have now been justified by [Christ's] blood..." Justification isn't simply some kind of commercial transaction whereby God winks at our sins and wipes the record clean. God warned our first parents that they would die if they disobeyed Him, so justification is a matter of life and death. Jesus bore our sins when He died for us on the cross, and when we trust Him, we receive His righteousness put on our account. Justification is costly.

RIGHTEOUSNESS THAT LEADS TO GOOD CHARACTER AND GOOD WORKS

False righteousness, such as Cain's, cloaks its sins in the garment of religious activities. The pretender can go to the altar, offer a sacrifice to God, and then walk away and murder his own brother, but the true believer leaves the gift at the altar and seeks reconciliation (Matt. 5:23–24). Because of his faith, Abel had experienced a change of heart and life that resulted in good character and good works. With Cain, deception reigned through hypocrisy, but for Abel, grace reigned through righteousness (Rom. 5:21).

Why did Cain murder his brother? "Because his own actions were evil and his brother's were righteous" (1 John 3:12). We don't know how God revealed his acceptance of Abel's sacrifice; perhaps fire came from heaven or God spoke to him audibly. By using the plural "offerings," Hebrews 11:4 may suggest that this divine approval was given each time Abel came to the altar; and perhaps each time Cain noticed it, he became angrier and more resentful. What a tragedy to come to worship God and then go away filled with thoughts of murder!

Had you questioned Cain, you probably would have discovered that his theology was fairly sound. He believed in God and believed that God had created all things. He believed that God wanted to receive worship and thanksgiving. He believed that he and his brother were supposed to work and carry their share of the family burdens. But the demons believe in one God, and they aren't saved; and when they think about God, they tremble—something Cain didn't do (James 2:19). That's why James added, "As the body without the spirit is dead, so faith without deeds is dead" (James 2:26).

Dead faith is deceptive faith, but it doesn't fool God. True saving faith makes the believer into a new creation, with a new Master, new motives, new priorities, and new desires to love God and one's neighbor. Jesus called Abel "righteous Abel" (Matt. 23:35), and John said that Abel's actions were righteous, so in both character and conduct, he proved to be a righteous man.

RIGHTEOUSNESS THAT BEARS WITNESS

The righteousness of God was seen not only in Abel's life and worship but also in his death. Abel was slain because he faithfully worshiped and served the Lord, and the crime was committed by a member of his own household (Matt. 10:36). It was obvious to Cain, the firstborn, that God had bypassed him and chosen his younger brother to carry on the messianic promise, an act the Lord frequently did in Jewish history. God rejected Ishmael, Abraham's firstborn, and chose Isaac (Gen. 17:17–20), and then He bypassed Esau, Isaac's firstborn, in favor of Jacob. Jacob replaced Reuben, his firstborn son by Leah, for Joseph, his firstborn son by his beloved Rachel (Gen. 49:1–4). Jacob had already "adopted" Joseph's two sons as his own, making Ephraim, the younger grandson, the firstborn instead of Manasseh, the elder grandson (Gen. 48:15–20). The message of these changes is clear: God rejects our first birth, and therefore we need a second birth, a "new birth" from above (John 3:3–7), if we are to enjoy God's blessing. In His sovereign grace, God chooses the least and gives them the most (1 Cor. 1:26–31).

Cain tried to conceal his terrible sin, but his brother's blood cried out to the Lord from the ground, bearing witness that Cain had murdered him (Gen. 4:9–12). The English word *martyr* comes from the Greek word that means "witness," for a martyr is one who bears witness by giving his life for the Lord. Abel was a martyr-witness for the Lord, the first martyr recorded in the Bible.

The name Abel (*hebel*) means "vanity" or "meaninglessness." It's the same word Solomon used in Ecclesiastes at least thirty-eight times. One of my seminary professors defined *hebel* as "what's left over after a soap bubble breaks." Why Adam and Eve chose that name for their second son is a mystery; perhaps life had become meaningless for them in the cruel world, especially when they recalled the delightful days they had spent in Eden.

But Abel's life and death were not meaningless or a tragic waste, for Abel is associated with the Lord Jesus Christ. As believers, we have come "to Jesus the mediator of a new covenant, and to the sprinkled blood that speaks a better word than the blood of Abel" (Heb. 12:24). While Abel's blood cried out from the ground for God to avenge his death, the blood of Jesus speaks from heaven of mercy and forgiveness, for His blood has obtained eternal redemption for all who will believe on Him (Heb. 9:12). Abel died as a martyr, but Jesus died as a victor and arose again to ascend to glory.

Paul's great desire was that Christ be exalted in his body "whether by life or by death" (Phil. 1:20). And it was Paul who gave us 1 Corinthians 15, that great resurrection chapter, which climaxes with this marvelous assurance: "Therefore, my dear brothers, stand firm. Let nothing move you. Always give yourselves fully to the work of the Lord, because you know that your labor in the Lord is not in vain" (v. 58).

"Utterly meaningless! Everything is meaningless," scoffed King Solomon at the opening of Ecclesiastes. Life is *hebel* from start to finish!

"Not so!" said Paul. "Your labor in the Lord is not in vain!"

Christ has been resurrected and glorified. Abel has been vindicated.

7

NOAH – *Rest*
walked w God. 5:22 6:9

Noah did everything just as God commanded him. *4x's*

GENESIS 6:22

*obedient. Builder. Preacher
walked w. God.*

*D*oing everything that God commands is not easy when the world around
you is rapidly turning into a cesspool and the only believers you know are the
members of your own family. Yet four times the narrative of Noah's life says that
he did everything just as God commanded (6:22; 7:5, 9, 16). *4x's*

Noah's father was Lamech, a descendant of Seth. He is not to be confused
with the Cainite Lamech who was a bigamist and murderer (Gen. 4:19–24).
Lamech was 182 years old when Noah was born. He was a farmer who was weary
of trying to coax a harvest out of the ground that the Lord God had cursed,
and that's why he called his son "Noah," which means "rest" or "comfort" (Gen.
5:8–29). "He will comfort us in the labor and painful toil of our hands," Lamech
said, but he didn't explain how his son would do this. Lamech remembered God's
promise that a Redeemer would come and overcome the Devil and the curse
(Gen. 3:14–15), and perhaps he hoped that little Noah was the fulfillment of
that promise.

Well, he wasn't, but he did point to the One who is, because there are similarities between Jesus and Noah. For one thing, Noah became a builder and a
preacher, and Jesus was a builder turned preacher. When Jesus began His public
ministry, his neighbors called Him "the carpenter" (Mark 6:1–3), so He must
have been helping Joseph in the carpentry shop during those growing-up years
in Nazareth. The apostle Peter connects Noah and the flood with Christ (1 Peter
3:18–22), for in the flood, the old earth experienced death, burial, and resurrection. When the flood came, the only salvation available was in the ark, and today
our only salvation is in Christ. Peter said that in Acts 4:12. *Builder
Preacher*

HIS WALK WITH GOD

Like his famous ancestor Enoch, Noah walked with God (Gen. 5:22; 6:9); he
was righteous toward God and blameless toward his neighbors. His righteousness
came from God because of God's favor and Noah's faith in God's promise. He
and his family were saved just as sinners are saved today — by grace (Gen. 6:8),
through faith in Jesus Christ (Eph. 2:8–9; Heb. 11:7) — and they proved their

faith by their works. "Do two walk together unless they have agreed to do so?" (Amos 3:3). Noah and his family agreed with the Lord, so they walked with the Lord.

When we consider how wicked society was in that day, we can understand how difficult it was for Noah's family to maintain their walk with God. Righteous people enjoy peace with God but conflict with those who hate God and disobey Him. "The fruit of righteousness will be peace; the effect of righteousness will be quietness and confidence forever" (Isa. 32:17). But light exposes the things of darkness, and those who do evil hate the light (John 3:20). We complain today because a few people persecute us for our faith, but Noah had an entire world against him and his family!

HIS PROCLAMATION OF GOD'S MESSAGE

People forget that Noah was not only a builder but also a "preacher of righteousness" (2 Peter 2:5). As a builder, he prepared for the coming judgment, and as a preacher, he called rebellious sinners to repent and invited them to find safety in the ark. Noah was a righteous man, so he had the right to declare God's message of righteousness (see Ezek. 14:14, 20), but the people didn't heed his message. God determined that humankind had 120 years of grace and then judgment would fall (Gen. 6:3), and at the end of that period, only Noah and his family—eight people—were saved from judgment. All preachers, teachers, missionaries, and Christian witnesses who feel that their efforts have failed should remember Noah's patience and keep being faithful.

Noah was called to preach ("herald") righteousness to an unrighteous population, so his message wasn't very popular. Enoch had preceded him in declaring God's message to an evil age (Jude 14–15), but after Enoch was taken to heaven, things didn't get any better on earth. "The LORD saw how great man's wickedness on the earth had become, and that every inclination of the thoughts of his heart was only evil all the time.... Now the earth was corrupt in God's sight and was full of violence" (Gen. 6:5, 11). The Cainite "civilization" had taken over, and God's longsuffering was about to come to an end.

HIS OBEDIENCE TO GOD'S ORDERS

The main purpose of the ark was the preservation of humankind and all creatures that had "the breath of life," but even its construction was a sermon in action. Apparently it hadn't rained prior to the flood (Gen. 2:4–6; Heb. 11:7), so the neighbors must have wondered why Noah and his sons were building a boat on dry land. His message about a coming storm of judgment no doubt gave them many a laugh as they ate and drank and attended wedding parties. Jesus said that society would be like that just before His return (Matt. 24:36–41).

The Lord gave Noah all the instructions he needed for the building of the ark, just as He gave Moses the plans for the tabernacle (Ex. 25:9, 40; Heb. 8:5) and David the plans for the temple (1 Chron. 28:11–19). Step by step, as we obey the Lord, He will show us the paths He has marked out for our lives (Pss. 16:11; 23:3).

When the work was completed, God brought the animals to the ark, and Noah put them in (Gen. 6:19–20; 7:8–9, 15). At the Lord's command, Noah led his family into the ark, and God closed the door (Gen. 7:1, 16). "Noah went in first, and his wife and family followed him," said D. L. Moody. "He had lived such a life as to give his children confidence in him. If you parents do not go into the ark yourselves, how can you expect your children to go in?"[1] It would be tragic to bring others to the faith but not your own family.

HIS PATIENCE

For 120 years, Noah patiently preached to the people and worked on the ark, always walking with the Lord and seeking to please Him. That's a long wait. Then God invited him and his family into the ark where they waited a week (Gen. 7:4). Finally, the rains began to fall, and they were in the ark with the animals for one year and seventeen days (Gen. 8:13–14). One of the church fathers is supposed to have said that being in the ark was something like being in the church on earth: if it weren't for the judgment on the outside, you could never stand the smell on the inside. Even after the water began to subside, Noah waited for the Lord's signal to disembark, and when it came, he and his family obeyed (Gen. 8:13–19).

The ability to wait upon the Lord is a mark of faith and spiritual maturity, and Noah had both. "Whoever believes will not act hastily" (Isa. 28:16 NKJV).

HIS WORSHIP

There is no record that the Lord commanded Noah to build the altar and offer the sacrifices. It was something Noah did from his own heart in response to the Lord's grace and mercy in saving him and his family. As we learned from the Cain episode, the value of the sacrifice depended on the heart of the worshiper, and Noah was a man of faith whose heart was fixed on the Lord. As lord of the renewed creation, his first act was to lift heart and soul to God and give Him all the glory.

God was delighted and gave Noah and his family, his descendants, and all creation the assurance that there would never be another flood and that the cycle of the seasons would not be interrupted. The sign of this covenant, the rainbow, reminds us today that God will never break His promise.

HIS REPROACH

"Noah did everything just as God commanded him"—except when he got drunk and shamefully exposed himself (Gen. 20–28). Unlike many biographies, the Bible tells the truth about its heroes, including their faults and failures. Twice Abraham lied about his wife, and his son Isaac followed his bad example. Moses

---

1. W. H. Daniels, *Moody: His Words, Work and Workers* (Chicago: Nelson and Phillips, 1877), 144–45.

lost his temper and struck the rock. David committed adultery with Bathsheba and arranged to have her husband slain in battle; and Peter lost his courage and denied Jesus three times.

Some students feel that Noah wasn't to blame for what happened. They suggest that, following the storm and the flood, dramatic changes occurred on the earth and in its atmosphere, and these changes produced fermentation, something Noah had never seen before. But if the novel taste of fermented wine excited Noah and caused him to drink more, it was still his own lack of discipline that led him into drunkenness and nakedness, and the two often go together (Lam. 4:21; Hab. 2:15–16).

When you compare Genesis 9:24 and 10:21, you learn that Ham was Noah's youngest son, Japheth his oldest, and Shem the son in between. Shem is named first because he was given the greatest blessing and was treated like the firstborn (Gen. 9:26). This is another biblical instance of the second-born being made the firstborn. Ham had dishonored his father, and Noah found out about it and prophesied that Canaan, Ham's youngest son (Gen. 10:6), would become slaves of the lowest kind. The Canaanite nations were indescribably wicked (see Lev. 18), which explains why Moses wanted Israel to wipe them out. Those who survived eventually became slaves to Israel. I shouldn't have to add this note, but this so-called curse of Noah has nothing to do with the black races and slavery.

Why did Moses include this account of Noah's drunkenness and indecency and Ham's disrespect? For one thing, the emphasis in Scripture is on the descendants of Shem, especially Abraham (Gen. 11:10–12:9), and the descendants of Canaan would play a big part in their history. But there is another reason: God wants to remind us that all heroes are human and all humans are sinners. Noah was a great man who did a great work, but he didn't end well, and that can happen to any of us. "Noah did everything just as God commanded him"—except for misusing the wine. If we want to end well, we must beware of permitting exceptions. They can be costly.

NOAH - REST COMFORT. NOAH WALKED W GOD. Preacher of Righteousness.

obedient when called by God.

8

ABRAHAM – *Faithful. Believed God.*
Faithful in spite of consequence.

By faith Abraham, when called ... obeyed.

HEBREWS 11:8

Just about the time a person finishes one test another pops up.

Poet and priest Geoffrey A. Studdart-Kennedy wisely wrote, "Faith is not believing in spite of evidence; faith is obeying in spite of consequence."

Daniel's three friends understood what it meant to live by faith. "The God
we serve is able to save us," they boldly told Nebuchadnezzar. "But even if he
does not, we will not serve your gods or worship the image of gold you have
set up" (Dan. 3:17–18 paraphrased). That's faith—obeying in spite of consequence. It's the kind of faith that Abraham practiced, and we should follow his
example.

Believing God doesn't mean sitting down and enjoying a comfortable feeling
while we think beautiful thoughts. Believing God means standing up and facing
an impossible challenge without fear of what might happen when we obey God's
will. It's Joshua and the people of Israel crossing the Jordan River and conquering
Canaan; it's young David on the battlefield defeating a giant single-handedly; it's
Esther in the palace saying, "If I perish, I perish"; and it's young Mary in Nazareth
saying, "I am the Lord's servant. May it be to me as you have said."

Next to our Lord Jesus Christ, perhaps the greatest example of faith in
Scripture is the patriarch Abraham. From Genesis 11:27 through 25:11, we follow his adventure of faith and seek to imitate his victories and avoid his mistakes. Abraham failed occasionally just as we all do, but the general trend of
his life was marked by faithful obedience. No matter what God called him to
do, he believed that God's calling involved God's enabling, and he obeyed God
by faith. If with the limited promises that Abraham had, he could successfully
walk by faith, what ought we be able to do who possess the entire Word of
God!

Let's learn from Abraham to respond in obedient faith to God's calling.

WHEN WE ARE CALLED TO AN UNKNOWN FUTURE

"By faith Abraham, when called ..., obeyed ..., even though he did not
know where he was going" (Heb. 11:8). At the age of seventy-five, Abraham said
farewell to Ur of the Chaldees, tarried in Haran, and then headed for Canaan

(Gen. 11:27–12:9). "They set out for the land of Canaan," says the record, "and they arrived there." How we would like to know more about that journey, but only a comma separates the departure from the arrival. This we do know: Abraham obeyed God a day at a time, a step at a time, trusting Him to lead the way, and the Lord didn't fail him.

We rarely travel that way today. The motor club, travel agent, or computer provides us with detailed maps that identify the best stopping places and the worst road construction sites, and fortified with this up-to-date information, our route and destination clearly identified, we bravely set forth. Some vehicles are even equipped with sophisticated global positioning devices that help you find the right neighborhood, the right street, and the exact house you're looking for.

But Abraham didn't know where he was going! And even if we today take advantage of all the travel aids mentioned in the previous paragraph, we have to admit that we don't know where we are going. We make plans, but they don't always work out as we expected. I was driving home late one evening but didn't arrive there until two weeks later. A drunk driver hit me going more than eighty miles an hour, and I ended up in the intensive care ward of a local hospital where I lived for a week before being transferred to my own room for another week. It was an interesting place to celebrate Father's Day, but praise God, I was still alive and could wave to the children from my window.

Occasionally I pick up my copy of the old *Keswick Hymnal* and read the nutritious lyrics of a hymn, such as #122, by J. Parker, a writer I have not been able to identify.

> God holds the key of all unknown, and I am glad;
> If other hands should hold the key,
> Or if He trusted it to me,
> I might be sad.
> What if tomorrow's cares were here, without its rest?
> I'd rather He unlocked the day,
> And as the hours swing open, say,
> "My will is best."
> I cannot read His future plans, but this I know:
> I have the smiling of His face,
> And all the refuge of His grace
> While here below.
> Enough — this covers all my wants, and so I rest;
> For what I cannot, He can see,
> And in His care I saved shall be,
> Forever blest.

Perhaps Abraham sang similar hymns as he traveled by faith, following the Lord. Called to an unknown future, he obeyed by faith.

WHEN WE ARE CALLED TO TAKE SECOND PLACE

Since we are focusing on Abraham's faith, we will not dwell on his unbelief and wretched conduct in Egypt. He had sense enough to return to Canaan, build an altar, and get right with the Lord. But in the life of faith, just about the time a person finishes one test, another one takes its place. For years I have threatened to write a book and call it *There's Always Something!*

When Abraham was called by God to leave his native city, he was commanded to leave his family as well (Gen. 12:1), but he took his father, his wife, and his nephew Lot with him. After Terah died in Haran, Abraham and Sarah resumed the journey and took Lot with them. This was a mistake, for they were supposed to leave their family. Lot created problems for them, because, while in Egypt, he picked up some ideas that no good Jewish boy should consider. It's likely that when Pharaoh gave gifts to Abraham, he also included Lot, so that both men became wealthy and had extensive flocks and herds. But their wealth was also a problem, because flocks and herds insist on having grass to eat and water to drink, and there just wasn't enough grass and water in that area for both men's animals.

Had Lot been mature and spiritual, he would have met Abraham at the altar, offered a sacrifice and prayed, and then worked the problem out, yielding his will to that of his godly uncle. But Abraham had to take the first step, and because he was a man of faith, he stepped down to second place and let Lot choose first! Lot was a troublemaker, but Abraham was a peacemaker. Lot measured everything by the values of Egypt (Gen. 13:10), while Abraham thought only of the glory of God. After all, the Canaanites and Perizzites were watching them (Gen. 13:7), and Abraham wanted to be a good witness. Lot walked by sight (Gen. 13:10), while Abraham walked by faith, knowing that the whole land belonged to him anyway! Lot was gazing at Sodom, but Abraham was looking by faith at that heavenly city that God was preparing for him (Heb. 11:10, 13–16). Abraham's values were based on the realities of eternity, not the passing fads of Egypt.

What difference does it make if we must take second place behind someone who isn't fit to lead, as long as Jesus Christ is first in our lives and He gets all the glory? The Lord was pleased with Abraham and reassured him that everything was in His control and there was nothing to fear. Abraham never read Matthew 6:33, but he did practice it. He just kept walking by faith.

WHEN WE ARE CALLED TO RESCUE SOMEBODY WHO MAY NOT DESERVE IT

Lot chose the fruitful plains of Jordan, not only because of its ample pastures and water supply, but primarily because he had his eye on Sodom. Eventually he moved closer to the city, forsook his tents and pilgrim life, and then became a resident of the city (Gen. 13:12; 14:12). When the four kings invaded and captured the cities of the plain, Lot was taken prisoner, but Abraham was not. Abraham in his tent was safer than Lot in a walled city. Lot received exactly what he deserved, but Abraham didn't abandon him. By faith, Abraham rallied the troops and rescued all the inhabitants of Sodom, and he did it for Lot's sake. Lot probably wouldn't have done that for Abraham.

This experience should have warned Lot to return to the tents and altar and to the God of Abraham, but he didn't get the message. When God decided to destroy Sodom and the other cities of the plain, it was Abraham outside of Sodom who first got the message and not Lot, who was sitting in the gate with the other leaders of the city. "The LORD confides in those who fear him" (Ps. 25:14), and Lot didn't qualify.

Knowing what kind of people lived in Sodom, most of us would have been happy to see them wiped out, but Abraham interceded for the city and the people he had witnessed to when he rescued them (Gen. 18:16–33). Of course, he was thinking again of his nephew. The Lord destroyed Sodom, but for the sake of Abraham, He permitted Lot to escape (Gen. 19; note especially v. 29). Abraham's faith and faithfulness meant salvation for Lot and Lot's two daughters. Lot's incest led to the founding of the Ammonite and Moabite nations, people who were enemies of the Jews. That was a fine way to thank Uncle Abraham!

Have you ever sacrificed to help somebody who didn't thank you but turned right around and got into more trouble? Have you ever prayed for people in trouble, only to watch them do everything they could to make it difficult for God to answer your prayers? Then you know that it takes faith to obey Matthew 5:38–48 and Galatians 6:1–2 and to pray with Jesus, "Father, forgive them, for they do not know what they are doing" (Luke 23:34).

WHEN WE ARE CALLED TO WAIT

The life of faith involves not only the Lord's ministry to others through us but also the Lord's ministry to us personally. He wants us to experience His love and receive His grace so that we may accomplish the purposes He has in mind. We walk by faith, but we also wait by faith, and the waiting is as important as the walking.

In Genesis 15, the Lord brought Abraham into an experience that spiritual directors call "the dark night of the soul." Abraham found himself in "a thick and dreadful darkness" (v. 12). As a result, this great man of faith was afraid, uncertain, and frustrated, and he asked the Lord why He hadn't sent the son He had promised to him and Sarah. God permits these midnight experiences so that it is dark enough for us to see the stars and quiet enough to hear His voice reaffirm the promises He has made to us. The Lord made a covenant with Abraham that night and assured him ownership of the land, even though the land was possessed at that time by ten pagan nations. A difficult experience for Abraham? Yes, but what a boost to his faith.

But as time went on, Abraham and Sarah became impatient and Sarah began to make her own plans for helping the Lord provide the promised child (Gen. 16). Faith is living without scheming, and Abraham should have put his foot down and said no. If Sarah thought Lot had caused problems as a neighbor, she had no idea what Ishmael would do living right in their family! Abraham trusted God in the darkness, but now he doubted God in the daylight.

Waiting on the Lord is essential for the growing life of faith. Running ahead of the Lord and trusting our own resources only creates problems; that means missing God's best blessings for our lives.

WHEN WE ARE CALLED TO SACRIFICE WHAT WE LOVE

1st mentioned

God kept His word and in His time sent Abraham and Sarah the son who would carry on the messianic promise. God instructed them to call his name "Isaac" (Gen. 17:19), which means "laughter," because both Abraham and Sarah had laughed over the prospect of two elderly people having a baby (Gen. 17:17; 18:13–15; 21:6–7). Everybody who heard about it would laugh too!

How strange it was that God should ask Abraham to sacrifice the very son He had given them, the one on whom rested the future of the Jewish nation and the salvation of a lost world. The first time the word *love* is found in the Bible is in Genesis 22:2, where the Lord affirms Abraham's love for his only son. (Note that Ishmael isn't included, though he was Abraham's firstborn.) The first time the word *love* is found in the New Testament is in Matthew 3:17, where the heavenly Father affirms His love for His Son. Why would the Lord share a gift of love with Abraham and Sarah and then ask Abraham to slay the boy?

This was Abraham's greatest test of faith, but a faith that can't be tested can't be trusted. The tests that God permits help us to discover whether our faith is true or false, whether we are standing solidly on God's character and covenant promises or sinking slowly in the quicksand of deceptive feelings and elusive circumstances. Abraham focused on God's covenant promises and trusted God to work things out for His own glory. As it has well been said, God didn't want Abraham's *son*; He wanted Abraham's *heart*.

It is a basic law of the Christian life that we must give back to the Lord whatever He gives to us; otherwise those blessings may become idols that come between the Lord and us. By faith, Abraham obeyed God and yielded up Isaac—and received him back as if raised from the dead (Heb. 11:17–19). The spiritual experience of death and resurrection has always been God's way for His people to enjoy the abundant life (Rom. 6; 8). When God calls you to surrender up to Him the most precious thing you possess, do it by faith, knowing that this is the only way to receive it back as a blessing and not a burden.

WHEN WE ARE CALLED TO WEEP

Genesis 23 records the first funeral and the first tears in the Bible, and, interestingly enough, Sarah is the only woman in the Bible whose age at death is recorded. Sarah was a woman of faith just as Abraham was a man of faith (Heb. 11:11 NKJV, NASB, NIV margin note), and they were a team as they served the Lord.

1st mentioned

Abraham's tears weren't a mark of unbelief or defeat; they were evidence of his great love for his wife. God's people sorrow but not as those who have no hope (1 Thess. 4:13). Abraham set a good example for all of us in the way he honored Sarah and buried her, and he used the event as an opportunity to witness to his unsaved neighbors. The cave he purchased ultimately held the bodies of Sarah, Abraham, Isaac, Rebekah, Leah, and Jacob. The book of Genesis ends with a full tomb (Gen. 49:29–32), but our faith is founded on an empty tomb, for Jesus Christ came forth from the tomb and conquered death (1 Cor. 15:12–28, 54).

The longer we walk this pilgrim trail, our loved ones and friends leave us to be with the Lord. If the Lord doesn't return in our lifetime, we will go to join them. But we have nothing to fear. "For this God is our God for ever and ever; he will be our guide even to the end" (Ps. 48:14).

WHEN WE ARE CALLED TO DIE

Abraham lived to be 175 years of age, which means he had been walking with the Lord for a century (Gen. 25:5–11). He died in faith just as he had lived by faith, anticipating entering the glorious city on which his eyes had been fixed since the day God called him (Heb. 11:13–16). But before Abraham died, he wanted to be sure that Isaac had the right wife and the wealth he needed for himself and the generations to come. Blessed are those who consider the future generations! What an example Abraham had set for his descendants!

Knowing he would soon die, Abraham transferred all his wealth to Isaac (Gen. 24:34–36; 25:5). Then he sent his chief servant to the town of Nahor, where his relatives lived, to find the wife that the Lord had chosen for Isaac. The account given in Genesis 24 reveals the love of God, the providence of God, and the faithfulness of God in keeping His covenant promises. Abraham's faith and the steward's faithfulness combined to bring Isaac just the wife he needed. Isaac was surely privileged to have a father who was a giant in the faith!

Because Abraham was concerned about the next generation and made provision for them spiritually and materially, you and I have a Savior and a Bible. Isaac, Jacob, and the whole Jewish nation were blessed because of faithful Abraham, and the Lord deigns to be known as "the God of Abraham, the God of Isaac and the God of Jacob." True faith overcomes circumstances, transcends generations, and never fears death. True faith is living faith in the living Word. To quote Studdart-Kennedy again, "Faith is not believing in spite of evidence; faith is obeying in spite of consequence."

SARAH *means princess*

mother of Kings.

"Look to ... Sarah, who gave you birth."

ISAIAH 51:2

woman of faith

Sarah's given name Sarai is used seventeen times in the Old Testament, but we aren't sure what it means. When God changed Abram's name to Abraham, He also changed Sarai's name to Sarah, which means "princess" (Gen. 17:15–16). It's found forty-one times, so she's named fifty-eight times in Scripture, which is more times than the apostle John is named. God promised she would be the mother of kings, so He made her a princess. The only time she is mentioned in the Old Testament outside the book of Genesis is in Isaiah 51:2, the verse I have chosen for her "life sentence."

When people look at Sarah, what do they see?

ABRAHAM LOOKED TO SARAH AND SAW LOVE

Abraham and Sarah were pagan idolaters when they lived in Ur of the Chaldees (Josh. 24:1–3), a city that worshiped the moon god Nannar. "The God of glory" appeared to Abraham (Acts 7:1–3) and told him to leave Ur and his family and go to a land that He would show him. The Lord bypassed other people in that great city and revealed Himself to Abraham. What amazing grace!

How did Sarah respond when Abraham came home and told her that Nannar was a fake, that the only true and living God had spoken to him, and that she should start packing? She probably asked, "Where are we going?" and when Abraham replied, "I don't know—God didn't tell me," Sarah may have had second thoughts. But Scripture indicates that she was a woman of faith (Heb. 11:11), so she abandoned her idols, trusted the Lord, and went with her husband. She submitted to her husband who in turn had submitted to the Lord, which is the proper thing for a husband to do if he wants the respect and obedience of his wife (Eph. 5:21–33). She loved him and was willing to exchange her settled home in a prosperous city for a pilgrim's tent on the dangerous plains of an unknown country.

So, off they went, but they made the mistake of taking Abraham's father and nephew along. We rejoice that Abraham and Sarah told their relatives about the true God, but they were supposed to leave their relatives behind as witnesses. After all, Abraham wasn't leading a tour to the Holy Land; he was striking out by faith, without map or compass, and he didn't need any extra baggage. But he did need Sarah, and he knew it. "Sarah was a princess in name and in nature," wrote James Strahan in his book *Hebrew Ideals*. "She understood her husband's divine vocation, shared his religious aspiration, and never ceased to be his true helpmeet."[1] No wonder the apostle Peter held her up as an example for Christian women everywhere (1 Peter 3:1–6).

Because Sarah loved her husband, she carried in her heart a lie that they had agreed upon: she would pass as his sister and not as his wife (Gen. 20:11–13). This scheme protected Abraham's life, but it certainly jeopardized Sarah's purity—and she was to be the channel through whom the promised son would come. Faith is living without scheming. Twice this family secret got them into trouble.

ISAAC LOOKED TO SARAH AND SAW FAITH

The faith of Abraham and Sarah made possible the conception of their promised son Isaac. It is unfortunate that the New International Version translation of Hebrews 11:11—an extremely difficult verse in the original—has demoted Sarah to the margin, but better there than not at all. "By faith even Sarah, who was past age, was enabled to bear children...." When Sarah and Abraham first heard the good news that God would give them a son, they both laughed in unbelief because they were well beyond the age of having children. But the God of hope gave them joy and peace as they trusted Him (Rom. 15:13), and soon their incredulous laughter became holy laughter as they accepted the absurdity and impossibility of the whole matter and rejoiced in the greatness of the God of glory. If you can explain what's going on, God didn't do it. If you can't explain what's going on, then God did it, and all you can do is joyfully praise Him and go ahead and laugh!

ISAIAH LOOKED TO SARAH AND SAW HOPE

Now let's focus on Sarah's "life sentence" verse. It comes from the second section of the book of Isaiah, which he addressed particularly to the Jewish exiles in Babylon (Isa. 40–66). They would be in exile for seventy years (Jer. 25:8–14; see Dan. 9:1–3) and then be allowed to return home—but there wasn't much to return to! The Babylonians had ruined Judah and Jerusalem, destroyed the temple, and greatly reduced the population. It wouldn't be easy for the exiles to travel that long distance from Babylon to Judah, and was it really worth it? Could a small remnant of prisoners of war restore their country and rebuild their nation? If ever a group of people faced an impossible task, those Jewish exiles were that group.

But Isaiah knew how to encourage them. First he told them to *look around* and contemplate the greatness of the Lord in creation (Isa. 40). We humans may be like grass that grows up in the morning and withers by evening, but the eternal

---

1. James Strahan, *Hebrew Ideals in Genesis* (Grand Rapids, Mich.: Baker, 1982), 111.

God created all things and sustains them by His mighty power. No one is greater than He. The Jews had abandoned the Lord and turned to idols, and that is why He disciplined them in Babylon; but helpless man-made idols could never accomplish what only Jehovah could do. The great God of creation was their God, and He would fulfill His purposes for them.

But did the Lord still love them? After all, they had disobeyed His will and broken His heart. Isaiah told them to *look up* and see the Lord as a loving shepherd who protected the sheep and carried the weary lambs (40:11). Then he repeated the same command four times: "Do not fear!" (41:10, 13, 14; 43:1–2). God is going to work on your behalf, so listen to His Word and claim His promises. Look up!

In Isaiah 51:2, he urged the people to *look back* and remember their humble beginnings. The nation of Israel didn't descend from heaven on a cloud; it was dug out of a pit like stones from a quarry! The nation began with a man seventy-five years old, whose wife was sixty-five years old, too old to have a family, and yet to them God gave the promise of descendants as numerous as the sand on the seashore and the stars in the heavens (Gen. 13:14–17; 15:5). If God could build a nation out of two elderly people, couldn't He rebuild the nation from the feeble remnant of Jewish exiles? The Lord kept His promise to Abraham and He would keep His promises to Abraham's descendants.

When the Jewish remnant began to rebuild their temple, it seemed an insignificant structure compared with the magnificent temple Solomon had built, and the old people wept (Ezra 3:11–13; Hag. 2:3), but the Lord sent the prophet Zechariah to ask them, "Who despises the day of small things?" (Zech. 4:10). Look back to Abraham and Sarah who founded the nation, and remember that out of that impossible beginning the Lord built a great and mighty people. From small beginnings, humanly speaking, the Lord can do great things that glorify His name. This is a good word of encouragement for anybody who has lost hope and wants to give up. "Not by might nor by power, but by my Spirit," was the promise God gave them through Zechariah (4:6), and that promise is still valid today.

GOD'S PEOPLE TODAY LOOK TO SARAH AND SEE FREEDOM

Paul took the accounts of Sarah and Hagar in Genesis 16 and 21 and wrote an inspired interpretation of them as a beautiful and profound allegory. What he wrote helps us understand who we are in Christ and the privileges we can enjoy in grace (Gal. 4:21–31). His purpose was to explain to the religious legalists in the Galatian churches that by mixing the law of Moses with the gospel of Jesus Christ, they were defying the very commandment of God. Here is the cast of characters:

Hagar, a slave girl, represents the law (earthly Jerusalem)
Sarah, a free woman, represents grace (heavenly Jerusalem)
Ishmael, a slave boy, born after the flesh
Isaac, a free son, born by God's grace and power

To begin with, Abraham was never supposed to take Hagar. In an hour of weakness, he disobeyed God, turning from faith to sight and from the Spirit to the flesh. From the sixth day of creation, when God made Adam and Eve, He did everything on the basis of grace, and this continued in His dealings with Noah, Abraham, Isaac, Jacob, and Joseph. God gave promises — that's grace; His people believed and obeyed Him, and He blessed them. The law was added (Gal. 3:19); it wasn't there from the beginning. Promise and grace go together and release God's power; law and self-effort go together and encourage the works of the flesh. "The power of sin is the law" (1 Cor. 15:56).

Sarah was wrong when she suggested her husband give her a child by Hagar, but Sarah was right when she told Abraham to cast out Hagar and her son. Grace sets us free, but law enslaves us. Law tells us that we need grace, and grace enables us to obey the law by the power of the Holy Spirit (Rom. 8:3). Believers today are not like Ishmael but like Isaac (Gal. 4:28). We were born by God's power in response to His promise, we were born rich, and we were born free. If Sarah represents grace and Abraham represents faith, then Isaac was born "by grace … through faith" (Eph. 2:8–9). No law ever given could enable two old people with "dead" bodies the power to produce a son! "For if a law had been given that could impart life, then righteousness would certainly have come by the law" (Gal. 3:21).

God didn't want Abraham to have a "blended family," mixing law and grace, freedom and bondage, God's power and human efforts. The old nature knows no law, and the new nature needs no law. "It is for freedom that Christ has set us free" (Gal. 5:1), so let's enjoy that freedom to the glory of God.

BELIEVING WIVES LOOK TO SARAH AND SEE BEAUTY

To escape the famine in the Promised Land, Abraham fled to Egypt, a sin that his descendants would commit many times (Ex. 16:1–3; 17:1–3; Num. 14:1–4; Isa. 30:1–5; 31:1–3; Jer. 37:1–10). As they entered Egypt, Abraham didn't want Sarah to become a widow, so he reminded her of their secret. Sure enough, the Egyptians said Sarah was beautiful, Pharaoh's officers said she was beautiful, and Pharaoh agreed with them and brought her into his harem (Gen. 12:10–16). This sin was repeated later in Gerar (Gen. 20), and that is where we learn about their secret. However, Peter used this story, not to blame Abraham (although Abraham was wrong to doubt God and imperil his wife) but to extol Sarah as a model of a believing wife.

Some of the Christian wives in Peter's day were trying to win their unsaved husbands by cultivating an artificial beauty and adopting a domineering attitude (1 Peter 3:1–6). They followed the worldly examples of the unconverted Greek and Roman women, but Peter urged them to follow the examples of the godly women in Scripture, especially Sarah. It wasn't necessary for these Christian wives to preach to their husbands or to show off their jewels, coiffeurs, and expensive clothing, because that's not what would bring them to Christ. True beauty comes from within; it's natural, not artificial, "the unfading beauty of a gentle and quiet spirit" (1 Peter 3:4). This is what pleases God, and when we please Him, we can trust Him to do the rest.

The wives were afraid that their husbands would dislike them and perhaps desert them if they weren't as "attractive" as their godless neighbors and friends, but Peter told them to calm down and submit to their husbands in love and faith. Sarah called Abraham "master" (Gen. 18:12) because she loved him and therefore submitted to him, and there was no fear in her heart. No matter how old she became, Sarah was always Abraham's "beautiful wife."

Every age has its fashions and fads that point the way to expensive artificial beauty that ultimately cheapens a person. Since the world does look on the outward appearance (1 Sam. 16:7), Christians should look as attractive as possible; but even more important is the beauty of the heart, the fruit of the Spirit that the world can't successfully imitate (Gal. 5:22–23). "Charm is deceptive, and beauty is fleeting; but a woman who fears the LORD is to be praised" (Prov. 31:30).

Whether we need to grow in love, faith, hope, freedom, or true beauty, we will be helped if we look to Princess Sarah, the mother of all who believe.

Woman of faith   Mother of kings.
Sarah - freedom   Hagar - law.
Princess!

10

ISAAC

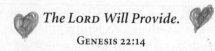 *The LORD Will Provide.*

GENESIS 22:14

Jehovah Jireh — "The LORD Will Provide" — is one of the compound names of the Lord found in the Old Testament. It is the name Abraham gave to the place where he offered his son on the altar and where the Lord supplied the ram to die in Isaac's place. But "The LORD Will Provide" also describes Isaac's experience, not just on Mount Moriah, but throughout his entire life, for God always supplied whatever he needed.

Isaac was the son of a famous father and the father of a famous son, and because of this seems to lack the luster and adventure that we associate with Abraham and Jacob. Isaac lived 180 years (Gen. 35:28–29), longer than his father or his son, and yet those years weren't especially eventful. "Abraham is more interesting than Isaac," said G. Campbell Morgan, "and Jacob is more interesting than Isaac — to us, but not to God."[1] We who have trusted Christ "like Isaac, are children of promise" (Gal. 4:28), and one of God's great promises is that He will supply our every need through the riches we have in Jesus Christ (Phil. 4:19). So, this sacred name describes the experience of believers today if we will but walk by faith.

PROVISION FOR ISAAC

As long as Isaac walked by faith, the Lord provided whatever he needed. To begin with, God provided Isaac with *an inheritance*. Abraham had to build his wealth year by year, and so did Jacob, but Isaac was born rich. Sarah was concerned that Ishmael might try to steal from Isaac's inheritance (Gen. 21:10). Abraham gave gifts to the sons of his concubines and of his second wife, Keturah, but he gave "everything he owned to Isaac" (Gen. 25:1–6). "My master's wife Sarah has borne him a son in her old age," Abraham's servant told Laban, "and he has given him everything he owns" (Gen. 24:35–36). Isaac's crops doubled and his flocks and herds were the envy of his neighbors (Gen. 26:12–14) because he trusted the God whose name is The LORD Will Provide.

This doesn't mean that God will make each of His children wealthy in the

---

1. G. Campbell Morgan, *26 Sermons* (Joplin, Mo.: College Press, 1969), 79.

material things of life, because that just doesn't happen. Christian investors don't miraculously double their money, nor do land owners automatically double their holdings. But David's testimony becomes the witness of every trusting child of God: "I was young and now I am old, yet I have never seen the righteous forsaken or their children begging bread" (Ps. 37:25). We have every spiritual blessing in Christ, and we share in "the riches of his glorious inheritance in the saints" (Eph. 1:3, 18). We are "heirs of God and co-heirs with Christ" (Rom. 8:17).

We have already noted that the Lord provided *a substitute* to die in Isaac's place, just as He provided His own Son Jesus Christ to die in our place. This in itself should convince us that God will meet our needs, for if He gave us His very best gift, why would He withhold any other blessing that we need? "He who did not spare his own Son, but gave him up for us all—how will he not also, along with him, graciously give us all things?" (Rom. 8:32). When we have Jesus Christ, what more do we need?

When Isaac was forty years old, God provided him with just *the wife he needed* and Rebekah was worth waiting for (Gen. 25:20). It was important that he have the right wife because he and Rebekah were involved in the messianic promise.

If Isaac's neighbors created problems for him, God enabled him to avoid conflict and ultimately win their friendship (Gen. 26:12–31). Unfortunately, his son Esau created conflict in the home by marrying pagan women (Gen. 26:34–35). More than one faithful child of God has had to bear this kind of burden.

Best of all, the Lord gave Isaac *the assurance of heaven.* The patriarchs lived by faith and died by faith, always anticipating the heavenly city God was preparing for them (Heb. 11:13–16). We today live in an increasingly dangerous world, but no matter what happens to us here on earth, we know we have a home in heaven. Jesus is in heaven now preparing this home for His people (John 14:1–6), and when the time comes, He will either call us home personally or return to take His whole church to glory. The future is secure.

PROVISION THROUGH JESUS

"Your father Abraham rejoiced to see My day," said Jesus to the religious leaders who opposed Him, "and he saw it and was glad" (John 8:56 NASB). To them, this statement was blasphemy and they wanted to stone Him, but it wasn't blasphemy, because through the eyes of faith, Abraham did see the day of Jesus. To a spiritually sensitive man like Abraham, the events in his own life would certainly point ahead to the promised Messiah. This would include the miraculous birth of his son Isaac, Isaac's obedience and willingness to be offered on the altar, his "resurrection" (Heb. 11:19), and the coming of Isaac's beautiful bride (Gen. 24). We today look back and recognize the messianic import of these events, but Abraham experienced them centuries ago and looked ahead and saw Jesus.

"The Father loves the Son and has placed everything in his hands" (John 3:35) reminds us of Genesis 24:35–36 and 25:5. This truth is repeated in John

13:3 and 16:15. Unlike Isaac, Jesus was born into poverty and lived the life of a poor itinerant teacher who had no place to lay His head. When He was born, his mother laid Him in a borrowed manger. During His ministry, He borrowed Peter's boat, a little boy's lunch, and an anonymous disciple's donkey; and after His death, He was buried in a borrowed tomb. But He enriched the world! "For you know the grace of our Lord Jesus Christ, that though he was rich, yet for your sakes he became poor, so that you through his poverty might become rich" (2 Cor. 8:9).

Without Jesus, people might be rich in this present world and yet poor in the next world. But with Jesus, it is possible to be poor in this world and rich in the world to come (Luke 6:20–23), or even rich in this present world and rich in the world to come (1 Tim. 6:17–19). Christians are supposed to be channels, not reservoirs; God blesses us that we might bless others. "For in Christ all the fullness of the Deity lives in bodily form, and you have been given fullness in Christ" (Col. 2:9–10). Isaac was born rich, and when we were born again through faith in Christ, we were born rich! Like Jesus and the apostles, God's people are "poor, yet making many rich; having nothing, and yet possessing everything" (2 Cor. 6:10). What a paradox—and what a privilege!

PROVISION GOD'S WAY

The thing we must remember is that our responsibility as God's children is to please the Father and do His will the way He wants it done. In his youth, Isaac sought to please his father, even to the point of surrendering his life, but toward the end of his life, he tried to manage things his own way (Gen. 27). It is the sad account of a man who began well but didn't end well.

For nearly twenty years after their marriage, Isaac and Rebekah waited for the Lord to give them children, but it never happened. What had happened to the messianic promise? Isaac did the right thing by asking God to give his wife conception, and God answered his prayers (Gen. 25:21–22). Disturbed by the unnatural movements of the babies in her womb, Rebekah asked the Lord what was wrong, and He gave her this answer:

> Two nations are in your womb,
>   and two peoples from within you will be separated;
> one people will be stronger than the other,
>   and the older will serve the younger.

GENESIS 25:23

God was doing the "firstborn reverse" again as He had done with Cain and Abel and with Japheth and Shem. The messianic line would bypass Esau and continue through Jacob.

Certainly Rebekah told her husband what God had said, and yet Isaac tried to give the blessing to Esau, the firstborn, instead of to Jacob! It was a well-known fact in the camp that Esau cared nothing for spiritual things and had even sold his birthright for a bowl of stew. Isaac favored Esau, the outdoorsman, the hunter, and he wanted Esau to have the blessing.

What Rebekah and Jacob did was wrong; they should have prayed and sought the Lord's help in changing Isaac's mind. The Lord permitted them to succeed in their plans, but they paid dearly for their success. Jacob had to flee from home to save his life, and he never saw his beloved mother again. Years later, Jacob's sons used the same deception on him that he and his mother had used on Isaac (Gen. 37:31–35).

However, Isaac was the cause of the trouble because he was partial to his first-born son. Isaac's reason (or excuse) for wanting to bless Esau was that he thought he was about to die, but he lived more than 40 years longer and was 180 years old when he died. Instead of living in the Spirit, Isaac was walking according to the flesh, depending on feeling, smelling, and tasting, and not on the leading of the Lord. Isaac knew that he was wrong and "trembled violently" when he learned that Jacob received the blessing after all (Gen. 27:33).

When God isn't allowed to rule, He overrules, and His will shall be accomplished. The old adage is still true: God always gives His best to those who leave the choice with Him.

Isaac — God will provide. Provision for Isaac. Provision thru Jesus. Provision God's way.

11

REBEKAH

"Just do what I say."

GENESIS 27:13

*B*efore he died, Abraham gave all his wealth to his son Isaac. Then he sent his trusted servant to find Isaac a wife. She couldn't be just any woman, for in marrying Isaac she would become a part of the messianic line, a living link in the salvation plan that would bring blessing to the whole world. The story of Isaac's marriage to Rebekah begins in great joy but ends in much sorrow as the family almost self-destructs. But out of it all, the Lord accomplished His purposes.

DIRECTION

Our English word "providence" comes from two Latin words (*pro* and *video*) that together mean "to see before" or "to see to it before." What the theologians call "divine providence" is the work of God in planning beforehand and going before us to accomplish His will for our lives. For the obedient child of God, life is not a series of accidents but an unfolding pattern of divine appointments, and Genesis 24 is one of the best illustrations of divine providence found in Scripture.

Obeying Abraham's orders, the anonymous servant took ten camels, loaded them with travel necessities and gifts, and headed for the town of Nahor. All he had to assure him of success was Abraham's promise that the Lord would direct him (Gen. 24:7), a promise he memorized (Gen. 24:40) and claimed by faith. Providentially, he came to the right place at just the right time and met Rebekah, the woman God had chosen for Isaac. The servant asked her the question every potential wife must be asked: "Whose daughter are you?" To us today, it means, "Are you a child of God or a child of this world?"

From the very beginning Rebekah appeared to be the perfect choice for Isaac. She was a beautiful woman, as was Sarah (Gen. 12:11–14), a virgin, industrious, generous, thoughtful, energetic (she ran, Gen. 24:20, 28), and respectful. She was a shepherdess, which suggests that she had patience, courage, and compassion. What more could Isaac want?

DECISION

Rebekah was a woman of decision and demonstrated it in the way she welcomed the servant, cared for him and his camels, and brought him to her house.

We become somewhat suspicious of her brother, Laban, when we read that the sight of the expensive golden gifts and the ten camels moved him to say to the servant, "Come, you who are blessed by the Lord!" This is the same Laban who years later tried to fleece Jacob out of everything he had earned and would have succeeded if the Lord hadn't intervened. As we shall see, under her great grace and beauty, Rebekah hid some of her brother's scheming ways.

In our modern world, friendship between a man and woman may lead to love, love may lead to engagement, and engagement may result in marriage. Not so in the ancient world, for marriage came first. Today we fall in love and get married, but back then two people got married and then learned to love each other. It was the prerogative of the bride's parents or guardians to select a husband and arrange for the marriage. So the servant had to meet the family, tell his story, and wait for a decision.

Do we begin to detect a family problem? Rebekah's father, Bethuel, was still alive (Gen. 24:50), but Rebekah "ran and told her mother's household" about the stranger (Gen. 24:28). The women lived in separate tents, but what news did Rebekah have for her mother? Only that Uncle Abraham's servant had arrived bringing valuable gifts. Did Rebekah's feminine intuition tell her that a marriage proposal was in the offing, or is it just natural for a daughter to share special news first with her mother? Apparently her mother sent her to tell her father and her brother, Laban, and it appears that Laban was the one in charge. Her father seems to be out of the leadership circle, but her mother joined the family council and with Laban made the decision. They asked that Rebekah remain ten days so they might send her off with proper festivities (Gen. 24:55). Bethuel was able to express himself along with Laban, "This is from the LORD" (Gen. 24:50), but the mother and Laban seem to be in authority. Is there a suggestion here that Rebekah inherited her forceful management ability from her mother? At least she wasted no time in deciding. "I will go," she said, and nobody argued with her.

DEVOTION

The events of the long journey are ignored, and the text goes right to the scene we are most eager to behold, the presenting of the bride to the groom. Again we see the providential hand of God at work, for Isaac was walking in the field meditating as the camel train approached. No license or special ceremony was required for Isaac to claim Rebekah as his wife. Taking her to himself and consummating the marriage was all that society expected.

Isaac placed Rebekah in his mother's tent, for she was now the wife of the leader of the clan. Isaac's love for his beautiful wife compensated for the pain he felt at the loss of his mother. To a certain extent, many wives have to "mother" their husbands, and Isaac comes across as a sensitive and fragile man. But if Rebekah's mother-in-law was always present in her husband's heart and memory, how much room was left for his wife? Well, we rejoice that Isaac loved his mother and felt deep pain at her death, but now he had a wife whom he loved, and she deserved all of his heart.

DIVISION

The happy couple had to wait twenty years before God gave them children, but even before the twins were born, family division began as the boys struggled in the womb (Gen. 25:19–34). Scripture literally says "they crushed one another." As the brothers grew older, the division widened because Isaac favored Esau, the outdoorsman, and Rebekah favored Jacob, the meditative stay-at-home boy. One would have expected just the opposite, for Isaac was the meditative type and Rebekah was the activist, but often parents try to experience in their children the life they desired but never could achieve.

Both Isaac and Rebekah knew that God had made Jacob the firstborn, which meant he would receive the birthright and the patriarchal blessing. Isaac should have given stronger spiritual leadership to the family and spent time preparing Jacob for his role as the family priest, but the aging father focused his attention on Esau. On Isaac's wedding night, he had two women in his heart, and now he had two conflicting families in his home. Trouble was coming.

DECEPTION

Almost every family has a "listening post," and in Isaac's family it was his wife, Rebekah. Perhaps it was a good thing that she did some discreet eavesdropping, because her husband was about to deliberately disobey the Lord and give Esau the patriarchal blessing. Everybody in the camp knew that Esau was a godless man who fraternized with the Hittites and even married two Hittite women who brought grief to his parents (Gen. 26:34–35). Surely Isaac remembered God's statement that "the older will serve the younger" (Gen. 25:23; Rom. 9:10–12), but he chose to ignore it.

If you knew you were going to die, what would your final activity be? Reading the Bible? Praying with friends and family? Praising God in song? Like a convict before his execution, Isaac chose to spend what he thought was his last hour eating his favorite dinner! It seems that his spiritual desires had disappeared. Always ready for action, Rebekah hatched a plot worthy of her brother, Laban, and took advantage of her husband's appetite. She wanted to make sure that the blessing went to her favorite son, Jacob, and not to that pagan bigamist Esau. The philosophy she followed is an ancient one: "Let us do evil that good may result" (Rom. 3:8). Or, in the words of the originator of a famous phrase, German theologian Hermann Busenbaum (1650), *"Cum finis est licitus, etiam media sunt licita,"* which means literally, "If the end is permitted, then the means is also permitted." In today's language, "The end justifies the means."

It is difficult to understand our own motives, so how can we understand the heart of Rebekah? She loved Jacob and knew that the blessing belonged to him, but she didn't have the courage to confront Isaac. God was on her side, and the future of the messianic promise rested on Isaac's blessing, but Rebekah didn't have the faith to take her hands off and let God do it His way. Rebekah had a decisive managerial mind, so she enlisted Jacob's help and said, "Just do what I say" (Gen. 27:13). Little did she realize that she was paving the way for her grandchildren to pull the same trick on Jacob and give Jacob twenty-two years of heartache because he thought Joseph was dead.

Her plan worked, and Jacob got the blessing, but almost everything else fell apart. Esau determined to kill Jacob, so Rebekah decisively shipped him off to her brother's house to find a wife, although she let Isaac think it was his idea. Isaac didn't die for several years, and when he did, Esau and Jacob were friendly enough to attend the funeral and together bury him. However, Rebekah never saw Jacob again, but their bodies rested together in the cave of Machpelah (Gen. 49:29–53).

"Who has known the mind of the Lord? Or who has been his counselor?" (Rom. 11:34). Both Isaac and Rebekah knew the mind of the Lord concerning Jacob, but Isaac didn't agree with the Lord and Rebekah thought God needed her help to make it happen. "In whatever man does without God," wrote George MacDonald, "he must fail miserably or succeed more miserably." Rebekah succeeded and lived to regret it.

"Just do what I say" is decisive and efficient. People today would call it good management and excellent leadership. But being out of God's will is dangerous, and the consequences could affect generations to come.

12

ESAU *means Red.*

Lest there be any ... profane person like Esau.
HEBREWS 12:16 NKJV

Esau - profane meaning irreverent, outside the temple. Secular - - nothing sacred.

This admonition in Hebrews is clear and definite: don't let people like Esau remain in your congregation or they will defile it and that defilement will spread.

This is a hard command to obey, because people like Esau are pleasant to be with, full of good stories about their outdoor experiences, very tolerant of what you do and believe, and are often pretty good cooks. Men like Esau are perfect for managing the men's breakfast or leading hunting or fishing trips, and women like Esau successfully direct the annual bazaar or Victorian tea with skill and success. Esau's nickname was Edom, which means "red" (Gen. 25:29–30), and any two-fisted he-man with the nickname Red can't be all bad.

But people like Esau are dangerous because they are "profane." Today the word *profane* means "guilty of taking God's name in vain," but that's not what it meant when the King James Version was translated four centuries ago. Modern versions of the Bible use words like *godless, irreligious, irreverent,* and even *careless about God,* all of which come close to the truth, but I still prefer "profane." Why? Because it is a noble Latin word that literally means "outside the temple."

Fine. But what does "outside the temple" mean? It means common, ordinary, secular, open to everything and everybody. It means without boundaries or walls so that anything can get in or out and anybody can walk on you. The Latin Vulgate Old Testament uses *profanus* as equivalent to the Hebrew word *hol,* which means "common, ordinary," and the word in the Greek New Testament is related to the word for "threshold." In other words, a "profane" person is like a threshold—open to all, walked on by all, very common and accessible. That describes Esau and all who follow him. They are secular; there is nothing of the sacred in their lives.

The aged Isaac was surprised when "Esau" showed up so quickly with the savory food he had requested. "How did you find it so quickly, my son?" he asked, and "Esau" replied, "The LORD your God gave me success" (Gen. 27:20). That's when Isaac got suspicious, because he knew that Esau wouldn't have given God the credit for anything. Everybody in the camp knew that Esau had no interest in God or in spiritual things. As far as the secular man is concerned, "in all his thoughts there is no room for God" (Ps. 10:4).

This is quite a contrast to the true children of God who have been set apart *by* the Lord and *for* the Lord. Their bodies are temples of the Holy Spirit, and they won't permit just anybody to walk on the soil of their hearts or invade the sacred precincts of their minds. They simply aren't open to everything and everybody. They aren't "outside the temple" but inside, living in the Most Holy Place (Heb. 10:19–25).

Realizing that he had forfeited the birthright (Gen. 25:29–34) and now had lost the blessing, Esau became angry and threatened to kill his brother. That's when Jacob found it convenient to leave home and go find a wife in Uncle Laban's household. Esau settled south of the Holy Land in Mount Seir and founded the nation we know as the Edomites. Although Esau personally abandoned his hatred for his brother and seemed to become reconciled to him, Jacob had his doubts and went his own way (Gen. 32–33). As far as the record is concerned, the last time they were together was at Isaac's funeral (Gen. 35:27–29), where we hope they got along, at least for their father's sake.

Whatever Esau may have done personally with reference to Jacob and his descendants, Esau's descendants took up the quarrel and kept it going. Edom was Israel's perpetual enemy and took every opportunity to annoy them and attack them. The prophets frequently pointed this out (see Jer. 49:7–22; Ezek. 25:12–14; Amos 1:11–12; Obad. 1:10–14). During the Babylonian attack on Jerusalem, the Edomites led the cheering section and urged the Babylonian army to "tear it down" (Ps. 137:7). Jeremiah promised that Edom would be punished for this sin against their brother (Lam. 4:21).

According to the prophet Malachi, what the other prophets announced about God's judgment of Edom came true (Mal. 1:1–5). Their violence against the Jews came back on their own heads, and though visitors to the Holy Land today can make the arduous trip to Petra and other sites in Edom, they won't be greeted by the descendants of Esau.

"But doesn't Malachi say that God had made a personal choice and there was nothing Esau could do about it?"

Jehovah said through Malachi, "Yet I have loved Jacob, but Esau I have hated" (Mal. 1:2–3), a statement Paul quoted in Romans 9:13 to confirm God's sovereign choice of Jacob over Esau. It was the "firstborn reverse" again—the second-born declared to be the firstborn—a choice that almighty God has every right to make. But Malachi was announcing God's judgment on the Edomites—the people of Esau—and not on the man Esau. God loves sinners and will save any sinner who repents and calls on Him. Esau tried to get the blessing from Isaac, but there is no evidence that Esau ever repented and turned from sin (Heb. 12:17). He left his father's tent determined to murder his brother! Is that proof of repentance? Esau was rejected for the same reason Cain was rejected: his heart was wrong before God. Esau's descendants were rejected because they followed in the footsteps of their founder.

Anybody who uses the sovereignty of God as an excuse for going to hell needs to remember that "[God is] not willing that any should perish" (2 Peter 3:9 NKJV) and that "[God] wants all men to be saved" (1 Tim. 2:4). According to Matthew 25:34, the eternal kingdom was prepared for God's people, those who belong to Jesus Christ; but hell was prepared for the Devil and his angels, not for people (Matt. 25:41). Or, as Dr. Donald Grey Barnhouse used to say, "Every person can either go to heaven God's way or go to hell their own way."

God's way is faith in Jesus Christ, and "the Father has sent his Son to be the Savior of the world" (1 John 4:14).

13

JACOB

...God of Jacob...
father of 12 tribes.

> *"You have struggled with God and with men*
> *and have overcome."*
>
> **GENESIS 32:28**

I cannot forecast to you the action of Russia," said Winston Churchill in a 1939 broadcast to the people of Britain. "It is a riddle wrapped in a mystery inside an enigma." What Sir Winston Churchill said about Russia, I sometimes relate to the man Jacob.

One Bible encyclopedia says that Jacob was "a scheming scoundrel in his earlier years," and perhaps he was; but the Lord has deigned to call Himself "the God of Jacob," and there isn't a higher honor than that. The Lord spoke to Jacob at Bethel when Jacob left home (Gen. 28) and also when he was laboring for Laban (Gen. 31:10–13). God wrestled with him at Peniel when he was about to meet his brother, Esau (Gen. 32). He appeared to him at Bethel (Gen. 35:9–15) and spoke to him at Beersheba when he was going to Egypt to live with Joseph (Gen. 46:1–4). He gave Jacob a great deal of personal attention! Jacob is the father of the twelve tribes of Israel, and they bear his name, and through them the Savior came into the world. What an honor!

As we examine Jacob's life, we must heed the wise counsel of Watchman Nee:

> Until God begins to deal with us, we are inclined to take a superior at-
> titude to Jacob's intrigues, but as we begin to encounter the deviousness
> of our own thinking, we soon recognize the man's essential character in
> ourselves. And remember, what changed Jacob's life from vanity to profit
> was nothing less than the power of the grace of God.[1]

In other words, our problem with Jacob may actually be a problem with ourselves. *We* are the riddle wrapped in a mystery inside an enigma! "The heart is deceitful above all things and beyond cure. Who can understand it?" (Jer. 17:9). The Hebrew word translated "deceitful" (*aᶜqob*) is related to the word *heel* (*aᶜqeb*),

1. Watchman Nee, *A Table in the Wilderness* (Fort Washington, Penn.: Christian Literature Crusade, 1965).

and both are connected to Jacob (*ya'aqob*) in Genesis 27:36, where Esau laments, "Isn't he rightly named Jacob? He has deceived me [supplanted me, taken me by the heel] these two times." We might translate Jeremiah 17:9, "The heart is Jacob," and then look in the mirror!

Centuries later the prophet Hosea addressed the people of the northern kingdom of Israel, pointing them back to their namesake, Jacob, and telling them to show the same kind of zeal for the spiritual that he displayed when he wrestled with the Lord. "In the womb he grasped his brother's heel; as a man he struggled with God. He struggled with the angel and overcame him; he wept and begged for his favor" (Hos. 12:3–4). In spite of his many weaknesses—and we all have them—Jacob had a heart for God and desired the blessings that He alone could bestow. Esau wasn't like that.

Since all of us have a "Jacob" heart, let's learn from this great man how to handle the challenges of life: struggling with people and circumstances, struggling with God, and finally overcoming ourselves.

STRUGGLING WITH PEOPLE AND CIRCUMSTANCES

Even before birth, Jacob struggled with his brother, Esau, in a battle that lasted throughout his life; and Esau's descendants, the Edomites, carried on the battle at every opportunity. Jacob struggled with his clever father-in-law, Laban, who tricked him into giving him fourteen years of service for Rachel and Leah and six years more so he could build his own flocks. All those years Jacob bore the losses, suffered out in the pastures, and had his wages changed ten times.

When after twenty difficult years Jacob finally left Paddan Aram, he and Laban had to put up a boundary marker called "Mizpah" (which means "watchtower") and swear that neither would cross it and attack the other. "The LORD will watch between us," they said, which means, "God sees what you're doing, so be careful!" People who sing the so-called Mizpah blessing at the close of a meeting don't realize that they are singing about an armed truce and not a cessation of hostilities.

But that isn't all. Jacob not only had trouble with Laban and Laban's sons, but he had to endure conflict and competition among four women—his wives, Rachel and Leah, and their handmaids, Bilhah and Zilpah. When a weary Jacob came home after long days with the sheep and goats, he never knew which wife would claim him. Add to this the management of eleven sons, and you can see that Paddan Aram was no Disneyland, yet Jacob patiently endured it all!

How did he do it? He told his secret to Laban in Genesis 31:42: "If the God of my father, the God of Abraham and the Fear of Isaac, had not been with me, you would surely have sent me away empty-handed. But God has seen my hardship and the toil of my hands, and last night he rebuked you." Jacob teaches us an important lesson: when people are difficult and abrasive, and circumstances unbearable, turn it all over to the Lord and trust Him to mature you and eventually prosper you. The wear and tear of mean people and miserable circumstances can either polish us or destroy us, and we must make the choice. Those twenty years of silence and submission were the making of Jacob, and he gave the glory to the Lord.

"Once we truly know that life is difficult—once we truly understand and accept it—then life is no longer difficult," wrote psychiatrist W. Scott Peck in the opening chapter of his bestseller *The Road Less Traveled*.[2] The mystical poet William Blake said the same thing two centuries ago: "Man was made for joy and woe / And when this we rightly know / Thro' the world we safely go."[3] The Lord was using difficult people and circumstances to perfect Jacob and to prepare him for the ministry he would have building the nation of Israel. It has well been said that what life does to us depends on what life finds in us; and in Jacob, life found faith and patience. Jacob worked, suffered, and waited, and when God's signal came, he obeyed.

STRUGGLING WITH GOD

Hosea said of Jacob that "as a man he struggled with God" (Hos. 12:3). The account is in Genesis 32:22–32, and the text uses the verbs "struggled" and "wrestled" (vv. 24–25, 28). Jacob was preparing to meet his brother, Esau, and was expecting a costly battle, but Jacob was at war with others and with himself because he was at war with God, and that battle had to be settled first before he could face Esau. (For a New Testament commentary on these three wars—with others, yourself, and God—see James 4:1–10.) Careful planner that he was, Jacob separated his immediate family from the rest of the camp and put them in a safe place, and then he stood guard, wondering what would happen next.

As Jacob stood alone, planning and praying, he was attacked by a stranger who wrestled with him until daybreak. Was this person an angel appearing as a human, or was he the Son of God in a preincarnate appearance? Verses 28 and 30, along with Hosea 12:3, seem to point to the latter; the Son of God had come down to defeat Jacob so he could win a victory. Jacob had struggled with his brother, Esau, with Laban and his family and with his wives, but now he had to defend himself by wrestling with God!

As the night wore on, Jacob discovered that he could never defeat his mysterious adversary, so he got a good grip on the man's body and just held on. "As the years go on," said F. B. Meyer, "we begin to cling where once we struggled." Why cling? Because Jacob wanted the stranger to bless him, and he wouldn't let go until He did. Jacob realized that he was wrestling with God! The Lord could have defeated Jacob in an instant, but it was important that Jacob discover that it was time to stop fighting and start yielding. John Calvin said, "God fights *against* us with His left hand and *for* us with His right hand." King David knew this secret: "To the pure you show yourself pure, but to the crooked you show yourself

2. W. Scott Peck, *The Road Less Traveled* (New York: Simon and Schuster, 1979), 15.
3. William Blake, "Auguries of Innocence," in *The Portable Blake*, ed. Alfred Kazin (New York: Penguin, 1946), 150–54, lines 55–62.

shrewd" (Ps. 18:26). God will stop using His left hand when we yield to His will, hold on by faith, and ask for the blessing He wants to give—"yet not my will, but yours be done" (Luke 22:42).

This is what leads to victory. "The Lord cannot fully bless a man," said A. W. Tozer, "until He has first conquered him."

OVERCOMING THROUGH DEFEAT

"He struggled with the angel and overcame him," says Hosea 12:4 of Jacob, but it was Jesus Christ, the Angel of the Lord, who was the true overcomer. It is only when we are conquered by the Lord that we can conquer ourselves and our circumstances. Jacob was at war with himself and the people in his life because he was at war with God, and when he stopped wrestling and began clinging, he turned defeat into victory. Like his grandfather Abraham in Genesis 15, Jacob experienced "the dark night of the soul," but it made a new man out of him.

First, he was given *a new weakness.* This seems to be a strange way to help a person succeed, but according to Paul, it is when we are weak in ourselves that we are strong in the Lord (2 Cor. 12:10). God touched Jacob's hip and made him lame, but as an old proverb puts it, "He who limps is still walking." When Jacob returned to his family, they noticed his limp and must have asked about it, and he had to tell them that he had seen the face of God and been changed.

But Jacob was also given *a new name.* The last time Jacob was asked, "What is your name?" was when he was impersonating his brother. He answered his father, "I am your son, your firstborn, Esau" (Gen. 27:32), and that lie led to trouble. But this time he didn't lie; he told the truth and simply said, "Jacob." He finally admitted to himself and to the Lord that he was a deceiver, a "heel-grabber," a schemer. The Lord gave him the new name of "Israel."

Hebrew scholars don't agree on the root meaning of "Israel," whether it comes from *śarah*, "to contend, to struggle," or from *śar*, "to be a prince." The explanation in the text seems to combine both meanings: "because you have struggled with God and with men and have overcome." G. Campbell Morgan combined both meanings when he called Jacob's experience "the crippling that crowns."[4] Jacob was overcome by God that he might become an overcomer for God. Some say that Israel means "a God-mastered man." The Bible speaks of the patriarch sometimes as Jacob and other times as Israel, but the name Israel (the man or the nation) is used more than 2,500 times in Scripture.

The Lord gave Jacob a *new blessing* because he asked for it by faith. God had blessed him at Bethel at the beginning of his pilgrimage (Gen. 28), and now He had blessed him at Peniel to prepare him for the burdens he would bear during the next years of his life. He had seen the face of God, and as Jacob-Israel limped back to his family, the sun rose above him. For him, it was the dawning of a new day, and so may it be for us.

---

4. G. Campbell Morgan, *The Westminster Pulpit*, vol. 7 (London: Pickering and Inglis, n.d.), 313.

Jacob's career began as a fugitive running from home. Then he became a stranger, because for twenty years he was away from home. But then he became a pilgrim who was heading home as he returned to the land of his father. Even as he was about to step into the heavenly city, he was still a pilgrim "as he leaned on the top of his staff" (Heb. 11:21).

The struggles were ended.

- JACOB - struggled w God & w men & has overcome.
- God gave a great deal of attention to Jacob.

RACHEL *Disappointed.*

"Give me children, or I'll die!"

GENESIS 30:1

*W*hen Jacob saw his beautiful cousin Rachel leading Laban's flock to the well, it was obviously love at first sight. He wanted to speak to her privately and did his best to persuade the waiting shepherds to water their sheep and move on, but they were interested in the stranger and curious about what might happen. Did Jacob recall how Abraham's servant met his mother Rebekah at the well? Would history repeat itself? Yes, Rachel would be married to Jacob; but, no, she wouldn't have the kind of life Rebekah enjoyed as the wife of a wealthy and powerful sheik.

The seven years during which Jacob was working to earn his wife were undoubtedly the happiest in Rachel's life, but after that, things began to change for the worse. Perhaps the word that best describes the rest of Rachel's life is *disappointment.*

DISAPPOINTED WITH HER FATHER

No sooner had Jacob identified himself as her cousin than Rachel ran to tell her father, Laban, and he hurried out to meet his nephew. Laban knew that Jacob's mother was married to a very wealthy man, and he was probably expecting to see a long train of camels bearing chests of expensive gifts. He was mistaken. Jacob didn't possess his father's wealth, and all he had in his hand was his staff (Gen. 32:10). I would like to have seen the look on Laban's face as he quickly began to work on Plan B.

Laban wasn't to be outsmarted. During the first month that Jacob was a guest in the household, everybody noticed the special feelings expressed between Rachel and Jacob, so Laban decided to take advantage of it. He knew that Jacob was too poor to pay the traditional bride price for Rachel, so why not ask him to work for her hand? Shrewd man that he was, Laban figured he would get free service from Jacob. He could adjust his wages as he pleased, and since it was a business deal, he wouldn't have to share the money with his daughter. Jacob was happy to have a home for seven years and give his brother time to cool off.

It was the deal of a lifetime, but it had one flaw. After the wedding, Jacob would take his wife and head for home where Isaac's wealth awaited him, so

Laban had to devise a way to keep him much longer. We aren't told how he managed to substitute Leah for Rachel, but Leah surely had to be in on the plot. Where was Rachel during this entire charade? Did Laban promise both girls a bigger bride price if they would cooperate with him? We don't know, and it's unwise to guess. The bride would be heavily veiled, of course, and perhaps Jacob had celebrated so much he didn't fully know what was going on. Leah could have disguised her voice as they whispered to each other during the night, and once the marriage was consummated, Jacob couldn't escape.

Twenty years later, Leah and Rachel expressed their true feelings about how their father had lied to them, robbed them, and used them to build up his own wealth (Gen. 31:14–16, 38–42). Laban wasn't a rich man when Jacob joined the family, but God's blessing through Jacob made him wealthy, and Laban admitted it (Gen. 30:27). Laban wasn't a believer in the true and living God, but he was willing to let a believer work for him and bring the blessing of God into his home.

When Rachel packed up to leave with Jacob and the family to go to Canaan, she stole her father's household gods and lied about it (Gen. 31:30–35). After all, Laban had stolen from her, so why shouldn't she steal from him? According to Laban's religion, the person possessing the gods would have success in life and would also inherit the family fortune. Jacob had provided that fortune for Laban, so it rightly belonged to Leah and Rachel. Was Rachel trusting the Lord or the idols, or was it just an act of revenge?

DISAPPOINTED WITH HER HUSBAND

When Jacob discovered what Laban and Leah had done, why didn't he raise more of a fuss? Why did he so readily accept Laban's offer when he might have done some bargaining for himself? For one thing, he was a stranger and a houseguest, and there was nobody from his family there to help defend him. Jacob didn't lack for shrewdness, but he had met his match in Laban. Whatever happened, Jacob didn't want to lose Rachel, and her future was in the hands of her crafty father. Was it true that the elder had to be wed before the younger? (Probably not.) Jacob loved Rachel and wanted her more than anything else, so he accepted Laban's offer and worked another seven years. (More time for Esau to calm down.) Rachel knew that Jacob loved her more than he loved Leah, and he proved it by enduring seven more years of difficult toil under an impossible taskmaster.

Perhaps a second factor was involved. It's possible that Jacob's conscience had reminded him that he had deceived his father seven years before. Leah the firstborn had pretended to be the second-born, and Jacob the second-born had pretended to be the firstborn. The deceiver had been deceived, and his sins had found him out. Jacob accepted this discipline from the Lord and went right on bearing his burdens, which shows he was growing spiritually and learning the ways of God.

But Rachel's greatest disappointment was that she didn't have any children, and for this she blamed Jacob. "Give me children, or I'll die!" She knew that Jacob loved her more than he loved Leah, but even that couldn't compensate for children of her own to love (see 1 Sam. 1:8). Leah already had borne four sons, and when Jacob took Rachel's maid, Bilhah, as his concubine, she conceived and bore two sons, so obviously Jacob wasn't the problem. Leah gave her maid, Zilpah, to him, and she bore him two sons, and then Leah had three more children of her own. Rachel thought that by eating mandrake roots she could encourage pregnancy, but it didn't work. Finally, she prayed about the matter, something she should have done sooner, and the Lord heard her cries and gave them Joseph (Gen. 30:22–24; and see 25:21). His name means "may he add" and indicates that Rachel was asking God for still another son. God answered years later and gave her Benjamin.

DISAPPOINTED WITH HER HOME

Rachel and Leah knew that their father was a schemer and treated them like servants and used them to achieve his selfish goals. Their desire had been to get married as soon as possible and leave home, but there was always some obstacle in the way. The marriage plot kept Jacob there fourteen years, but when he was free to leave, he had no flocks of his own with which to support his large family. Building his own financial base took another six years. Rachel and Leah dreamed of going to live with Isaac and Rebekah and enjoying their wealth.

It's difficult to imagine the atmosphere of a home with one father, four mothers, and at least a dozen children, especially when two of the mothers were sisters who didn't get along, and the other two mothers were second-class wives elevated from being servants (Prov. 30:20–23). And all of them were under the thumb of a heartless man whose main ambition was to get rich—at any cost. The undercurrents of intrigue, envy, and rivalry involving the four women must have been very strong, and surely all of this affected the children. No wonder Jacob stayed with the flocks day and night (Gen. 31:40)!

DISAPPOINTED WITH LIFE

Jacob finally fulfilled his contract with Laban and was free to return to his father's home in Canaan, but he left secretly so his father-in-law couldn't set any more traps. On that journey, Jacob's beloved wife Rachel died in childbirth near Bethlehem (Gen. 35:16–20), an event that broke Jacob's heart. Years later, while talking with Joseph about the place of his sons in the family, Jacob brought up Rachel's death (Gen. 48:1–7). Had she not died, she might have given birth to more sons, so Jacob adopted Joseph's two boys to make up for this loss. Joseph, his firstborn by Rachel, replaced Reuben, his firstborn by Leah (Gen. 49:1–4).

There's something poignant about Rachel's last words, something like "His name is Ben-Oni," which means "son of my sorrow" or "son of my trouble." Imagine growing up with that kind of a name! Every time somebody addressed you, it would remind you that your birth helped to cause your mother's death.

Rachel had known seven years of joy as she anticipated marrying Jacob, but those years were followed by thirteen years of trouble before Jacob became a pilgrim and headed for Bethel. They had escaped trouble with Esau, but Dinah was raped at Shechem and Simeon and Levi slaughtered the men of that city.

Rachel had wanted another son, and God gave him to her, but at a very great price. "Give me children, or I'll die" (Gen. 30:1). We wonder if her last words didn't go beyond the immediate occasion and reflect her estimate of her life—trouble and sorrow. Jacob wisely gave his youngest son a new name—Benjamin, "the son of my right hand." In that culture, the right hand was the place of honor and power. Jacob now had twelve sons, and they would become the twelve tribes of Israel. By the way, Benjamin was the only child of Jacob who was born in the Holy Land.

The Jewish people honor Rachel and Leah as the women "who together built up the house of Israel" (Ruth 4:11). Watching the Jewish prisoners being marched off to Babylon, the prophet Jeremiah heard Rachel "weeping for her children" (Jer. 31:15), "sons and daughters of my sorrow." Matthew heard the same weeping when Herod ruthlessly killed the Bethlehem children in his attempt to kill Jesus (Matt. 2:16–18). Benjamin's two names remind us of our Lord Jesus Christ in His suffering (Ben-Oni) and in His glory (Benjamin). First the suffering, then the glory; first the cross, then the crown. Let's remember this truth the next time we conclude that life is only a painful battle.

One final comfort for Rachel: her two sons were used of God to accomplish His great purposes in this world. Joseph rescued the nation of Israel from extinction and sheltered them in the land of Egypt. Joseph also gave Israel the tribes of Ephraim and Manasseh. The tribe of Benjamin gave the church the apostle Paul (Phil. 3:5), and Paul wrote half of the books in the New Testament.

Rachel, why are you weeping?

Disappointed Rachel :
\# with her father \# with her husband \# her home
\# with Life.

15

JOSEPH *suffered because of others. ⁇*

♡

♡ *"God intended it for good."* ♡

GENESIS 50:20

♡

Although Joseph spent most of his life in Egypt, he represents Jewish manhood at its best. He had clean hands and a pure heart, yet he suffered considerably because of what others did to him. His father pampered him and his older brothers hated him and sold him as a slave. His master's wife lied about him, and he was imprisoned and forgotten by everybody except God. "They bruised his feet with shackles, his neck was put in irons," wrote the psalmist (105:18). The *Anglican Prayer Book Version* of 1877 reads, "The iron entered into his soul." I have a feeling that Joseph experienced both kinds of suffering. What a man!

It has well been said that what life does to us depends on what life finds in us, and this truth is no better demonstrated than in the history of Joseph. Here we will focus primarily on Joseph, but to appreciate his response to what God permitted him to experience, we must take time to examine the responses of his father and his ten brothers.

THE BROTHERS: "WHAT IS GOD DOING TO US?"

Their actual response was, "What is this that God has done to us?" (Gen. 42:28), and they said it when one of them found his money for grain returned in his full grain sack. What a shock! Each man's conscience was smiting him, and each man was afraid of what the Lord was going to do. Had they thought about the justice of the Lord when they sold Joseph, they never would have sinned as they did, but they were sure they could get away with it.

When they arrived home, they all found their money in their sacks; and then they had to tell their father that Simeon was being held hostage in Egypt. But the news got worse: the Egyptian lord would release Simeon only if they brought Benjamin along on their next trip. Joseph had learned from his dreams that all eleven brothers had to bow before him (Gen. 37:5–11), so he kept Simeon and demanded to see Benjamin.

The brothers' evil conduct was catching up with them. They had hated Joseph and couldn't speak to him without showing their hostility. Jacob, Joseph, and Benjamin had each other, but the ten older brothers made life miserable for

Joseph. According to Genesis 50, they wronged him (v. 15), treated him badly (v. 17), and intended to harm him (v. 20). In spite of his tears and entreaties, they threw him into a pit, plotted to kill him, and then sold him—their own brother!—as a slave (Gen. 42:21–22).

In being cruel to Joseph they were also cruel to Jacob. They lied to him and told him that Joseph was dead, and they even manufactured "evidence" to convince their father they were telling the truth. Sir Walter Scott was right—"O what a tangled web we weave when first we practice to deceive." Jacob didn't see his beloved son Joseph for more than twenty years, and he grieved for his son, thinking he was dead. How wicked for those brothers to lay this fictitious burden of sorrow on their father in his old age! Yes, Jacob was being paid back for lying to his own father, but that doesn't excuse the brothers for their lies and cruelty.

What was God doing? He was bringing them to the place of truth, repentance, confession, and forgiveness. God was using Joseph to deal with them in a wise and patient way. *INTERESTING.*

JACOB—"GOD IS DOING NOTHING!"

Jacob didn't say that God was doing nothing, but that's the way he felt in his heart. What he said was, "Everything is against me!" (Gen. 42:36), and it certainly looked that way.

Consider his trials. There was a famine in the land, and his sons had to travel to Egypt for food to sustain the large family. Jacob thought his beloved son Joseph was dead, and now his son Simeon was being held hostage in Egypt. Even worse, the ruler of Egypt said he wouldn't release Simeon until the brothers brought Benjamin with them on their next trip. Both Benjamin and Joseph were the only sons of Rachel, Jacob's favorite wife, now deceased, and Jacob couldn't bear losing both of them. No matter where he turned, Jacob faced painful problems and had to make difficult decisions. Where was the Lord?

Jacob was forgetting the promise God made to him long ago at Bethel. "I am with you and will watch over you wherever you go, and I will bring you back to this land. I will not leave you until I have done what I have promised you" (Gen. 28:15). When Jacob fled from Laban, God said to him, "Go back to the land of your fathers and to your relatives, and I will be with you" (Gen. 31:3). "I will not leave you"—that's the negative. "I will be with you"—that's the positive. And the night that he wrestled with the Lord, Jacob's name was changed from Jacob to Israel. He had struggled with God and was now an overcomer, a prince with God. Surely his ever-present limp would remind him of this. "If God is for us, who can be against us?" (Rom. 8:31).

Let's not be too hard on Jacob; after all, where would he get spiritual help in his family? Furthermore, you and I already know how the story ends, and that makes it easier for us to smile and quote Romans 8:28. "Jacob, don't say that everything is working against you! God says it is all working for your good." But Jacob didn't know Romans 8:28, and he was a man with a broken heart. The next time our own world is shattered and we wonder if God really cares, maybe we'll better understand how he felt.

JOSEPH—"WHAT GOD DID HE INTENDED FOR GOOD"

At least five times in Scripture we are told that "the Lord was with Joseph" (Gen. 39:2, 3, 21, 23; Acts 7:9), which means that God was in control of events so that everything would work out for the good of Joseph and his family and for the glory of God. It's important to note that God worked everything together for good throughout the entire experience and not just at the end. Romans 8:28 doesn't say, "And we know that God will work out everything for good in the end," but that He is always at all times working things out for good, no matter how we feel or what we see.

The most important "good thing" that God was accomplishing was the preservation of the nation of Israel (Gen. 50:20), because through them, God would give the world the Word of God and the Son of God. Joseph was God's chosen servant to shelter Israel and to save a lost world. God "sent a man before them" (Ps. 105:17).

What happened was good for Jacob and his sons. Surely Jacob realized that he was reaping the bitter fruit from some of the seeds of deception he had sown years before, and the brothers were finally brought to the place where their mouths were stopped and they had run out of lies and excuses. "What can we say to my lord?" said Judah. "What can we say?" (Gen. 44:16). Every mouth was silenced as the men (Benjamin excepted) stood guilty before the Lord and Joseph (Rom. 3:19). It took twenty-two years for the brothers' sins to find them out, and then Joseph forgave them and assured them of his love. A few years before, when Joseph's first son was born, Joseph named him Manasseh—"forget"—which means Joseph was not holding any grudges or looking for ways to avenge himself. F. W. Robertson said, "The only revenge which is essentially Christian is that of retaliating by forgiveness." How could Joseph hate his brothers when he knew that God intended everything to produce good?

Perhaps Joseph himself was the recipient of more good than anybody else. Psalm 105:17 says that God sent "a man" before them, but Joseph was only a somewhat pampered seventeen-year-old boy when his brothers sold him. God gave him two dreams to sustain him, but dreams without disciplines become nightmares; so the Lord sent one discipline after another to form him and polish him.

Joseph knew the pain of family rejection, the humiliation of being sold as a slave, and the sorrow of separation from loved ones at home. He endured the demands of hard work in a foreign land, the temptations of the world, the helplessness of condemnation by false accusation, the misery and shame of imprisonment, and the seeming absurdity of the whole thing. But these experiences were used by God to turn a boy into a man and a servant into a ruler. He was faithful over a few things, so God entrusted him with many things (Matt. 25:21).

I have counted seven times in this narrative when Joseph wept. He wept and pleaded when he was thrown into the pit (Gen. 42:21–22). He wept when his brothers admitted their sins to each other (Gen. 42:24) and when he saw his brother Benjamin (Gen. 43:30). He wept loudly when he was reconciled to his brothers (Gen. 45:2, 14–15) and "for a long time" when he saw his father after more than twenty years (Gen. 46:29). As any son would do, he wept when his father died (Gen. 50:1). When he read his brothers' message asking for forgiveness, he wept and assured them that they were forgiven. They wanted to become slaves, but he assured them they were sons. Does that sound familiar? (See Luke 15:19, 21.)

The disciplines of Joseph's life, plus his faith in the Lord, transformed him into one of the most beloved characters in the Bible, a man who is very much like Jesus Christ. Like Jesus, Joseph was beloved by his father but hated by his brethren. He was illegally sold, he was falsely accused, and he was condemned and imprisoned. Joseph went from the prison to the throne, from suffering to glory, and he provided bread for the known world. (Joseph merely sustained life; Jesus *gives* life.) Joseph also gave forgiveness to his brethren and provided a home for them. There is much more, but I'm sure you get the point: it is only as we suffer for and with Jesus that we become more like Him. On the other side of Romans 8:28 is Romans 8:29, which says that God's purpose is that we "be conformed to the likeness of his Son."

In the midst of pain and trouble, it takes faith for us to say, "God intends this for good," but that's just what we must do. To say that "everything is against me" when everything is working for me, is to rebel against the loving heart of God. To ask, "What is God doing?" when we know His purpose is to make us more like Jesus, is to make our situation worse.

In the midst of danger and difficulty, David wrote, "But I trust in your unfailing love; my heart rejoices in your salvation. I will sing to the LORD, for he has been good to me" (Ps. 13:5–6).

"God intended it for good," says Joseph.

We reply, "God is good—all the time!"

16

JOB

"There is no one on earth like him."

JOB 1:8

JOB was Righteous -- Blameless & Upright.

As a friend and I drove through Pennsylvania, we kept seeing signs that read, "Beware of falling rocks!" We were glad for the good advice, but how were we supposed to put it into practice? If we saw some falling rocks, should we immediately stop the car and perhaps cause an accident? Or should we speed up and try not to be a target? Or should we just "watch and pray" and trust God to keep the rocks from falling? We never did find out.

The rocks fell on Job, and he couldn't see them coming. He suffered as few men have suffered. In one day, all his great wealth was taken from him and his ten children died. Then he was afflicted with sores from head to foot, painful festering sores that disfigured him grossly and kept him awake at night. He left his home and sat outside the town on the ash heap where the trash was collected, and there he mourned and meditated, talked with some friends, and waited for the Lord to help him.

But the remarkable thing is that God said He found no fault in Job! "There is none on earth like him" was God's evaluation of this man. That commendation from God is better than the highest recognition anybody on earth can give or receive. Job lived in Uz about the time the Jewish patriarchs were journeying in Canaan. He was a man greatly blessed by God, and yet he seemed to be a man greatly cursed by God.

All of us want life to run smoothly. We want the road signs to read, "Relax! No danger of falling rocks!" We don't want delays or interruptions, problems or emergencies, pains or disappointments. But life doesn't work that way. Life seems to be made up of all of the above plus many more nuisances and detours and distresses that I haven't listed but that most of us have experienced. To be sure, from time to time, pleasure and peace are squeezed into our lives and the sea is calm, but it doesn't take long for a storm to blow up when we least expect it.

The plot in the book of Job involves God, Job, his three friends, and a fellow named Elihu. However, the story also involves us, the readers, because this is the Word of God and we dare not ignore it. As these key characters look at Job and his situation, what do they see? And what do we see?

WHAT GOD SEES

The Lord looks at Job and sees a man unique in his character and conduct, so much so that God said there was nobody else like him. God told Satan that Job was "blameless and upright, a man who fears God and shuns evil" (Job 1:8). Job was open before God (Job 6:21) and confessed that he wasn't perfect (Job 7:21), but he was a man of integrity who practiced justice and mercy in his dealing with others. He was what the Old Testament Jew would call "a righteous man," and there was nobody like him in all the earth. (Centuries later the prophet Ezekiel agreed with this estimate; see Ezek. 14:14, 20.)

It is easy for us to make mistakes about people, but God doesn't make mistakes. "Man looks at the outward appearance, but the LORD looks at the heart" (1 Sam. 16:7). The Lord knows the secrets of every heart (Ps. 44:21), so Job couldn't fool God, nor can we. This truth is both an encouragement and a warning. People may misunderstand us, and the Devil may accuse us, but if God knows our hearts are right, we have nothing to fear. But if our hearts are not right, and if we are lying to the Lord and to others, then we are heading for trouble.

As you read the book of Job, it is important to note that Job maintained his integrity before God. Job didn't try to please his friends by inventing some kind of sin that would explain why he was suffering so much (Job 2:9; 6:29; 13:15; 27:5). What sin could he have committed that would demand that magnitude of suffering? It was like killing a mosquito with a cannon!

Reputation is what people think we are, but character is what God knows we are. You can make or ruin a reputation in a moment, but it takes years to build character, and God is concerned about character. At the very outset of the book, God made it clear that He wasn't chastening Job for his sins. At the end of the book, God said that Job had spoken rightly about Him (Job 42:7), while his friends had not spoken rightly about either God or Job. All this suffering wasn't Job's fault, because God had a much higher purpose in mind.

WHAT SATAN CLAIMS TO SEE — opposes

"Satan" means "adversary"; "devil" means "slanderer, accuser." The Devil is a created being, a fallen angel, who opposes God by attacking God's people (Rev. 12:7–12). It surprises people to discover that Satan is neither all-knowing nor all-powerful, nor is he present everywhere. These divine attributes belong only to the Lord. During this present age, Satan has access to God's throne in heaven where he accuses God's servants (Zech. 3:1–7). However, the Devil must get the Lord's permission before he can attack the Lord's people (Job 1:12; 2:6). It's encouraging to know that Satan can't touch us apart from the will of God, and that if he does attack us, God has a special purpose to fulfill and will give us the strength we need to overcome (Luke 22:31–32).

Satan stalks the earth looking for victims (Job 1:7). He may come as a serpent to deceive (2 Cor. 11:3), as a lion to devour (1 Peter 5:8–9), or even as an angel of light to delude (2 Cor. 11:13–15). Apparently he had tried to attack Job in the past but the Lord had protected His servant. Satan had his eyes on Job, for Job was an influential man in his community, and if Job turned from the Lord, it could lead many to abandon their faith. This would please Satan.

Satan couldn't speak a word until first the Lord had challenged him. We wonder if the Lord can point to us and use our faith and faithfulness to silence the accuser. Keep in mind that Job knew nothing about this conversation at the throne of the Almighty! He had no idea that his body would become a battleground where God and Satan would wage war. There are unexplained experiences in the visible world that grow out of spiritual conflicts in the invisible world, and we must be ready to trust God and rest on His promises. We walk by faith and not by sight — or feeling.

"It's no surprise that Job serves you," Satan said to the Lord. "After all, you've built a hedge around him, and I can't touch him. The only reason he serves you is because you're paying him to be obedient. You give him everything good and protect him from everything bad. He doesn't love you and serve you because of who you are but because of what you do for him."

This is the central theme of the book. In spite of what's been said in books and sermons, the book of Job doesn't wrestle with the question, "Why do the righteous suffer?" That wasn't Satan's attack at all. Satan was accusing Job of worshiping and serving God only because God was rewarding him. At the same time, Satan was accusing God of not being worthy of man's worship and obedience, and that's why He has to reward His worshipers. If He didn't pay Job, Job wouldn't worship God at all. In other words, the big question is not "Why do the righteous suffer?" but "Is the God for whom we suffer worthy of our suffering? Do we suffer for Him because He pays us or because He is worthy?"

God knows our hearts, Satan and his demonic hosts watch our conduct, and we must examine our motives. Satan was wrong about Job, but he may be right about us.

WHAT HIS FRIENDS NEED TO SEE

Bad news seems to spread faster than good news, and the report quickly went out that Job had lost his family, his wealth, and his health. Three of Job's older friends (Job 15:10) agreed to meet and travel together to visit Job and offer their comfort and encouragement. At first we admire them for their display of sorrow and their willingness to sit silently on the ground by their friend and share his pain. Had the situation remained like that, they might have consoled him; but when Job opened his mouth and began to describe his suffering and the seeming lack of purpose behind it, they felt they needed to discuss the matter, disagree with him, and then accuse him. Later Elihu, a younger man, joined the discussion and pretty much sided with the three visitors.

But Job didn't appreciate the lectures given by his so-called friends. He called them undependable streams (Job 6:14 – 21) that promised water but failed to produce it. They were "worthless physicians" (Job 13:4) who spent all their time diagnosing his case but failed to provide a remedy. Finally, he called them "miserable comforters" (Job 16:2), which is an effective oxymoron. Spurgeon said that the three friends poured vinegar into Job's wounds and increased his agony tenfold.

What the friends failed to see was that Job was in great pain and that their words were hurting him more than healing him. He hurt physically, with painful running sores (Job 2:7–8), nightmares (Job 7:13–14), weight loss (Job 19:20), chills and fever (Job 21:6), and an upset stomach and diarrhea (Job 30:27). He was so changed physically that his friends could barely recognize him (Job 2:12). But Job was also suffering emotionally, for he had lost all his children and all his wealth. He had no loved ones to care for him and his wife, and he had no money to pay somebody else to do it. His situation was hopeless.

But even worse, his faith in God was under attack as he wrestled with questions. *What have I done to deserve so much suffering? Why would God give us ten children and then allow a storm to kill them all at once? Why did He enrich me and then suddenly rob me? If I'm so bad, why didn't the Lord warn me and give me opportunity to repent?* Day and night these questions pounded at his brain.

And what did his friends do? They argued theology and tried to prove that Job was a hypocrite who had at last been found out. Their logic went like this: (1) God is holy and must punish sin. (2) God is punishing Job. (3) Therefore, Job is a sinner. But they forgot that God is also longsuffering, gracious, and loving, and that He is willing to forgive sin. God is also wise and works in ways we can't always understand. These men acted as though they had an inside track into the counsel of almighty God.

There is nothing wrong with discussing theology if we remember that we don't live on explanations but on promises. When the surgeon showed me the X-rays and explained why my gall bladder hurt, that didn't make me feel any better. But when he said he would operate and I'd be home pain-free in three days, he gave me a promise that encouraged me. We live on promises, not explanations. Promises are God's medicine for the heart, and they bring healing to the inner person. But Job's friends had no promises to share. All they had were arguments and philosophical statements that were like knives that cut deep into Job's already bleeding heart.

Why did the friends do this? Here is one suggestion: they needed arguments to assure themselves that such affliction could never happen to them because they were righteous before the Lord, and He had to bless them. That was their theology: God does good to the righteous and punishes the wicked. But Jesus said that the Father "causes his sun to rise on the evil and the good, and sends rain on the righteous and the unrighteous" (Matt. 5:45). The friends were not righteous men; they were self-righteous men. They needed their false theology to bolster their own courage and assure themselves, "This can never happen to us."

At the end of this entire episode, God said to Eliphaz, "I am angry with you and your two friends, because you have not spoken of me what is right, as my servant Job has" (Job 42:7–8). The friends didn't have such good theology after

all. They also lacked sympathy and love, not to speak of tact. They should have
been witnesses to the love and grace of God, but they became prosecuting at-
torneys and judges instead.

WHAT JOB WANTED TO SEE

As you read the long speeches recorded in the book of Job, you sense that
the ash heap had become a court of law, and this is true. The book of Job is filled
with legal terminology. The friends wanted to see Job confess his sins and get
right with God, so they kept repeating their accusations. But Job wasn't about to
surrender to their false theology and confess sins he hadn't committed. He never
claimed to be sinless, but he was a man of integrity when he spoke about himself
and about God (Job 42:8). But Job didn't know how to find God and get Him on
the witness stand to testify, "There is nobody on earth like My servant Job!"

Throughout his speeches, Job expresses his desire to meet God face-to-face,
to get Him into court and make Him present the evidence for Job's guilt. He
wanted to "dispute with him," which in Hebrew means "enter into litigation,"
and force the Lord to answer, which means "testify in court" (Job 9:3). He wanted
to plead with the Judge for mercy (9:15). He longed to find a "daysman," an um-
pire or arbitrator, who could settle the dispute fairly (9:33). Job wanted to plead
his own case (13:18–19), but there was no way to set a time and place where he
and the Lord could talk together (13:3).

Since Job wanted to meet with God and defend himself, God deigned to
come to see him and speak to him (Job 38:1–40:2). But when God showed up
and began to ask Job questions, Job had nothing to say! He put his hand over his
mouth and said, "I will say no more" (Job 40:5). The solution to Job's problems
wasn't a profound explanation from the Lord, but a personal revelation of the
Lord. Psychiatrist Paul Tournier wrote, "For God's answer [to human needs]
is not an idea, a proposition, like the conclusion of a theorem; it is Himself. He
revealed Himself to Job; Job found personal contact with Him."[1] The hurt child
doesn't want to hear a lecture on bicycle safety; the child wants to feel Mother's
arms and kiss and to hear Father's assuring voice. Theology is important but only
if its truths bring us closer to the Lord.

The hymn "Break Thou the Bread of Life" says, "Beyond the sacred page I
seek Thee, Lord. / My spirit pants for Thee Thou living Word." Job never sang
those words, but he did experience the blessing they describe. What Job wanted to
see—a righteous Judge—he never saw; but he did meet a wonderful, loving God
who solved the problems and answered the questions just by being there. "I had a
million questions to ask God," wrote Christopher Morley in his book *Inward Ho!*
"but when I met Him, they all fled my mind, and it didn't seem to matter."[2] Job's
mouth was shut, but his heart was opened and he began to experience healing.

1. Paul Tournier, *Guilt and Grace* (New York: Harper and Row, 1962), 46.
2. Christopher Morley, *Inward Ho!* (Garden City, N.Y.: Doubleday, Doran and Co.,
1931), 9.

WHAT BELIEVERS TODAY MUST SEE

Let's start with our own needs and then move on to how we can meet the needs of others.

First, we must see that suffering is a part of life. We are a fallen people, living in a fallen world, and God never promised that this earth would always be a friendly place. But while suffering is the result of Adam's sin, our own suffering isn't always punishment for our personal sins. Yes, sometimes it is; we disobey God and He has to discipline us because He loves us. But the Devil wants people to think God is punishing us, because the Devil is the accuser of God and God's people. What we think is "undeserved suffering" may be exactly what we need to prepare us for our next assignment. Both Joseph and David went through those experiences.

So, when you are struck by falling rocks, or when you are in your own Gethsemane, always respond with, "Not my will but Your will be done." Remember that the will of God comes from the heart of God (Ps. 33:11) and is a demonstration of His love. When He puts us into the furnace, He keeps His eye on the clock and His hand on the thermostat, and He knows how long and how much. See the Lord and rest on His promises. Spurgeon said that "we are sure to get into mischief as soon as we begin catechizing God and asking 'Why?' and 'Wherefore?'" God turns question marks into exclamation points when we focus on Him in all His grace and greatness.

God sometimes permits us to suffer so that we can help encourage others. God "comforts us in all our troubles, so that we can comfort those in any trouble with the comfort we ourselves have received from God" (2 Cor. 1:4). Paul didn't say that, in order to help others, we must experience exactly the same suffering as they did, for that's not always possible. He said that God's imparted grace to us can "overflow" through us and bring comfort to others (2 Cor. 1:5). Let's not complain about our suffering; after all, Jesus suffered far more than we ever could, and He did it because He loved us. He is able to sustain us and see us through.

But let's not follow the bad example of Job's friends. No matter how much people complain or resist suffering, let's love them for Jesus' sake and patiently share the promises of God and His healing grace. Let's not work for Satan and be omniscient accusers. God is looking for comforters. If the sufferers are lost, see them as those for whom Jesus died. If the sufferers are believers, see them as those in whom Jesus lives. It is our love for Christ that makes the difference and motivates us (2 Cor. 5:14), and "love never fails" (1 Cor. 13:8). Remember what our Lord said: "I tell you the truth, whatever you did for one of the least of these brothers of mine, you did for me" (Matt. 25:40).

There's so much suffering and need all around us that we must be careful not to become judgmental, isolated, and insulated. Pious talk can never substitute for sacrificial ministry (James 2:14–17; 1 John 3:16–20). Each of us needs to "become Jesus" in the life of someone who is suffering, who may never meet Him any other way.

17

MOSES

> *"Now show me your glory."*
> EXODUS 33:18

At the time Moses asked God to show him His glory, Moses was with God on Mount Sinai, interceding for the people of Israel. He had just asked the Lord not to abandon His sinful people but to go with them on their journey, and God said, "I will do the very thing you have asked, because I am pleased with you and I know you by name" (Ex. 33:17). At this point, Moses could have asked the Lord for almost anything, but all Moses prayed was, "Now show me your glory."

What people pray for is one indication of what they live for, what's really important in their lives. More than anything else, Moses wanted to see God's glory in person. The glory of God is a repeated theme in the life of Moses, the faithful servant of God. I believe that his lifelong focus on God's glory was one of the secrets of his faithfulness and endurance as he led the nation of Israel. He didn't have an easy calling, and there were times when he felt like quitting, but focusing on the glory of God strengthened him and kept him going.

Let's trace these "glory experiences" and apply them to our lives so that we, too, might run the race with endurance and finish our course with joy.

THE BURNING BUSH (Ex. 3)

To an Israelite, fire was one of the images of Jehovah God. "For the LORD your God is a consuming fire" (Deut. 4:24; Heb. 12:29). When fire came down from heaven and consumed the sacrifice on the altar, it meant that God had accepted the sacrifice and was pleased with the worshiper. Moses saw the bush burning but not being consumed and was naturally attracted to it. Then he discovered that God was there, waiting to speak to him.

Did the burning bush symbolize Moses, insignificant in himself but a powerful servant when ignited by God? Or did the bush picture Israel, a small weak people who would take the light of God's glory and truth to the nations? Perhaps the burning bush signified both. Moses gave the Lord many reasons why he wasn't the best man for the job, but God persisted and Moses finally said yes. He was an eighty-year-old shepherd, a fugitive from Egypt where he'd killed a man (possibly in self-defense). He didn't think he was capable of rescuing Israel from Egypt, but he was willing to believe that God was able.

The next time we tell God He has made a mistake in calling us, let's remember Moses and the burning bush. We might see ourselves as only flickering candles, but God sees us as bushes that can burn and not be consumed. Ministry is a miracle. As the late Dr. Bob Cook, president of King's College, used to say, "If you can explain what's going on, God didn't do it."

THE FIERY CLOUD (Ex. 13:21–22)

The Lord delivered Israel from Egypt and went before them to lead them where He wanted them to go. They had no maps or compasses nor did they hire any wilderness guides. The Lord God went before them in a cloud of glory by day and a pillar of fire by night (Deut. 1:33). Traveling by night wasn't too convenient, especially for the aged and the very young, but the people knew they were following God's plan. They didn't have to fear surprise enemy attacks because the Lord of the universe was both guiding and protecting. The same angelic hosts that protected them from the army of Egypt guarded them in their journey (Ex. 14:19–20).

When Moses erected the tabernacle in the center of the camp and then dedicated it to the Lord, the glory of God moved into the Most Holy Place and the cloud rested over the tent during the day and the pillar of fire by night (Ex. 40:36–38). Israel was the only nation on earth that actually had God's glorious presence with them in the midst of the camp (Rom. 9:4). The other nations had sanctuaries, but they were empty. What an awesome privilege to have the Lord Jehovah dwelling with them! What a great responsibility!

Every child of God can claim the promise: "He guides me in paths of righteousness for his name's sake" (Ps. 23:3). We may not see a billowy cloud or a pillar of fire, but God is going before us just the same, so long as we seek His will and obey it. Jesus goes ahead of us and we follow Him as He speaks to us from the Word (John 10:4).

Even more, God dwells in the bodies of His people (1 Cor. 6:19–20) and with His people when they assemble to worship Him (1 Cor. 3:16–17; the pronouns are plural). The church worldwide is a holy temple, a dwelling in which God by His Spirit lives with His people (Eph. 2:19–22).

THE FLAMING MOUNTAIN (Ex. 19:16–19)

The glory is increasing! Moses began with seeing a burning bush, and then God gave Israel a pillar of fire to follow, but now Israel was encamped around a flaming mountain at Sinai. "Mount Sinai was covered with smoke, because the LORD descended on it in fire" (Ex. 19:18). The glory of the Lord came down on the mountain, and "to the Israelites the glory of the LORD looked like a consuming fire on top of the mountain" (Ex. 24:17). "The mountain was ablaze with fire" (Deut. 5:23), and Moses confessed that he was so terrified that he trembled with fear (Heb. 12:21).

Why did God put on this frightening display of fire and smoke and thunder and loud trumpets? Israel was a people in the infancy of their faith, and they had to learn to respect God, to hear His voice and obey what He commanded. At Sinai they learned that Jehovah was Lord, they were His people, and He was in command. They were about to be taught God's wonderful law, and "the fear of the LORD is the beginning of wisdom" (Prov. 9:10). By giving Israel His law, God set them apart as His people; and by obeying His law, the nation would enjoy His blessings. Believers today are citizens of a heavenly city (Heb. 12:18–24), but we must still respect the holy will of God and seek to glorify Him. "See to it that you do not refuse him who speaks ... for our 'God is a consuming fire'" (Heb. 12:25, 29).

THE RADIANT COUNTENANCE (Ex. 34:29–35; 2 Cor. 3)

Moses saw God's glory in the bush, in the fiery cloud, and on the flaming mountain, but he couldn't see the glory on his own face!

As he communed with the Lord, Moses incorporated some of the divine glory, and it radiated from his face, but after a time it faded away. Paul interpreted this event for us in 2 Corinthians 3 and explained why Moses put on a veil to cover the glory. It wasn't because the people were frightened but because the glory was fading. Who wants to follow a leader whose glory is fading? Paul saw this as a contrast between the ministry of law and the ministry of grace. In Paul's day, the glory of the law was fading, and soon the temple itself would be destroyed; but the glory of the grace of Jesus Christ was increasing. Our message today isn't "Obey Moses" but "Believe on the Lord Jesus Christ and you will be saved!"

Paul closed his discussion by giving a personal application (2 Cor. 3:18). Moses spent time with the Lord and went from His presence with the glory on his face. As we spend time with the Lord in His Word, the Holy Spirit radiates the glory of Jesus through us because the Spirit teaches us the Word and reveals Jesus to us. To paraphrase 2 Corinthians 3:18, "When the child of God looks into the Word of God, he or she sees the Son of God and is transformed into the image of God by the Spirit of God to the glory of God." Moses had to climb a mountain to spend time with the Lord, but we can come to Him at any time in any place and experience that glorious communion. Our times of meditation in the Word ought to result in a burning heart (Luke 24:32), a glowing face, and growing likeness to Jesus Christ.

One of God's purposes in saving us is that we might be "conformed to the likeness of his Son" here and now (Rom. 8:29). Yes, "we shall be like him, for we shall see him as he is" (1 John 3:2), but we aren't supposed to wait until then. We must "take time to be holy" and allow the Spirit to transform us into His likeness. The word translated "transformed" that Paul used in 2 Corinthians 3:18 is the same word translated "transfigured" in Matthew 17:2. It means a change on the outside that comes from within. The word is also used in Romans 12:2: "Do not conform any longer to the pattern of this world, but be transformed [transfigured] by the renewing of your mind." We can experience our own personal transfiguration day by day as we spend time in the Word learning about Jesus.

The word *transfiguration* brings us to the fifth "glory experience" of Moses.

THE HOLY MOUNT (Matt. 17:1–8; 2 Peter 1:16–18)

Has it ever struck you that the life of Moses ended rather sadly? In the book of Deuteronomy, he taught the new generation the law and told them how to conquer the land and enjoy its blessings. He warned them what would happen if they disobeyed the Lord (Deut. 32), and then he gave them his blessing (Deut. 33). As the people watched, he left the camp and climbed Mount Nebo, and they never saw him again. No farewell banquet, no tributes, not even a long obituary listing his achievements. He died on the mount, and God buried him in a grave nobody could find. How unlike the "great leaders" of our day whose burials are televised around the world and to whose expensive tombs the world beats a path.

If anybody deserved a world-class funeral, it was Moses. He had sacrificially served the people of Israel for forty years. He had listened to their constant complaining, interceded for them when they sinned, settled their disputes, and taught them God's law. On two occasions, God offered to destroy the nation and create a new nation from Moses, but Moses said no (Ex. 32:9–10; Num. 14:10–12). Moses even offered to die to preserve the nation (Ex. 32:30–32; Ps. 106:23). Because of his own sin, Moses wasn't allowed to enter the Promised Land; all he could do was view it from Mount Nebo (Num. 20:1–12).

But Moses finally made it to the Promised Land! He and Elijah came down from heaven to an unidentified mountain (perhaps Mount Hermon) where they saw Jesus in His glory and talked with Him about His impending death on the cross (Matt. 17:1–8). Moses had seen God's glory manifested in many ways, but now he saw the greatest revelation of the glory of God "in the face of Christ" (2 Cor. 4:6). All other glory fades into shadows when compared with the glory of Jesus Christ.

The visit of Moses to the Mount of Transfiguration should be an encouragement to anyone who has experienced disappointments in this life. Like Moses, you may have given your very best in serving Christ and yet had nothing but trouble and seeming failure. You may never have received the recognition and rewards that rightfully were yours. Fret not. When you see your Savior in glory, the books will be opened and the accounts will be balanced accurately. "It will be worth it all when we see Jesus."

Meanwhile, find encouragement and enablement in seeing the glory of God today! When the work seems too difficult for you and the people too much for you, do as Moses did and retreat to your own "mount" and behold the glory of the Lord. Like Moses and Stephen (Acts 6:15), become a person like Jesus, a person with a shining face. And may the Lord never write over your life and work, "Ichabod—'the glory has departed'" (1 Sam. 4:21–22).

One more thought about Moses and God's glory. Until he was forty years old, Moses lived in Egypt when it was the world's leading empire. He learned their wisdom (Acts 7:22) and beheld their power and splendor, but it never took hold of him. He could have been a powerful man in Egypt, but he gave it all up to identify with the Jews, a nation of slaves who seemed to have no future. What motivated him to reject the transient glory of Egypt and seek only the glory of God?

May I suggest that it was the godly influence of the woman who raised him, his mother, Jochebed? Her name means "Jehovah is glory." Whenever Moses heard his mother's name, he was reminded that "Jehovah is glory." The glory of men and nations lasts as long as the flowers and grass in the backyard, but the glory of God lasts forever. That's the glory we want to choose.

18

AARON

Aaron, who was consecrated to the LORD.

PSALM 106:16

$\mathcal{A}$aron is remembered as "the brother of Moses," just as Andrew the apostle is remembered as "Simon Peter's brother." In the Pentateuch, God says, "Aaron your brother" eleven times. Aaron was three years older than Moses and therefore should have been the more prominent of the two, but as with Jacob and Esau, God decreed that the elder should serve the younger. We don't know how Aaron personally responded to this arrangement. For the most part, he seems to have accepted it as the will of God.

But there were times when Aaron had problems handling authority. Since exercising authority in life and in ministry is an important matter, let's learn as much as we can from Aaron.

USING AUTHORITY

Aaron had remained in Egypt during the forty years Moses was shepherding his father-in-law's flock in Midian. Now he would join Moses and, with the Lord's help, deliver the people of Israel from bondage. Moses had a tough job ahead of him and needed someone at his side to assist him. "Two are better than one" (Eccl. 4:9), which may explain why Jesus sent out His disciples two by two (Mark 6:7). As they traveled along, Aaron would be able to bring his brother up to date on people and events in Egypt.

Some Bible students minimize the ministry of Aaron and claim he gave Moses more trouble than he did help, but a careful reading of the record proves that this accusation is exaggerated. God called Aaron just as He called Moses, and there was divine authority behind these calls. In fact, before God called Moses, He had already prompted Aaron to leave Egypt and meet his brother in the desert (Ex. 4:14, 27). God didn't send Moses alone to Egypt; He sent "Moses and Aaron" together (Josh. 24:5; Pss. 77:20; 105:26; Mic. 6:4). Moses was the primary leader, and he and Aaron shared the divine authority to lead the people of Israel.

Aaron also had authority to speak for the Lord. Moses claimed that he himself couldn't speak well, so Aaron became Moses's spokesperson (Ex. 4:16; 6:12; 7:1). He and Moses spoke initially to the elders of Israel (Ex. 4:29), and then they spoke many times to Pharaoh. Along with Moses, Aaron performed signs and wonders that proved they were true messengers of Jehovah. Eventually Moses discovered that he could deliver his own messages, so Aaron stepped aside. Aaron probably didn't feel "demoted" when this happened, for as Israel's high priest, he was still an important man in the camp.

Aaron also had authority with Moses to intercede for the people. When the nation asked for bread, Aaron and Moses turned to God for help (Ex. 16). While Joshua fought the enemy on the battlefield, Aaron and Hur held up Moses's hands to guarantee victory for Israel (Ex. 17:8–16). When the people criticized Moses and Aaron because Korah and his fellow rebels were slain by God, it was Aaron who "stood between the living and the dead" and stopped the plague (Num. 16:41–50). That took faith and courage. At Kadesh Barnea, when the nation refused to trust God and enter the land, Aaron joined Moses in falling down before the Lord and pleading for Him to show mercy to His people (Num. 14:1–5).

As long as he was with Moses, Aaron exercised his authority in a mature and constructive way; but when his brother wasn't at his side, he fell apart and did foolish things. This takes us to the tragedy of the golden calf (Ex. 32).

ABUSING AUTHORITY

The Lord demonstrated His great power and glory at Mount Sinai and told Moses to approach the mountain while the rest of the nation stayed at a distance (Ex. 19:16–19; 20:21). The Lord gave Moses the book of the covenant (Ex. 20–23) and then commanded him to come up to Him on the mountain along with Aaron, Aaron's two sons, and seventy of the elders of Israel (Ex. 24:1). There they saw God and even ate and drank in His presence (Ex. 24:9–11). Then Moses and Joshua went higher to further commune with God while the others returned to the camp, and he told Aaron and Hur to take charge in his absence (Ex. 24:13–14).

People who are not *under* authority should not *exercise* authority, because acting independently is the first step toward abusing others and sinning against God. That's how dictators get their start. Aaron was under the authority of Moses, and both men were under the authority of God, so the absence of Moses should have made no difference in Aaron's attitude or conduct. God was watching even though Moses was absent. This was Aaron's opportunity to glorify God by watching over the nation just as Moses always did.

Moses stayed with God on the mountain forty days and nights (Ex. 24:18). He was getting instructions from God about building the tabernacle and establishing the holy priesthood. Since Aaron would be the high priest, what Moses was receiving applied directly to him and his ministry; therefore, when Aaron sinned, he hurt himself and his sons who would be serving with him. He manufactured a golden idol and allowed the people to worship it and give themselves to the most licentious kind of behavior.

Three times the text reminds us that what the Israelites did was "a great sin"

(32:21, 30, 31). Why was it so great? Because of where they were, at the mountain of the Lord, where they had beheld His power and glory and where three times they had promised to obey Him (Ex. 19:8; 24:3, 7). Because of what they had heard in the law that Jehovah was the only true and living God. In making an idol, worshiping it, and engaging in lustful orgies, the nation broke four of the Ten Commandments, and if they broke even one, they had broken the entire law.

God had said of Aaron, "I know he can speak well" (Ex. 4:14), and what Aaron said to defend himself reveals what a smooth talker he was (Ex. 32:22–24). First he blamed the people for being prone to sin; then he blamed Moses for staying away so long; and then he blamed the furnace for producing the calf! It was everybody's fault but Aaron's, and yet God said that Aaron made the calf (Ex. 32:35). Twentieth-century evangelist Billy Sunday said that an excuse is the skin of a reason stuffed with a lie, and he was right. Moses had to return to the Lord on the mountain and intercede for the people, and especially for Aaron whom the Lord was ready to kill (Deut. 9:20). But sin still pays wages, and three thousand people were slain by the Levites (Ex. 32:25–29) plus an unidentified number by a plague from the Lord (Ex. 32:35).

Nothing erodes and destroys authority like giving people what they want instead of what they need. When spiritual ministry becomes market driven and culture driven, when the motto is "Give the customers what they want," then ministry has become business, and no matter how many customers come through the doors, the glory of the Lord has departed.

TESTING AUTHORITY

From time to time, leaders must be tested to remind them of how valuable their authority is and how it must be protected, and Aaron was involved in three such tests. The first was at Sinai when Moses left Aaron in charge and he made the golden calf. Aaron failed that test. The second was private, when he and his sister, Miriam, criticized their brother, Moses, for his choice of a new wife (Num. 12; see the chapter on Miriam). The third was when Korah, Dathan, and Abiram, and 250 other tribal leaders led a revolt against both Moses and Aaron, challenging their authority. Korah was a Levite who wanted the privileges of the priesthood, and the others wanted some of the authority that God gave Moses. The rebels used the old argument that "the whole community is holy" (Num. 16:3), so everybody is on the same level. They forgot that God appoints leaders and expects His people to follow them as they follow the Lord.

Moses tried to reason with them, but it was a waste of time. Moses even offered to conduct an experiment to see if the Lord would accept the 250 would-be priests with their censers. When God announced that judgment was about to fall, Moses and Aaron fell on their faces and pled for mercy for the people (Num. 16:22), but it was too late for intercession. The ground split open, and the leaders and their households were swallowed up. Then fire fell from heaven and killed the 250 men with the censers. God made it clear that Moses and Aaron were his leaders.

But some of God's sheep never get the message, and the next day the entire camp grumbled against Moses and Aaron. Once again, Moses and Aaron let the Lord defend them, and He sent a plague that killed 14,700 people. There would have been more deaths, but Aaron took his censer and courageously stood among the people and stopped the plague (Num. 16:41 – 50). Patiently, Moses performed another test and asked for a staff from the leader of each tribe with the leader's name written on it. These were put before the veil in the tabernacle, along with Aaron's rod; and the next day, Aaron's rod had sprouted, budded, blossomed, and produced almonds! He was God's chosen priest!

It is sad to realize that most of the people of Israel never understood the price Moses and Aaron had to pay to be their leaders. They had to endure the unbelief and disobedience of the people, the rebellion of the leaders, and the repeated murmuring and complaining of both people and leaders. If leaders are ever in danger of becoming proud, there is enough trouble around them to make them humble!

But challenging the authority of godly leaders who are serving the Lord faithfully is a serious matter.

19

MIRIAM

Set a guard over my mouth, O Lord;
keep watch over the door of my lips.

Psalm 141:3

*M*iriam, Aaron, and Moses were privileged to have godly parents who had faith in the true and living God, the God of Abraham, Isaac, and Jacob (Heb. 11:23). Amram and Jochebed feared God more than they feared Pharaoh, and they trained their children to follow their example (Heb. 11:23).

The three occasions in Scripture that feature Miriam suggest that she was a determined person who knew how to use words effectively. Even as a child, she didn't hesitate to approach Pharaoh's daughter and offer to provide a nursing mother for the crying baby boy in the basket. Exodus 15:20 calls her a "prophetess," a title she shared with nine other women in the Bible: Deborah (Judg. 4:4), Huldah (2 Kings 22:14), Noadiah (Neh. 6:14), the wife of Isaiah (Isa. 8:3), Anna (Luke 2:36), and the four daughters of Philip the evangelist (Acts 21:9). That title gave her the privilege of speaking officially for the Lord.

But persons who have the ability to speak well and the authority to do it must always be on guard. "The tongue has the power of life and death," warns Proverbs 18:21; and James 3:8 describes the tongue as "a restless evil, full of deadly poison." On the other hand, human speech can be like "food and medicine" and help heal troubled hearts (Prov. 10:11, 21; 12:18; 15:4, 23). We learn from Miriam that there must be a guard at the door of our lips, and that guard is the Lord.

WORDS OF WISDOM (Ex. 2:1–10)

Big sisters usually have a special attachment to little brothers, and besides, the family knew that Moses was "no ordinary child" (Acts 7:20; Heb. 11:23). When she put the baby in the basket in the Nile River, did Jochebed lift a prayer to the God of Israel that He would protect her little boy? I think she did, and then she backed up her faith with works by leaving Miriam on the scene to report what happened. At just the right time, the princess came to the water to perform her daily ablutions, and at just the right time, little Moses began to cry. The heart of a king is in the hand of the Lord (Prov. 21:1) and so is the heart of a princess. She couldn't resist the tug of the baby at her heart.

But see the alertness of Miriam. Without revealing that she was the little boy's sister, Miriam wisely offered to find a Hebrew nursing mother for the child, and she brought Jochebed! By the goodness and grace of God, Moses was raised in a godly home and prepared spiritually for his time in a pagan palace. Behold the greatness of the Lord! He used two women, a little girl, and a crying baby to take the first step toward defeating Egypt and setting Israel free. God uses the "weak things of the world to shame the strong" (1 Cor. 1:27).

How did Miriam know what to say to the princess? Did Jochebed coach her or did the Lord put those wise words in the little girl's mouth? "The preparations of the heart belong to man, but the answer of the tongue is from the LORD" (Prov. 16:1 NKJV). Her words were used by God to preserve the life of the person who would bring Israel to freedom and be their leader for forty years. In my own pastoral ministry, there were occasions when I had to give counsel to people and didn't always know what to say, but the Lord gave me the right words just when I needed them. If our hearts are prepared, we are ready to hear what the Lord wants to say.

How do we prepare our hearts? By reading God's Word, memorizing it, meditating on it, learning God's wisdom from it, and obeying what it says. If we are praying, walking in the Spirit, and ready to obey the Lord by faith, it is remarkable what the Lord can do with our hearts and our lips when they are dedicated to Him.

WORDS OF PRAISE (Ex. 15:1–21)

The first time we meet Miriam in the Bible, she is standing on the banks of the Nile River in Egypt, where the baby Moses was taken *out of the water.* The second time we meet her, she is on the far shore of the Red Sea where Moses had led the Israelites *through the water* to freedom on the other shore. Ever since that awesome night, the people of Israel have celebrated Passover annually and remembered the exodus, God's gracious act of deliverance. Imagine walking through the sea on dry land! Jesus celebrated the Passover before He was arrested, tried, and crucified; but on that cross, He provided a spiritual "exodus" for all who trust Him. (See Luke 9:31, where "departure" in the Greek is "exodus.")

But back to the worship service. The Jewish people were singing praises to the Lord, with Moses leading the men and Miriam leading the women, and they had every reason to praise Jehovah. Pharaoh had made them slaves, but now they were free! Pharaoh had ordered them to drown their boy babies, but now Pharaoh's crack troops had been drowned in the Red Sea! What a victory! True praise is not about us; it is about the Lord. "Then they believed his promises and sang his praise" (Ps. 106:12).

"The LORD is my strength and my song; he has become my salvation" (Ex. 15:2) is also found in Psalm 118:14 and Isaiah 12:2. All three passages emphasize the greatness of God and His marvelous works on behalf of His people. In Exodus 15 God is exalted in victory (vv. 1–10), in His glorious attributes (vv. 11–16), and in His wonderful promises to His people (vv. 17–18). He brought them out that He might bring them in (v. 17)!

This hymn of praise is called "The Song of Moses" and is referred to in Revelation 15:3. John saw, not the Red Sea, but a sea of glass mixed with fire, and he heard the victorious saints praising God. The scene relates to Passover because their hymn is also "the song of the Lamb," that is, Jesus Christ. Moses and Miriam led the people in praising the God who had judged Egypt with His awesome plagues, but the scene in Revelation 15 takes place *before* God sends plagues on earth, and those plagues parallel the plagues God poured out on Egypt.

The worship of God is the highest activity we can engage in and the greatest privilege we can experience. In too many churches, the sanctuary has become a theater and the worship leaders are polished performers. The congregation is now an audience, and what once was worship is now shallow entertainment. The measure of success isn't the awesome presence of God but the size of the crowd and the enthusiasm of their applause. We have forgotten the slavery of the old life, the death of the Lamb, and the greatness of God and His salvation—and we are the losers.

WORDS OF ENVY (Num. 12)

The nation was at Kadesh Barnea, preparing to enter the Promised Land and claim their inheritance. In Bible history, God's appointed leaders were often threatened by false accusations just before they faced a great opportunity, in this case, entering Canaan. We aren't told when Moses's wife Zipporah died, but Moses had married again, and Miriam didn't like the woman he chose. The issue wasn't race or the color of her skin, even though the King James Version erroneously translates this word as "Ethiopian." (The biblical Cushites lived in what we today know as Sudan.) No, Miriam's problem was deeper than the skin and certainly wasn't the fault of Moses or his new wife. If Miriam had kept her feelings to herself, she might not have caused so much trouble, but she won Aaron to her point of view, and that made it an official family concern.

The real issue was territorial; it was a matter of leadership and authority, as their questions in Numbers 12:2 make clear. Was Moses's new wife beginning to take charge and influence her husband too much? Was his sister losing some of the prestige and authority that Miriam felt were hers alone? Miriam is mentioned first (v. 1), and only she was disciplined, so we can assume that she was the originator of the problem. In Exodus 2, Miriam had protected her brother Moses, but now she was attacking him and making his job more difficult. Our foes may arise from our own households, as Joseph, David, and even Jesus discovered.

However, Moses in his meekness didn't defend himself but left his defense to the Lord. The name order in verse 1—Miriam, Aaron, Moses—was rearranged in verse 4 by the Lord to Moses, Aaron, and Miriam. God met the three leaders at the Tent of Meeting, rebuked Miriam and Aaron, and then displayed His holy anger by giving Miriam leprosy. Aaron immediately confessed their sin, which spared him from being punished, but the Lord refused to answer the brothers' plea that He immediately cleanse Miriam. He quarantined her outside the camp with the other unclean people, and this kept the whole camp from moving forward. Nothing hinders the progress of God's people like sin among the leaders. A week later, she was declared clean and allowed back in the camp. As the high priest, Aaron had to supervise his sister's examination and order her isolation, and this must have embarrassed him greatly.

Envy among God's people is a cancerous sin, and envious words spoken against God's servants especially grieve the Lord. Each of us must gladly accept the gifts, ministries, and spheres the Lord has assigned to us and be faithful to do our work for His glory alone. There is no competition in the work of the Lord, and each of us will give an account of our own ministry and not somebody else's (Rom. 14:9–12). The world at large is filled with "envy, murder, strife, deceit and malice" (Rom. 1:29), sins that must not even be named among God's people. Peter admonishes us to rid ourselves of "all malice and all deceit, hypocrisy, envy, and slander of every kind" (1 Peter 2:1). Envy means we are miserable when others succeed, and malice means we are happy when others fail, and both can lead to murder, strife, and deceit. The first step is to recognize these sins and admit that we are guilty; then we must confess them and forsake them.

When Miriam criticized Moses, she had no idea that her sin would be written in the official Jewish law for every generation to read. Nor did she realize that God would use her as an example! "Remember what the LORD your God did to Miriam along the way after you came out of Egypt" (Deut. 24:9). This reminder is given in connection with the laws concerning leprosy, but it is also a warning concerning the terrible sins of envy and false accusation. "Remember what the LORD your God did to Miriam" joins our Lord's warning, "Remember Lot's wife!" (Luke 17:32) as a warning we all must heed.

The next time we are tempted to envy, let's remember not only Miriam but also our Lord Jesus Christ, for envy was one of the sins that sent Him to the cross (Matt. 27:18).

20

JOSHUA

So Joshua overcame.

EXODUS 17:13

Those three words describe Joshua's first recorded military victory. The Amalekites attacked when Israel was marching from Egypt to Sinai, and Joshua defeated them with the help of Moses, Aaron, and Hur who interceded for him. Those three words could well describe Joshua's whole life, for in every way he was an overcomer.

His original name was Hoshea, which means "salvation," but with prophetic insight, Moses changed it to Joshua, which means "Jehovah is salvation" (Num. 13:8, 16). The Greek form of his name is Jesus (Matt. 1:21). With a name like that, how could the son of Nun be anything but an overcomer?

However, to be an overcomer, you must face obstacles and overcome them. What obstacles did Joshua overcome, and how can his victories encourage us to be overcomers today?

THE DEMANDS OF LEADERSHIP

The nation of Israel knew that Joshua had been chosen by the Lord to succeed Moses. In his youth, he began as Moses's humble servant (Ex. 24:13; 33:11; Num. 11:28; 27:15–23; Deut. 31:1–8; 34:9; Josh. 1:1), for when God wants to build a leader, He starts with a servant (Matt. 25:21). Scripture says that "no prophet has risen in Israel like Moses" (Deut. 34:10). Imagine following a leader like that! Moses was a man of great faith, courage, and conviction, a leader who performed mighty miracles, a prophet who spoke with God face-to-face and delivered God's Word to the people.

But Joshua was smart enough to know that, while every leader must trust God and obey His will, no two leaders are alike. But it often takes a new leader to challenge and guide a new generation, and Joshua's task was to bring the new generation into the Promised Land. He had the past years with Moses to instruct him, the promises of God to encourage him (Josh. 1:1–9), and the presence of God to assist him, so he was equipped for the battles that lay ahead.

Three times the Lord told Joshua to "be strong and courageous" (Josh. 1:6, 7, 9), and once He commanded him not to be discouraged (v. 9), because without courage, he would be frightened by the enemy and fail. "Courage is necessary in Christian work," said evangelist D. L. Moody. "I have yet to find a man who is easily discouraged that amounts to anything anywhere." The nation of Israel often tried to discourage Moses, but he kept right on going and obeyed the Lord, and Joshua followed that example. When you know God has called you to your task, you are on the winning side.

THE EVIL INFLUENCE OF EGYPT

If you have the idea that all the Jewish people who left Egypt were sanctified, you are badly mistaken. God had to say to them, "Each of you, get rid of the vile images you have set your eyes on, and do not defile yourselves with the idols of Egypt" (Ezek. 20:7). Did they obey Him? No! "But they rebelled against me and would not listen to me; they did not get rid of the vile images they had set their eyes on, nor did they forsake the idols of Egypt" (Ezek. 20:8). Read Ezekiel 23 and note how many times it mentions "prostitution," referring to the worship of false Gods in the place of Jehovah (vv. 3, 8, 18, 19, 21, 27, 29, 35).

After Joshua and the people had crossed the Jordan River, he set up twelve stones at Gilgal to remind the people that it was there that God opened the waters and brought them safely into the land (Josh. 4). The former generation experienced an exodus from Egypt, but the new generation experienced an exodus from their wilderness wanderings and defeats. Then Joshua had all the males circumcised as they reaffirmed the Lord's covenant with the nation, and in so doing, "the reproach of Egypt" was taken away. The nation was making a new beginning. Egypt no longer held dominion over them.

But if you are worshiping the gods of Egypt, you are not free, you are still a slave; and Joshua knew that the people were prone to worship false gods secretly. In his farewell speech, Joshua warned them about this: "Now fear the LORD and serve him with all faithfulness. Throw away the gods your forefathers worshiped beyond the River and in Egypt, and serve the LORD" (Josh. 24:14). Joshua and his elders must have done a good job, because during the years of their leadership and the leadership of the elders they trained, the people faithfully served the Lord; but the third generation abandoned the faith and turned to idols (Judg. 2:6–23).

As Joshua worked to settle Israel in their inheritance, his biggest challenge wasn't that the people measured Joshua next to Moses. His biggest problem was that they were prone to measure the Promised Land next to Egypt! The hidden sins of Egypt were still being nurtured in the hearts of some of the people. Moses had taken the Jews out of Egypt; in the new land, God had to take Egypt out of the Jews.

THE ENEMY ARMIES

The Lord promised His people that He would give them victory over the pagan nations in Canaan. "I will drive out the enemy" is a recurring theme (Ex.

23:20–33; 33:1–2; 34:10–14; Lev. 18:24–25; 20:23–24; Num. 33:50–56; Deut. 4:35–38; 7:17–26; 9:1–6).

God kept His promise, and Joshua defeated thirty-one kings and took the land (Josh. 12).

It is unfortunate that some religious folk ballads and even some hymns use the crossing of the Jordan River as a picture of believers dying and going to heaven, because Canaan with its wickedness and warfare is not a picture of heaven. It symbolizes claiming our spiritual inheritance in Christ and defeating Satan and his hosts who want to keep us wandering around and getting nowhere. We don't fight *for* victory in our own natural strength; we fight *from* the victory Jesus has already won in His death and resurrection. "And having disarmed the powers and authorities, he made a public spectacle of them, triumphing over them by the cross" (Col. 2:15). Claim that by faith!

The first four chapters of the book of Hebrews focus on claiming our spiritual inheritance in Christ, and the writer reminds us that it was Joshua, not Moses, who brought Israel into their inheritance. There were two reasons for this change in leadership. First, Moses had sinned by failing to give God the glory (Num. 20), and the Lord allowed him to see the land but not enter it. But second, Moses is identified with the law, and we don't claim our inheritance by obeying rules and practicing rituals. Jesus, our Joshua, fulfilled the law for us and nailed it to His cross, and we claim our inheritance by faith as we follow Christ. Israel's experience both in Egypt and in the wilderness was one of bondage and futility, but in the Promised Land, they enjoyed freedom and fullness.

HIS OWN MISTAKES

Joshua 7–9 records twice that Joshua ran ahead of the Lord and failed to wait, pray, and walk by faith. After the great victory at Jericho, Israel was humiliated and defeated at Ai (Josh. 7–8); and when the men of Gibeon fooled Joshua into thinking they were from a far country, he made a covenant with them (Josh. 9; Deut. 20:10–15). The Lord had admonished Joshua to "be courageous" (Josh. 1:6–7), but to have courage, one must wait before the Lord and get his or her orders from Him. "Wait on the LORD; be of good courage, and He shall strengthen your heart" (Ps. 27:14 NKJV). Had Joshua waited before the Lord, he would have learned about Achan's thievery and the Gibeonites' deception.

Because leaders are human, leaders make mistakes. How they handle those mistakes reveals their true character. Do they blame others? Do they try to cover things up? Do they make excuses? When Joshua made a mistake, he turned to the Lord for forgiveness and wisdom, and then he made his mistakes work for him! Israel's defeat before little Ai was turned into a clever plan of ambush that wiped out the town. As for the clever Gibeonites, Joshua put them to work as servants (Josh. 9:22–27). He literally made his mistakes work for him.

People who don't make mistakes usually don't make anything. People who make mistakes and give up are quitters, but people who make the best of their mistakes are overcomers. "Life, like war, is a series of mistakes," said F. W. Robertson, "and he is not the best Christian nor the best general who makes the fewest false steps. He is the best who wins the most splendid victories by the retrieval of mistakes. Forget mistakes; organize victories out of mistakes."[1]

UNBELIEF

Joshua discovered the key to victory when he believed the promises of God, acted upon them, and became an overcomer. "By faith the walls of Jericho fell" (Heb. 11:30). "This is the victory that has overcome the world, even our faith" (1 John 5:4).

In Joshua's farewell speeches, he claimed no honor for himself but reminded the leaders and the people that he simply believed the promises of God. "You know with all your heart and soul that not one of all the good promises the LORD your God gave you has failed. Every promise has been fulfilled; not one has failed" (Josh. 23:14; and see 21:45). Certainly there were times when Joshua was weary and discouraged (see Josh. 7:6–9), but he always cast his troubles on the Lord and claimed His promises. This was also true of Moses, who in many respects had a more difficult challenge than Joshua did. When we believe God's promises, God gives us the grace we need to get the job done.

In our Lord's messages to the seven church of Asia Minor, He challenged believers in each church to become overcomers (Rev. 2:7, 11, 17, 26; 3:5, 12, 21). He still challenges us today. Will we overcome—or be overcome? Will we be victors or victims? Everything depends on what we do with the promises of God.

---

1. Frederick W. Robertson, *Sermons*, First Series (London: Kegan Paul, Trench, Trubner and Co., 1900), 66.

21

RAHAB

"Salvation is from the Jews."

JOHN 4:22

*B*y the time your Bible reading brings you to Joshua 2, you might recall Israel's tragic failure at Kadesh Barnea (Num. 13–14), and you may say to yourself, "Here we go again!" But don't jump to conclusions. If Bible history seems to be repeating itself in Joshua 2, just look a little deeper and you'll discover that something wonderfully new is happening.

Nearly four decades before the events of Joshua 2, Moses had sent twelve men to spy out Canaan, all of whom are identified in Numbers 13; but Joshua sent in only two anonymous men to check out Jericho. The twelve spies looked over Canaan for forty days, and ten of the men decided Israel couldn't conquer the land. The two unnamed men in Joshua 2 made a quick visit to Jericho and learned that the hearts of the Canaanites had melted in fear of Israel. The discouragement caused by the ten spies sent Israel back into the wilderness where a whole generation died during a long funeral march; but the encouragement of the two spies gave Joshua and the people the extra confirmation they needed for attacking Jericho.

No, history wasn't repeating itself—but there's even more. The twelve spies sent by Moses came back bearing grapes, figs, and pomegranates, but Joshua's two spies came back to announce that they had met a prostitute who had put her faith in the true and living God! If it hadn't been for the Jews, Rahab's name wouldn't even be found in four books of the Bible, including the genealogy of Jesus Christ and the list of the heroes of faith in Hebrews 11.

Let's discover how Rahab was impacted by the Jewish people and lifted to such a notable position in Bible history. Let's learn how "salvation is from the Jews."

SHE MET THE JEWISH SPIES (Josh. 2:1–7)

Rahab is called a "prostitute" in Joshua 2:1 and 6:17, 22, and 25, and those who want to sanitize the story a bit remind us that the Hebrew word can also be translated "innkeeper." True, but Hebrews 11:31 and James 2:25 call her a "prostitute," and that's what the Greek word means. She may have been both.

When the spies entered the city, Rahab may have been lingering in the street near the gates looking for customers (Prov. 7:10–13). But there were also official guards there who saw the strangers go to her house, and this looked suspicious. The spies risked their lives going into the city, but Rahab took her life in her hands when she invited them to her house, hid them, and then lied to protect them.

But consider the meeting in that house. Two men met a woman. Two Jews met a Gentile. Two believers met what they were sure was an unbeliever. But God was also there! The two guests soon discovered that Rahab had put her faith in the true and living God, the God of Israel, and that changed the whole situation. Now there was no longer Jew or Gentile, male or female, friend or enemy, but they were one in their faith in the living God. Rahab had risked her life to save them, and now they would risk their lives to help save her and her believing loved ones. "Salvation is from the Jews."

SHE ACKNOWLEDGED THE GOD OF THE JEWS (Josh. 2:8–11)

Jericho's strategic location made it a convenient stopping place for travelers, and visitors gave the citizens opportunities both to make money and to hear the news from "outside." Rahab mentioned two unforgettable news items she had heard about the Jews—the opening of the Red Sea forty years before and the more recent defeat of the Amorite kings Sihon and Og as Israel approached the Jordan River. No matter how others may have interpreted these events, Rahab saw them as proof that the God of the Jews was indeed "God in heaven above and on the earth below" (Josh. 2:11). What the Jews had sung about on the far shore of the Red Sea had actually happened!

> The nations will hear and tremble;
> anguish will grip the people of Philistia.
> The chiefs of Edom will be terrified,
> the leaders of Moab will be seized with trembling,
> the people of Canaan will melt away;
> terror and dread will fall upon them.
>
> EXODUS 15:14–16

The Lord had said to Moses, "I will send my terror ahead of you and throw into confusion every nation you encounter. I will make all your enemies turn their backs and run" (Ex. 23:27). "This very day I will begin to put the terror and fear of you on all the nations under heaven. They will hear reports of you and will tremble and be in anguish because of you" (Deut. 2:25).

The fear of the Lord is indeed the beginning of wisdom, at least in Rahab's heart. She had been converted to faith in the true and living God, thanks to the Jews.

SHE MADE A COVENANT WITH TWO JEWISH MEN (Josh. 2:12–24)

Rahab knew that Israel would capture Jericho and that there would be no survivors. They would do to Jericho what they had already done to all the cities of the Amorites, because God had commanded them to destroy anything that breathed (Ex. 23:20–23; Deut. 20:16–18). Thus her greatest concern was her survival and the survival of her family. Hers was a practical faith: she protected the spies (Heb. 11:31; James 2:25), and she had a burden for her loved ones. No wonder James used her as an example of true faith.

The men covenanted to spare her and her family or forfeit their own lives. Note that they said "when the LORD gives us the land" and not "if the LORD gives us the land," for they were certain of victory. All they asked was that Rahab gather her family into her house and identify her house by hanging a scarlet cord out the window. Since the house was on the city wall, the Jewish soldiers would know where she was and be able to protect her and her loved ones. As yet, the spies didn't know what the battle plan was for the conquest of Jericho or even when the attack would take place.

Gentiles like Rahab were "excluded from citizenship in Israel and foreigners to the covenants of the promise" (Eph. 2:12), but Rahab's faith made her a partner in a covenant with the Jews and eventually brought her into full citizenship in Israel. This was all an act of grace on God's part in response to her faith. It reminds us of the cross where Jesus reconciled sinners with God and believing Jews and Gentiles with one another.

SHE WAS RESCUED BY A JEWISH GENERAL
(Josh. 6:15–27)

When Joshua gave the orders to his soldiers on the seventh day, he reminded them not to take any spoil from the city and not to leave anybody alive except "Rahab the prostitute" and all in her house (Josh. 6:17–19). After circling the city for the seventh time that day, the priests blew their trumpets, the people shouted, and the wall collapsed—except for the part of the wall that held Rahab's house, the house that had the red cord hanging out the window. Joshua's men rescued Rahab and her family and put them in a safe place outside the camp. Thus, Rahab and her family were rescued by Joshua, "Jehovah Is Salvation." This was a type of salvation that would later come through Jesus. "Give him the name Jesus [Yeshua], because he will save his people from their sins" (Matt. 1:21).

SHE MARRIED A JEWISH HUSBAND

Rahab married a Jewish man named Salmon mentioned in Ruth 4:20–21; 1 Chronicles 2:11; Matthew 1:4–5; and Luke 3:32. Of course, Salmon and the rest of the men in the family were circumcised and received into Israel as sons of the covenant. Salmon and Rahab had a son named Boaz who married a woman named Ruth. Boaz and Ruth had a son named Obed, and he had a son named Jesse who had a son named David. Jesus was born in the city of David because He belonged to David's family.

SHE HAS HER NAME IN TWO JEWISH GENEALOGIES
(Matt. 1:4–5; Luke 3:32)

These genealogies belong to Jesus Christ, the son of David, the Son of God! Rahab is one of four women mentioned in Matthew's genealogy, an unusual thing, because the Jews focus on the fathers and not the mothers.

Tamar is there, a woman who posed as a prostitute and lay with her father-in-law, Judah (Gen. 38). Ruth the Moabitess is there. No person from Moab could be received into the Jewish congregation even to the tenth generation (Deut. 23:3), but, like Rahab, she married a Jew. Bathsheba is there (Matt. 1:6), and you probably know what happened between her and David (2 Sam. 11–12). Rahab is there, in spite of the fact that she was a Gentile prostitute. Four women, four sinners, four women who were social and religious outcasts—yet there they are in the family record of Jesus Christ!

That's what the Bible means when it says, "For it is by grace you have been saved, through faith … it is the gift of God" (Eph. 2:8).

22

DEBORAH

"I, Deborah, arose, arose a mother in Israel."

JUDGES 5:7

*W*hen Moses looked at the nation of Israel, he saw an army. As the people left Egypt on Passover night, Moses viewed them as "the Lord's divisions," marching in victory (Ex. 6:26; 12:17, 41, 51). David looked at his people and saw a flock of sheep (2 Sam. 24:17), and Asaph the choir director saw a fruitful vine (Ps. 80:8). But Deborah the judge saw the people of Israel as a family—and she was the mother.

The period of the judges was a difficult time in Jewish history. The godly leaders had died who were trained by Joshua and his elders, and a new generation had appeared that rejected the traditions and turned to the false gods of the nations around them (Judg. 2:10–23). The Lord disciplined them for their sins by bringing Gentile nations to pillage the land and oppress the people. Then the Jews would cry out to the Lord for help and He would raise up judges in different places who would deliver the people from their oppressors. These were regional leaders and not rulers over the entire nation, and they didn't work together because they ruled at different times. This cycle of sin, suffering, repentance, and deliverance was repeated at least six times, and God raised up Othniel, Ehud, Deborah, Gideon, Jephthah, and Samson to set the people free. The only woman among the judges was Deborah, a mother in Israel.

LIKE A MOTHER, SHE SETTLED THEIR DIFFERENCES (Judg. 4:4–5)

Israel didn't have a centralized government until the appointment of King Saul, and people had to go to the nearest judge to have their disputes settled. Deborah's court was located under a palm tree between Bethel in Ephraim and Ramah in Benjamin. She knew the law of the Lord and was able to listen to the problems and give wise decisions based on God's law. Leadership of the society in those days was strongly masculine, and it was unusual for a woman to hold such a high office, but Deborah was a remarkable person, chosen and used by the Lord.

LIKE A MOTHER, SHE CHALLENGED THEM TO DO THEIR BEST (Judg. 4:6–10)

Jabin, one of the kings in Canaan, was the oppressor at that time, and the Lord told Deborah He wanted to deliver His people. Instead of taking on the task alone, she sent for Barak and challenged him to recruit an army. Barak was from the northern tribe of Naphtali, and he was able to get volunteers not only from his own tribe but also from Zebulun and Issachar, two adjacent northern tribes. The battle against Jabin would take place near Mount Tabor where the borders of Issachar, Zebulun, and Naphtali met. Deborah was able to recruit soldiers from the central tribes: Ephraim (her own tribe), Benjamin, and Manasseh west of the Jordan. Barak wouldn't lead the attack unless Deborah was with him, so she turned her forces over to an unknown leader and joined Barak.

A true leader challenges others and brings out the best in them. Travel and communications were difficult in those days, but Deborah managed to mobilize a large army.

LIKE A MOTHER, SHE ENCOURAGED THEM TO TRUST THE LORD (Judg. 4:11–16)

God gave Deborah the battle plan, and she followed it. Barak would assemble his troops at Mount Tabor where the rolling country would hinder the success of the enemy chariots. When the southern army arrived, it would draw some of Jabin's chariots to the open plain in the region of the Kishon River. Then the Lord would send a torrential rain that would turn the plain into mud, and this would halt the movement of the chariots (Judg. 5:4–5, 20–22). The Lord would give Israel victory over the Canaanites.

"Go! This is the day the LORD has given Sisera into your hands!" (Judg. 4:14). On the basis of that promise, Deborah and Barak and their troops defeated Jabin and Sisera and the Canaanite forces. The chariots that Sisera thought would bring him victory turned out to be useless in the heavy rain and mud, and when the river Kishon flooded and the streams of water came pouring down Mount Tabor, the Canaanites were helpless.

LIKE A MOTHER, SHE REPROACHED THE SLACKERS (Judg. 5:15–17)

Four tribes failed to respond to the call to arms. Reuben and Gad (Gilead) were east of the Jordan River and didn't feel Jabin's oppression quite as much, and Dan and Asher were along the Mediterranean coast and not as involved. The citizens of the city of Meroz in the tribe of Naphtali also refused to volunteer (Judg. 5:23; see 5:18). By remaining home, these people failed their fellow Jews as well as their God.

LIKE A MOTHER, SHE LET OTHERS TAKE THE CREDIT
(Judg. 4:17–24; 5:24–31)

A true leader doesn't care who gets the credit as long as the Lord gets the glory, and Deborah closed her song by pointing to the Lord. "So may all your enemies perish, O Lord! But may they who love you be like the sun when it rises in its strength" (Judg. 5:31). The total defeat of their enemies (Judg. 4:16) meant the dawning of a new day for the Israelites.

Deborah gave special credit to Jael who killed General Sisera in her tent. In that day, it would be most unusual for an unaccompanied man to enter a woman's tent, so it would be a perfect place to hide. Jael belonged to a neutral tribe that was friendly with Jabin, and her invitation seemed sincere. She gave him milk to drink, waited until he was in a deep sleep, and then drove a tent peg through his head. Barak showed up in time to see the corpse covered with a robe. Yes, Jael was deceptive, but this was war and Sisera was the enemy.

It's strange that neither Deborah nor Jael is mentioned in Hebrews 11:32 where Barak is named, along with Gideon, Samson, Jephthah, David, and Samuel. If it hadn't been for Deborah and Jael, Barak might not have won such a great victory. Of course, we have the record in Judges 4–5, but it is still a puzzle that the writer of Hebrews overlooked two great women. God won the victory using two brave women and a rainstorm, and Barak got the credit.

Deborah was a mother in Israel and was willing for others to get the credit. That's the way mothers are.

23

GIDEON

"The LORD is with you, mighty warrior."

JUDGES 6:12

*W*henever Old Testament Jews wanted to describe great victories, they would compare them either to God's triumph over Egypt at the exodus or to Gideon's conquest of the Midianites in the days of the judges. "The day of Midian" was indeed a glorious experience in Jewish history, and they never forgot it (Ps. 83:9, 11; Isa. 9:4; 10:26). The author of the book of Judges devoted a good deal of space to Gideon, and the writer of Hebrews 11 honored Gideon by associating him with great heroes like Samuel and David (Heb. 11:32).

But Gideon didn't begin as a "mighty warrior," and none of his neighbors in the tribe of Manasseh would have given him that title. We get the impression that his family was fairly well-off financially, with at least ten servants (Judg. 6:27), and that Gideon was the youngest in the family (Judg. 6:15). It is likely that his father was one of the leaders of the local Baal cult, yet Gideon seemed to know who the Lord was and what He had done for Israel in the past (Judg. 6:13). How did the Lord transform Gideon from a fearful young man into a "mighty warrior" who delivered Israel? God dealt with him the same way He deals with us when He wants us to serve Him.

GOD CHALLENGES US (Judg. 6:1–14)

Many scholars believe that the angel of the Lord who appeared to Gideon was the second person of the Trinity, our Lord Jesus Christ. The visitor is called "the Lord" (Judg. 6:14, 16, 18) and even accepted worship (vv. 17–22), something no angel would dare to do. (We find a similar scene in Judg. 13.) But whether it was God Himself or His special angel who visited Gideon, the fact that the messenger came at all is very significant. It meant that God had a special work for Gideon to do.

God knew who the young man was—the youngest son of a fairly prosperous farmer; and He knew where he was—hiding in a winepress, threshing wheat. Hiding! Yet the Lord called Gideon a "mighty warrior" and assured him that God was with him. Mighty warrior indeed! But the Lord wasn't using a cheap psychological trick to try to improve Gideon's self-image. God knew the potential that lay hidden in Gideon, and He was going to set it free. Jesus spoke to Simon Peter in a similar way: "'You are Simon son of John. You will be called Cephas' (which, when translated, is Peter)" (John 1:42). Both Peter and Cephas mean "a rock." That's the way God challenges us: "You are—you shall be." And Peter did become a rock, and Gideon did become a mighty warrior.

Like Gideon, we are prone to argue with God and try to convince Him that His statement of our potential is greatly exaggerated. Moses took that approach when God called him (Ex. 3–4), and so did young Jeremiah (Jer. 1); but both of them finally gave in and surrendered to the Lord's will. It's a good thing they did, because that was the making of them. "Who has known the mind of the Lord? Or who has been his counselor?" (Rom. 11:34). Since when does God need our input about ourselves? After all, long before we were born, He planned our genetic structure and our purpose in life, and when we were conceived in the womb, He equipped us to make it all happen (Ps. 139:1–16). The will of God is the expression of the love of God for us (Ps. 33:11), so let's accept what He says and let Him have His way.

GOD STRENGTHENS OUR FAITH (Judg. 6:16–7:14)

No matter what Gideon thought of himself, God told him he would become a great warrior. The Lord's promise and presence guaranteed success if only Gideon would trust and obey. God's commandment always includes His enablement, because that's what it means to live by faith. But Gideon was very weak in his faith, so the Lord had to begin strengthening His servant for his appointed task.

God spoke to Gideon at least twelve times in chapters 6 and 7, because true faith comes by hearing the "word of faith" and receiving it into one's heart (Rom. 10:8, 17). The Lord also revealed His glory and power to Gideon when He touched the offering with His staff and fire from the rock consumed it. Then the messenger disappeared! First we hear and believe, and then faith is confirmed by seeing. In response, Gideon built an altar to the Lord. When you trust God, you want to worship Him.

But that was just the beginning of the lessons on faith. The next step was God's command that Gideon destroy his father's altar dedicated to Baal and also the pole dedicated to the goddess Asherah. Then he was to offer his father's second bull on the altar he dedicated to Jehovah. Faith doesn't mature instantly, so don't criticize Gideon for obeying this command at night. The next morning, the men of the town wanted to kill Gideon because of what he did, but his father pointed out that it was foolish to worship a god who can't even protect himself. All Gideon received from the skirmish was a nickname—Jerub-Baal, which means "contender with Baal." The Lord first tested Gideon at home, because that's where the life of faith must begin.

The Lord then strengthened Gideon's faith by filling him with the power of the Spirit. Faith is living without scheming and without depending on our own experience and resources. Now that He had a Spirit-filled leader, the Lord brought together an army of 32,000 volunteers from the Abiezrites in Manasseh (his own tribe) as well as from Asher, Zebulun, and Naphtali (Judg. 6:34). But how could 32,000 men defeat an army that looked as thick as locusts in the valley and whose camels were like the sand on the seashore (Judg. 7:12)? Perhaps Gideon was having second thoughts.

But now for lesson three: God condescended to stoop to Gideon's weakness and do what he asked with the fleece (Judg. 6:36–40). When Christian people talk about "putting out a fleece," they are confessing doubt and fear, not faith. Gideon knew God's promise (Judg. 6:36), but he wanted the Lord to back it up with a demonstration. How gracious the Lord is, "for he knows how we are formed, he remembers that we are dust" (Ps. 103:14).

Gideon had tested God, so God proceeded to test Gideon and remove more than 99 percent of his army! The number went from 32,000 to 300! The Lord wanted Gideon to trust in Him and not in what men, weapons, and tactics could do. Deuteronomy 20:1–9 gives God's instructions for preparing the army for battle, and fainthearted soldiers weren't needed. I see no deep meaning behind the drinking test at the river. It was simply God's way of quickly identifying for Gideon the 300 men He had chosen. Once more, the Lord promised Gideon that he would defeat the enemy (Judg. 7:7).

The Lord graciously gave Gideon one last encouragement by allowing him to hear the Midianite guards discuss and interpret a dream (Judg. 7:9–15). Barley was a cheap grain, used mostly by the poor, so Gideon's identification with a barley cake wasn't very flattering. The Lord was reminding him that in spite of himself, if he would trust God, he would win the battle. If the enemy guards believed that Gideon would win, why should Gideon doubt it? But Gideon must not exalt himself, for he was only a barley cake!

GOD BLESSES OUR OBEDIENCE (Judg. 7:15–8:35)

The 300 soldiers were certainly armed with their swords, but they started their attack by using pitchers, trumpets, and torches. God still uses foolish and weak things to put to shame the "great things" of this world (1 Cor. 1:26–31), because that is the way He glorifies Himself the most. Gideon could have called a staff meeting and debated the Lord's strategy all night, but it would have been a dangerous waste of time. The sudden bursts of light, blasts of the trumpets, and shouts of the troops all caught the Midianites by surprise, and they began to fight each other and then to flee. Gideon called for reinforcements, so the rest of the army showed up along with fresh volunteers (it is much easier to volunteer when you know the army is winning), and they chased the enemy for miles and killed 120,000 of them (Judg. 8:10).

The way Gideon handled the Ephraimites (Judg. 8:1–3) shows that he knew how to use the soft answer (Prov. 15:1; 17:14), and the way he punished the men of Succoth (Judg. 8:4–21) reveals that he had wisdom and discernment. The Ephraimites had expressed a private complaint against Gideon, but the men of

Succoth had rebelled against the Lord's commander. In his "mopping up" strategy, Gideon knew who to forgive and who to punish. But it was clear to all that God had done a marvelous thing in a most remarkable way, and that Gideon had acted by faith.

If the story had ended there, it would have been much better for Gideon and for Israel; Gideon won the battles but lost the victory. Andrew Bonar said, "Let us be as watchful after the victory as before the battle," but Gideon didn't have or heed that warning. He seemed very spiritual when he refused to accept the crown and said, "The LORD will rule over you" (Judg. 8:23), but in his heart he was about to collect his dividends from the nation. He didn't become a king, but he certainly spent his last years living like a king! After delivering Israel from the bondage caused by their idolatry, he led them right back into a homemade brand of idolatry!

Gideon missed a glorious opportunity to lead the nation back to God and the law of Moses. It wasn't enough to defeat an enemy; they had to commit themselves to the Lord and live to please Him. No sooner was Gideon off the scene than the nation returned to Baal worship. Their bodies were set free from bondage, but their hearts were still enslaved to idols. By his faith, the "mighty warrior" had led Israel to victory, but by his pride and covetousness, he led them back into defeat.

24

SAMSON

He is a double-minded man, unstable in all he does.

JAMES 1:8

$\mathcal{S}$amson has been accused of being "indecisive," but the accusation is incorrect. He could be very decisive, but his decisions were often wrong. Very early in life, he decided he wanted to serve two masters—himself and the Lord—and that's what ultimately destroyed him. "His whole life is a scene of miracles and follies," said Charles Spurgeon. "He had but little grace, and was easily overcome by temptation. He is enticed and led astray. Often corrected, he still sins again."[1] Jesus said that nobody could serve two masters (Matt. 6:24), but like many others, Samson tried it.

Samson had a wonderful beginning, but a good beginning isn't a guarantee of a happy ending. He had godly parents, and the angel of the Lord announced his birth to them. Samson was especially called by God and given the opportunity of judging Israel (Judg. 16:31) and beginning the conquest of the Philistines (Judg. 13:5). Samuel and David eventually completed this task. Samson was a Nazirite, especially dedicated to the Lord (Num. 6), and "the Lord blessed him" (Judg. 13:24). Hebrews 11:32 honors him for his faith but not for his faithfulness, because he wasn't a faithful servant. He was endued with divine power and fought entire armies, yet when enticed by women, he was as weak and unstable as water.

Granted, we must be cautious because we don't have the whole story of his twenty years of judgeship. But Samson vividly illustrates how we may forget our choices, but our choices won't forget us. Let's make the right choices in life; for after all, the will of God and our destiny are involved.

CHOOSE THE SPIRIT, NOT THE FLESH

The book of Judges records four times when the Holy Spirit worked in Samson's life (Judg. 13:25; 14:6, 19; 15:14), and there were doubtless many more; but it is one thing to have the occasional *enablement* of the Spirit and quite something else to experience the moment-by-moment *ennoblement* of the Spirit. The first relates to service, but the second relates to personal character, and the Lord is concerned about what we are as well as what we do. If we are completely yielded

---

1. Spurgeon, *Metropolitan Tabernacle Pulpit*, vol. 4, 474.

to the Lord and not double-minded, then our walk with God and our working for God will blend together and build our Christian character as we seek to accomplish God's purposes in this world.

Samson wanted the Spirit to help him slay the enemies around him but not to help him kill the appetites within him, the fleshly desires that controlled and eventually destroyed him. "So I say, live by the Spirit, and you will not gratify the desires of the sinful nature" (Gal. 5:16). Double-minded people compartmentalize their lives, living primarily for themselves but occasionally serving the Lord, but this kind of inconsistency doesn't build godly character or lasting service.

CHOOSE TO DO GOD'S WILL, NOT TO PLEASE YOURSELF

Of all the nations that God sent to chasten Israel for their sins, the Philistines stayed the longest—forty years (Judg. 13:1)—and they established themselves as Israel's masters in the land. God raised up Samson to "irritate" the Philistines and also to remind Israel that these idolatrous people were their enemies. Samson never raised an army or tried to expel the invaders; that wasn't his calling. His job was to aggravate the Philistines and distract them from attacking Israel. Sad to say, the people of Israel had gotten so accustomed to being servants, they didn't want Samson to upset the "peace." They were even willing to turn him over to the enemy (Judg. 15)!

But Samson's problem was that he wanted his own way. Whatever pleased him was the most important thing, and his parents obeyed him. Samson was "going with the flow," because at that time "everyone did as he saw fit" (Judg. 17:6; 21:25). We don't find Samson asking God for guidance. As a Nazirite, Samson was supposed to live in a way that honored God, but that doesn't seem to have been his greatest concern. He ate defiled honey taken from the carcass of a lion, and Nazirites weren't supposed to touch dead bodies (Judg. 14:8–9; Num. 6:6, 9). He even made a joke out of the lion incident (Judg. 14:14). He fought the Lord's battles by day and visited prostitutes by night.

But even when Samson did God's will, his motives weren't always pure. Even when he fought the Lord's battles, he acted more out of revenge than out of righteous anger. "Since you've acted like this, I won't stop until I get my revenge on you" (Judg. 15:7), he told the Philistines after they had killed his wife and father-in-law. His last prayer was that he might slay the Philistines because they had blinded him, not because they were God's enemies (Judg. 16:28). Granted, he had been treated severely, but he had also gotten himself into those situations and had to bear the consequences. You take what you want from life and you pay for it. "You go out, like Samson, against the enemies of God and His church," wrote Alexander Whyte, "but all the time you make your campaign an occasion for your own passions, piques, retaliations and revenges."[2] Religious zeal and even patriotism can cover a multitude of sins.

2. Alexander Whyte, *Bible Characters from the Old and New Testaments* (Grand Rapids, Mich.: Kregel, 1990), 198.

CHOOSE TO LIVE BY FAITH, NOT BY SIGHT

Samson not only had "I" trouble but also "eye" trouble. He saw a woman in Timnah and insisted that his parents arrange a wedding (Judg. 14). He saw a prostitute in Gaza and spent the night with her (Judg. 16:1–3). He saw Delilah in the Valley of Sorek and let her entice him into disobedience. The lust of the eyes and the lust of the flesh work together. After capturing Samson, the Philistines put out his eyes to keep him from causing more trouble, but surely he was reaping the sad consequences of his lustful looks.

Samson had the faith to trust God's power when he saw physical danger, but he lacked the discernment to see spiritual danger. Living by faith isn't something we turn on and off like a stereo; it's something we practice all the time. When you live by faith, it's as normal to pray and praise God as it is to breathe or wash your hands, but we find only two recorded prayers of Samson (Judg. 15:18; 16:28) and only one instance of praise (Judg. 15:18). People who walk by faith don't trust their own wisdom but learn to lean on the Lord (Prov. 3:5–6).

Check your map of Israel and you will see that Samson didn't stay in the Promised Land but wandered along the Philistine border and even penetrated enemy territory to find pleasure. His home in Zorah was five miles from Timnah, near the Philistine border. Gath was on the border. Ashkelon was twenty-four miles from Timnah. When we start to see how close we can come to the enemy, we are bound to meet the enemy. We get the impression that Samson didn't take sin too seriously and was perhaps too overconfident of his own powers.

CHOOSE THE LIGHT AND NOT THE DARKNESS

The name Samson means "sunny," yet he died in the darkness. In the Bible, light is a metaphor for God and holiness (John 8:12; Eph. 5:3–14; 1 John 1:5–10), while Satan is identified with darkness (Luke 22:53; Eph. 6:12; Col. 1:13). As long as we follow Jesus, the Light of the World, we walk in the light of life; but once we move into the darkness of disobedience, we are in the path of death and not the path of life.

Night after night, Samson visited Delilah, indulged in sin, put himself in danger, and eventually was trapped. He lost his separation and his Nazirite crown (Num. 6:7), and with them, he lost his strength. He lost his freedom, his sight, his testimony, and eventually his life. He thought that the Lord would rescue him as He had done time after time, but "he did not know that the LORD had left him" (Judg. 16:20). Until then, he had been special, even unique; but now he was as weak as any other man. Instead of judging Israel, he ended up entertaining the enemy. "For God's watchmen to become the world's showmen is a miserable business," wrote Charles Spurgeon.[3]

Even though his motive was revenge and not the glory of God, Samson did a courageous thing when he sacrificed his own life to inflict one last defeat on his

---

3. Spurgeon, *Metropolitan Tabernacle Pulpit*, vol. 37, 87.

enemies. The most important Philistine leaders were attending the celebration, and the nation was considerably crippled when these people died. At least nobody hindered his relatives from claiming the body and giving it a decent Hebrew burial. He was laid to rest "between Zorah and Eshtaol" near where God had begun to work in his life (Judg. 16:31; 13:25). Samson had come full circle.

The collapse of the building and the death of Samson bring to mind Proverbs 25:28: "Like a city whose walls are broken down is a man who lacks self-control." Long before the Philistine arena was destroyed, Samson had allowed the walls of separation and self-control to crumble in his own life, and like a city without walls, anything could get in and anything could get out. He left behind nothing permanent. Israel wasn't necessarily a better nation; the people still did what was right in their own eyes, and they were content to let the enemy rule over them.

But where sin abounds, grace much more abounds; and for the most part, Samson accomplished the work God assigned to him: he aggravated the enemy and distracted them from abusing the Jews. Others would take up the quarrel with the foe and eventually set Israel free.

Few people are called to be commanding generals, but each of us can do our part in contributing to the victories of some future Samson or David.

25

RUTH

"You are a woman of noble character."

RUTH 3:11

Each time you read the book of Ruth, remind yourself of two important facts. First, this beautiful story takes place during the difficult and dangerous days when the judges ruled and the Lord was repeatedly chastening Israel. The times were tough. Circumstances may be distressing in our own world today, but God's love story is still going on, and one day the Lord will claim His bride. The world's hatred and selfishness can't hinder the working of God's love, and that encourages me.

Second, this book is about ordinary people involved in the ordinary activities of life. It reports no miracles, except the miracle of God's providential leading and timing, and that miracle goes on in the lives of God's obedient people today. When it seemed like everything had fallen apart and couldn't get worse, God fulfilled His plan for Ruth and Naomi and everything came together. Ruth, Naomi, and Boaz experienced Romans 8:28 centuries before Paul wrote it down. We can still claim that assurance today.

Ruth's story begins with three funerals and ends with the birth of a baby — but not just any baby, for the son of Boaz and Ruth was an ancestor of King David who was an ancestor of our Lord Jesus Christ.

Ruth is described as "a woman of noble character," the same phrase that is used to describe Solomon's "perfect wife" (Prov. 31:10, 29). Noble character is something that everybody needs and everybody can have if we yield to God's will and let Him use His tools in our lives.

PERSONAL SUFFERING

The nations of Moab and Ammon came out of Lot's incestuous relationship with his two daughters (Gen. 19:30–38), so the Israelites and the Moabites were distantly related. However, in spite of this, they were still mortal enemies. No Moabite or Ammonite could enter the congregation of Israel "even down to the tenth generation" (Deut. 23:2–6), which meant "never." When the Jews returned to their land after their captivity, their leaders had to discipline the men who had married Moabite women (Ezra 9; Neh. 13:23). Yet here was Naomi returning to Bethlehem and bringing a Moabite daughter-in-law with her.

Ruth, however, was not only a citizen of Moab, she was also a young widow with no hopes of ever marrying a Jew in Bethlehem. God commanded the Jews to show kindness to "the alien, the fatherless and the widow" (Deut. 24:19–21; 26:12–13), and Ruth was all three. But she had come from Moab! Were the Jews obligated to show her any kindness?

It is an ancient truth and almost a cliché that personal suffering either makes us or breaks us. Ruth could have rejected Naomi's God and adopted her bitterness, but the grace of God changed Ruth's heart, and the love and example of Ruth gradually changed Naomi. When we trust the Lord, troubles work for us and not against us. "For our light and momentary troubles are achieving for us an eternal glory that far outweighs them all" (2 Cor. 4:17). "We know that suffering produces perseverance; perseverance, character; and character, hope" (Rom. 5:3–4).

SAVING FAITH

Why did Naomi not want to take her two daughters-in-law to Bethlehem with her? The three of them started out together, but then Naomi stopped and urged Orpah and Ruth to return to their own homes and their own gods and let her go on alone. Could it be that Naomi didn't want to take to Bethlehem evidence that her sons had disobeyed the law and married foreign women? Orpah obeyed Naomi's command and went home, but Ruth clung to her mother-in-law because Ruth had come to trust in the true and living God. "Your people will be my people and your God my God" (Ruth 1:16). Those who put their faith in Jesus Christ become God's "workmanship," and He works for them, in them, and through them to make them what He wants them to be (Eph. 2:8–10; Phil. 2:12–13).

When we consider Ruth's situation, it is really remarkable that she should come to such strong faith in Israel's God. She was living in a Jewish family that evidenced very little faith in the God they professed to serve. After all, when the famine came, they fled Bethlehem and went to get help in enemy territory. Couldn't they trust their God? And what kind of God allows three men to die and leave three widows almost helpless in the world? Naomi was very bitter and not much of an example for Ruth to follow. Remember, Naomi wanted her two daughters-in-law to return to their paternal homes and to their pagan gods. In spite of all this painful negative influence, by the grace of God, Ruth became a believer, so much so that Naomi came to depend on her!

Boaz said it best, when he addressed Ruth in the field: "May you be richly rewarded by the LORD, the God of Israel, under whose wings you have come to take refuge" (Ruth 2:12). We usually associate "wings" with the picture of a hen protecting her chicks, but I wonder if Boaz wasn't referring to the wings of the cherubim in the Most Holy Place (see Ex. 25:17–22; Pss. 36:7–8; 61:4). According to Ephesians 2:11–12, Ruth was a spiritually bankrupt outsider who had none of the spiritual blessings of the Jews, but her faith brought her not only into the commonwealth of Israel, but also into the fellowship of the Lord! Spiritually speaking, instead of being outside the camp with the rejects, she was within the Most Holy Place with the Lord.

CARING SERVICE

In Ruth 1, Ruth put the Lord first and wouldn't alter her decision to accompany Naomi. In Ruth 2, she lovingly cared for Naomi and gleaned in the fields to provide food. The barley harvest began in mid-April and the wheat harvest in early June, so Naomi and Ruth had arrived in Bethlehem just in time. "The Lord watches over the alien and sustains the fatherless and the widow" (Ps. 146:9). But that wasn't the only evidence of God's providential care, for the Lord directed Ruth to glean in the fields of Boaz, the most eligible bachelor in Bethlehem. And Boaz showed up while she was working there!

"Whose young woman is that?" he asked, and his question seems to announce love at first sight. Like everybody else in Bethlehem, Boaz had heard the news about the trials of Naomi in Moab and the remarkable conversion and character of her daughter-in-law Ruth. As Ruth bowed at the feet of the lord of the harvest, she manifested such gracious humility that Boaz was greatly impressed.

Had Ruth sat home mourning and complaining, she never would have met Boaz and become his wife. Have you noticed that God gives some of His best blessings to those who are busy at work? Moses was caring for Jethro's sheep when he heard God's call, and Gideon was threshing wheat. David was obeying his father's orders when he went to Israel's camp, and there God used him to slay the giant Goliath. Peter, Andrew, James, and John were working in their boats when Jesus called them to follow Him, and Matthew was busy in his tax office when his call came. You can't steer a car when the gears are in neutral. Get busy helping others, and the Lord will guide you.

There's something about old-fashioned work that clarifies the mind, warms the heart, and builds the character. "Hard work is a thrill and a joy when you are in the will of God," said Dr. Bob Cook, and he is right. Ruth's work was not only difficult, but it was also somewhat humiliating, for in gleaning she was declaring her poverty and helplessness. Gleaners were people who lived on leftovers, but she didn't care. She was living in the Most Holy Place, under the wings of Jehovah, and He was working on her behalf.

LOVING SUBMISSION

While Naomi was waiting at home, she was doing her share of the work as she prayed and planned for her daughter-in-law's future well-being. Naomi knew that Boaz was a near relative and that Ruth had the right to put her case before him and request his protection and care as her husband. She had bowed at his feet in his field and thanked him for his kindness and generosity (Ruth 2:10), but now she was going to come to his feet and claim him as her kinsman-redeemer (Ruth 3:5–8).

God owned the land and permitted the Jews to live on it and benefit from its riches. If a Jew fell into hard times and had to sell his land, a near relative could rescue him and buy back the land. Also, if the owner died and the widow was destitute, a near relative could purchase the land if he married the widow. It's explained in Leviticus 25:23–55. Because Naomi knew the Word of God, she was able to tell Ruth exactly what to do. Ruth submitted to Naomi, and the Lord did the rest. The law of the kinsman-redeemer is a beautiful picture of what Jesus Christ has done for us. We are poverty-stricken spiritually and have lost our inheritance, but He became a "near relative" and with His own life purchased our inheritance for us. What love!

Boaz was startled when he awakened to find a woman at his feet, but when he discovered who it was, he was filled with joy. "Spread the corner of your garment over me," Ruth requested (Ruth 3:9), which was a code phrase that meant "I am claiming you as my kinsman-redeemer and husband." The word translated "corner" in Ruth 3:9 is the same word translated "wings" in Ruth 2:12. Ruth was not only under the wings of the Lord because of her faith, but also under the wings of Boaz because of her loving submission. She was once again at the feet of the lord of the harvest.

PATIENT WAITING

"Wait, my daughter," Naomi counseled Ruth. "For the man will not rest until the matter is settled today" (Ruth 3:18). So Ruth waited. Little children and childish adults are notoriously guilty of fretting and running ahead of the Lord. "Be still, and know that I am God" (Ps. 46:10). In that verse, the verb "be still" means "take your hands off; leave it alone." There are times when we immediately obey what He tells us to do, and there are times when we take our hands off while He works for us.

For many of us, patient waiting is a difficult challenge, whether we are in the physician's waiting room or in a neighborhood traffic jam. But the Lord is never in a hurry, and His timing is never off. It has well been said that His delays are not His denials. Ruth knew that Boaz loved her and would pay any price to have her as his wife. The unknown "other kinsman" refused to marry Ruth because he would have risked his own inheritance; Jesus, however, not only accepted us but also made us a part of His inheritance!

Boaz purchased the property and his bride and settled the matter quickly. He could confidently say, "It is finished!" From this happy union Obed was born, and Obed became the father of Jesse, who was the father of David the king. This is how Ruth the Moabite alien got her name in the Messiah's genealogy (Matt. 1:5–6), along with rejects like Tamar and Rahab and Bathsheba.

> Amazing grace! How sweet the sound
> That saved a wretch like me;
> I once was lost, but now am found;
> Was blind, but now I see.
>
> JOHN NEWTON

26

ELI

"You have not set your heart to honor me."

MALACHI 2:2

*W*hen Malachi wrote, "You have not set your heart to honor me," he was speaking primarily to the priests of Israel. They were ministering in the restored temple after the nation had returned from captivity, but they were not serving in a godly manner. However, his words of warning can be applied to unfaithful priests at any time in Israel's history and even to believers today who need to be rebuked. After all, the church is "a holy priesthood … a chosen people, a royal priesthood, a holy nation" (1 Peter 2:5, 9), and it is a serious responsibility to serve God as a priest.

The Hebrew word *kabod* is a key word in Eli's story. Its basic meaning is "heavy" or "weight," and it is translated that way in 1 Samuel 4:18 where Eli is described as "an old man and heavy." A second meaning is "glory," as in 1 Samuel 4:19–22 where the newborn baby boy is named Ichabod, which means "no glory" or "the glory has departed." In 2 Corinthians 4:17, Paul connected the two concepts of glory and weight when he wrote about "an eternal glory that far outweighs them all." The word is also translated "honor" because honorable people "carry weight" and usually own weighty possessions.

How does this theme of "honoring God" reveal itself in the life and ministry of Eli?

GOD HONORED ELI

To begin with, God sovereignly arranged for Eli to be born a Jew. This meant that he came to know the true and living God of Abraham, Isaac, and Jacob; that he was a son of the covenant; and that he shared in the spiritual privileges that belonged only to Israel (Rom. 9:1–5). When Jesus came and completed the work of redemption, these privileges were shared with believing Gentiles (Eph. 2:11–22). It was a privilege to be a Jew, but it was an even greater privilege to be a high priest and serve at the altar. Eli was descended from the family of Ithamar, Aaron's fourth son.

The Lord further honored Eli by giving him a wife who bore to him at least two sons. Married couples in Israel wanted children, especially sons, to carry on the family name and to protect the family inheritance. It was especially important that there be sons in the high priest's family so that the office of high priest might be filled in each generation.

But perhaps the greatest honor God gave Eli was the privilege of mentoring young Samuel and preparing him to serve the people of Israel. Samuel would be the one who would anoint David to be king of Israel, and our Savior would come from the family of David. Indeed, Eli was a man honored by the Lord. When Samuel heard the voice that awesome night, Eli was discerning enough to know that it was the voice of God. Samuel wasn't living with the most spiritual family in Israel, yet God protected him and prepared him for his own ministry. His parents had given him to the Lord, and the Lord cared for him. Can't He do the same for our children and grandchildren who today are surrounded by all kinds of ungodly influences on campuses and in workplaces?

ELI DID NOT HONOR GOD

God honored Eli, but Eli failed to honor God in his heart. We move now from grace to disgrace. "A son honors his father, and a servant his master. If I am a father, where is the honor due me? If I am a master, where is the respect due me?" (Mal. 1:6). Because he was very old and growing blind, Eli turned the ministry over to his two sons, but he failed to supervise them according to the law. They failed to offer the sacrifices the way Moses commanded but saved the best for themselves. They treated the Lord's holy sacrifices with contempt and "fattened themselves" on the best parts of the animals (see 1 Sam. 2:12–17, 29; Mal. 1:8–9).

But even worse, the two sons slept with the women who served at the door of the tabernacle (1 Sam. 2:22; see also Ex. 38:8). We are not sure what religious services these volunteers performed, but Eli's sons seduced them and violated God's laws. They were acting like the pagan priests of the Gentile nations around them who conducted filthy rituals with shrine prostitutes (Deut. 23:17–18). What a shameful thing for the priests of Jehovah to do!

Eli knew that these things were going on, but he didn't take steps to discipline the men, and his mild rebukes made no difference in their conduct (1 Sam. 2:22–25). God even sent an anonymous prophet to warn Eli that by condoning his sons' evil conduct, he was as guilty as they were and would be punished by the Lord (1 Sam. 2:27–36). The pronoun "you" in verse 29 is plural, so it refers to Eli as well as his sons. Eli honored his sons more than he honored the Lord, and this meant he was dishonoring the Lord and would pay for it.

When the Israeli army confronted the Philistine army, Israel lost the first battle, so they decided to bring the ark of the covenant from the tabernacle to the battlefield and use it like a "good luck charm" (1 Sam. 4:1–11). The soldiers knew that the ark represented the throne of God and the presence of God with His people, and that it had often brought victory to Israel in the past (see Num. 10:33–36; Josh. 6:6–27; Ps. 80:1). But Eli's sons Hophni and Phinehas were defiled priests, not godly leaders like Moses and Joshua; and to get the ark, the two men had to enter the Most Holy Place of the tabernacle! That privilege was granted only to the high priest, and only once a year on the Day of Atonement. These two worldly priests usurped authority and acted in an ungodly manner, and Eli didn't call on the Lord to stop them or try to stop them himself.

No matter how we look at the situation, Eli was a careless and disobedient priest who had failed to raise his two sons in the fear of the Lord. Malachi describes God's ideal priest in Malachi 2:5–6: "My covenant was with him, a covenant of life and peace, and I gave them to him; this called for reverence and he revered me and stood in awe of my name. True instruction was in his mouth and nothing false was found on his lips. He walked with me in peace and uprightness, and turned many from sin."

GOD DISHONORED ELI

"Those who honor me I will honor, but those who despise me will be disdained" (1 Sam. 2:30). The word translated "disdained" means "to be cursed, to be humbled, to be made contemptible." The priests were supposed to bless the people and be a blessing, but Eli and his sons had despised the Lord, His laws, and his sacrifices, and now it was time for God to judge them.

That one day in Eli's life brought one judgment after another. First, the Philistine army defeated Israel and captured the ark, the throne of God. Then Hophni and Phinehas were both killed, and the wife of Phinehas died in childbirth. She named her orphaned son Ichabod, which means "the glory has departed." When Eli heard the news brought from the battlefield, he had a stroke or fainted, fell over backward, broke his neck and died, all of this aggravated by his excessive weight.

But that wasn't the end: God removed the priesthood from the family of Eli. In the time of King Saul, the priests massacred at Nob were descendants of Eli (1 Sam. 22:18–19), and Solomon removed the last priest of that line when he deposed Abiathar for siding with Adonijah in his conspiracy to seize the throne (1 Kings 2:26–27). Zadok took his place (1 Kings 2:35), so the prophecy announced by the man of God against Eli and his family was at last fulfilled (1 Sam. 2:30–36).

The greatest tragedy wasn't that Eli lost his sons, his daughter-in-law, or his own life, but that he disgraced the name of the Lord and robbed his descendants of the privilege of serving as priests of the Lord. The men would die young and not be able to serve as priests, and those who lived longer would be disqualified because of personal blemishes.

GOD WANTS TO HONOR US

"Those who honor me I will honor" is God's promise, and we can depend on it. Our Lord lived and died that He might honor the Father, and this is the example for us to follow. "I have brought you glory on earth by completing the work you gave me to do" (John 17:4). These were the words of Jesus when He "reported" to His Father before He went into the garden where He was arrested and taken to be tried, condemned, and crucified. No matter what people said *about* Him at the trial or *to* Him as He hung on the cross, He knew that He had been faithful to honor the Father and do His will.

Let's pray that our lives will close with that same glad assurance, and let's live so that the Father will delight to honor us. This means paying attention to the following essentials:

- prayer — Psalm 50:15 and 91:15
- thanksgiving — Psalm 50:23
- generosity — Proverbs 3:9 – 10
- obedience — Psalm 84:11
- dedicated service — John 12:23 – 26

Read those verses and ponder them.

It is really not important that people honor us, because much of human praise is cheap and temporary. When we live to honor God, we build our lives and ministries with "gold, silver [and] costly stones," but when we live and work only for the praises that people can give, we live for "wood, hay or straw" (1 Cor. 3:12). Human honor and praise will be burned up like wood, hay, and straw. But the gold, silver, and jewels will be made into glorious crowns that we will give to Jesus, because He alone is worthy of all honor and praise. As we lay our crowns at His feet, together in heaven we will sing: "Worthy is the Lamb, who was slain, to receive power and wealth and wisdom and strength and honor and glory and praise!" (Rev. 5:12).

27

HANNAH

Weeping may remain for a night,
but rejoicing comes in the morning.

PSALM 30:5

Hannah was experiencing another painful day. The family's annual visit to the tabernacle was always a depressing time for her, even though her husband was a spiritual man who loved her dearly. Hannah was barren, and her husband's second wife, Peninnah, never let her forget it. Hannah had no appetite and couldn't enter into the joy of the feast. She left the table and went to stand before the tabernacle and pray, and even there she found little sympathy. Eli the high priest thought she was drunk and rebuked her, but all she was doing was weeping and praying silently for a son. The Lord saw her heart and heard her prayer and gave her assurance that it would be answered.

The name Hannah comes from a Hebrew word that means "grace" or "favor." God was gracious to Hannah and gave her what she requested, and the night of sorrow was replaced by the sunlight of joy. In due time, she conceived and gave birth to a son whom she named Samuel—"heard of God." Throughout this entire experience, God graciously gave Hannah all that she needed, and He will do the same for us.

THE LORD GIVES US THE PATIENCE TO ENDURE

The text calls Peninnah Hannah's "rival" (1 Sam. 1:6–7), a Hebrew word that is related to words like *distress*, *anguish*, *enemy*, and *hostility*. When we examine the words that describe Peninnah's attitudes and actions, we can easily see that Hannah didn't have an easy time in the home. Peninnah provoked and irritated her until Hannah was bitter in her soul and could only weep (1 Sam. 1:6–7, 10). "I am a woman who is deeply troubled," she told Eli, for she was in "great anguish and grief" and was only "pouring out [her] soul to the Lord" (1 Sam. 1:15–16). Imagine living with that kind of emotional pressure day after day! "I pour out my complaint before him; before him I tell my trouble" (Ps. 142:2). That was Hannah's daily experience.

Like every married woman in Hebrew society, Hannah wanted to bear children, especially a son to carry on the father's name; but the Lord hadn't seen fit to open her womb. She was in the company of Sarah, Rebekah, and Rachel, barren women whom the Lord finally blessed with children. When her work was done each day, Hannah must have spent much time in prayer asking the Lord to do for her what He did for those women—give her a child.

Many of us have people in our lives who are abrasive and difficult to live with or work with. Peninnah didn't see Hannah as a woman with a broken heart; she saw her as a rival, competing for the affection of Elkanah. Peninnah used Hannah to elevate herself in the home and to inflate her own ego. Peninnah had to be first. She didn't care and wouldn't share. She must not have loved Elkanah very much or she wouldn't have added to his burdens. Only the grace of God sustained Hannah in those very difficult days.

THE LORD GIVES US THE FAITH TO ASK

Elkanah saw a change in Hannah's attitude and gave thanks. She told him that she had prayed for a son who would serve the Lord, and that the Lord assured her that her prayer would be answered. Elkanah agreed with her decision, and they united in asking the Lord to give them a son (1 Peter 3:7). We find here the name "LORD of hosts" or "LORD Almighty" for the first time in the Bible (1 Sam. 1:3, 11 NIV, NASB). The Lord of Hosts is the Lord of the armies of heaven and earth, the sovereign King of the universe. "The LORD of hosts is with us" (Ps. 46:7, 11 NASB), and He can do great things!

Was Hannah making a bargain with the Lord? I don't think so. If her prayer was that kind of bargain, then she didn't benefit much from it, because she didn't keep her son but gave him back to God. I think Hannah and Elkanah were greatly concerned about the low spiritual state of the nation and prayed that God would use their special son to bring Israel back to the Lord. It was common knowledge that Eli's sons were wicked men, but God would use their son to turn things around.

Faith isn't something we have to work up; it is something God sends down to let us know He is pleased with our request. True faith is strengthened by the promises of God that the Holy Spirit shows us in Scripture. As we pray, there is a growing confidence in our hearts that the Bible calls "joy and peace in believing" (Rom. 15:13 KJV). As Hannah and Elkanah prayed together for what they knew God wanted to give them, they realized that God was about to do something very wonderful for His people.

THE LORD GIVES US JOY TO PRAISE HIM FOR THE ANSWER

Hannah's song, recorded in 1 Samuel 2, is a remarkable expression of worship and praise. Centuries later, the Holy Spirit would direct the mother of our Lord to pattern her song after it (Luke 1:46–55). Hannah had just parted from her beloved firstborn son, and yet she was praising God and exalting Him! Yes, she came to visit Samuel annually, but that was a poor substitute for having the lad in the home, teaching him, hugging him, and watching him mature. Both

Hannah and Mary would go through deep pain and sorrow, yet they both praised God. "My heart rejoices in the LORD," sang Hannah, and centuries later, Mary sang, "My soul glorifies the Lord and my spirit rejoices in God my Savior" (Luke 1:46–47).

But even more, Hannah had left her innocent son in a den of thieves, a place where evil men were dishonoring God and abusing the people. What might they do to her son? And if Eli did such a poor job of raising his two sons, what would he do with Samuel? As my wife and I sent our four children to the public school each day and then watched them go off to college, we committed them to the Lord for His protection; and now we pray the same blessing for our grandchildren. The Lord did keep Samuel pure in character and obedient in conduct in spite of the bad examples around him, and He can do it for children today.

The songs of Hannah and Mary emphasize the remarkable ministry of God's grace: it turns everything upside down! Proud rulers are dethroned, but the humble take their places. The destitute are filled, but the wealthy go away empty. What kind of world is that? It is a world living under the grace of God, for grace always upsets human cleverness and classifications.

THE LORD GIVES US THE LOVE WE NEED TO RETURN THE GIFT TO HIM

"If you give us a son," prayed Elkanah and Hannah, "we will give him back to you." And they did. Their love for the Lord exceeded even their love for their precious son. Like the heavenly Father, they gave their only son.

It is a basic principle of the Christian life that we lose whatever we keep for ourselves and we keep whatever we give to God. God gave Abraham and Sarah a son and then asked Abraham to sacrifice the boy on the altar. Because Abraham obeyed, Isaac was given back to him; had Abraham disobeyed, he would have lost Isaac. "The man who loves his life will lose it," said Jesus, "while the man who hates his life in this world will keep it for eternal life" (John 12:25). The man we call the rich young ruler wouldn't part with his wealth so he could follow Jesus, and as far as we know, he eventually lost Jesus, his wealth, and his own life. What did he gain? "For whoever wants to save his life will lose it, but whoever loses his life for me and for the gospel will save it" (Mark 8:35).

One of the dangers of answered prayer is that we permit the gift to become more important than the Giver, and this is idolatry. Whatever God gives us must be placed on the altar and dedicated to Him, or it will become a stumbling block in our lives. Our own lives, our plans, our loved ones and friends, our possessions, our opportunities, our achievements, our abilities — all of these things and more must be placed at the feet of Jesus before God can bless and use them for His glory. Like seeds, we must be buried and experience death before we can produce fruit (John 12:24), for it is out of death to self that we discover life for others.

God's promise is that "rejoicing comes in the morning." It may come on the morning after the night when you wept and pled with God for His help. Or it may be the morning after a night of wrestling and consecration, when you put your all on the altar for the Lord to use. However, it may not be until that morning of resurrection glory when the Lord returns and we see Him as He is. But there will be a morning of rejoicing, so be of good cheer and don't give up. "Weeping may remain for a night, but rejoicing comes in the morning."

The Lord said so—and He knows!

28

SAMUEL

"I have been your leader from my youth until this day."

1 SAMUEL 12:2

One of the marks of true servants of God is that people usually resist them and abuse them and sometimes end up killing them. After they have buried them, the people lament and honor them.

Samuel is a good example. From youth to old age, Samuel faithfully served God and Israel, and yet at the hour when the nation needed him most, they fired him!

Everybody admitted that his record was spotless, but they still fired him! Why? Their excuse was that Samuel's sons weren't qualified to succeed him, but the real reason was because Israel wanted a king so they could be like the other nations. They no longer wanted God as their ruler. They wanted a human super-hero they could follow and brag about. All the other nations had kings, and it was a shame for God's people not to be up-to-date. But when God's people are like other people, they are usually out of the will of God. God's people are supposed to be different.

God gave Israel what they asked for, a handsome young man named Saul, and he just about wrecked the nation. Sometimes the Lord judges nations (and churches and individuals) by giving them exactly what they deserve. Samuel spent the rest of his life mourning over Saul and the decline of the nation.

When the new generation decides to retire old, experienced godly leaders and start doing things differently, what should these leaders do? They should do just what Samuel did.

OBEY THE LORD

When it came to learning life's lessons the hard way, the nation of Israel was at the head of the class. They rarely listened to God's Word and obeyed it; instead, they usually offered God an alternative. Often the Lord let them have their way, and then they would get into trouble and cry out for His help. Some of God's people are like that today.

Samuel asked God what he should do, and the Lord told him to give the people what they wanted. One of God's greatest punishments is just to let people have their own way. He gives them over to the consequences of their deliberate sins (Rom. 1:24, 26, 28). God told Samuel to warn the Israelites about what life would be like under their king, but when he did, the people didn't believe him. "No! We want a king over us!" was their response, and the Lord said, "Listen to them and give them a king" (1 Sam. 8:19–22).

The times were changing, and old Samuel knew it. He would be the last of the judges (Acts 13:20). The ages were colliding, and it was Samuel's lot to help make the transition as easy as possible for the people. "It is very certain that the coming age and the departing age seldom understand each other," wrote Ralph Waldo Emerson in his essay "Education," and his observation is a valid one. Samuel knew the past and learned from it; the nation forgot the past and didn't care to hear about it. But those who don't know the past have a difficult time understanding the present and preparing for the future. We have a similar situation in some of the churches today.

If the younger generation sets you aside, stay true to the Lord and obey what He tells you. They haven't rejected you; they have rejected God. Israel would do it again when they rejected Jesus and cried out, "We have no king but Caesar" (see John 19:15).

PRAY TO THE LORD

Samuel was born because his parents knew how to pray. When Hannah brought her son to give him to the Lord, she said to Eli, "I prayed for this child" (1 Sam. 1:27). The name Hannah gave her son means "asked of God," so as a little child, he learned the importance of prayer every time his mother spoke his name. "Moses and Aaron were among his priests, Samuel was among those who called on the LORD" (Ps. 99:6). The prophet Jeremiah wrote, "Even if Moses and Samuel were to stand before me, my heart would not go out to this people" (Jer. 15:1). That's the kind of reputation Samuel had in God's sight, so why worry about what people think? Samuel would pray and the weather would change. He would pray again and armies would be defeated.

The nation was rejecting the old and pleading for the new, but they had forgotten the eternal. They forgot the words of Moses, "Lord, you have been our dwelling place throughout all generations" (Ps. 90:1). God heard Samuel's prayers for Israel, for King Saul, for young David, and for the new generation, and God answered in His time and in His way. "As for me," Samuel said in his farewell sermon, "far be it from me that I should sin against the LORD by failing to pray for you" (1 Sam. 12:23). The new generation may not have wanted Samuel's leadership, but they couldn't stop him from praying.

One of the greatest ministries the older generation can have to the new generation is to pray for them. It's not an option; it's an obligation.

TEACH THE LORD'S WORD

But Samuel didn't stop with prayer; he added, "And I will teach you the way that is good and right" (1 Sam. 12:23). This reminds us of the priorities of the apostles: "We ... will give our attention to prayer and the ministry of the word" (Acts 6:3–4). These two essentials must never be separated. "If you remain in me and my words remain in you," said Jesus, "ask whatever you wish, and it will be given you" (John 15:7). He unites the Word of God and prayer.

This pattern is found throughout the Bible. Moses would go up the mountain to intercede for the Jews and then come down and share God's Word with them. Daniel studied the words of the prophets and then prayed about the truth he had learned (Dan. 9). Paul commended the Ephesian elders to God—that's prayer—"and to the word of his grace" (Acts 20:32); and in his description of the believer's armor, he connected the sword of the Spirit—the Word—with prayer (Eph. 6:17–18). Our Lord arose early in the morning to pray, and then He went out to teach and preach the Word (Mark 1:35–39). All Bible and no prayer gives you light but no power, and all prayer but no Bible gives you zeal without knowledge; so we need the balance of the Word and prayer.

When Samuel was dismissed from office, he did a beautiful thing: he organized "schools of the prophets" and taught those of the next generation how to serve God. He established a school at his hometown of Ramah (1 Sam. 19:18–24) and at Saul's hometown of Gibeah (1 Sam. 10:5–7). Later schools were established at Gilgal, Bethel, and Jericho (2 Kings 2; and see 1 Kings 20:25). Clovis Chappell wrote: "This wise prophet particularly became interested in the youth of his day. There are few surer signs that one has grown old and sour on the inside than his wholesale condemnation of youth.... For these he established divinity schools."[1] Samuel was simply obeying the Word of God, for God commands the older generation to teach the younger generation His ways and His Word (see Deut. 11:18–21; 32:46; Pss. 34:11–14; 78:1–8; and note 2 Tim. 2:2).

GRIEVE BEFORE THE LORD

"Until the day Samuel died, he did not go to see Saul again, though Samuel mourned for him. And the LORD was grieved that he had made Saul king over Israel" (1 Sam. 15:35). Samuel was a man after God's own heart. They grieved together.

This wasn't a matter of magnifying "the good old days" the way some older folks like to do. Someone has said that "the good old days" are usually a combination of a bad memory and a good imagination, and often that's true. No, Samuel grieved over the low spiritual state of the people and over the folly of Saul in wasting his opportunities to serve the Lord and build the nation. Even Saul's son Jonathan said, "My father has made trouble for the country" (1 Sam. 14:29). One of the problems churches face today is that the younger people don't want to mingle with "the old fogeys" and learn their wisdom and spiritual insight. David was an exception: he visited Samuel and sought his direction (1 Sam. 19:18). Samuel mentored the next king.

---

1. Clovis Chappell, *More Sermons on Biblical Characters* (New York: Richard Smith, 1930), 32.

Where today is the grieving remnant that holds the future in their hands? Like Samuel, we had better be weeping, praying, teaching, and encouraging, even if we have to minister "outside the system." Jeremiah wished he could weep even more as he prayed for the backslidden people of God (Jer. 9:1–6). "Woe to me because of my injury!" he cried. "My wound is incurable!" (Jer. 10:19). In Ezekiel's time, God put a mark on the people in Jerusalem "who grieve[d] and lament[ed] over all the detestable things that [were] done in it" (Ezek. 9:4), and He commanded Ezekiel to groan before the people "with broken heart and bitter grief" (Ezek. 21:6). Jesus wept over the city of Jerusalem because they were ignorant of their own sad condition and the judgment that was coming (Luke 19:41–44).

Yet today, as in Jeremiah's day, the house of God is filled with laughter, and God's people want to be entertained, not edified. The sanctuary has become an auditorium and the platform a stage as "worship experts" perform and make sure everything goes on schedule. God forbid that the Lord should break in and upset things! Saints today need to hear the words of James, "Grieve, mourn and wail. Change your laughter into mourning and your joy to gloom. Humble yourselves before the Lord, and he will lift you up" (James 4:9–10). Have you heard that message lately? Probably not.

Prayer is a spiritual investment in the future. Yes, Samuel prayed for Saul to be delivered from his pride and pretending, but he also prayed for David whom he had anointed to be the next king. Samuel prayed for the young men he had taught in the schools, that they might be faithful to the Lord in such a decadent day. He prayed for himself, that he might end well—and he did.

A Greek proverb says, "The old age of an eagle is better than the youth of a sparrow." Samuel was an eagle. He can teach us sparrows how to fly.

29

SAUL

So, if you think you are standing firm,
be careful that you don't fall!

1 CORINTHIANS 10:12

The people of Israel repeatedly wanted things they weren't supposed to have, things that would only get them into trouble.

When Moses tarried too long on Mount Sinai, the people begged Aaron, "Come, make us gods who will go before us" (Ex. 32:1). We know the tragic consequences of that foolish idea. Later, when they failed to enter Canaan at Kadesh Barnea, they said, "We should choose a leader and go back to Egypt" (Num. 14:4). If Moses hadn't interceded for them, the Lord would have wiped out the whole nation and started over with Moses as the new founder. As it was, the Lord sent them off wandering in the desert for the next thirty-eight years until the older generation died off.

Now, years later, they were pressuring old Samuel, "Appoint a king to lead us, such as all the other nations have" (1 Sam. 8:5). This time God gave them their request, but it wasn't long before the wise people wished He hadn't.

THE KING

Samuel was familiar with the law of Moses, so the idea of kingship wasn't foreign to him. God told Abraham and Sarah that kings would be among their descendants (Gen. 17:6, 16), and dying Jacob told his sons that the royal scepter belonged to the tribe of Judah (Gen. 49:10). That strange prophet Balaam saw kings in Israel's future (Num. 24:7, 17–19), and in Deuteronomy 17:14–20, Moses wrote regulations for Israel's future king to obey. Samuel read these verses to Saul and the people when Saul was crowned (1 Sam. 10:25).

The problem with their request for a king was that it came from them and not from the Lord, and their motives were selfish. They wanted to be like the other nations when God wanted them to be separate from the nations (Num. 23:9). Furthermore, they wanted a king to protect them from their enemies (1 Sam. 12:12), which meant that Israel didn't have living faith in the God of Israel. They weren't rejecting Samuel; they were rejecting the Lord (1 Sam. 8:6–9). Jehovah had cared for Israel since the day He called Abraham and Sarah, but Israel didn't trust Him. "Give us a king!"

A third factor was the Israelites' desire to bring unity to the nation, which might help them defeat their dangerous neighbors. "In those days Israel had no king; everyone did as he saw fit" (Judg. 21:25). But surely the people had God and His tabernacle at the heart of their nation, His law as their guide, and Samuel as their prophet. Their disunity came from disobedience, not from bad government. How prone we are to tinker with the machinery when the heart of the problem is the problem in the heart.

God had a king in mind for the Israelites, a godly young man named David, but it wasn't time for him to ascend the throne. As a temporary measure, God gave them Saul, the kind of superhero they desired. Saul wasn't expected to establish a dynasty in Israel because he came from the tribe of Benjamin, not Judah. God used Saul to teach His people how dangerous it is to try to second-guess the Lord. By the time Saul finished his reign, Israel was better prepared to receive David, God's first choice for the throne. "So in my anger I gave you a king, and in my wrath I took him away" (Hos. 13:11).

THE KING STANDING

Samuel had been the spiritual leader of Israel for years, yet it was Saul's servant, not Saul, who knew who Samuel was. That kind of ignorance certainly isn't the mark of a spiritual man. Saul and Samuel met for the first time at Ramah, Samuel's hometown, and there Samuel anointed Saul as the king of Israel. It was at sunrise, as though the Lord was announcing to the nation the dawning of a new day (1 Sam. 9:26–10:1).

When Saul left Samuel and turned to make his way home to Gibeah, the Lord "changed Saul's heart" (1 Sam. 10:9–10). I don't think this is a description of spiritual conversion, even though the Spirit did come upon Saul in power and he joined the sons of the prophets in praising God. According to Matthew Henry, this "new heart" meant that Saul no longer thought and felt like an ordinary farmer but like a statesman and a general.[1] Alexander Whyte said, "The Spirit of God came upon Saul for outward and earthly acts but never for an inward change of heart.... Saul all along was little better than a heathen at heart."[2]

"I do not think that he ever did really, in his innermost soul, know the Lord," said Charles Spurgeon. "After Samuel anointed him, he was 'turned into another man,' but he never became a new man; and the sense of God's presence that he had was not, for a moment, comparable to that presence of God which a true saint enjoys."[3]

1. Matthew Henry, Commentary on 1 Samuel 10:9.
2. Whyte, Bible Characters, 231.
3. Spurgeon, Metropolitan Tabernacle Pulpit, vol. 48, 521.

John Henry Newman commented:

Some men are inconsistent in their conduct, as Samson, or as Eli, and yet may have lived by faith, though weak faith. Others have sudden falls, as David had. Others are corrupted by prosperity, as Solomon. But as to Saul, there is no proof that he had any deep-seated religious principle at all; rather, it is to be feared, that his history is a lesson to us, that the "heart of unbelief" may exist in the very sight of God, may rule a man in spite of many natural advantages of character, in the midst of much that is virtuous, amiable and commendable.[4]

Those sentences are worth reading again and pondering.

Samuel called the people to Mizpah, where they had previously met to confess their sins and seek God's help (1 Sam. 7:5–13). There he did a roll call of the tribes and chose Benjamin; then he selected the clan of Matri; then he focused on the family of Kish and named Saul as the king. But Saul's first official act was to hide himself among the baggage! The word describes the miscellaneous equipment and supplies that are kept at the fringes of a camp. Somewhat embarrassed, Samuel had to ask the Lord where the king was. The Lord told him and the men brought him out—and here is the key passage: "as he stood among the people he was a head taller than any of the others" (1 Sam. 10:23). He stood tall, but eventually he fell.

"If God has called a man to kingship," said G. Campbell Morgan, "he has no right to hide away.... [I]f that man out of any sense of modesty shall hide away and try to escape the responsibility, therein is the first evidence of his weakness. So it was with Saul."[5] I agree, because I have a feeling that Saul's hiding wasn't humility, it was hypocrisy, a false humility that covered a cancerous pride. On that day, Saul began the great charade, the pretending and performing that led to the deterioration of his character and the ruin of his life.

As he stood there before Samuel and the people, Saul had many things in his favor, along with his strong body and good looks. He had been called by God, anointed by Samuel, and accepted by the people who cried, "Long live the king!" (They had heard their pagan neighbors say that.) He had been born into a leading family (1 Sam. 9:1). Saul had a wonderful friend in Samuel and a choice son in Jonathan. (Later he would have a gifted son-in-law in David.) He had been helped by God's Spirit, and a band of men devoted themselves to following him (1 Sam. 10:26). The Lord had handed him a glorious opportunity to defeat Israel's enemies and transform a group of scattered people and tribes into a solid nation.

Yet Saul failed to accomplish what God ordered him to do. He began well by standing tall at his coronation, but he ended by falling in shame on the battlefield.

---

4. John Henry Newman, *Parochial and Plain Sermons*, vol. 3 (London: Rivingtons, 1885), 35–36.

5. Morgan, *Westminster Pulpit*, vol. 9, 14.

THE KING STUMBLING

Saul made a good beginning when he rallied the troops and rescued the city of Jabesh. Samuel had ordered Saul to meet him at Gilgal and to do nothing until Samuel arrived (1 Sam. 10:8). Here Saul revealed his impulsive nature and his ability to make excuses and blame other people. When he beheld the large Philistine army, he was greatly frightened, so he offered sacrifices to the Lord, hoping that this would win the blessing of the Lord and victory over the enemy (1 Sam. 13). Again, it was all part of the act.

Saul had already taken Samuel's place as leader of the nation; now he took his place as God's priest. But it was Jonathan and his armor-bearer who took the first steps in attacking the Philistines, and the Lord did the rest. Saul merely watched. Adding more pretense to his artificial spirituality, Saul made a foolish vow that appeared spiritual but was downright impractical and almost cost Jonathan his life. The Lord was not in the vow.

The turning point was Saul's refusal to obey the Lord in the battle against the Amalekites (1 Sam. 15). He didn't destroy the people or the animals, and he spared King Agag—and then he lied about it! "But I did obey the Lord," he argued (1 Sam. 15:20), but Samuel turned a deaf ear and walked away. Saul must have been bowing very low when he grasped the hem of Samuel's robe and tore it. But it only gave Samuel a text for a sermon to Saul: "The LORD has torn the kingdom of Israel from you today and has given it to one of your neighbors—to one better than you" (1 Sam. 15:28).

Now the truth came out as Saul pleaded, "But please honor me before the elders of my people and before Israel" (1 Sam. 15:30). He was more concerned about his reputation—the popularity polls—than his character, having his way than doing God's will. Samuel reluctantly went to the altar with him and offered a sacrifice, and then he turned and went home. Until he returned from the dead, Samuel never confronted Saul again.

THE KING FALLS

From that time forward, it was downhill all the way—Saul's fear of David and his futile attempts to kill him; his growing paranoia that everybody was out to get him; his bribery of his leaders who were nothing but bootlickers and cheerleaders. The climax came when he visited the witch's house at night and asked her to bring up Samuel. However, it was God who allowed Samuel to return; the witch was surprised and frightened because she had nothing to do with it. At that point, Saul fell prostrate on the ground (1 Sam. 28:14) and then got up and listened to Samuel's message. When Saul heard that Israel would be defeated and that he and his sons would be slain, again he fell on the ground in fear. But there was no escape. Saul had to go lead the Israeli army against the Philistines, because that's what the people expected him to do (1 Sam. 28:18).

Three of Saul's sons were killed in the attack, and then some anonymous Philistine archer critically wounded Saul. The king's young armor-bearer wouldn't end his agony, so Saul fell on his own sword and died (1 Sam. 31). Saul had once plotted for David to fall in battle (1 Sam. 18:25), but the Lord had other plans—it was Saul who died in battle. When David heard the news, he grieved for Saul and Jonathan and three times lamented, "How the mighty have fallen!" (see 2 Sam. 1:19, 25, 27).

The report given to David by the Amalekite was likely a pack of lies (2 Sam. 1). The man thought he would ingratiate himself with David by claiming he killed his enemy, when instead the Amalekite only forfeited his own life. However, one poignant truth came out of the event: the man took Saul's crown. This brings to mind the warning Christ gave to the believers in Philadelphia:

I am coming soon. Hold on to what you have,
so that no one will take your crown.
REVELATION 3:11

How the mighty have fallen!
2 SAMUEL 1:19, 25, 27

So, if you think you are standing firm,
be careful that you don't fall!
1 CORINTHIANS 10:12

To him who is able to keep you from falling
and to present you before his glorious presence
without fault and with great joy.
JUDE 24

30

DAVID

David shepherded them with integrity of heart;
with skillful hands he led them.

PSALM 78:72

It is unfortunate that whoever wrote the epistle to the Hebrews didn't have time to describe David's life of faith. "I do not have time to tell about Gideon, Barak, Samson, Jephthah, David, Samuel and the prophets" is the way he excused himself (Heb. 11:32), although some of the victories described in verses 33 and 34 certainly belonged to David.

It is also unfortunate that too few people realize the richness of David's spiritual contribution to the church today. Mention the name "David," and the average Bible reader will respond with either "Goliath" or "Bathsheba" and stop. But there is much more to the personality and ministry of Israel's greatest king than a remarkable adolescent victory and a costly midlife failure. When you look carefully at his varied experiences with the Lord, you will soon discover that David is one of the truly great heroes of faith in Scripture, a person with whom we would be wise to spend some time.

Paul reminded a synagogue congregation that David "served God's purpose in his own generation" (Acts 13:36). Paul didn't have time (or take time) to explain that David not only served his own generation but every generation since! He left Solomon with the plans for the temple as well as the materials needed to build it. He organized the temple staff, arranged the liturgy, invented instruments for the musicians, and wrote psalms for the choirs. We read and sing those psalms today, and the New Testament contains more than four hundred quotations from the Psalms.

The life of David recorded in Scripture has brought instruction and inspiration to God's people for centuries. Most important, David established the dynasty that brought Jesus Christ into the world to be our Savior. God made an unchanging covenant with David, promising him an everlasting kingdom (2 Sam. 7), and that covenant is fulfilled in Jesus Christ, the Son of David. "The Lord God will give him the throne of his father David, and he will reign over the house of Jacob forever; his kingdom will never end" (Luke 1:32–33).

LET'S HEAR IT FOR DAVID!

However, like the writer of Hebrews, I don't have time to deal with the entire record of David's journey of faith, nor is it necessary. As for his sins, God put them away and we'll set them aside. If you feel qualified, you can cast the first stone. Instead, I want to consider four images that are found in David's "life sentence." These images will be like four windows through which we can see this great man and learn from him how to have a heart that delights the Lord.

SHEEP

The Old Testament writers saw the people of Israel as a flock of sheep, with the Lord as their Shepherd. Jehovah was addressed as "Shepherd of Israel" (Ps. 80:1). This is how the temple musician Asaph described the exodus from Egypt: "He brought his people out like a flock; he led them like sheep through the desert" (Ps. 78:52). David himself prayed, "Save your people and bless your inheritance; be their shepherd and carry them forever" (Ps. 28:9). During troublesome times, Asaph asked the Lord, "Why does your anger smolder against the sheep of your pasture?" (Ps. 74:1); and at a time of national judgment, David said to the Lord, "I am the one who has sinned and done wrong. These are but sheep. What have they done?" (2 Sam. 24:17). In worship services today, both Christians and Jews confidently sing, "We are his people, the sheep of his pasture" (Ps. 100:3).

Jesus saw the people of His day as a scattered flock, like sheep without a shepherd (Matt. 9:36), an image that goes back to the time of Moses, who himself was a shepherd (Num. 27:17). The church adopted the image and called their spiritual leaders "pastors," which means "shepherds" (Eph. 4:11), and the congregation was known as the Lord's flock (1 Peter 5:1–4). Paul admonished the Ephesian elders, "Be shepherds of the church of God, which he bought with his own blood," and he warned them that "savage wolves" would come among them "and not spare the flock" (Acts 20:28–29).

That God's people should be compared to sheep shouldn't surprise us if we are really honest with ourselves. Sheep are relatively defenseless creatures that lack the keen eyesight of other animals. They must be led and guarded or they may be injured, go astray, or be killed by predators. Sheep are useful animals that provide milk, wool, and young for their owners, and occasionally meat. Lambs and sheep were needed for sacrifices, and Christian believers today are admonished to be "living sacrifices" (Rom. 12:1), wholly yielded to the Lord.

"I am sending you out like sheep among wolves," Jesus told His apostles (Matt. 10:16), and our status in society hasn't changed since then. "Yet for your sake we face death all day long; we are considered as sheep to be slaughtered," wrote the sons of Korah (Ps. 44:22). Paul quoted that statement in Romans 8:36 and then reminded us that "we are more than conquerors through him who loved us." Conquering sheep! The lamb becomes a lion!

Though he was God's chosen shepherd-king, David never forgot that he was still one of the Lord's sheep, and he wrote, "The LORD is my shepherd" (Ps. 23:1).

Whenever David forgot this important truth, the Lord sent some challenge or trial into his life and reminded him of his weaknesses. Jeremiah said that "it is not for man to direct his steps" (Jer. 10:23), and that applies to kings as well as commoners. We all need Jesus as our Shepherd, but many people are following the wrong shepherd.

SHEPHERDS

Some of the most important people in Bible history were shepherds, including Abel, the first martyr, as well as Abraham, Isaac, Jacob, Moses, and at the top of the list, David. In the ancient world, rulers were called shepherds because they were expected to love their people, care for them, and lead them wisely. Unfortunately, too many of these shepherds abused and slaughtered the sheep. "Woe to the shepherds of Israel," cried Ezekiel, "who only take care of themselves! Should not shepherds take care of the flock?" (Ezek. 34:2). That entire chapter is devoted to God's indictment of the selfish rulers who mistreated God's flock as though it were their own.

In New Testament times, the shepherd image wasn't that glamorous; in fact, shepherds were considered among the lowest in society, along with widows, prostitutes, and lepers. Because they had to spend many days and nights out in the fields and away from home, shepherds couldn't participate in the religious activities of the temple and synagogue, and because they worked with animals, they were usually ceremonially unclean. In spite of this, the first announcement of the Savior's birth was made to shepherds in the fields (Luke 2), and Jesus identified with shepherds by calling Himself the "good shepherd" (John 10:11).

In that chapter, Jesus named three kinds of people and defined their relationship to the sheep. The shepherd knows the sheep by name and they know his voice, so they follow him and he cares for them. Because he loves them, he is willing to lay down his life for them. The hireling is just the opposite: he is in it only for the salary. When danger arises, he runs away and doesn't care what happens to the sheep. The thieves and robbers want to scatter the flock and destroy it, taking whatever they want for themselves. The nation of Israel had many religious and civil leaders who were both hirelings and robbers, and assisting them were some false prophets. Is the situation much different today?

Sheep need shepherds, and this includes God's flock, the church. Every pastor and church leader ought to regularly read Paul's address recorded in Acts 20:18–35 and take it to heart, especially the words of Jesus that he quotes in verse 35, "It is more blessed to give than to receive." That's the life verse for every true shepherd.

What do shepherds do for the sheep? They go before the flock and lead it; they don't march behind and drive it. They lead the sheep away from danger and into the rich pastures and still waters. (Sheep don't like running water.) They check the pastures for dangerous rocks or holes where sheep might be hurt, and they watch out for predators. They keep their eyes open and go after the sheep that heedlessly stray and are in danger of getting lost. Shepherds cleanse the wounds that the sheep incur and soothe them with oil. They pay special attention to the young of the flock, the lambs that still have much to learn. Shepherding isn't a nine-to-five job for loafers; it is a full-time job for people who know how to work and sacrifice.

David was that kind of shepherd. To protect his father's sheep, David killed a lion and a bear; and to bring honor to the God of Israel, he killed a loudmouthed giant and cut off his head. How many times did David risk his life on the battlefield, all the while crying out to God for a victory that would glorify His name? Day after day, David had to make difficult and unpopular decisions that pleased some and angered others, but he sought to follow the Lord, his Shepherd. The one place where he failed to shepherd faithfully was in his own family, and as a result, his daughter Tamar was raped, and his sons Amnon, Absalom, and Adonijah were killed. When the shepherd goes on the wrong path, he encourages others to go astray.

Shepherding God's people is a high and holy calling that deserves our very best, and the Chief Shepherd will reward us accordingly (1 Peter 5:1–4).

HEARTS

Even godly Samuel had to be corrected by the Lord when he went to Bethlehem to anoint the next king. As Jesse's seven sons passed before Samuel, the Lord reminded him, "Do not consider his appearance or his height.... The LORD does not look at the things man looks at. Man looks at the outward appearance, but the LORD looks at the heart" (1 Sam. 16:7). The Lord had examined David's heart and concluded, "I have found David son of Jesse a man after my own heart" (Acts 13:22; see 1 Sam. 13:13–14).

Integrity is the word Asaph used to describe David's heart. In one of his prayers, David asked the Lord, "Teach me your way, O LORD, and I will walk in your truth; give me an undivided heart, that I may fear your name" (Ps. 86:11). Saul had a divided heart, and that kind of person is "unstable in all he does" (James 1:8). This helps to explain why Saul made such a mess out of his opportunities as king of Israel, why he said one thing and then turned around and did something else and then lied about it. On the one hand, he wanted to obey the Lord, but at the same time, he wanted to please the people and himself. That's not integrity; it's duplicity. David's son Solomon wrote, "The integrity of the upright guides them, but the unfaithful are destroyed by their duplicity" (Prov. 11:3). David wasn't sinless—nobody is—but in his heart, he was blameless before the Lord and the people (Ps. 18:20–24).

We call whole numbers "integers" and divided numbers "fractions." David's heart was an integer, and Saul's heart was a fraction. David's heart was wholly devoted to the Lord, and therefore he had strength and stability and God used him mightily. Saul's heart was divided, so he was marked by weakness of character and instability of conduct. David knew that the Lord couldn't help disobedient people but only those who had "clean hands and a pure heart" (Ps. 24:4).

Jesus made it clear that we cannot serve two masters (Matt. 6:24), whether God and money, God and the pursuit of fame, God and the possession of great authority, or God and the enjoyment of "happiness." Money, fame, authority, and happiness are either idols that take the place of God or blessings God may grant us when Jesus is our Lord and these things are in their rightful place in our hearts. "But seek first his kingdom and his righteousness, and all these things will be given to you as well" (Matt. 6:33).

Duplicity—a divided heart—begins with hypocrisy. Hypocrisy means "play acting," lying to other people, but duplicity means lying to ourselves. "If we claim to be without sin, we deceive ourselves and the truth is not in us" (1 John 1:8). People with a divided heart are so adept at lying that they don't realize how serious their condition is. The next step is to start lying to God. "If we claim we have not sinned, we make him out to be a liar and his word has no place in our lives" (1 John 1:10).

Even during the years David was a fugitive hiding from Saul, he obeyed the law of the Lord and kept his life pure. In his hymn of praise for God's deliverance, David wrote, "All his laws are before me; I have not turned away from his decrees. I have been blameless before him and have kept myself from sin" (Ps. 18:22–23). Wherever David went, he was on holy ground, and he kept himself pure before the Lord.

We have learned in our previous studies that great leaders often fail in their greatest strength—Abraham in his faith, Moses in his meekness, and now David in his integrity. As soon as David's heart lusted for Bathsheba, he became double-minded, lied to himself, and said, "I can get away with this." He moved from hypocrisy to duplicity. He schemed and tried to trap Uriah, her husband, but the scheme didn't work. Then he arranged to have Uriah slain in battle. He married Bathsheba to give the baby legitimacy, and he covered his sin all during her pregnancy, but then the baby died. David finally confessed his sins, and God forgave him, but the price David paid was a costly one.

"Surely you desire truth in the inner parts," David said to the Lord (Ps. 51:6), and he was speaking about conscience and integrity. The enemy wants to attack us in our area of greatest strength, for if that falls, other things will fall with it. David was restored, and his last years were spent, not grieving over the past, but investing in the future. He got everything ready for the building of the temple and encouraged Solomon to finish the work. Solomon was the son of David and Bathsheba. "But where sin increased, grace increased all the more" (Rom. 5:20).

HANDS

God's hand and God's anointing were on David (Ps. 89:21), and David's hand was available for the Lord to use. Consider what David had in his hand as he served the Lord.

A shepherd's crook. God trained both Moses and David by making them shepherds. After all, the people of Israel acted like sheep, just as people do today! As a lad shepherding the flock, David served the Lord by serving his father. When he led them to food and water, cared for the ewes and their young, and killed a lion and a bear, he had no idea that the Lord was preparing him for a much more important ministry. The principle enunciated in Matthew 25:21 — "You have been faithful with a few things; I will put you in charge of many things" — was being played out.

A sling. Saul loaned David his own armor and sword, but David knew he couldn't win using somebody else's equipment. He had his trusty sling with him, picked up five stones, and used one of them to kill Goliath (1 Sam. 17:38 – 50). Then he took Goliath's sword and cut off the giant's head. God uses strange and interesting tools to accomplish His purposes — David's sling; Moses's staff; Samson's jawbone of a donkey; Gideon's trumpets, torches, and pitchers; Jael's hammer and tent peg; a widow's pot of oil; and a little boy's lunch.

A harp. David was a poet and a musician. The Lord used his harp music to calm King Saul when he was about to fall apart, and He used his poetry to express great worship and theology in the Psalms. It is too bad that some congregations have abandoned the kind of worship found in the Psalms and have followed the world's entertainers instead of "Israel's singer of songs" (2 Sam. 23:1).

A sword. David turned out to be a mighty warrior and a great military strategist, so much so that the singing women praised David more than they did Saul (1 Sam. 18:6 – 9). This didn't sit well with Saul, who kept his eye on David from then on. David was certainly a unique combination of soldier, musician, poet, administrator, and worshiper of God. David's sword led the way for Israel's armies to defeat their enemies, enlarge their national borders, and bring security to the nation. David wasn't afraid to be in the heart of the battle, for he knew the Lord would give him success.

It is important to remember that God trained David's hands and gave him the strength to fight His battles (Ps. 18:32 – 34). First a lion, then a bear, then a giant, then the enemy armies. He said, "Praise be to the LORD my Rock, who trains my hands for war, my fingers for battle" (Ps. 144:1).

A cup. One of the most beautiful episodes in David's life occurred in the cave of Adullam (2 Sam. 23:13 – 17). Almost under his breath, David sighed for a cup of cold water from the well near the Bethlehem gate where he had drunk as a lad. Three of his crack soldiers heard his request and risked their lives to get the water and bring it to him. David refused to cheapen their sacrificial exploit by drinking the water, for he saw it as their very blood; so he poured it out as a drink offering to the Lord. This reminds me of what General Robert E. Lee said when he refused to write a book about the Civil War: "I should be trading on the blood of my men." David was a master of making great experiences out of seemingly small matters, and this endeared him to his men. "Great services reveal our possibilities," said George H. Morrison; "small services reveal our consecration."

The temple plans. Just as God gave Moses the plans for the tabernacle, so He gave the plans for the temple to David (1 Chron. 28:11). More than anything else,

David had wanted to build a house for the Lord, but the Lord said no. David did the next best thing: he asked for the privilege of receiving the plans, and these he handed over to his son Solomon.

The temple materials. Throughout his successful military career, David took a portion of the spoils and put it into the Lord's treasury to be used for building the temple (2 Chron. 29:1–9). Solomon didn't need to hire a fund-raiser or even increase the taxes.

David risked his life so that his people might have a glorious house of God.

God asks each of His children, "What is that in your hand?" (Ex. 4:2). Give Him what you have and watch Him do wonders. Whatever He gives you, learn to use it skillfully as David did, and give your hands, your heart, your tools, and your skills to the Lord.

Michelangelo's seventeen-foot statue of David was placed in Piazza Signoria in Florence, Italy, in 1504. Since that time, it has been stoned by protesters and struck by lightning. An arm was broken when rioters threw a bench out of a window, and nobody bothered to repair the statue. Well-meaning people tried to clean it with hydrochloric acid and steel brushes and only removed the protective finish. A crazy man attacked it with a hammer, and the unprotected statue stood in the freezing rain for centuries. Then the people decided it was time to restore and rededicate the statue in honor of its five-hundredth anniversary in 2004, and this was done at a cost of an estimated $500,000.

No matter what happens to the statue, the man David, as described in the Bible, will always stand tall and strong and will command our respect. May the Lord raise up more like him!

31

JONATHAN

A friend loves at all times,
and a brother is born for adversity.

PROVERBS 17:17

*N*o one can develop freely in this world and find a full life without feeling understood by at least one person," wrote psychiatrist Paul Tournier. British preacher Charles Spurgeon said, "Friendship is one of the sweetest joys of life. Many might have failed beneath the bitterness of their trial had they not found a friend."

Friends are essential for all of us but especially for those to whom God has given places of leadership. There is loneliness in leadership that is known only by those who have experienced it, and there is strength and comfort in friendship that encourages leaders to keep going in spite of obstacles. No matter what our position in life, talking things over with a friend and praying together helps us to get perspective on our problems and on the resources God has available for us in Christ.

The friendship of David and Jonathan ranks above all the famous friendships of literature and history. King Saul had four sons, of whom Jonathan was the oldest and therefore heir to the throne (1 Chron. 8:33). A man had to be at least twenty years old to serve in the Jewish army (Num. 1:3), and Jonathan was in charge of a thousand men (1 Sam. 13:2), so it is likely he was ten years older than David. But the ties that bound them together were much stronger than age or rank, and even stronger than death.

THEY LOVED EACH OTHER

Jonathan and David met after the defeat of Goliath, and immediately the two men "became one in spirit" (1 Sam. 18:1–2). In his victory over the giant, David had demonstrated the very qualities that Jonathan admired and also possessed—faith in God, courage, humility, a desire to glorify God, and a willingness to take risks. Jonathan found none of those virtues in his father, and we have no evidence that his brothers qualified. A prince can't afford to get friendly with everybody, but here was a man with whom Jonathan could identify and sincerely love. Their hearts were bound together.

But to make David his friend was a dangerous step for Jonathan. Samuel had already anointed David to be the next king of Israel (1 Sam. 16), and the Spirit of God was at work in his life. David's father and seven brothers had witnessed the ceremony, but we don't know how many other people knew about it. Three of David's brothers were in Saul's army (1 Sam. 17:13–15), but it is not likely they bragged about their little brother. Eliab, David's oldest brother, told David he was conceited and wicked (1 Sam. 17:28). As time went on, Saul became jealous of David's military skill and popularity and tried various ways to kill him. Finally David's future kingship came into the picture (1 Sam. 20:30–31).

Surely, in their quiet conversations, David opened his heart to Jonathan and told him of the Lord's leading in his life. But this only strengthened their friendship, and neither man felt threatened. Love "does not envy, it does not boast, it is not proud" (1 Cor. 13:4). The other soldiers seemed to appreciate Jonathan and notice that he wasn't at all like his father. Even Jonathan's armor-bearer was willing to die with him (1 Sam. 14:7).

In his touching lament for Saul and Jonathan (2 Sam. 1:17–27), David openly confessed, "I grieve for you, Jonathan my brother; you were very dear to me. Your love for me was wonderful, more wonderful than that of women" (v. 26). To read erotic overtones into this statement, as some have tried to do, is both ridiculous and blasphemous. Saul tried to kill both David and Jonathan, and if he had suspected they were breaking God's law, he would have had all the evidence he needed to destroy them. No, the friendship between Jonathan and David was pure and wholesome, like the devotion of a wife who left mother and father and remained faithful to her husband.

THEY WERE BOUND TOGETHER IN A COVENANT

Jonathan made a secret covenant with David that they would be loyal friends for life, and he sealed the covenant by giving David his royal garments and weapons (1 Sam. 18:3–4). Later that covenant included two other important matters: when David became king, he would not destroy Jonathan's family (1 Sam. 20:14–17, 23, 42), and Jonathan would reign with him and be second in command (1 Sam. 23:17). David showed extraordinary kindness to Jonathan's lame son, Mephibosheth (2 Sam. 9), but David wasn't able to provide a throne for Jonathan because Jonathan died on the battlefield with his father and three brothers (1 Sam. 31:1–6).

Whenever I think about this beautiful covenant of friendship, I find myself pondering the covenant Jesus has made with those who have trusted Him. David and Jonathan were equals, one a prince and the other a future king, but when Jesus invited me to enter into a covenant relationship with Him, I was a failure and a condemned sinner. Nevertheless, He loved me, and that love was greater than any human love, even the love of a husband and wife. Jonathan gave David a royal robe, but Jesus gave me a robe of righteousness and forgave all my sins. Even more, Jesus died for me and paid the penalty for my sins. He didn't make me "second" on the throne but invited me to sit on the throne with Him and "reign in life" (Rom. 5:17; Eph. 2:6). Jonathan interceded with his father on behalf of David, but Saul never kept his promises. Our heavenly High Priest and Advocate represents us before the throne and shares the Father's blessings with us. When Jonathan died, the covenant ended between him and David, but the salvation covenant we have from Jesus will never end, because He lives by the "power of an indestructible life" (Heb. 7:16). David and Jonathan were friends for a few years, but Jesus has made us His friends forever (John 15:13–15).

Jonathan didn't abandon his father or his thousand men when he covenanted to be David's friend, but on several occasions he helped bring victory to Israel. His father wasn't doing anything to attack the enemy, so Jonathan attacked a Philistine outpost and apparently killed the officer in charge. This so angered the Philistines that they moved their troops into the land of Israel and began to threaten the Jews. This was what Jonathan wanted, because it gave him opportunity to attack the enemy, which he did, and the Lord gave Israel a great victory (1 Sam. 13–14). One can't help but admire Jonathan's faith when he said to his armor-bearer, "Nothing can hinder the LORD from saving, whether by many or by few" (1 Sam. 14:6). Jonathan had spiritual discernment and knew what the Lord wanted him to do. Saul was sitting under a tree planning to ask God what He wanted done. Jonathan was number two in rank but was doing the work of a general, and Saul got all the credit.

THEY ENCOURAGED EACH OTHER

I wonder if Jonathan didn't teach David the finer points of using the sword and the bow. Before he met Jonathan, David knew how to use a sling and had killed a lion, a bear, and a giant; and being from the tribe of Benjamin, Jonathan would admire David's skill with a sling (1 Chron. 12:1–2). But there is no evidence that David had been trained to use a sword or a bow. Of course, it was the Lord who trained David's hands for battle and gave him strong arms to wield a sword and bend a bow (Ps. 18:34). First Samuel 20 suggests that David and Jonathan were accustomed to doing target practice together, and perhaps they also worked together on their swordsmanship.

Their friendship survived many tests and trials because they loved and trusted each other and the Lord. It must have pained David to have to disagree with his friend over Saul's intentions, and it hurt Jonathan even more to find out that David was right in saying that Saul was out to kill him and keep him from ascending the throne of Israel (1 Sam. 20). Saul even tried to kill Jonathan! By standing up for David, the people in Jonathan's own household became his enemies (Matt. 10:36).

When David had to flee into the wilderness, he had two dependable friends in Jonathan and Samuel (1 Sam. 19:18–22), and he learned firsthand that "a brother is born for adversity" (Prov. 17:17). When David was in the Desert of Ziph, Jonathan risked his life and came to him "and helped him find strength in God" (1 Sam. 23:16). A true friend doesn't just tell us to "keep a stiff upper lip" or to "hang in there" but points us to the Lord and encourages us to trust in His promises. This was probably the last time David and Jonathan met on this earth. Later, when David faced a crisis at Ziklag and his men wanted to stone him, "David found strength in the LORD his God" (1 Sam. 30:6), something Jonathan had helped him to learn. We never know when we might see friends for the last time, so let's be an encouragement to them.

THEY HONORED ONE ANOTHER

Jonathan died in battle on Mount Gilboa with his father and three of his brothers (1 Sam. 31). Samuel had told Saul that this would happen (1 Sam. 28:16 – 19). Did the two men who accompanied Saul to the witch's house also hear what Samuel said? If so, did they tell others? Did Saul tell his sons? Then why go to battle? Why not surrender and save your life and the lives of your sons?

Israel had asked for a king who would fight their battles (1 Sam. 8:19 – 20), so Saul didn't dare back out, nor did he dare send his sons elsewhere. How do you lead your army into battle when you know you are going to lose? How do you show courage when you know an arrow has your name on it? You do the best you can, and Saul was always a good pretender anyway.

But why would the Lord allow godly Jonathan to die with his apostate father? Not because he was a great sinner, but because it wasn't God's plan that Israel have two kings from two different tribes. Jonathan was willing to be second to David, and David was willing for this to happen, but the Lord wasn't willing. The king had to come from Judah (Gen. 49:10), and David was that king.

David not only honored Saul and Jonathan with his beautiful elegy, but he also saw to it that their bodies were given proper burial. The Philistines cut off Saul's head and hung the four bodies on the wall of Beth Shan, and then they paraded Saul's head and armor throughout the land, boasting of their great victory. The men of Jabesh Gilead risked their lives to rescue the bodies, burn them, and bury the ashes in Jabesh. Later, David disinterred the ashes and buried them in the family plot in Benjamin (2 Sam. 21:12 – 14).

The lament in 2 Samuel 1:17 – 27 is a remarkable expression of David's devotion for both Saul and Jonathan. He doesn't mention that Saul made six attempts to kill him, or that Saul was a paranoid dictator who oppressed people, or that Saul even wanted to kill his own son Jonathan because Jonathan was David's friend. He calls them "[God's] glory" (v. 19), "the mighty" (vv. 19, 25, 27), "loved and gracious ... swifter than eagles ... stronger than lions" (v. 23). David may have been Saul's enemy, but David didn't consider Saul his enemy. David had a forgiving heart.

We wonder what went through Jonathan's mind as he lay dying on the battlefield at Mount Gilboa. Perhaps he said, "Lord, I've been loyal to You, to my father, to Israel, and to David. Thank You that this is not the end. Your servant David will defeat the enemy, unite the people, and reign for Your glory. With my last breath, Lord, I pray that You will bless my friend David, the beloved one, and lead him on to victory."

The name Jonathan means "the Lord has given."

"The LORD gave and the Lord has taken away; may the name of the LORD be praised" (Job 1:21). In all this, Jonathan did not sin by charging God with wrongdoing.

32

SOLOMON

If only they were wise and would understand this
and discern what their end will be!

DEUTERONOMY 32:29

In spite of David's fasting and praying, the baby born from his adulterous relationship with Bathsheba lived only a week and died nameless. But the second son she bore him was given two names. His parents named him Solomon, which means "peaceful," and the Lord named him Jedidiah, which means "loved by the Lord." (David's name means "beloved.") It was obvious from the beginning that the Lord had a special love for Solomon and special tasks for him to accomplish. After the painful experiences of his disobedience, David was happy to have this reaffirmation of the Lord's love.

"Our beginnings never know our ends," wrote T. S. Eliot in his poem "Portrait of a Lady," and this was especially true of Solomon. If anybody was born to privilege and surrounded with God's best gifts, it was Solomon. He was a young man who gave every evidence of great promise, but he ended far from where he started. "Solomon may well be described as the wisest fool in the Bible," said American preacher, Clarence McCartney. This means that Solomon never really made much progress in the school of life but remained a sophomore—a "wise fool."

Let's look at four portraits of Solomon, each one identifying a different stage in Solomon's life and teaching us an important lesson.

THE SPIRITUAL MAN, SERVING THE LORD

Solomon's early years brought good to the people and glory to the Lord, although his reign began with palace intrigue and bloodshed. David, now on his deathbed, assumed that everybody knew that God had chosen Solomon to be the next king, but Adonijah challenged his father and half brother and declared himself king. This led to Adonijah's death and also to the death of General Joab, his coconspirator. Solomon's name might mean "peaceable," but he knew how to deal with troublemakers. Perhaps he had seen the sad consequences of David's leniency with Amnon and Absalom and was determined to act justly but decisively. "The wisdom that comes from heaven is first of all pure; then peace-loving..."

(James 3:17). During the early years of his reign, Solomon would not tolerate "peace at any price."

We are impressed with Solomon's humble request that God give him wisdom to know how to lead the nation. We are also impressed with God's bounty in giving him both the wisdom he asked for and the things other people would have asked for. It's an Old Testament illustration of Matthew 6:33, "But seek first his kingdom and his righteousness, and all these things will be given to you as well." Solomon had his priorities in order.

Solomon was a good example to his people. He faithfully obeyed the schedule of public worship established by Moses and celebrated the feasts of Passover, Pentecost, and Tabernacles each year (1 Kings 9:25; Ex. 23:14–17) and took of his own wealth and provided thousands of sacrifices for these national celebrations. In short, he gave every evidence of being a spiritual man.

The Lord appeared to Solomon twice (1 Kings 3:5 and 9:2) and "the LORD his God was with him and made him exceedingly great" (2 Chron. 1:1). The king was required to write his own copy of the Law—probably the book of Deuteronomy—and meditate on it (Deut. 17:14–20). Solomon must have obeyed, for when we read his prayer offered at the dedication of the temple (1 Kings 8), we can tell that he was familiar with the covenants God made with Israel. How tragic that later he gradually began to ignore God's Word and deliberately disobey the Lord.

In the fourth year of Solomon's reign, he began to build the temple, an assignment that involved nearly 200,000 workers and took seven years to complete. David had provided the plans, materials, and money, so Solomon didn't have to conduct a fund-raising campaign. He had in the treasury 3,750 tons of gold, 37,500 tons of silver, and metals, wood, and stones, the value of which couldn't be measured. The non-Israelite aliens in the land did the heavy work, but the king drafted 30,000 Jewish men to cut down trees in Lebanon, with each man devoting every third month to the project. That was a big price for them to pay, but the work was for the Lord and for David. After Solomon died, the people complained about this conscription to King Rehoboam, but he showed them no sympathy (1 Kings 12:1–10).

THE SECULAR MAN, IMITATING THE WORLD

Solomon was a man with many interests. He was keenly interested in wisdom—we'd probably say "philosophy" today—and during his lifetime wrote 3,000 proverbs. He was a musician and wrote more than a thousand songs. He understood botany, biology, and zoology, and people came from distant lands to ask him questions. What a talk show host he would have been!

Once the temple was completed, Solomon launched into an expansion program that left the people breathless—and almost penniless. He had spent seven years building the temple; now he spent thirteen years building a three-story official complex called "The Palace of the Forest of Lebanon" (1 Kings 7:2–5). It included his own palace, a house for his Egyptian wife, a throne room, and "the Porch of the Pillars." It was surrounded by a "great court" that tied in with the court area around the temple. When people visited Jerusalem, they weren't sure which structure was more magnificent, the temple or "The Palace of the Forest of Lebanon."

Solomon also went into the import-export business. He assembled a fleet of ships and manned them with experienced sailors from other nations (the Jews weren't known for their maritime skills) and sent them to distant lands to sell products from Israel and gather exotic merchandise to bring back to Israel. He made trade agreements with other nations in return for the privilege of importing their goods, and this brought vast wealth to the king and the kingdom.

Of course, all these expensive enterprises had to be protected, so Solomon raised a standing army, strengthened the walls of Jerusalem, and placed fortifications in Hazor, Megiddo, and Gezer, making sure his borders were protected. In spite of the Lord's commandments in Deuteronomy 17:16–17, he imported chariots and horses from Egypt (he forgot what his father wrote in Pss. 20:7; 33:16–17) and took seven hundred wives "of royal birth," among them the daughter of Pharaoh. He also had three hundred concubines. Solomon was imitating the Gentile rulers to whom a large harem was a mark of wealth and great honor. Many of these marriages were only guarantees for treaties that Solomon had made with the kings of other nations, assuring peace and cooperation between them and Israel. After all, your father-in-law isn't likely to declare war on you or block the trade routes if his daughter is living under your protection. But the Israelites weren't supposed to intermarry with pagan nations, and this is what eventually brought Solomon's ruin.

When we add to all these costly accomplishments the amount of food consumed in the palace daily (1 Kings 4:22–28), it all leads to one word—*luxury*. Of course, if you had a thousand women in your house, plus the officers and retainers, you would need plenty of food. Where did it come from? Solomon drew a new map and divided the land into twelve districts, and each district provided food for one month. (This included food for all of Solomon's horses.) He also taxed the people heavily (see 1 Kings 4:7; 12:1–19) and received annual tribute from neighboring rulers whose lands his father had conquered.

The people of Judah and Israel "ate, they drank and they were happy" (1 Kings 4:20). But all was not well, for the glitter and glamour on the outside only covered up the decay on the inside. As Alexander Whyte said, "The secret worm ... was gnawing all the time in the royal staff upon which Solomon leaned."[1] The English poet Oliver Goldsmith said it best in "The Deserted Village":

> Ill fares the land, to hast'ning ills a prey,
> Where wealth accumulates, and men decay.

LINES 51–52

---

1. Whyte, *Bible Characters*, 284.

The nation appeared to be strong and prosperous, but it was slowly decaying because the Lord was not being given first place.

The Jews were never supposed to be like the other nations, and Solomon knew this. In his temple prayer, he said, "For you singled them out from all the nations of the world to be your own inheritance" (1 Kings 8:53). In his study of the law of Moses, surely he read Numbers 23:9, "I see a people who live apart and do not consider themselves one of the nations." He also must have read the warnings God gave Israel not to imitate the Canaanite peoples. But Solomon ignored these divine instructions and built a nation and a capital city that were the envy of his neighbors, and people traveled long distances to see the wonders in Israel. Everybody was impressed but the Lord.

But before we pass judgment on an ancient king, let's look at our own lives and churches to see if perhaps we may be guilty of the same sins today. Are the churches imitating the world in their feeble attempt to attract the world? Are we worshiping the Lord or just staging a production? Is there any evidence of the fear of the Lord and the awesome character of God? Is the large congregation a sign of blessing or compromise? Does anybody feel a conviction of sin? These are serious questions that can't be ignored. The worm may already be gnawing.

THE SKEPTICAL MAN, HATING LIFE

There were no copyrights or publication dates in the ancient world, so we have no idea when in his life Solomon wrote Proverbs, Ecclesiastes, and the Song of Songs. I have always assumed that the Song of Songs, extolling human love, was written early in his life. It emphasizes the love of one man for one woman. The book of Proverbs was penned during his lifetime and compiled after his death (Prov. 25:1). But Ecclesiastes definitely seems to belong to the closing years of his life, when he stopped to look back and evaluate what had occurred. It is a record of his personal projects and successes, his "experiments" with life and the lessons he learned the hard way.

Ecclesiastes chronicles Solomon's frustrations with life, not only his own life but also the lives of the people he studied out in the marketplace and even in the palace. He uses the word *vanity* thirty-eight times in his book; it is the translation of a Hebrew word that means "futility, emptiness, vapor." He was having an end-of-life crisis, and all his philosophical pondering made a skeptic—almost a cynic—out of Solomon. He wrote, "So I hated life, because the work that is done under the sun was grievous to me. All of it is meaningless, a chasing after the wind" (Eccl. 2:17).

Solomon discovered that you can have power, wealth, wisdom, and opportunity—all the things that make up what the world calls success—but if you don't have God, life doesn't satisfy you or even make sense. In broad strokes, that is the message of Ecclesiastes; and when you read the book, you aren't surprised that Solomon looked at life and became skeptical and at times cynical. (Skeptics raise their eyebrows and say, "You can't prove it!" Cynics sneer and mutter, "Even if you could prove it, it isn't worth it!") He'd lost faith in people, in life's challenges and pleasures, and in his wealth and wisdom. Even more, whether he knew it or not, he was gradually losing his faith in God. He had nothing to hold on to as he tried to navigate his last voyage on the stormy sea of life.

Keep in mind that before Solomon arrived at this place, he had been involved in activities that were driven primarily by selfish ambition. He didn't need pleasure parks and zoos or golden goblets and expensive meats, and he certainly didn't need a thousand women to do his bidding. Jesus warns us that "the worries of this life and the deceitfulness of wealth" can choke God's Word and keep us from being fruitful (Matt. 13:22). Solomon got too busy in his secular projects and began to neglect God's Word, and this resulted in faith being replaced by skepticism.

It was this skepticism that made it easy for him to look at the religions of his foreign-born wives and ask, "Maybe they have something to offer."

THE SINFUL MAN, TURNING FROM GOD

I don't believe that Solomon was an apostate who completely abandoned the Lord God of his fathers. "As Solomon grew old, his wives turned his heart after other gods, and his heart was not fully devoted to the LORD his God, as the heart of David his father had been" (1 Kings 11:4). He still worshiped the Lord publicly with his people, but it was not sincere worship. David was a man after God's own heart, but Solomon was a man whose heart was torn between the Lord who had blessed him abundantly and the pagan wives who comforted him in his old age. He didn't have the energy to resist their influence, so he compromised and then he fell. The king had told the people at the dedication of the temple, "Your hearts must be fully committed to the LORD our God" (1 Kings 8:61), and now he wasn't obeying the command himself.

I suppose the enemy found the first chink in the royal armor when Solomon married the Egyptian princess, although Jewish tradition tells us she was converted to the Jewish faith. The pagan high places were off-limits to the Jews, but high places dedicated to Jehovah were acceptable until the temple was built (see 1 Sam. 9:11–25). At least God didn't rebuke Solomon when he worshiped at the high place at Gibeon (1 Kings 3:4). It was when Solomon began to multiply foreign wives that his heart began to turn from the Lord (1 Kings 11:1–13). The preparation for this move had been made during those "secular years" when Solomon was working hard to impress his neighbors and his people and wasn't cultivating a heart of love toward the Lord.

God still loved Solomon, even though Solomon couldn't enjoy that love, and because God loved him, He chastened him (Heb. 12:4–11). Solomon knew the warnings that God had given (2 Sam. 7:14–15; 1 Kings 3:14; 6:11–13; 9:3–9), but he chose to ignore them. God permitted his enemies to rise up against him, and then God announced that ten of the tribes would be torn away from Solomon's son and given to another (1 Kings 11:14–40). God let Solomon's successors keep one tribe only because of God's love for David.

Did Solomon ever face reality and return to the Lord? I like to think that he did. I feel that one day he woke up to the fact that he was living on substitutes — reputation, not character; lust, not love; prices, not values; confidence in himself, not faith in God; making a living, not making a life — and that he turned back to the Lord in repentance. At least Ecclesiastes 11:9 – 12:14 points in that direction. Perhaps he read Deuteronomy again and was arrested by 32:29.

Solomon was now an old man whose physical powers were rapidly waning, and his life would soon end. In Ecclesiastes he had looked around and seen how futile life was without the Lord, so he spoke to his readers, especially the young ones, and gave them three admonitions: rejoice (11:7 – 9), remove (11:10), and remember (12:1 – 8). Then he summed it all up in 12:13: "Fear God and keep his commandments, for this is the whole duty of man." There is no need to add the word "duty," because "the whole of man" makes good sense. Solomon had looked at various parts of life "under the sun," and he found it difficult to put the fragments together. What he needed — and what he recommends to us — is to see life from heaven's point of view and get the whole picture.

The Westminster Shorter Catechism says it well: "What is the chief end of man? To glorify God and to enjoy Him forever."

Meanwhile, the Lord "richly provides us with everything for our enjoyment" (1 Tim. 6:17). What more could we ask?

33

REHOBOAM

He did evil because he had not set his heart
on seeking the LORD.

2 CHRONICLES 12:14

*W*hen you study English history, you soon learn that many of the kings not only had numbers but also nicknames. Richard I was also Richard the Lionheart, and William I was William the Conqueror. You will meet Edward the Martyr, Edward the Exile, and Edward the Confessor. But my favorite is Ethelred II who ruled England from 978 – 1016 and was called Ethelred the Unready. The word "unready" is a translation of the Anglo-Saxon word *redeless* which meant "without counsel." (The English word "ready" comes from *rede*.) When the Danes attacked England, Ethelred wouldn't listen to the counsel of his nobles but chose to bargain with the enemy. He established the first general tax in England and robbed his people to buy off the Danes. But it didn't work. His nobles abandoned him twice and, in the end, the Danes took over the country. Ethelred the Unready should have listened to his leaders and become Ethelred the Ready.

This slice of history reminds me of King Rehoboam, son of Solomon and grandson of David. He also rejected the advice of his elders and ultimately robbed God's temple so he could pay a ransom to Shishak, king of Egypt. I don't know what Rehoboam was doing during the years his father, Solomon, was reigning, but when it came his time to ascend the throne, he wasn't prepared and he didn't know how to make the right decisions. He was Rehoboam the Unready.

Using the experiences of "Rehoboam the Unready" as our guide, let's try to determine the essentials for effective leadership. How can a person be ready?

SEEK THE LORD

The inspired historian bluntly states that Rehoboam "had not set his heart on seeking the Lord" (2 Chron. 12:14). To seek the Lord means to trust Him and want to fellowship with Him and please Him in all things. This involves prayer, worship, and meditation on His truth. It means hungering and thirsting after God just as we hunger for food and thirst for water. It leads to obedience and a constant personal experience with the Lord that enables Him to mold us and direct us.

When David brought the ark of the covenant to Jerusalem, he wrote a special psalm of thanksgiving for the occasion. It is found in 1 Chronicles 16 and says, among other things, "Glory in his holy name; let the hearts of those who seek the LORD rejoice. Look to the LORD and his strength; seek his face always" (vv. 10–11). When David prepared Solomon to take the throne, he said, "Now devote your heart and soul to seeking the LORD your God" (1 Chron. 22:19). Did anybody tell Rehoboam about these events? Did they try to teach him and find him unwilling to listen? "Those who seek the LORD lack no good thing." Had Rehoboam ever read those words of David in Psalm 34:10?

For a person to seek the Lord means to fix the heart on Him and not have a divided heart and mind. The word "set" in 2 Chronicles 12:14 means to fix, to determine, not to waver. "My heart is steadfast, O God," wrote David. "I will sing and make music with all my soul" (Ps. 108:1). Solomon knew about the Lord's personal dealings with his father because David told him (1 Chron. 28; 1 Kings 8:15–21), but did anybody tell Rehoboam about this rich spiritual heritage? Rehoboam's mother was an Ammonite (1 Kings 14:21, 31), probably one of Solomon's "treaty wives" who helped to lead him into idolatry. With all his projects and appointments, Solomon was perhaps too busy to prepare his son for leadership, but the boy undoubtedly spent much time with his mother. What could she teach him?

Leaders must expect to be high-profile public people, but the most important part of any person's life is the part that only God sees. That's the part Rehoboam neglected. Nations change, leaders change, circumstances change, but the eternal God never changes and wants to be our "dwelling place throughout all generations" (Ps. 90:1).

OBEY GOD'S WILL

It was customary at a coronation for the kings of Israel to renew the royal covenant with the Lord and the people, promising to obey the law of God and to serve the nation faithfully. Solomon was crowned at Gihon on Mount Zion, but knowing the division in the nation, Rehoboam chose to go to Shechem in the tribe of Ephraim. That would please the ten northern tribes, who took more than seven years to accept David and, led by Jeroboam, had protested Solomon's heavy-handed administration (1 Kings 11:26–40). They were just on the verge of revolting and fulfilling Ahijah's prophecy and forming their own kingdom. Jeroboam returned home from Egypt and presented their case for lightening the heavy load of taxation, conscription of workers, and provision of food for the royal family and horses. Rehoboam listened and promised to act in three days. Had he been in touch with the Lord, he would have had the right answer for them.

The new king then consulted the court officials, the elders who knew the inner workings of Solomon's administration. I see this as strictly a political move to give the impression that Solomon's cabinet was in agreement with what the king did. Rehoboam's mind was already made up, and when he consulted with his friends whom he had put into office, they agreed with him.

I get the impression that Rehoboam had spent more time laughing with his young friends than he did learning from the wise elders of the land. This wasn't a "generational problem"; it was a spiritual problem. Age is no guarantee of wisdom, and youth is no mark of folly. Joseph, David, and Daniel and his friends made some very wise decisions in their youth. "He who walks with the wise grows wise, but a companion of fools suffers harm" (Prov. 13:20). "Listen to advice and accept instruction, and in the end you will be wise" (Prov. 19:20). The principles laid down in Scripture aren't dated and apply to every generation, but Rehoboam ignored them.

CARE FOR GOD'S PEOPLE

Three days later, when the delegates met the king, Rehoboam's only concern was that they respect his authority and accept his decision. He forgot (or never learned) that effective leadership demands *stature* as well as *authority*, and Rehoboam was a pygmy, not a giant. His grandfather David had defeated many enemies and won the hearts of the people, and even Solomon had national respect for his wisdom and achievements, but who was Rehoboam? He didn't even have a voice of his own, because he was only the echo of his friends. He thought that a domineering dictatorial approach would impress the people, but it only made them more hostile. Didn't Solomon write something about harsh words? "A gentle answer turns away wrath, but a harsh word stirs up anger" (Prov. 15:1). "Words from a wise man's mouth are gracious, but a fool is consumed by his own lips" (Eccl. 10:12).

David saw the people of Israel as a flock of sheep, and a shepherd doesn't drive sheep or whip them. He loves them and leads them. Solomon began his reign with that attitude, but once the temple was completed, his attitudes changed and he began to "use" the people to accomplish his projects. It's too bad Rehoboam didn't model himself after his grandfather.

The elders advised Rehoboam to be a servant (1 Kings 12:7), but he preferred to have the people do the serving and he the commanding. When the Son of God came to earth, He came as a servant, and He is the example for us to follow (Phil. 2:1–10). When we serve the least of His brethren, we serve Him (Matt. 25:31–46). In the family of God, we lead by serving and we receive by giving. The world doesn't understand this approach, and many professed believers ignore it, but that's still the way God works. Rehoboam wouldn't serve the people, so he ended up serving the king of Egypt and paying him for the privilege of doing it!

REMEMBER YOUR MISSION

The nation of Israel was chosen by God to be His servant to bring truth into the world—the truth of the one true and living God, the truth of the Scriptures, and the Messiah who is the truth. Every privilege He gave them was His gracious way of helping them fulfill their responsibilities. They were a people separated from the world and even persecuted by the world, but they had an important job to do. Each time the leaders forgot their high and holy calling, they got themselves and their people into trouble and God had to chasten them.

He chastened Rehoboam. When Rehoboam sent Adoniram, one of his oldest and most trusted officers, to negotiate with Jeroboam and his people, they stoned him to death, and that was the signal that trouble was coming. As the prophet Ahijah predicted, the nation divided into the southern kingdom of Judah and Benjamin (1 Kings 12:23) and the northern kingdom of the ten remaining tribes. Rehoboam could have been king of a great nation, but he ended up the ruler of two tribes. There could have been peace, but Israel and Judah had border disputes and wars from then on (1 Kings 14:30).

The kingdom of Judah had the temple and the Levitical priesthood, but Rehoboam permitted the people to set up pagan idols and even to visit the high places with their male shrine prostitutes (1 Kings 14:22–24). Do we see here the influence of the Ammonite queen mother? In the fifth year of Rehoboam's reign, the Lord sent the king of Egypt to invade the land and loot the temple of its treasures, including the costly gold shields of Solomon (1 Kings 10:16–17; 14:25–28). This event did humble the king, but nothing really changed. Eager to keep up appearances, Rehoboam had them replaced with bronze shields that were carried by the guards whenever the king went to the temple. Little by little, everything in the kingdom was being cheapened, and it was only because of God's covenant with David that the Lord didn't destroy the kingdom.

There is a message in all this for the church today. The Lord has given us the important mission of carrying the good news of Jesus Christ to a lost world, and those who lead us must set the example and encourage us to follow. When the church becomes like the world, the church can't effectively reach the world. Do we still have our golden shields, or are they made of brass or painted papier-mâché? Are we only keeping up appearances?

Rehoboam was in the third generation from David, the founder of both the dynasty and the kingdom, and frequently it is the third generation that begins to tear things apart. I have seen it happen in businesses, parachurch ministries, volunteer organizations, and especially churches. It was true of the third generation of Israelites after the conquest of Canaan (Judg. 2:6–15) as well as the third generation of David's dynasty. More than one church or parachurch ministry has started to fail with the third generation of leadership. If we don't obey 2 Timothy 2:2, this will keep on happening: "The things you have heard me say in the presence of many witnesses entrust to reliable men who will also be qualified to teach others." Everything rises or falls with leadership, and leaders must be prepared to lead.

"I hated all the things I had toiled for under the sun," wrote Solomon in Ecclesiastes 2:18–19, "because I must leave them to the one who comes after me. And who knows whether he will be a wise man or a fool?" We know that his son was a fool—and we had better take heed that we don't follow Rehoboam's bad example. Unless we know the past and understand the present, we can't lead people into the future.

34

ELIJAH

"You are God in Israel and ... I am your servant."

1 KINGS 18:36

The name Elijah means "my God is Jehovah." That's important, so remember it.

During the reign of King Ahab and his evil wife, Jezebel, Elijah and seven thousand other Israelites were the only ones who could honestly say, "My God is Jehovah." Practically the whole nation was worshiping Baal. Queen Jezebel was a Sidonian princess who brought Baal to Israel when she married Ahab, and she demanded that the Jewish people worship her god. She murdered the true prophets of Jehovah and used government funds to subsidize hundreds of the priests and false prophets of Baal and his consort, the fertility goddess Ashtoreth. The nation of Israel was officially apostate.

Why should the people want to worship Baal when the Lord God Jehovah was all they needed? Baal and Ashtoreth were man-made idols, but Jehovah is the true and living God. The story of Elijah is really about God, and from what Elijah did and said, we discover what kind of God Jehovah really is.

THE GOD WHO IS FAITHFUL TO HIS COVENANT

The Lord owned the land, and the people were allowed to live on it and benefit from its resources as long as they honored the terms of God's covenant. They knew what these terms were and what God would do if they violated them, so their idolatry was inexcusable. One of the terms of the covenant was that God would turn off the rain if the people failed to acknowledge Him and Him alone as God. If they started worshiping idols, the Lord would send drought and famine (see Deut. 11:8–21; 28:9–14, 23–24).

The Lord appointed Elijah to call this breach of contract to their attention and to warn them that judgment was about to come. One day Elijah appeared from out of nowhere and told King Ahab that God was sending a drought that wouldn't end until Elijah said the word. James 5:17 indicates that Elijah had first prayed about this, and Luke 4:25 tells us the drought lasted three and a half years. Since the farmers depended on the early and latter rains, that is a long time to be without water.

The Lord is always faithful to keep His promises, whether to bless us or chasten us. "All the ways of the LORD are loving and faithful for those who keep the demands of his covenant" (Ps. 25:10). The Jewish people were like little children who understood only rewards and punishments. If they obeyed, they were rewarded; if they disobeyed, they were punished. What could be simpler than that?

THE GOD WHO GUIDES AND PROVIDES

Elijah never had to flip a coin or study the stars to find out what God wanted him to do. God always told him. The phrase "the word of the LORD came to Elijah" is used six times in the account of his life, and twice we read that God's angel directed him (2 Kings 1:3, 15). Three times Elijah said to Elisha, "The LORD has sent me" (2 Kings 2:2, 4, 6). Even when Elijah disobeyed God's will, the Lord still spoke to him and lovingly dealt with him (1 Kings 19:9). Baal couldn't guide his followers because he was dead, he couldn't see them or hear their prayers, and he couldn't speak to them because he had no vocal cords (Ps. 115:4–8).

During the three and a half years of drought, Elijah always had food and water because he trusted the Lord and obeyed His commands. This was a great encouragement to God's faithful servants. "My servants will eat, but you will go hungry; my servants will drink, but you will go thirsty; my servants will rejoice, but you will be put to shame" (Isa. 65:13). The ravens fed him in the Kerith ravine, and when the brook dried up, God sent Elijah a hundred miles to Zarephath where a widow cared for him. Zarephath was in Jezebel's home country, but Elijah wasn't afraid. Ahab searched diligently to find Elijah (1 Kings 18:10), but God protected His servant. The safest place in the world is in the will of God.

THE GOD WHO ANSWERS PRAYER

The same Lord who told Elijah to go hide himself (1 Kings 17:3) now told him to go show himself to Ahab and call for a public meeting (1 Kings 18:1). Ahab called Elijah "you troubler of Israel" (1 Kings 18:17), but it was Ahab and Jezebel who caused the trouble. The contest between Jehovah and Baal on Mount Carmel (on the border between Israel and Phoenicia) was really no contest at all, because Jezebel and her false priests and prophets didn't have a chance. By the time the meeting ended, there was no question that Jehovah was God and Elijah was His servant.

At the meeting were Elijah, the prophet of Jehovah, along with representatives of the ten tribes of Israel, and 850 priests and prophets of Baal. We don't know how many spectators belonged to the faithful remnant that still honored Jehovah, but when the people saw the fire consume the sacrifice, they fell on their faces and cried, "The LORD — he is God! The LORD — he is God!" (1 Kings 18:39). Then they helped Elijah by killing all the priests and prophets of Baal, which was another covenant command (see Deut. 13:13–18; 17:2–5).

But there was still one more task for the prophet to perform: he had to pray and ask God to end the drought and send the rain. God answered prayer and sent a heavy rain, another proof that Jehovah is the only true and living God. Baal was the Phoenician storm god, but he wasn't even able to send fire to consume the sacrifice let alone send the rain to heal the land! James 5:16–18 uses this to prove that "the prayer of a righteous man is powerful and effective."

THE GOD WHO IS LONGSUFFERING

"Elijah was a man just like us," says James 5:17, and 1 Kings 19 supplies the evidence. "Elijah had a heavenly name," said Alexander Whyte, "but he had, to begin with, but an earthly nature."[1] Jezebel could have sent an executioner instead of a messenger, but her real desire was to scare the prophet away and prevent him from rallying the faithful. Elijah's martyrdom would have unified the people and challenged them even more to carry on his war against Baal. When Elijah vanished from the scene, the faithful remnant was left without a leader, and Elijah had won the battle but lost the victory. Like many a leader in Bible history, he failed in his strongest point, which, in his case, was his courage. Fear and faith cannot dwell for long in the same heart.

What caused this whirlwind prophet to fail when he was on the verge of such great success? He had been stretched to the max by the confrontation at Mount Carmel; his nerves were taut, and he was hungry, thirsty, and weary. He made his worst decision in his weakest hour. He was experiencing what we today would call "burnout," and it was the opportune hour for the enemy to attack. By leaving his servant behind and walking through the wilderness alone, Elijah made his situation even worse, because lonely people are especially vulnerable. "Two are better than one," advised Solomon (Eccl. 4:9–12), which explains why Jesus sent out His disciples in pairs. In times of fear and seeming failure, we need somebody to talk to and to pray with and to give us a clear perspective on the situation. Eventually God would give Elijah a friend in his successor Elisha, and then things would be better.

Elijah journeyed 100 miles to Beersheba and then 250 miles more to Mount Sinai. Perhaps at Sinai he hoped to catch some of the spirit of Moses when Moses met God on the mountain after Israel's tragic lapse into idolatry (Ex. 32–34). But instead of interceding for Israel, as Moses did, Elijah had a "pity party" and told God he was the only faithful Jew left in the world. "Everybody else has failed, but I am still your faithful servant." Faithful? After abandoning the battlefield?

God is longsuffering, and He patiently worked with His servant to bring him back to reality. During Elijah's journey, God sent an angel to give him food and water and to protect him while he slept. As Elijah hid in the cave, God demonstrated various kinds of power—a stormy wind, an earthquake, a fire—but none of these moved the prophet; and then God spoke in a gentle whisper, and Elijah left the cave. The Lord was reminding His servant not to judge divine work by human standards, such as noise and size. Tornadoes, earthquakes, and fires may

1. Whyte, *Bible Characters*, 363.

be awesome, even frightening, but they don't change the human heart. That's where God's still small voice comes in. The spectacular may draw a crowd, but it can't build a godly people.

Let's give thanks that God is longsuffering toward His children and gently speaks to us when we are running away and feeling hurt. "The LORD is compassionate and gracious, slow to anger, abounding in love" (Ps. 103:8).

THE GOD WHO JUDGES SIN

The Lord had more work for Elijah to do. The prophet called Elisha to be his successor (1 Kings 19:19–21), and later Elisha would anoint Hazael and Jehu, and Jehu would wipe out Baal worship in Israel. Elijah had one more meeting with wicked King Ahab to rebuke him for allowing Jezebel to have Naboth slain and then confiscating his property for her husband. Ahab was eventually slain in battle at Ramoth Gilead, and Jezebel was pushed from a second-story window and died in the fall, and the dogs ate her body and drank her blood.

There is a difference between reformation and spiritual revival. It is one thing to destroy all the idols and slay the false prophets, but it is quite something else to change the hearts of the people. Israel was a covenant nation, and God had every right to judge their sins, but unless the people humbled themselves and turned back to God, they would soon return to their wicked ways. Both Israel and Judah tried to serve God and their idols at the same time, and both kingdoms eventually were destroyed.

THE GOD WHO WAS, AND IS, AND IS TO COME

Our God is eternal, the God of the past, the present, and the future. "Jesus Christ is the same yesterday and today and forever" (Heb. 13:8). Elijah revisited some of the important historic places in the land that reminded him and Elisha of God's faithfulness in the past. At Gilgal, Israel "rolled away the reproach of Egypt" (Josh. 5:9); at Bethel Jacob had life-changing experiences with God (Gen. 28, 35); at Jericho, Joshua won a great victory (Josh. 6); and at the Jordan River, the people of Israel had passed through the water and entered the Promised Land (Josh. 1–4). Let's remind ourselves that the church annually celebrates what God has done for us in the past—Jesus' birth, life, death, resurrection, and ascension, and the coming of the Spirit at Pentecost. What a history!

But these events in the past can have a spiritual impact in our lives today. Elisha learned that the Lord God of Elijah wasn't dead but was able to take His servant home in great power and glory. Elisha was Elijah's "spiritual son," so he asked for the double portion that belonged to the firstborn son (Deut. 21:17), and he received it. God is not dead, and whenever His people exercise faith, He demonstrates His great power. Elisha marched into the future confident that God was with him and that the work of the Lord would go on.

It did go on! John the Baptist came "in the spirit and power of Elijah" (Luke 1:11–17; cf. Mal. 4:5–6) and prepared the way for the Lord Jesus Christ. Elijah met with Jesus and Moses on the Mount of Transfiguration (Matt. 17:1–13), and they discussed His coming death on the cross. All would be fulfilled just as the Scriptures promised!

"Where now is the LORD, the God of Elijah?" asked Elisha (2 Kings 2:14), and he struck the water of the Jordan River and it opened up for him to walk across. But the important question today isn't "Where now is the Lord God of Elijah?" but *"Where are the Elijahs?"* Where are the men and women who will say to the Lord, "You are God … and I am your servant," and then trust Him to work?

35

ELISHA

*Continue to work out your salvation
with fear and trembling.*

PHILIPPIANS 2:12

$\mathcal{P}$aul wrote the words "Continue to work out your salvation with fear and trembling" to a congregation of believers in Philippi, urging them to do their ministry as God directed them and not to copy some other church. However, since congregations are made up of individuals, the admonition has its personal application as well, and it is beautifully illustrated in the life and ministry of Elisha. It wasn't easy to take the place of a great man like Elijah, but Elisha made a success of it. Not every successor is a success, so let's look at Elisha and discover essentials for making a success out of our lives and ministries.

WE NEED THE COURAGE TO BE OURSELVES

Elisha's master, Elijah, was a strong personality, and as Elisha lived and served with him for perhaps ten years, it would have been easy to become like the fiery prophet, whether deliberately or unconsciously. But Elisha chose to be himself. "Elisha is a different personality," said George W. Truett. "Elisha is not the copyist. Elisha is not the echo. Elisha stands out in his own unspoiled individuality."[1]

One of the encouraging things about Bible personalities is their variety. The Lord is "the God of Abraham, the God of Isaac and the God of Jacob" (Ex. 3:6) — three different kinds of men, yet each one a believer who served the Lord. When Jesus selected His twelve apostles, He deliberately chose an assortment: John the poetical, Peter the impulsive, Thomas the questioning, and even Judas the treacherous. Look around at the world God made and you will be convinced that God loves variety.

Legalistic fellowships manufacture cookie-cutter Christians who are all alike, but where the Spirit of God is at work through the Word, there will be unity in the midst of diversity. Elijah was a loner, while Elisha needed and wanted

---

1. George W. Truett, *The Prophet's Mantle* (Nashville, Tenn.: Broadman Press, 1948), 17.

other people. Elijah went to a cave, but Elisha called for a minstrel and waited for the Lord to speak to him. Elijah had a dramatic departure from earth in a whirlwind, but Elisha simply died and was buried. (After Elisha died, a man was raised to life when the man's body was thrown into Elisha's tomb.) Each of them was an original, and both accomplished the work of God. Elijah's ministry was identified with the storm, the fire from heaven, and the earthquake, but Elisha's work was more like the still small voice.

As we walk with Jesus by faith, we become more like Him, but we also become more like ourselves and accomplish all that the Lord called us to do. Why be imitations when we can be originals? God created us individually (Ps. 139:13–16), saved us individually, and mapped out an individual faith journey for each of us (Eph. 2:10). Let's have the courage to be ourselves, and together we will bring glory to the Father. Yes, certain spiritual principles and precepts apply to all of us, and we don't want to be eccentric rebels, but the work God wants to do in us and through us is unique, personal, and individual.

WE NEED OBEDIENCE TO GOD'S CALL (1 Kings 19:19–21)

Like many others in Scripture—Moses, Gideon, David, Peter, Andrew, James, and John—Elisha was working when God called him. Elisha was at the end of a line of twelve men who together were plowing his father's field. This suggests that Elisha's father was well-off and that he raised his son to know the importance of hard work. The rabbis used to say, "He who does not teach his son to work, teaches him to steal." They found that thought in Proverbs 18:9, "One who is slack in his work is brother to one who destroys." The Bible has nothing good to say about lazy people.

When God's call suddenly and unexpectedly came to him, Elisha made a complete break with his past and followed Elijah with no intention of turning back. Today we would say that "he burned his bridges behind him," except that Elisha burned his plow equipment, just as our Lord's first disciples left their fishing boats and nets behind them when Jesus called them. "No one who puts his hand to the plow and looks back is fit for service in the kingdom of God," said Jesus (Luke 9:62).

Between the record of his call in 1 Kings 19 and that of the sudden departure of Elijah in 2 Kings 2, Elisha's name isn't once mentioned in Scripture! Elisha went from being the son of a wealthy landowner to the servant of a singular prophet, and his name drops out of the annals. He was first a servant and then a leader (Matt. 25:21), a pattern the Lord usually follows as He trains His workers. But it all begins with obedience to His call.

WE NEED RESPECT FOR THE PAST (2 Kings 2:1–8)

Elijah knew that he was going to be taken to heaven (2 Kings 2:5), and he wanted to have one final meeting with the men who belonged to the schools of the prophets that Samuel had founded. Elijah let Elisha decide for himself whether he wanted to make the journey, and Elisha wisely went with his master. New leaders may do things in new ways, but some things don't change and must be conserved. Leaders who don't conserve the best of the past are upsetting the present and threatening the future. Elisha took the students to his heart and cared for them.

But much more was involved: each of the geographic locations the two men visited was important to Israel's past. They started at Gilgal, and that's where Israel "rolled away the reproach of Egypt," renewed their covenant with the Lord, and celebrated the Passover (Josh. 5:1–12). The covenant sign of circumcision, the deliverance from Egypt, and the covenant given at Sinai were precious possessions of the Israelites, and Elisha needed to be reminded of this.

From Gilgal they traveled to Bethel, sacred to the memory of Abraham and Jacob (Gen. 12:8; 13:3; 28:10–22; 35:1–8) and Samuel (1 Sam. 7:16; 10:3). However, in Elisha's day, Bethel was a center for the idolatrous worship of the golden calf that King Jeroboam had set up there and in Dan (1 Kings 12:26–33). Elijah and his servant hated the idolatry, but they didn't abandon the city, and the day came when King Josiah removed the idols and called the people to worship Jehovah alone (2 Kings 23:15–23).

As the two men walked together and conversed for the last time, they headed for Jericho and the Jordan where Joshua and Israel had experienced great miracles (Josh. 3; 6). Like Joshua, Elijah trusted God to open the river so he and Elisha could pass over to the other side. Elijah would leave the Promised Land near the place where Israel had entered it centuries before, and Elisha would reenter the land like a second Joshua.

In ancient times, some kings began their reigns by wiping out the names and records of their predecessors, forgetting that their own successors might do the same thing to them; but God doesn't work that way. The past is not an anchor to hold us back but a rudder to direct us, and the leader who ignores the past is destined to be remembered as a failure. As someone has said, "Methods are many, principles are few; methods always change, principles never do."

The Lord had used Elijah to prepare Elisha for his ministry, and the same God who blessed Elijah would bless his successor.

WE NEED LIVING FAITH IN THE LIVING GOD
(2 Kings 2:9–18)

Elijah had poured his life into Elisha, but he wanted to leave him one last gift, so he asked what the younger man wanted. Elisha's reply shows that he was a spiritually-minded man with discernment. The phrase "a double portion of your spirit" doesn't mean twice as much of the Holy Spirit, because the Spirit isn't measured out in that way, nor does his request mean twice as much enthusiasm as Elijah displayed. Elisha was referring to the Jewish inheritance law that gave twice as much to the elder son (Deut. 21:17). "Let me be your spiritual heir and have the privilege of continuing your ministry in the power of God" was the import of his request. More than anything else, he wanted the blessing of God upon his life and ministry. But he had to keep his eyes on his master or the blessing would not be his. When Elijah was suddenly snatched away by the Lord, Elisha saw it happen! The Lord answered his prayer!

Elijah was gone, but the Lord God of Elijah was still on the throne and He could be trusted. Elisha's words in 2 Kings 2:12 compare Elijah to the whole army of Israel, and this image would be used for Elisha at the end of his life (2 Kings 13:14). Yes, every servant is important to God, and each member of the body is needed, but whether we like it or not, some men and women are more important than others and have a more strategic work to do for the Lord. Elisha trusted God to open the waters of the Jordan for him as He had done for Joshua and for Elijah, and God rewarded his faith. God changes His workers, but every worker must serve by faith, trusting God to guide and empower. Elisha didn't try to do anything more spectacular than what Elijah had done. He simply began his ministry where Elijah had left off and let God get the glory.

WE NEED TO EXPECT OPPOSITION (2 Kings 2:23–25)

He had no sooner begun his ministry when the enemy arrived and began to ridicule Elisha before the eyes of the people. We shouldn't be surprised at this, because "everyone who wants to live a godly life in Christ Jesus will be persecuted" (2 Tim. 3:12), and this is especially true of godly leaders.

Those who reject the Bible like to use this passage to argue that God is an evil tyrant if He killed forty-two innocent children just for joking about the preacher, but there is more involved than this. First of all, these were responsible young men and not innocent little children. The word translated "youths" is also applied to Joseph, Isaac, and Solomon. These young men knew what they were saying and doing, and they did it deliberately. That there were so many of them together at one time, all saying the same thing, indicates that this was likely a planned meeting that may have been organized by some of the adults.

But consider what these young men did. To begin with, they poked fun at God's servant by calling him "baldhead." They also made a joke out of Elijah's ascension to heaven. The men who saw this miracle surely reported it to others, and the youths heard their parents talking about it. Bethel was a center for false worship, and these people needed a demonstration of the power of the true and living God. They also needed to be reminded of God's covenant with His people, a covenant that had not changed or been revoked (Lev. 26; Deut. 28–30). If the people disobeyed God's laws, He promised to chasten them in various ways, including sending wild beasts to attack their children (Lev. 26:21–22).

If Elisha had ignored a flagrant public attack like this, made by a gang of disrespectful ruffians, he would have begun his ministry in weakness and not strength. What kind of authority would a prophet have if smart-aleck young people were allowed to call him "baldhead"? There are times when we overlook what foolish people say, but there are also times when we must exercise authority and rebuke those who speak against the Lord and His servants. In Philippi, Paul used his Roman citizenship to protect the gospel and the infant church in the city (Acts 16:35–40).

WE NEED A SERVANT'S HEART (2 Kings 2:19–8:6)

Until he became frightened and started majoring on saving his own life, Elijah was a servant to his people, but according to the record, Elisha served them even more. Following the opening of the Jordan, there are at least fifteen miracles attributed to Elisha, including a posthumous miracle at his tomb (2 Kings 13:20–21). He healed the water of the spring at Jericho, and this helped to restore productivity to the land. He provided water for the king's army and animals, which in turn helped them defeat the army of Moab.

Like Elijah, he helped a poor widow by multiplying the oil as she poured it into jars, and he empowered a barren wife to bear a son. When that son died, Elisha raised him from the dead. He healed the poisoned pottage at the Gilgal school of the prophets, and he multiplied the bread and grain to feed a hundred people. One of his greatest miracles was the healing of Naaman's leprosy, but he also afflicted his own servant Gehazi with leprosy to cure him of his covetousness.

One of the schools had to expand its facilities, and during the construction, a student lost a borrowed ax head, but Elisha caused it to float on the water so it could be recovered. He closed the eyes of the Aramean soldiers but opened his servant's eyes so he could see the hosts of angels protecting Elisha. Instead of slaying the captured soldiers, Elisha treated them kindly and sent them home. He predicted the end of the famine in the besieged city of Samaria, and this was accomplished by the Aramean army being frightened by a heaven-sent sound and fleeing away. While he was on his deathbed, Elisha enabled King Jehoash to win three victories over the Arameans (2 Kings 13:14–19). A corpse touched Elisha's dead body in his tomb and came back to life again!

All of this speaks of compassion and personal concern for the needs of others. A leader must sacrifice and serve, for these are the hallmarks of true leadership. We must be leaders who serve and servants who lead. You and I may not have the prophetic or apostolic power to perform miracles, but we can still use our abilities and resources to serve others, and we can pray. In the leadership ranks of the church today, there are too many celebrities and too few servants. "I am among you as one who serves," said Jesus (Luke 22:27), and He is the example for us to follow (Phil. 2:1–12).

36

JEZEBEL

"Everyone who sins is a slave to sin."

JOHN 8:34

*M*ost parents would violently oppose the suggestion that any of their children be called Jezebel or Judas. Both names have been too defiled to be attached to a newborn infant—one by a murderous queen and the other by a treacherous false apostle. Your dictionary probably lists Jezebel as "the wife of King Ahab," with a second listing that reads, "jezebel (lower case): a wicked and shameless woman." My thesaurus lists her three times, once under "wicked" and twice under "unchastity," and I can think of a few other categories where she could be included. But before we condemn her and her husband and brag about ourselves, let's pause to ponder some of the lessons she teaches us, wicked as she was. After all, we may be in danger ourselves!

PEOPLE CAN CHOOSE TO BE WICKED

Jezebel was born into the pagan household of Ethbaal, king of the Sidonians and high priest of Baal, but that is not what made her wicked. Like all humans, she was born with a sinful nature that gradually expressed itself as she got older and began to make decisions. True, coming into a home and a culture that both honored the filthy false god Baal made it easier for her to conform, but even in idolatrous Phoenicia, God had not left Himself without a witness. Jezebel could see the hand of the Creator in the world around her, and surely she knew what Jehovah had done in the past for the nation of Israel. God saved Rahab the prostitute in Jericho, and He could have saved Jezebel, but she chose to be wicked and wasn't ashamed of her decision.

When Jezebel moved to the palace in Samaria, the capital city of the northern kingdom, she brought with her 450 prophets of Baal and 400 prophets of Asherah, the consort of Baal, and she supported them out of the royal budget. Ahab built a temple for Baal and let it be known that the new religion was the official religion of the land. It appears that most of the people in Israel chose to worship Baal, for the Lord's census revealed only 7,000 who hadn't bowed the knee to Baal (1 Kings 19:18).

God has given us the privilege of choice, and it brings with it an awesome responsibility. Every decision leads to consequences, and both our decisions and their consequences will one day be judged by the Lord. Let's not imagine that God's divine will and our human responsibility are enemies at war with each other, because our privilege of choice is part of our bearing the image of God. Dedicated Christian believers "reign in life through ... Jesus Christ" (Rom. 5:17), which means that we sit on the throne with Him and together make decisions and act upon them. Jesus works in and through us, not instead of us or in spite of us.

DELIBERATE WICKEDNESS LEADS TO BONDAGE

King Ahab, ruler of the northern kingdom of Israel, knew Jezebel's character and idolatrous beliefs, and that's why he chose her to be his queen. Ahab and Jezebel were soul mates and sin mates. Another reason for the marriage was political: by marrying Ethbaal's daughter, Ahab sealed a peace treaty with the Sidonians and enlisted them as allies. Ahab had already sold himself to do evil before the eyes of the Lord, and the evil influence of his wife only enslaved him more (1 Kings 21:20, 25). The two of them would bring Israel into some of its darkest days of unbelief and rebellion.

There are many pictures of sin in the Bible — darkness, disease, debt, defilement, and even death — but bondage is the consequence of all of them. Jezebel and Ahab deliberately sold themselves into bondage, and the longer they rejected the truth of God's law, the worse their slavery became, but they thought it was freedom! Sin always promises freedom but eventually brings slavery (2 Peter 2:19).

A familiar proverb says:

> Sow a thought and reap an action.
> Sow an action and reap a habit.
> Sow a habit and reap a character.
> Sow a character and reap a destiny.

That principle is illustrated throughout secular and sacred history, whether you examine the biographies of Ahab and Jezebel, Samson, King Saul, King David, or Judas. "The evil deeds of a wicked man ensnare him; the cords of sin hold him fast" (Prov. 5:22), and only Jesus Christ can set us free from the bondage of sin (John 8:32, 36). To know Him personally by faith and to receive His truth and obey it is the only sure way to avoid the snares of Satan. "I will walk about in freedom, for I have sought out your precepts" (Ps. 119:45).

WICKEDNESS SPREADS AND DESTROYS

There were three kinds of citizens in Ahab's kingdom: those who gladly worshiped Baal, those who worshiped Baal in public but privately worshiped Jehovah, and those who let it be known that they worshiped only Jehovah because He was the true and living God. Jezebel had killed many of the Lord's prophets (1 Kings 18:13), so there weren't too many spiritual leaders left to shepherd the dwindling remnant, but the remnant remained faithful through it all. The fact that Ahab could "frame" Naboth, have him killed, and then confiscate his vineyard (1 Kings 21) is proof that most of the people in the northern kingdom weren't interested in obeying the laws of the Lord. Evil spreads from person to person and brings destruction wherever it goes.

Israel's first contact with the Canaanite god Baal was in Moab, at the border of Canaan, when the Moabites invited the Jews to share in a special feast (Num. 25). Worshiping Baal was such flagrant disobedience on the part of Israel that God sent a plague that destroyed 24,000 Jews, and the courageous tribal leaders killed many others who were indulging in immorality and idolatry. The memory of that crisis should have restrained the people from following Baal in Jezebel's time. During the time of the judges, Baal came back on the scene (Judg. 2:11; 3:7; 8:33), and before the kingdom was established in the time of Samuel, the Jews had to put away their images of Baal (1 Sam. 7:4). From generation to generation, the prophets had to call the Jews back to Jehovah and away from worshiping Baal.

Is the situation any different today in the professing church? Like yeast in bread dough, false teaching has been secretly introduced into the church and is quietly growing until lies replace truth in the pulpit and the classroom. But even worse is the leaven of false living. Pollsters tell us that professing Christians hold the same false values and practice the same despicable sins as people outside the evangelical church. Jezebel has been dead for centuries, but what she believed and practiced is still with us and has poisoned the church! Jesus warned the church in Thyatira that there was a Jezebel in their midst doing exactly what Queen Jezebel did in her day: encouraging believers to compromise their faith by worshiping false gods and practicing immorality (Rev. 2:18–29). He called these teachings "Satan's so-called deep secrets" (v. 24). Imagine a professed believer seeking a "deeper life" with the Devil!

How careful we must be to make sure no Jezebels or Ahabs creep into the local church and defile it with their false teachings and godless living.

THE WICKED AND THEIR WICKED DEEDS ARE JUDGED

There were times during the twenty-two-year reign of Ahab that the faithful in the land were sure that the true faith would disappear forever, what poet James Russell Lowell described in "The Present Crisis" as "Truth forever on the scaffold, wrong forever on the throne." But the Lord never forsook His people, and there came a day when "by chance" King Ahab was killed in battle (1 Kings 22:29–38) and another day when Queen Jezebel was thrown out a window and trampled to death by horses (2 Kings 9:30–37). Then King Jehu wiped out Ahab's descendants as well as the priests of Baal. The death of Ahab and his wife, and the extermination of their family, had been predicted by Elijah (1 Kings 21:17–26) and an anonymous prophet (2 Kings 9:1–10, 30–37).

Sometimes God judges the wicked during their lifetime, but not always. Many godless and arrogant people seem to escape both human law and divine wrath and die peacefully, leaving their wealth to their children. But no sinner will escape that last judgment, when the books will be opened and their works judged. Like the evil deeds of Ahab and Jezebel, the deeds of lost sinners will exert strong influence on people for years to come, and the full consequences of their sins will be known only at the end, when time is no more. The same principle applies to the good works of believers. The seeds that God's people have planted over the centuries will continue to bear fruit, and God will give His servants their full reward at the judgment seat of Christ. You never know all the good you are doing as you serve Jesus Christ, so walk and work by faith, not by sight.

And as for the Ahabs and Jezebels of this age, turn them over to the Lord, fix your eyes on Jesus Christ, and don't be detoured from the work God has called you to do.

37

JONAH

"Your sins have deprived you of good."

JEREMIAH 5:25

*W*hat the apostles said to Jesus about Mary and her lavish gift, we might say about the prophet Jonah and his foolish behavior: "Why this waste?" He was certainly an unprofitable prophet who cheapened himself greatly as he disobeyed God and wasted the opportunities the Lord had given him. But that is what happens when we rebel against the Lord and choose to go our own way. We pay a terrible price.

Jonah was court chaplain to Jeroboam II who reigned over the northern kingdom of Israel for forty-one years. Jeroboam expanded the borders of the nation—Jonah predicted that he would—but Jeroboam also followed the bad example of his namesake and "did evil in the eyes of the LORD" (2 Kings 14:23–24). The kingdom of Israel was politically secure and economically prosperous but spiritually bankrupt. Because the people ignored the king's bad character and focused on his great accomplishments, they failed to see that their "prosperity" was but a thin veneer covering a rapidly decaying foundation.

But back to Jonah. Assyria was the rising power in his day, and the Lord called him to go to Nineveh, Assyria's key city, to warn them that God would destroy it within forty days. Knowing the compassion of the Lord and being a popular court preacher and a patriotic Jew, Jonah had no desire to see Nineveh spared, so he resigned his commission as a prophet and took off in the opposite direction for Tarshish in Spain. In the days that followed, he wasted three wonderful opportunities.

HIS OPPORTUNITY TO PLEASE THE HEART OF THE LORD

Jonah acted just like the prodigal son who went to a far country, wasted his inheritance, and broke his father's heart (Luke 15:11–32). To begin with, Jonah wasted his high and holy calling as a prophet of God. He enjoyed the privilege of walking with the Lord and learning His secrets, yet he abandoned that privilege and boarded a ship going to Tarshish. God didn't speak to him as before; instead, He sent a storm that got everybody's attention except Jonah's, because Jonah was asleep! When he awakened, did Jonah recall Psalm 29?

> The voice of the LORD is over the waters;
>> the God of glory thunders,
>> the LORD thunders over the mighty waters....
> The LORD sits enthroned over the flood;
>> the LORD is enthroned as King forever.
>
> VERSES 3, 10

Jonah was ruling his own life; the Lord wasn't his King. It is a sad day in our lives when our stubbornness makes us deaf to the loving voice of God and He has to send a storm to wake us up and start us thinking. Jonah had been cheapened. He was no longer a man of God; he was only another passenger on a ship. He had lost God's voice, his power in prayer, and his witness for the Lord.

But it grew worse. Being a Jew, Jonah was supposed to be a source of blessing, because that was part of God's covenant with Abraham: "I will bless you ... and you will be a blessing" (Gen. 12:1–3). But instead of bringing blessing, Jonah caused a storm that nearly drowned the crew. This is what usually happens when people rebel against God's will. Think of Abraham in Egypt (Gen. 12:10–20), Achan on the battlefield (Josh. 7), and David's family after he sinned with Bathsheba and arranged for her husband's death (2 Sam. 11–18). The name Jonah means "dove," but Jonah certainly wasn't a harbinger of peace.

Jonah continued to cheapen himself and was treated like a piece of cargo! He said, "Pick me up and throw me into the sea, and it will become calm" (Jonah 1:12). The pagan sailors had more compassion for him than he had for them or for the people of Nineveh! But things deteriorated even more, because the "Jonah cargo" became food for a great fish—and eventually it became vomit! How low can a person get? Where did it all start? It started when Jonah rejected God's will and decided to go his own way.

One of the most important aspects of the Christian life is our relationship to the will of God. "Your will be done on earth as it is in heaven" is a key request in the Lord's Prayer because it is linked to God's name and God's kingdom and bridges into our own personal requests (Matt. 6:9–13). What right do we have to ask the Father for food, forgiveness, and guidance if we aren't really concerned about doing His will? The only time Jonah wanted God's will was when he prayed for deliverance from the great fish (Jonah 2), and like him, many people seek God's will only in emergencies.

The will of God comes from the heart of God and is the expression of the love of God. "But the plans of the LORD stand firm forever, the purposes of his heart through all generations" (Ps. 33:11). Therefore, to ignore His will or deliberately disobey it is to reject His love and grieve His heart. "As the Father has loved me," said Jesus, "so have I loved you. Now remain in my love. If you obey my commands, you will remain in my love, just as I have obeyed my Father's command and remain in his love" (John 15:9–10).

To obey God is to be enriched; to disobey Him is to be cheapened.

HIS OPPORTUNITY TO MAGNIFY THE GRACE OF GOD

God in His grace kept Jonah alive in the great fish, heard his prayer for help, and rescued him from death. Jonah recalled the promise of 1 Kings 8:46–51, looked toward the temple in Jerusalem (Jonah 2:4), and asked for God's forgiveness. As disobedient people often do when they are asking for God's help, Jonah made some promises to the Lord. "What I have vowed I will make good," he said (Jonah 2:9), and the great fish vomited the prophet onto dry land. Whether anyone saw this miracle occur isn't revealed in Scripture, but if people did see it, they carried the news quickly to Nineveh, and the city would be prepared to see and hear this unusual stranger. Perhaps Jonah's appearance was changed because he had been in the great fish for three days and nights, and that certainly would attract attention. He was like a man raised from the dead. The Lord graciously gave him a new commission and a message to deliver to the city. We must keep in mind that this book is not so much about Jonah, a great fish, or the city of Nineveh, but about God. The fish is mentioned four times, the city nine times, and Jonah eighteen times, but God is mentioned thirty-eight times. This is an account of God's grace and mercy.

In Jonah 1 and 2, the prophet acted like the Prodigal Son and ran away and wasted what he had, but in chapters 3 and 4, he behaved like the prodigal's elder brother (Luke 15:25–32). To begin with, he obeyed the Lord and served Him *only because he had to.* His obedience didn't come from a joyful heart of love or from a surrendered will. Like the elder brother, he did only what he was told to do, but his motives weren't pure. Of course, he didn't want the Lord to chasten him again, and perhaps he was hoping that the Ninevites would turn a deaf ear and eventually be destroyed. Obeying God means "doing the will of God from your heart" (Eph. 6:6), and that's what Jonah lacked.

Jonah's announcement was one of warning: "Forty more days and Nineveh will be overturned" (Jonah 3:4). As far as the record is concerned, he gave no message of grace or forgiveness, but the Lord used his words to bring conviction to the Ninevites, and they repented and turned to God in faith. Had Jonah really appreciated God's grace and been motivated by His love, he could have told them what the Lord had done for him, but there is no record that he gave that kind of witness. Like the elder brother, he just did his job and nothing more.

But God accepted the repentance and faith of the Ninevites! That's grace! Jonah may have expected the Lord to require them to first become Jewish proselytes, perhaps to make a pilgrimage to the temple in Jerusalem, or at least to send for a company of priests to come and offer sacrifices. Another servant of God—Peter—was in Joppa when God called him to preach to the Gentiles, and his first response was, "Surely not, Lord!" (see Acts 10). But then Peter learned that Gentiles didn't have to become Jews before they could become Christians. "All the prophets testify about him [Jesus] that everyone who believes in him receives forgiveness of sins through his name," said Peter, and Cornelius and his family and friends believed and were saved (Acts 10:43–48).

Jonah suffered from narrowness and blindness, and both were foreign to the message of God's grace. A patriotic Jew, he wanted to see Israel's enemies destroyed and his own nation blessed. He preached the message of impending judgment, and the entire city, people and beasts, repented and turned to God. "Where sin abounded, grace did much more abound" (Rom. 5:20 KJV).

HIS OPPORTUNITY TO MATURE IN THE LOVE OF GOD

"But Jonah was greatly displeased and became angry" (Jonah 4:1). Instead of using his time to instruct the new believers about the Lord, Jonah abandoned them and sat in a shelter he had made for himself east of the city. He was probably hoping that the Ninevites would do something that would anger the Lord and He would wipe them out anyway. The elder brother in our Lord's parable was angry because his wasteful younger brother had been welcomed home and forgiven, and even more, because he had been given new shoes, a ring, the father's best robe, and a feast in his honor. The party that the obedient elder brother always wanted for himself was given for the prodigal and his friends.

Had Jonah been a faithful servant and ministered to the Ninevites, he would have gained new insights into the love of God and grown in godly character. Actually, Jonah needed Nineveh as much as Nineveh needed Jonah. Peter learned new truths about the Lord and grew in spiritual stature because of his ministry to Cornelius and his family in Caesarea (Acts 10), and Jonah could have grown in the same way. But instead of being *childlike* and serving others, he became *childish* and started pouting and complaining. He had pity on the gourd that withered and died, but he had no pity for the thousands of men, women, and children — as well as their animals — who would have perished had Nineveh been destroyed. What an opportunity he wasted!

If we obey the difficult things God asks us to do, that obedience will lead us to the most wonderful truths He wants us to learn, and they will guide us to exciting spiritual growth and to becoming more like Jesus Christ. Let's not waste our opportunities. They may never come again.

According to Matthew 12:38–42, Jonah's deliverance from the great fish is an Old Testament picture of the resurrection of Jesus Christ. Jonah pictures Jesus as the Suffering Servant in His death, burial, and resurrection. This is grace indeed! Jonah certainly wasn't worthy of being chosen as a type of the Son of God, but the Lord chose him just the same. Matthew 12 describes Jesus Christ as greater than Jonah (v. 41), greater than the temple (v. 6), and greater than Solomon (v. 42), for He is Prophet, Priest, and King.

It was the sign of Jonah that Peter and the other apostles preached in the book of Acts (2:22–26, 32; 3:15; 5:30–32; 10:39; 13:26–37), and that is the heart of the message of the gospel (1 Cor. 15:1–8).

Jesus is certainly "greater than Jonah" in His person, for He is the eternal Son of God, and in His message, for it is a message of salvation and not judgment. Jonah had a message for only one city, but Jesus speaks to the whole world.

Jonah did not die, but Jesus did die and was buried and arose from the dead as He promised. The death of Jonah could not save anybody, but the Father gave His Son to be the Savior of the world (1 John 4:14). Jonah was willing to be thrown from the ship and to die for his own sins, but Jesus willingly died for the sins of the world — and He had no sin! Jonah was unwilling to make a trip to Nineveh, yet Jesus left heaven and came all the way to earth to reveal God's love and grace to us. Jonah prayed for himself and not his enemies, but Jesus prayed for His enemies: "Father, forgive them, for they do not know what they are doing" (Luke 23:34). God spared Jonah but did not spare His own Son. Rather, He delivered Jesus up to die for us (Rom. 8:32).

As Jonah wasted his opportunities, he became less and less, but God still used him to picture His own Son in death, burial, and resurrection! What a miracle of grace!

If I sent to one of my publishers a manuscript crafted like the book of Jonah, they probably would return it to me with a memo saying, "Where is the ending?" The book ends with God's question to Jonah, but we don't know how Jonah answered. Did he repent and finally learn the important lesson that God can save pagan Gentiles as well as religious Jews, and they don't have to become Jews to be saved? (That was the big debate at the Jerusalem conference recorded in Acts 15.) Did Jonah confess his anger and narrowness and go home with a loving heart? We hope so, but we don't know. We can't do much about Jonah's decisions, but we can do something about our own decisions. Are the lost a nuisance or a burden to us? Do we wish God would destroy them, or do we pray for Him to save them? Do we believe that God's grace is great enough to save the worst sinners?

> *The Lord is ... not wanting anyone to perish,*
> *but everyone to come to repentance.*
> 2 Peter 3:9

> *God our Savior ... wants all men to be saved and*
> *to come to a knowledge of the truth.*
> 1 Timothy 2:3–4

Between these two verses, there is room for everybody. Where and what is your Nineveh, and are you willing to go there?

38

ISAIAH

He saw Jesus' glory and spoke about him.

JOHN 12:41

The "he" in this life sentence is the prophet Isaiah. The apostle John is referring to the prophet's life-changing experience recorded in chapter 6 of Isaiah's prophecy. I suggest you take time now to read that important chapter.

Isaiah was "the son of Amoz," a fact mentioned thirteen times in the Old Testament. This suggests that Isaiah's father was a well-known person in the Jewish community and probably held a prominent government position. We note that his son had easy access to kings and other people in high places.

The important thing, however, isn't the name of his father but the name of the King that Isaiah saw in his vision of heaven. John makes it clear that Isaiah saw Jesus, the Son of God. Abraham had seen Jesus as a traveler (Gen. 18), Jacob had seen Him at the top of a ladder (or staircase) that reached from earth to heaven (Gen. 28:10–22; John 1:51), and Joshua had seen Him as a soldier (Josh. 5:13–15). But like the apostle John's experience in Revelation 4–5, Isaiah was allowed to look into the throne room of heaven and see the Son of God reigning in glory.

This scene reveals four basic truths about God: He is "high and exalted," He is holy, He is glorious, and He is sovereign. But if He is so exalted, how can we approach Him? If He is holy, how can He receive sinners like us? If He is glorious, why should He be concerned about things on this earth where there isn't much glory? And if He is sovereign, what need has He of weak creatures like us? The answer to all these questions is Jesus Christ.

GOD IS HIGH AND EXALTED, BUT HE CAME TO US IN CHRIST (Isa. 6:1–4)

"No one has ever seen God, but God the One and Only, who is at the Father's side, has made him known," wrote John (John 1:18), and Jesus said, "Anyone who has seen me has seen the Father" (John 14:9). Our access to God is through Jesus alone.

In Jesus' incarnation, He came to earth as a man and as a servant to reveal the Father and die on the cross. Isaiah wrote about His miraculous birth. "The virgin will be with child and will give birth to a son, and will call him Immanuel [God with us]" (Isa. 7:14; Matt. 1:23). "For to us a child is born [His humanity], to us a son is given [His deity]" (Isa. 9:6). "A shoot will come up from the stump of Jesse; from his roots a Branch will bear fruit. The Spirit of the LORD will rest on him" (Isa. 11:1–2).

Isaiah also wrote about His ministry, starting with the witness of John the Baptist. "A voice of one calling: 'In the desert prepare the way for the LORD; make straight in the wilderness a highway for our God'" (Isa. 40:3; Matt. 3:1–3). Isaiah saw Jesus as God's faithful servant: "Here is my servant, whom I uphold, my chosen one in whom I delight.... A bruised reed he will not break, and a smoldering wick he will not snuff out" (Isa. 42:1, 3; Matt. 12:18–21).

The prophet also wrote about His preaching. "The Spirit of the Sovereign LORD is on me, because the LORD has anointed me to preach good news to the poor. He has sent me to bind up the brokenhearted, to proclaim freedom for the captives and release from darkness for the prisoners, to proclaim the year of the Lord's favor and the day of vengeance of our God, to comfort all who mourn" (Isa. 61:1–2). Jesus selected this as the text for the message He gave in the synagogue in His hometown of Nazareth (Luke 4:16–21). The people admired His preaching but rejected Him and His message, and Isaiah also wrote about that: "For both houses of Israel he will be a stone that causes men to stumble and a rock that makes them fall" (Isa. 8:14). "See, I lay a stone in Zion, a tested stone, a precious cornerstone for a sure foundation; the one who trusts will never be dismayed" (Isa. 28:16; cf. Ps. 118:22; Matt. 21:42–44; Rom. 9:33; 1 Peter 2:4–8).

Yes, God is high and exalted, but Jesus Christ has bridged that great gulf and made it possible for us to know the Father and fellowship with Him. The children of God are invited to "approach the throne of grace with confidence, so that we may receive mercy and find grace to help us in our time of need" (Heb. 4:16).

GOD IS HOLY, YET THROUGH JESUS HE FORGIVES OUR SINS (Isa. 6:5–7)

"Holy, holy, holy is the LORD Almighty," called the seraphs above the throne as they worshiped the Lord, and Isaiah heard their words. When the doorposts and thresholds of the temple shook and the building filled with smoke, the prophet may have been reminded of the scene at Mount Sinai when the Lord gave Moses the tables of the law (Ex. 19:16–20; Heb.12:18–21). The result? Isaiah saw himself as a sinner and cried out in fear and conviction, "Woe to me! I am ruined!" (Isa. 6:5).

The events in chapter 6 precede those described in chapters 1–5, so Isaiah said, "Woe to me!" before he pronounced the woes recorded in chapter 5. The prophet had to deal with his own sins before he could confront his people with their sins, which is a good principle for all of us to remember. Both Abraham and Job confessed that they were but "dust and ashes" when they saw the Lord

(Gen. 18:27; Job 42:6), and Peter admitted that he was a "sinful man" after seeing Jesus miraculously fill his nets with fish (Luke 5:8).

One of Isaiah's favorite names for the Lord is "the Holy One of Israel," used twenty-five times in his book. The word *holy* carries the ideas of purity, dedication, and separation ("wholly other, wholly different"). Israel was to be "a holy nation" (Ex. 19:5–6), separated to the Lord and different from the neighboring nations. Isaiah knew that he and his people were anything but holy, but was there any hope for them?

Yes, there was hope, because there was an altar near the throne, and the blood of the sacrifices was shed on that altar for the sins of the people. On the annual Day of Atonement, the Jewish high priest carried hot coals and incense into the Most Holy Place of the temple, and this filled the room with smoke. Then he sprinkled the blood of the sacrifice on the mercy seat, and this brought cleansing for himself (Lev. 16:11–14). The seraph from the throne of God brought Isaiah a live coal from the altar, and when it touched his lips, he was cleansed and forgiven. The entire temple became like the Most Holy Place as the smoke filled the building.

All of this speaks of the work of Jesus Christ on the cross when He died for the sins of the world, and Isaiah has much to say about this great work. "The Song of the Suffering Servant" in Isaiah 52:13–53:12 is his inspired description of what Jesus experienced and accomplished on the cross. Our Lord was humiliated and disfigured (52:13–15), despised and rejected (53:1–3), smitten by God for our sins (53:4–6), and obedient even to death on the cross (53:7–9). But from His death and resurrection, sinners can be justified because God's holy law has been satisfied!

When you cry out to the Lord for salvation and believe on Jesus Christ, "your guilt is taken away and your sin atoned for" (Isa. 6:7). The Lord washes away our sins and makes us "as white as snow" (Isa. 1:18). Our sins are forgiven (Isa. 33:24), put behind the Lord's back (Isa. 38:17), forgotten by the Lord (Isa. 43:25), and swept away like a cloud (Isa. 44:22). He is "the Lamb of God, who takes away the sin of the world" (John 1:29).

GOD IS GLORIOUS, YET HE IS GRIEVED BY THE WORLD'S SIN (Isa. 6:3b)

"The whole earth is full of his glory," the seraphs cry even today as they call to one another and praise God continually. Glory? *Full* of glory? *God's* glory? There are days when you and I are sure that what is happening on the earth is anything but glorious. We seem to be living in the days of Noah, when the only thing great about humanity was its wickedness, when the earth was filled not with glory but with corruption and violence (Gen. 6:5–13). In Isaiah's day, God looked down at the religious people crowding into the temple courts with their sacrifices, and He wasn't impressed. He saw that their hands were "full of blood" and that their city was filled with injustice (Isa. 1:10–17). Religion was popular, but personal and civic righteousness were very unpopular and uncommon. The land was full of wealth, but the people were spiritually bankrupt, and superstition and idols filled the land (Isa. 2:6–22). "Full of glory" indeed!

But the heavenly worshipers can't be wrong. According to Romans 1:18–20, God's "eternal power and divine nature" are clearly seen in creation, and David affirmed that the silent voice of creation declares God's glory and proclaims God's works day and night (Ps. 19:1–6). This doesn't mean that God is ignorant of what is going on in the world. "The LORD is in his holy temple; the LORD is on his heavenly throne. He observes the sons of men; his eyes examine them" (Ps. 11:4). Sinful human beings have no glory of their own but are like grass and flowers that live for a short time and then fade and die (Isa. 40:6–8). God created us for His glory (Isa. 43:7), but "all have sinned and fall short of the glory of God" (Rom. 3:23). There are no exceptions.

In Isaiah's day, the Lord was grieved with the sins of His people, and today He is grieved with the sins of professed believers and the wickedness of a lost world. "You have burdened me with your sins," the Lord said through His servant Isaiah, "and wearied me with your offenses" (Isa. 43:24). Jesus wept over Jerusalem, and Paul's heart was broken because of the blindness of Israel (Luke 19:41–44; Rom. 9:1–5). But are there many people today who grieve over the state of society and the church? If the Lord sent another Ezekiel to find out how many people were grieving and lamenting over the sins of His people, how many would he find (see Ezek. 9)?

When Jesus returned to the Father, it wasn't to bask in the praise and glory of heaven but to help His people on earth extend the glory of God by winning the lost and building the church. He sent the Holy Spirit to His church to teach us the Word, empower us to witness, and enable us to live for His glory in an evil world. The exalted High Priest is today equipping His yielded servants to do His will (Heb. 13:20–21), and without Christ and the Spirit, we can do nothing. In our Lord's great High Priestly Prayer, His first request was, "Glorify your Son, that your Son may glorify you" (John 17:1). One happy day when Jesus returns, "the earth will be full of the knowledge of the LORD as the waters cover the sea" (Isa. 11:9).

Until then, we have a work to do, and that's our next topic.

GOD IS SOVEREIGN, AND THROUGH JESUS WE CAN SERVE HIM (Isa. 6:8–13)

Isaiah probably wasn't surprised when he heard the seraphs praising God, because praise and worship fill the atmosphere of heaven. But he must have been surprised when he heard the voice of the Lord ask, "Whom shall I send? And who will go for us?" (Isa. 6:8). Must the sovereign Lord ask for volunteers? Isn't He able to command and expect His sovereign will to be obeyed?

When Jesus ministered here on earth, He exercised divine power and did many wonderful works. The wind and waves obeyed Him, the fish and birds obeyed Him, disease germs and demons obeyed Him, and even death obeyed Him. But when it came to sharing the Word and extending His kingdom, He enlisted the help of men and women who trusted Him and followed Him. He borrowed Peter's boat so He could teach the crowd standing on the shore. Generous women ministered to His needs (Luke 8:1–3). Peter caught a fish and helped Jesus pay the temple tax. An anonymous child helped Him explain the meaning of humility and service. An unknown man allowed Him to borrow his animals so He could ride into Jerusalem, and another unknown man let Him use his upper room to celebrate Passover. A visitor from Cyrene carried His cross, and a respected member of the Sanhedrin prepared a tomb for His dead body.

Yes, the sovereign Lord has humbled Himself so as to need the help of His people. The Lord of glory allows us to help Him accomplish His will and His work in this world!

But the work isn't easy. People who hear the Word won't understand the message. Their hearts are calloused, their eyes are blind, and their ears are deaf. What Isaiah wrote in 6:9–10 is quoted by Jesus in Matthew 13:14–15; Mark 4:12; and Luke 8:10; by John in John 12:39–41; and by Paul in Acts 28:25–27 and Romans 11:8. The Lord didn't promise Isaiah a national revival, but just the opposite. The kingdom of Judah would be ruined and the people taken into exile, and only a remnant would remain. But even though that godly remnant was only a "stump in the land" (Isa. 6:13), from that stump would one day come a shoot and a Branch (Isa. 11:1). The promised Redeemer would come!

Isaiah was faithful in his ministry even though the work was difficult and discouraging. He preached the Word and wrote his wonderful book for us to read, and tradition tells us that he died a martyr during the reign of wicked King Manasseh. Hebrews 11:37 may refer to the event. Yes, the Redeemer *did* come! He read publicly from Isaiah's book, He quoted from it, and He fulfilled the prophecies Isaiah wrote about His birth, ministry, life, and death. And He will come again and fulfill the prophecies Isaiah wrote about His kingdom and His glory!

The work is still difficult and the laborers are few. People's hearts are still hard and they don't want to hear. But we must be faithful.

The Father waits to hear us say, "Here am I. Send me."

39

JEREMIAH

Who will listen to me?

I was only in second grade, but I can remember in 1936 the concern felt in our home and expressed in the newspapers when war was brewing in Europe. I was too young to understand all that was involved, but I can still hear Adolph Hitler's menacing voice as it came out of our Zenith radio in the living room and the announcer translating the German into English, "And Hitler has said..."

About that same time, a battle was going on in the British Parliament. Winston Churchill was struggling to get the leaders to act effectively to prevent World War II. On November 12, 1936, Churchill said, "So they [the British Government] go on in strange paradox, decided only to be undecided, resolved to be irresolute, adamant for drift, solid for fluidity, all-powerful to be impotent." Eventually Churchill won out and they got the message.

But back in the sixth century BC, the prophet Jeremiah wasn't that successful. The brutal Babylonian army was poised to invade the kingdom of Judah, and Jeremiah told the Jewish leaders God's solution to the problem: repent of your many sins, turn to the Lord in humility, and surrender to the Babylonians. But the leaders vacillated and then refused to listen. "Surely God would not permit pagan Gentiles to destroy His holy city and His holy temple," the king and his cabinet argued. "To surrender to the Babylonians is ridiculous, for the Lord will protect His chosen people!" Their indecision was a decision, and it was the wrong decision; within a few years, everything the politicians said wouldn't happen *did* happen. Why? Because people wouldn't listen.

The Hebrew word *šama* means "to hear, to listen, to obey" and is used nearly two hundred times in the prophecy of Jeremiah. Like the prophet Isaiah, Jeremiah quickly discovered that the people of Judah had eyes that could not see and ears that could not and would not hear (Jer. 5:21; cf. Isa. 6:9–10). No wonder Jeremiah cried out, "Who will listen to me?"

Yet Jeremiah didn't quit. For forty years he faithfully proclaimed God's Word to the spiritually blind and deaf people of Judah. His example teaches us how to keep on going when we are obeying God's will but nothing good seems to be happening.

WE MUST LISTEN OBEDIENTLY TO THE LORD
WHEN HE SPEAKS (Jer. 1)

Jeremiah was born into a priestly family in the town of Anathoth, about three miles from Jerusalem. When he was in his late teens and ready to start serving as a priest, the Lord called him to become His prophet. Ezekiel, Zechariah, and John the Baptist all had the same experience of going from priest to prophet. It would have been much easier to serve as a priest, for the duties were fairly routine and were explained in the books of Moses. A priest's job was to conserve the past, while a prophet's task was to change the present so as to guarantee the future. Both vocations were important, but the priest's work was much easier. The offerings of the people met the needs of the priests, and the priests weren't expected to meddle in politics or make speeches. The people respected the priests but usually rejected the prophets and sometimes killed them. To be God's messenger to a rebellious nation was a frightening challenge to a sensitive young man, and it is no wonder Jeremiah imitated Moses and began by resisting the call.

When God first spoke to him, Jeremiah argued that he was too young to represent the Lord before the nation. The people, and especially the leaders, would never listen to the words of "a child." But God assured him He had appointed him before he was conceived and had equipped him to be His prophet. A seraph had touched Isaiah's mouth with a coal from the altar, but the Lord Himself touched the mouth of Jeremiah and gave him the words to speak. God also gave him a great promise: "I am watching to see that my word is fulfilled" (Jer. 1:12). Like Samuel, none of Jeremiah's words would fall to the ground and be lost (1 Sam. 3:19). Our words are but a puff of air and a bit of sound, and then they're gone, but not so when we speak the words God gives us. "It will not return to me empty, but will accomplish what I desire and achieve the purpose for which I sent it" (Isa. 55:11). His Word shall not pass away.

The message the Lord gave to Jeremiah was anything but good news to the nation, for he announced that disaster was coming from the north. The Babylonian army would invade Judah, devastate the land, destroy the temple and the city of Jerusalem, and carry away thousands of captives to exile in Babylon. If the Jewish people repented of their sins, turned from their idols to the Lord, and surrendered to Nebuchadnezzar, the city and temple would be spared; but the people believed the lies of the false prophets and expected the Lord to rescue Judah from the enemy.

When God called young Jeremiah to be a prophet, He called him to be a destroyer, a builder, and a planter (Jer. 1:10), an assayer (Jer. 6:27), a physician (Jer. 8:21–22), and a shepherd (Jer. 13:17). Ponder those vocations as they relate to prophetic ministry. The leaders would oppose and attack him, but the Lord would make him a fortified city, an iron pillar, and bronze walls (Jer. 1:18). Jeremiah saw himself as a sacrificial lamb being led to the slaughter (Jer. 11:19) and a religious troublemaker that everybody would hate (Jer. 15:10). When he complained to the Lord and thought about resigning (9:2), the Lord only told him that the work was going to get harder! "If you have raced with men on foot and they have worn you out, how can you compete with horses? If you stumble in safe country, how will you manage in the thickets by the Jordan?" (Jer. 12:5).

What kept Jeremiah going? He listened to the Word of the Lord, fed on it (Jer. 15:16), and fearlessly declared it to the people. He knew that he was called of God and that the Lord would keep His promises. That is the way ministry still works today. God watches over His Word and accomplishes His will, even if we don't see anything happening. Our responsibility is to listen to the Lord and declare His truth, and He will do the rest. Ours is a work of faith, and "faith comes by hearing, and hearing by the word of God" (Rom. 10:17 NKJV).

WE MUST TRUST THE LORD, FOR HE LISTENS TO US

If we are quick to hear the Lord when He speaks, He will be quick to listen to us when we speak. Jeremiah was a man of prayer, and at least fifteen times in his book we find him speaking to the Lord (Jer. 1:6; 4:10; 9:1–2; 10:23–25; 12:1–4; 14:7–9, 19–22; 15:10, 15–18; 16:19–20; 17:12–18; 18:19–23; 20:7–18; 32:16–25; 42:1–22). Jeremiah must have been a faithful intercessor, for at least three times the Lord commanded him to stop praying for the nation (Jer. 7:16; 11:14; 14:11; and see 15:1). Like the apostles, Jeremiah devoted himself to prayer and the Word of God (Acts 6:4).

There were times when Jeremiah was spiritually on top of the mountain, and then he would suddenly plummet down into the valley of despair. "Why does the way of the wicked prosper?" he asked (Jer. 12:1–2), referring to those who lied about him and opposed him. He praised God for delivering him, and then he cursed the day he was born (Jer. 20:13–18). He decided that the Lord couldn't be depended on and called the Lord "a deceptive brook" and "a spring that fails" (Jer. 15:18). On more than one occasion, Jeremiah asked the Lord to avenge him against his enemies (Jer. 11:20; 15:15; 20:12). "Drag them off like sheep to be butchered," he prayed (Jer. 12:3). "Let my persecutors be put to shame ... let them be terrified" (Jer. 17:18). He reminded the Lord that he was suffering reproach for His sake (Jer. 15:15), and that included being put into the stocks (Jer. 20:1–6), arrested illegally (Jer. 37:11–21), dropped into an abandoned cistern (Jer. 38:1–13), and having his precious scrolls of prophecy burned by the king (Jer. 36:1–32).

But in all these experiences, no matter how much he was humiliated or hurt, Jeremiah prayed to the Lord and was honest in describing his own feelings. He was bold before the people but broken before the Lord, and that's the way it ought to be. "God is our refuge and strength" (Ps. 46:1), and we can run to Him and hide and at the same time receive the strength we need to go back into the battle. He hides us to help us, not to pamper us. "Listen to me, O LORD!" was the prophet's cry (Jer. 18:19), and the Lord listened and answered. He will do the same for us.

WE MUST LISTEN DISCERNINGLY TO OUR OWN TIMES

The effective servant of the Lord must be like the men of Issachar "who understood the times and knew what Israel should do" (1 Chron. 12:32). It isn't enough to know God's Word; we must also know the times and be able to apply that Word to the needs of the people. The false prophets in Jeremiah's day preached that God would defeat Babylon and rescue Jerusalem and the people, but both their diagnosis and prognosis were wrong. "They dress the wound of my people as though it were not serious," said Jeremiah. " 'Peace, peace,' they say, when there is no peace" (Jer. 6:14; 8:11). Jeremiah was an honest physician who wept over the sick nation and gave the people the true remedy. "Is there no balm in Gilead? Is there no physician there? Why then is there no healing for the wound of my people?" (Jer. 8:22).

40

EZEKIEL

The heavens were opened and I saw visions of God.

EZEKIEL 1:1

In the year 597 BC, when Ezekiel was twenty-five years old, he was taken captive to Babylon along with weak King Jehoiachin and about 10,000 skilled Jewish people (2 Kings 24:14). Five years later, when he should have begun his ministry as a priest, Ezekiel was called by the Lord to be His prophet to the exiles in Babylon, just as He had called Jeremiah to minister to the poor people left in Judah. Like Jeremiah, Ezekiel had to minister to a rebellious people with hard hearts and closed minds, but God gave Ezekiel the encouragement He needed.

Jeremiah had already sent a letter to Babylon instructing the Jewish exiles to settle down in the land, build houses, plant gardens, and give their children in marriage, because the exiles would be in Babylon for seventy years (Jer. 29:1–14). It was Ezekiel's task to help the people remain true to the Lord because they had to prepare the next generations to return to Judah and rebuild the nation. But there were false prophets in Babylon just as there were in Jerusalem, deceived men who were preaching a popular message of triumphant deliverance that contradicted the messages declared by Jeremiah and Ezekiel. But the Lord gave Ezekiel visions of Jerusalem so that he knew more of what was happening there than did the people who lived in Judah!

Surrounded by pagan idolatry, the Jews in Babylon heard God speak through Ezekiel and remind them, "I am the Lord!" (We find the statement fifty-nine times in his book.) At least fifty times he writes, "The word of the LORD came," and he was faithful to declare that word to the people. "The most pathetic person in the world," wrote Helen Keller, "is someone who has sight but has no vision." Ezekiel was a man of both sight and vision. We want to consider three of the many visions God gave him and learn from them how we can be faithful servants of God, ministering to difficult people in difficult places in difficult times. It's always too soon to quit.

A VISION OF ENCOURAGEMENT: THE LORD REIGNS IN GLORY (Ezek. 1)

Isaiah was called to ministry after he saw God's glory in the temple (Isa. 6), and Jeremiah's call was accompanied by visions of an almond tree and a boiling pot (Jer. 1:13–19). But to Ezekiel was given perhaps the most complex vision of all.

He saw a violent storm coming from the north (Babylon), with dark billowing clouds and flashes of lightning. At the heart of the storm was an intense fire like molten metal, and in the fire were four "living creatures," identified in Ezekiel 10 as cherubim. They each had four wings and four faces — the face of a man, a lion, an ox, and an eagle — and under each cherub were sparkling crystal intersecting wheels that were alive and moved under their own power, and the wheels had eyes in them! The creatures moved like lightning and the wheels moved with them. Because each pair of wheels intersected, the wheels could instantly go forward or backward, to the right or to the left, without having to make wide turns like an automobile would today.

Ezekiel looked over the creatures and the wheels and saw a large expanse of crystal, like sparkling ice, and then he realized that he was beholding the chariot of the Lord. For on the expanse was a throne of sapphire, and on the throne was the Lord God of Israel! This was the Lord's glorious "throne chariot" appearing to His servant in a foreign land. God's glory and God's government were present and at work in Babylon! Ezekiel was so overwhelmed that he fell on his face stunned, something he would do several times during his ministry (see Ezek. 1:28; 3:23; 9:8; 11:13; 43:3; 44:4).

As frightening as this vision was, it brought a message of encouragement. Ezekiel knew that Jerusalem would be destroyed, the temple would be ruined, and the people of Judah would be scattered, but now he saw that God was still on the throne and was reigning in glory! The radiance around the throne was like a rainbow (Ezek. 1:28), and the rainbow reminds us of God's covenant with creation that a flood would never again destroy life on the earth (Gen. 9:8–17). Now we see the significance of the four faces on each of the cherubim, for God's covenant was with humankind, wild creatures, and domesticated creatures (Gen. 9:10). Noah saw the rainbow *after* the storm, but Ezekiel saw the rainbow *in* the storm, and it told him that all was well. God's people would be chastened, but the nation would not be destroyed.

Consider this quotation from F. W. Robertson: "To be independent of everything in the universe is God's glory, and to be independent is man's shame. All that God has, He has from Himself — all that man has, he has from God. And the moment man cuts himself off from God, that moment he cuts himself off from all true grandeur."[1]

Man's glory is feeble and temporary, dependent on this earth like the grass and the flowers of the field (Isa. 40:6–8), but God's glory is eternal and powerful and doesn't depend on anybody or anything. God alone rules, and He rules in glory. The wheels in the vision speak of God's presence everywhere and His ability to act quickly. The eyes remind us that He sees and knows everything, and the

1. Frederick W. Robertson, *Sermons*, Third Series (London: Kegan Paul, Trench, Trubner, and Co., 1898), 237.

fiery storm demonstrates His great power. Our "true grandeur" is to submit to the will of God and seek only to glorify Him. The next time the situation is too much for you, remember what Ezekiel saw and accept it by faith.

A VISION OF JUDGMENT: THE LORD REMOVES THE GLORY (Ezek. 7–11)

In Romans 9:1–5, Paul lists eight wonderful blessings God has given to Israel and to no other nation. He begins with "the adoption as sons," referring to God's choice of Abraham and his descendants to be His very own people. The second blessing is "the divine glory" (v. 4), His presence with His people in His sanctuary. God also gave Israel the covenants, the divine law, and the form of worship He would accept. He gave them His promises, first to the patriarchs and then to the prophets. But the greatest blessing of all was that His own Son came into the world through the nation of Israel to fulfill God's promises and bring salvation to lost sinners. Israel is a rich nation indeed.

Six of these eight blessings cannot change, but two of them could change and did change: the temple worship (John 4:19–24) and the presence of God's glory with His people. Other nations had temples, priests, and sacrifices, but only Israel had the glory of the true and living God dwelling with them. When Moses dedicated the tabernacle, God's glory moved in (Ex. 40:34–38; Lev. 9:22–24) and traveled with Israel as they marched to the Promised Land. But centuries later, the nation sinned and the glory departed (1 Sam. 4:12–22).

Then Solomon built the temple and dedicated it to the Lord, and once again the glory came to dwell with God's people (2 Chron. 7:1–3). But Israel once more departed from the Lord and began to worship idols, and the Lord showed Ezekiel how defiled the temple had become (Ezek. 8). "Son of man," said the Lord, "do you see what they are doing—the utterly detestable things the house of Israel is doing here, things that will drive me far from my sanctuary?" (Ezek. 8:6). The glory of God that had dwelt between the cherubim in the Most Holy Place moved from there to the threshold of the temple (Ezek. 9:3; 10:4) and then to the south side of the temple court where the throne of chapter 1 was hovering. From there it moved to the east gate of the temple (Ezek. 10:3, 18–19), and then the cherubim and the throne and the glory all left the temple and went to the Mount of Olives east of the city. God's glory had abandoned the temple! God no longer will dwell in houses made by human hands (Acts 7:48–50).

The glory of God returned to this earth when Jesus came in human flesh and by His words and deeds glorified the God of Israel (John 1:14; 13:32; 17:4). What did we do to that glory? We crucified the Lord of glory (1 Cor. 2:8)! But the work of redemption He wrought on the cross made it possible for God's glory to dwell in the lives of those who put their faith in Jesus. Through the Holy Spirit, the glory of God dwells in each believer's body, in each local church body, and in the church body collectively (1 Cor. 6:19–20; 3:16–17; Eph. 3:21–22). We are sanctuaries of God on earth.

It is a great privilege for us to have the glorious presence of the Lord dwelling in us and in our assemblies, but it is also a great responsibility. God's glory departed from the tabernacle and the temple because God's people had sinned, and the Spirit can be so grieved with our sins today that He would remove His power from us and take away the glory. I remember hearing A. W. Tozer say, "If God were to take the Holy Spirit out of this world, most of what the church is doing would go right on and very few people would know the difference." What a tragedy!

Over the doors of many ministries today the Lord could write, "Ichabod, the glory has departed." Our public services are enthusiastic and entertaining, but where is the glory of God? Is God pleased with our ministry? Do lost sinners fall on their faces before the Lord and cry out, "God is really among you" (see 1 Cor. 14:23–25)? Vance Havner used to remind us that God's last word to His people is not "Go and make disciples of all nations" (Matt. 28:19–20) but the warning of Revelation 2 and 3, "Repent or else!" God warns us that He may take away our lampstand and terminate our witness if we don't clean out His temple and make it fit for the glory to return. We need to ponder our Lord's messages to the seven churches to discover the sins we must confess and the changes we must make.

A VISION OF FULFILLMENT: THE LORD RETURNS THE GLORY (Ezek. 40–48)

Ezekiel doesn't close his book on a negative note, for he describes the glory of the Lord returning to the land and to the temple in the future kingdom. God had departed from the temple through the eastern gate and had gone to the Mount of Olives, but Ezekiel saw the glory cloud enter the temple at the eastern gate and fill the temple (Ezek. 43:1–5). In the chapters that follow, Ezekiel gives the details of the new temple, the restored land, the divine worship, and the holy city; and he says that the name of the city will be Jehovah Shammah, "THE LORD IS THERE" (48:35). Where is the Lord? Wherever He is glorified in and by His people.

No matter how bleak the situation may be among God's people today, the Lord wants to return to us and share His glory with us. According to Ezekiel, there is coming a day when He will return permanently and fill His temple with glory. Meanwhile, He longs to dwell with us and magnify Himself by blessing our lives and ministries. We call this "revival," which means "new life." And when this new life comes to us, there is also new glory for the Lord.

Years ago when I was ministering with Youth for Christ International, many of us on the headquarters staff were out on weekends preaching at YFC rallies and in local churches. When we returned to the office, the conversation at morning coffee breaks often focused on what God was doing out in the fields. One of our staff evangelists always asked us the same question: "Did God come to the meeting?" At first, I didn't understand what he was talking about, but then it became clear to me. He was asking, "Did the ministry please the Lord? Was Jesus glorified? Did sinners trust Jesus? Was it obvious to everybody that God came to the meeting?" The important thing isn't just that the auditorium is filled with people or that the offering plates are filled with money; it is that the place is filled with the power and glory of the Lord and everybody knows God is there!

We don't have to wait until a future kingdom for this to happen, for today we can experience "the kingdom and the power and the glory" if we will only prepare for the Lord a temple fit for His presence.

Repent—or else!

41

DANIEL

We are more than conquerors through him who loved us.

ROMANS 8:37

ention the name of Daniel among people who read the Bible and you will get a variety of responses. Prophecy students will say, "An inspired interpreter!" Businesspeople will reply, "He was also an efficient administrator." A youth pastor might say, "A model young man," and the prayer warriors will add, "But don't forget he was a faithful intercessor."

These assessments are true, but behind them is the most important characteristic of all: Daniel was a conqueror. In fact, he was a "more-than-conqueror" kind of person who believed God and became an overcomer. George Washington Carver said that success is measured not only by where people end up in life but also by how much they had to overcome to get there. Daniel had to meet and overcome many enemies and obstacles in order to survive and continue serving the Lord and His people in a pagan kingdom. "The story of Daniel is fascinating," said G. Campbell Morgan, "because it reveals the possibilities of godliness in the midst of the circumstances of ungodliness."[1]

Daniel was a teenager when he was taken to Babylon in 605 BC, and he served successfully for at least sixty years under four different Gentile rulers. While Jeremiah was helping the poor remnant in Judah and Ezekiel was encouraging the exiles in Babylon, Daniel was at the center of political power bearing witness of the one true and living God. He was serving the Lord by witnessing to the lost, advising the king, and writing the book that today teaches God's people. He did his work faithfully, and God honored him.

Let's look at our own lives through the lens of Daniel's life and discover how to be more than conquerors through faith in the Lord who loves us.

THE ENEMIES WE FACE

It wasn't easy for Daniel and his three friends to be uprooted from their homes in Judah and be taken to Babylon, but the enemy always wants those who

---

1. Morgan, *Westminster Pulpit*, vol. 8, 221.

are among the very best. These four young men were healthy and handsome, good students, and more than qualified to be trained as leaders. They belonged to "the nobility" in every sense of the word (Dan. 1:3–4), and Nebuchadnezzar wanted them to be trained for his service. This led to the first enemy Daniel and his friends had to overcome—conforming to and compromising with the pagan world around them, a world controlled by idolatry, deception, violence, and pride.

Had they so desired, Daniel and his friends could have rationalized their way into compromising with the enemy, which from the human point of view looked like a wise move. From the Lord's point of view, however, to compromise would have been to sin. The men might have asked, "Why should we obey God when He allowed our nation to be defeated by the enemy? Maybe the gods of Babylon are greater." The men were far from home and the godly influence of their elders, so they might have concluded, "When in Babylon, do as the Babylonians do." The other young men in the training program were going along with the crowd (Dan. 1:15), so why not join them? Why not obey their all-powerful ruler openly but at the same time serve God secretly?

Nebuchadnezzar's officers did all they could to encourage the men to conform to the Babylonian way of life. They started by giving them new names associated with the Babylonian gods, and then they gave them new diets, which the men wouldn't accept. They knew that the king's food came from unclean animals, was prepared in an unclean manner, and was then dedicated to false gods. To eat such food would mean disobedience to Jehovah and compromise with idolatry, but not to eat it would get them and their official guard into trouble. The men didn't have the right to jeopardize the guard's life because of their convictions, but the guard did permit them to be tested with a vegetable diet. It worked, and the four Jewish students ended up at the head of the class in health, good looks, intelligence, and ability. Matthew 6:33 worked in Old Testament days and it still works today.

So much for the conformity problem. The next obstacle the young Hebrew men faced was the need for wisdom in dealing with the king and his advisers. Eastern rulers were usually proud and dictatorial and held in their hands the power of life and death over all their subjects. They were often temperamental and impulsive, and they expected their advisers to be able to interpret dreams, explain mysteries, and give counsel that was always correct. If that wasn't difficult enough, Nebuchadnezzar expected them to describe the dream that he had forgotten and explain what it meant. The Lord gave Daniel the insight and wisdom he needed to unravel all these mysteries, and by so doing, he exposed the foolishness and ineptitude of the pagan astrologers who were on the king's payroll.

But that led to another problem: the other advisers (astrologers) hated Daniel for his integrity, wisdom, and success, so they plotted against him. I have a friend who lost a job because he worked too hard and showed up the laziness of the others in his department. Some of the loafers got together and lied to the foreman about my friend, and the foreman found an excuse for firing him. There is nothing new under the sun, because this is the way the astrologers treated Daniel, but the Lord vindicated him.

Believers today still have to fight the world, the flesh, and the Devil. Even though we don't fight against flesh and blood (Eph. 6:12), we still have to live and work with people the Devil uses to create problems for us and to tell lies about us. Young Joseph faced them in Egypt, David had them in his kingdom, the early church had them, and Jesus had one disciple who was serving the Devil.

Paul assures us in Romans 8:37 that "in all these things" we can experience victory, but what "things" is he referring to? The things mentioned in verses 35 and 36—trouble, hardship, persecution, famine, nakedness, danger, the sword, and even martyrdom. We not only conquer these things and the people who cause them, but we conquer the Devil who uses these people and things to oppose Christ, and this makes us "more than conquerors." By faith we defeat Satan and his hosts—demonic and human—and that is real victory.

THE RESOURCES WE USE

The heart of every problem is the problem in the heart, and a divided heart is a defeated heart; so the first resource for victory is a heart totally yielded to the Lord. "Daniel resolved not to defile himself" (Dan. 1:8). As well-taught Jews, surely he and his three friends had studied the book of Proverbs and could quote Proverbs 4:23: "Keep your heart with all diligence, for out of it spring the issues of life" (NKJV). The *New Living Translation* reads, "Above all else, guard your heart, for it affects everything you do."

In Mark 7, Jesus preached a sermon based on this text proving that sin is a matter of the wickedness of the heart and not the uncleanness of the hands. "What comes out of a man is what makes him 'unclean,'" said Jesus (Mark 7:20), and therefore the heart must be changed and cleansed by the Lord. "Surely you desire truth in the inner parts.... Create in me a pure heart, O God" (Ps. 51:6, 10). David had it right.

Because he had a united and devoted heart, Daniel was *a man of prayer.* "Three times a day he got down on his knees and prayed, giving thanks to his God" (Dan. 6:10). Even when it was declared a capital crime to pray to anyone except the king, Daniel opened his window toward Jerusalem and prayed just the same. Daniel prayed for wisdom to discover and explain the king's forgotten dream, and God gave the answer (Dan. 2). His prayer of confession recorded in Daniel 9 stands with Ezra 9 and Nehemiah 9 as an example of humility and contrition, and the Lord ranked Daniel's intercessory prayers along with those of Noah and Job (Ezek. 14:14, 20). Yes, we must put on the whole armor of God, but we must also "pray in the Spirit on all occasions with all kinds of prayers and requests" (Eph. 6:18).

However, Daniel also depended on the resource of the *Word of God.* God gave him His Word directly, and he wrote it down for our learning. But Daniel also read and understood what his fellow prophet Jeremiah had written (Dan. 9:1–2; Jer. 25:11–12), and this motivated him to intercede for the Jewish nation. The Word of God and prayer must always go together (John 15:7; Acts 6:4; Eph. 6:17–18). God's Word is a light to direct and protect us in this dark world (Ps. 119:105) and a sword to defeat the prince of darkness (Eph. 6:17; Heb. 4:12). The Holy Spirit can take the sword of the Spirit and enable us to wield it victoriously. Daniel obeyed God's truth in his daily life and work (Dan. 6:4–5), and the Lord honored him for it.

But all of these spiritual resources would have been ineffective in Daniel's life had he not been *a man of faith*. When Daniel prayed he had faith to believe that God would answer, and He did. When he opened the scroll of Jeremiah, he trusted God to teach him, and He did. Daniel trusted God to guide him, for faith is living without scheming. He asked God to direct him, and he left the plots and intrigues to his enemies. When Daniel was taken out of the lions' den, "no wound was found on him, because he had trusted in his God" (Dan. 6:23). His enemies' schemes failed, but Daniel's faith succeeded (Prov. 3:5–6).

THE BLESSINGS WE RECEIVE

The number one blessing that came to Daniel—and can come to us—is the privilege of glorifying the Lord God of Israel. Nebuchadnezzar's victory over the kingdom of Judah seemed to prove that the false gods of Babylon were greater than the true and living God of Israel, but Daniel put a stop to that lie. The Babylonian astrologers and magicians couldn't describe the king's dream. Daniel, on the other hand, not only described it but also interpreted it (Dan. 2). The king honored Daniel and said to him, "Surely your God is the God of gods and the Lord of kings and a revealer of mysteries" (Dan. 2:47). When Daniel's friends were delivered from the fiery furnace, the king said, "Praise be to the God of Shadrach, Meshach and Abednego" (Dan. 3:28).

Daniel interpreted the king's "tree dream," and what he predicted came true. Nebuchadnezzar lived like an animal for seven years and then was delivered. "Then I praised the Most High," he wrote; "I honored and glorified him who lives forever.... Now I, Nebuchadnezzar, praise and exalt and glorify the King of heaven" (Dan. 4:34, 37). What a testimony from a pagan king! When King Darius learned that Daniel was still alive in the lions' den, he released him and issued an edict commanding all the people in his empire to "fear and reverence the God of Daniel" (Dan. 6:25–27).

Not all of us can attain the high positions that were given to Daniel, but we can still so live, work, and witness that those in authority over us will recognize that God helps us, and they will glorify the Lord. That's what Jesus taught in Matthew 5:16.

Daniel not only glorified God, but he also was especially loved by God. The angel Gabriel came from heaven and told Daniel that he was "greatly beloved" by God (Dan. 9:23 NKJV). This phrase is repeated in Daniel 10:11 and 19. But all true believers can enjoy God's special love if they do what Daniel did—pray, meditate on the Word, cultivate a heart wholly devoted to the Lord, and obey His commands. "Whoever has my commands and keeps them is the one who loves me," said Jesus. "Anyone who loves me will be loved by my Father, and I too will love them and show myself to them.... Anyone who loves me will obey my teaching. My Father will love them, and we will come to them and make our home with them" (John 14:21, 23 TNIV). Jude 21 summarizes Jesus' teaching: "Keep yourselves in God's love...." My "life sentence" for Daniel reminds us that we can be more than conquerors, as he was, "through him who loved us."

As God's faithful servant, Daniel had the *joy of helping others*. He shared his honors with his three friends and saw to it that they were promoted (2:49). By interpreting the dreams and visions, he helped kings understand God's ways and God's plans, although not every king accepted the message. Daniel's life and character have been an example and encouragement to God's people for centuries, and his insights into the future have helped us better understand the Scriptures. To know the book of Daniel is to be prepared to better understand the book of Revelation.

Jeremiah helped the poor Jews left in Judah, and Ezekiel taught the exiles in Babylon, but it was undoubtedly Daniel who opened the door for those exiles to return to Judah when the captivity ended. He understood the timetable in Jeremiah 25:11–12 (Dan. 9:1–3), prayed, and undoubtedly spoke to Cyrus about God's plan. Cyrus then issued the edict that freed the Jews to leave Babylon and return home (Dan. 1:21; 2 Chron. 36:22–23; Ezra 1:1–4). Out of that struggling remnant came a restored nation and a rebuilt temple, and from that small beginning came the prophets, the written Word, and eventually the Messiah.

Thank You, Lord!

Thank you, Daniel, man greatly beloved!

42

ESTHER

God chose the weak things of the world to shame the strong.

1 CORINTHIANS 1:27

God always has servants ready to care for His people.

After the Babylonians defeated Judah, Jeremiah ministered to the poor Jews left in the land. Ezekiel ministered to the exiled Jews in Babylon, and Ezra, Nehemiah, Haggai, and Zechariah ministered to the 50,000 Jews who returned to their land. But what about the many Jews who didn't return to the Holy Land? Cyrus had given them permission to go home, so why did they stay in the lands of their exile? That's not an easy question to answer.

Daniel and his friends were in their teens when they were exiled, so they were much too old seventy years later to make the trip back to Judah. But at least two generations of Jews, possibly three, had been born during the seventy years of captivity, so there were younger people who could have gone back and helped restore the nation and rebuild the temple. Perhaps the younger Jews decided to stay put until their grandparents or parents died ("Let me first bury my father"), and then they would return to the land, but we don't know how many of them actually did so. No doubt many were involved in business and just couldn't break away or didn't want to.

Among those remaining were Mordecai and his beautiful cousin, Hadassah ("myrtle"), an orphan he had adopted and raised. She was also called Esther, which means "star." Since Mordecai sat "at the king's gate" (2:21), it is possible that he held a minor office in the government. It isn't for us to pass judgment on the Jews who didn't go back home, but it is obvious from the book of Esther that God had a special reason for Mordecai and Esther to stay right where they were.

The cast of characters in the book of Esther may be divided into two groups: the somebodies and the nobodies. From the human viewpoint, the Persians were the somebodies and the Jews were the nobodies, but before long, that situation would be reversed.

A GATHERING OF THE SOMEBODIES (Est. 1)

The book begins with the report of an opulent banquet hosted by the Persian ruler Xerxes (in the Hebrew, *Ahasuerus*), hosted for his officers and nobles at his gorgeous palace in the citadel of Susa. Daniel had predicted that the Babylonian Empire would be succeeded by the empire of the Medes and the Persians (Dan. 2:31–39; 7:5; 8:19–20). This occurred when Darius the Mede, representing King Cyrus, entered the city of Babylon in 539 BC, killed King Belshazzar, and took over the Babylonian kingdom (Dan. 5). The Persians ruled until 330 when they were defeated by the Greeks (Dan. 8:21). An estimated fifteen million Jews lived in the Persian Empire, which stretched from the upper Nile region to India. It was Darius, the son of Xerxes, who in 538 issued the proclamation that permitted the Jews to return to Palestine, thus ending the seventy years of captivity (Dan. 9; Ezra 1; Jer. 25:11–12; 29:10).

But back to the banquet. It was indeed a gathering of the somebodies, the very important people in the empire, at least in their own eyes. For the most part, they maintained their jobs and reputations by means of political intrigue and personal flattery. The king had called them together from the 127 provinces to discuss his plans for declaring war on Greece. He wanted to impress his nobles and officials with his wealth and power, and he must have succeeded, because they agreed to his plan. Unfortunately, the Persians didn't win the war, and their defeat was costly and humiliating.

But during the banquet itself, the king had a personal embarrassing defeat of his own. His wife, Queen Vashti, would not obey his command to come to the men's banquet to display her great beauty. You can't blame her. The somebodies had been feasting for a week, and many of them were drunk, including the king, and no respectable woman would want to be on display at such a gathering. Three cheers for Vashti!

The result of Vashti's disobedience was that she was deposed from her throne. The king also sent an edict to all the provinces admonishing each man to be "ruler over his own household" and each woman to be respectful to her husband (Est. 1:16–22). The text doesn't explain how the king planned to enforce the ruling, but the edict at least helped him get out of an embarrassing situation. Off he went to war and came back a beaten man. But all this activity—eating and drinking, dethroning the queen, issuing edicts, and losing the war—was part of God's plan to rescue His people from annihilation. If God's ways sometimes seem complicated, just remember Ezekiel's vision of God's "chariot throne" with the wheels within the wheels (Ezek. 1). "How unsearchable his judgments, and his paths beyond tracing out!" (Rom. 11:33). We don't have to explain God's will or even fully understand it, but we do have to obey it.

A NOBODY BECOMES A SOMEBODY (Est. 2)

When the king returned home after the war, there was no queen to greet him and help nurse his wounded ego. Of course he had his choice of women from the royal harem, but he was smart enough to know that he needed a wife. His counselors appointed commissioners in each province to stage "beauty contests" and bring the winners to Susa. Who knew? Perhaps one of the contestants might make an ideal wife for the king. It is important to note that Esther didn't volunteer, nor did Mordecai encourage her to do so. She was chosen by the local commissioner and didn't have the privilege of refusing. This was the king's order, and disobeying it would have been dangerous.

Esther was an orphan, and she and Mordecai were both Jewish nobodies. After Esther was conscripted, it is likely they both thought she would be back home as soon as the preliminary tests ended, but they were wrong. The Lord had chosen Esther to be His special servant to deliver His people from death. A nobody was about to become a somebody, in fact, the next queen. God chooses the weak nobodies to defeat the somebodies of this world and to bring glory to His name.

God's name isn't mentioned anywhere in the book of Esther, but God's presence is very obvious, and His providence is at work from beginning to end. The theologian Augustus Hopkins Strong called providence "God's attention concentrated everywhere." Thank you Father

Almighty God is the Lord of the universe, and therefore nothing happens by chance. "The earth is the LORD's, and everything in it, the world, and all who live in it" (Ps. 24:1). "The LORD has established his throne in heaven, and his kingdom rules over all" (Ps. 103:19).

Esther didn't tell anybody that she was a Jewess, which meant that she ate what the other women ate and did what they did. It wasn't a kosher situation at all, but the Lord still worked on her behalf and then worked through her. God blessed Daniel and Ezekiel because they obeyed His laws concerning food, but He blessed Esther in spite of the fact that she didn't obey His laws governing "clean" and "unclean." Had the commissioners known she was a Jewish nobody, they might have sent her home, so she kept quiet. So did Mordecai.

During the year that the finalists were being prepared to meet the king, Mordecai walked back and forth in the courtyard of the harem to learn how his cousin was doing. Perhaps he got his information from the eunuch Hathach who eventually served Esther (Est. 4:5–6). When he wasn't checking on Esther, Mordecai sat at the king's gate, and it was there that he uncovered the plot of two disgruntled officers to kill the king. He reported this to Queen Esther who told the king, and the two officers were hanged. Esther gave Mordecai credit for the discovery, and this was written into the royal annals, but no special recognition came to Mordecai. Never mind—God was saving it for later. Mordecai was still a nobody, but the day would come when, like Esther, he would be publicly recognized.

We must never try to force the hand of divine providence. God has His times and His reasons, and we must walk and wait by faith. Faith is living without scheming. Our times are in His hands (Ps. 31:15).

A NOBODY THINKS HE'S A SOMEBODY (Est. 3–6)

Haman is suddenly introduced into the story without any explanation of who he is or why the king promoted him. Mordecai had saved the king's life and received no reward, but for no apparent reason, Haman was made the highest of the appointed royal officials. Haman had no doubt flattered his way into the king's favor and subtly influenced him into making this appointment, but, of course, the Lord was at work to prepare Haman for his execution. "Pride goes before destruction, a haughty spirit before a fall" (Prov. 16:18).

At a glance, Mordecai saw through Haman and refused to treat him like a god. Bowing politely to somebody wasn't forbidden to the Jews. Abraham bowed before the Hittites (Gen. 23), Jacob and his family bowed before Esau (Gen. 33), and David bowed before Saul (1 Sam. 24:8). Wanting to please the king and perhaps receive promotions, the officials at the king's gate knelt before Haman, but Mordecai didn't join them. This discerning Jewish nobody knew that Haman was an Amalekite, and the Amalekites were the sworn enemies of the Jews (Ex. 17:8–16; Deut. 25:17–19; 1 Sam. 15). The longer Mordecai ignored Haman, the angrier Haman became, not just toward Mordecai but toward all the Jews in the empire. His hatred grew into an obsession.

Haman easily could have hired some rogues to kill Mordecai, but being a crafty man, he developed a plan that would ingratiate him to the king, destroy all the Jews, and put a great deal of wealth into his own pocket. If the king would permit him to destroy all the Jews (although he didn't identify the people to the king), he could confiscate their wealth and end up with far more money than he gave the king—and Mordecai and his people would be gone! The king's Greek war had been costly, and he needed money badly, so he was ready for Haman's generous offer. He gave Haman carte blanche to carry out his plan. "Many are the plans in a human heart, but it is the LORD's purpose that prevails" (Prov. 19:21 TNIV).

Once the edict was announced, Mordecai went into public mourning. He got word to Esther that she too would perish unless she interceded with the king, but she knew she couldn't approach the king unless he permitted it by holding out his scepter. Once again the providence of God was at work, for the king received her and agreed to come to her banquet with Haman. But why include that wicked man? Perhaps Esther was buying time as her people prayed for her and she made her plans, and perhaps she wanted to inflate Haman's ego and get him off his guard. He had cast lots to find the right day for the attack on the Jews, but he didn't know Proverbs 16:33: "The lot is cast into the lap, but its every decision is from the LORD." Haman thought he was really a somebody and boasted to his family and friends of his intimacy with the king and queen, and he even built a gallows high enough for everybody to see Mordecai when Haman would hang him.

God's providence continued to work. The king couldn't sleep, so he had the latest royal records read to him—what is more boring than reading the minutes of a meeting?—and he discovered that Mordecai had saved his life but had not been honored for it. At that moment, Haman came to see the king and in his pride thought he was the man the king wanted to honor. Instead, Haman ended up humiliated by having to honor the man who would not honor him! This event plus the words of his wife, Zeresh, should have warned and humbled Haman, but he didn't get the message. Anyway, it was time for the second banquet with the king and queen, and the king's servants hurried Haman to the palace. It would be his last meal.

It is easy to hate and despise Haman for his arrogance and malice, but I fear there is a bit of Haman in all of us, and some people are controlled by it. Moses encountered it in Pharaoh, David saw it in Saul, and Jesus saw it in His disciples. "Who among us is the greatest?" was a frequent topic of conversation, and James and John wanted to call down fire from heaven to burn up a Samaritan village. The apostle John had to deal with a man named Diotrephes who was disturbing a church because he loved to be first (3 John 9), and there seems to be a Diotrephes in every church.

THE NOBODIES OVERCOME (Est. 7–10)

It took a great deal of courage and faith for Esther to approach the king; if he didn't recognize her, that was the end. At the first banquet, she had to appear calm and content before the king, and then, at the second banquet, she had to confront him with the awful truth. She had to tell him of the terrible plot of his favorite courtier and then inform her husband that she was a Jewess and in danger of losing her life. She had surrendered herself and the crisis into the Lord's hands and said, "If I perish, I perish" (Est. 4:16). This was dedication, not resignation, the kind of dedication Jesus described when He said, "Whoever wants to save his life will lose it, but whoever loses his life for me will find it" (Matt. 16:25). Ahasuerus was an unpredictable man, as were many Eastern rulers. If he deposed Vashti for refusing to obey him, what might he do to Esther for accusing the second highest official in the land of being a murderer?

The king was so deeply stirred by what he heard that he left the banquet and went into his garden to think. But consider all that he had to process in that short time. Without knowing that his queen was Jewish, he had impetuously given Haman the right to destroy all the Jews. A Jewish man named Mordecai had saved his life, and he too would be slain along with the queen. He was embarrassed, angry, and overwhelmed, but by the grace of God, he did the right thing. He ordered Haman to be hanged on the gallows Haman had built for Mordecai, but he promoted Mordecai and asked him to draft an edict that would give the Jews the right to protect themselves. (The king couldn't annul the old law, but he could proclaim a new one.) "The righteous is delivered from trouble, and it comes to the wicked instead" (Prov. 11:8 NKJV).

The new law stated that the Jews had the right to defend themselves, and the Persians knew what the king was saying: ignore the first edict, and don't attack the Jews. But the Jews took advantage of the new law and got rid of their enemies, including the ten sons of Haman. Mordecai was such a great man that the Persians feared him and helped the Jews. In fact, some of the Persians "became Jews" because it was safer to be a Jew than a Gentile! What should have been

3 Celebrations

a day of mourning for the Jews became a day of celebration, a tradition that is remembered even today as the Feast of Purim. At Passover the Jews remember their deliverance from Egypt, on Hanukkah the victory of Judas Maccabaeus over the Syrians and the restoration of the temple, and at Purim the defeat of Haman and the preservation of the nation. On the Feast of Purim, our Jewish friends assemble in the synagogue where the book of Esther is read publicly. Each time Haman's name is mentioned, the congregation calls out, "May his name be blotted out!" The next day, the people feast, exchange gifts, and rejoice at what the Lord did for them.

The nation of Israel has been attacked by the enemy many times and has always survived to begin again. The Egyptians enslaved the Jews and tried to drown the Jewish male babies, but Pharaoh's army was drowned instead and the Jews were set free. During the time of the judges, Israel was attacked and invaded seven times, but the nation survived. In modern times, nations have imitated Nebuchadnezzar and tried to destroy the Jews in the furnace (Dan. 3), but Israel is still with us. God's covenant promise "Whoever curses you I will curse" (Gen. 12:3) has never been repealed.

But God used a woman, not an army, to deliver her people from destruction. As Charles Spurgeon said, "What wonders can be wrought without miracles!" God is hidden in the book of Esther but His work is seen on every page. Many of the Jews in Susa may have been assimilated into the population and were neglecting the Lord, but God blessed the faith and courage of Esther and Mordecai and answered the prayers of the remnant of true believers. God still uses the weak things of this world to shame the strong, if only we will yield to Him and trust Him to work. The somebodies may seem in charge these days, but don't despair, for the nobodies become somebodies when they follow their Lord.

43

EZRA

*For Ezra had devoted himself to the study and
observance of the Law of the LORD.*

Ezra 7:10

Ezra was an academic, a scholar, yet he became one of the greatest leaders in the history of Israel. The Jewish people call him "the second Moses," which is high praise indeed, and Jewish tradition says that Ezra helped to assemble the Hebrew Scriptures and to organize the first synagogue. Some people claim that real leaders don't come from academic ivory towers but from the trenches, yet Ezra proves that the statement is a myth. He clearly demonstrates that scholarship and leadership are friends, not enemies, and that leaders need brains as well as biceps.

Ezra was born in captivity in Persia but grew up to become Israel's leading scribe. In the original text of Ezra 7:11, the king calls him "the scribe." The Lord used him to lead some of the Jewish people back to their own land to help establish the struggling nation. The first half of his book describes the return of about 50,000 exiles in 538 under the leadership of Joshua and Zerubbabel (Ezra 1–6), and the last half tells how Ezra led about 2,000 Jews back to Jerusalem to assist in reforming the nation and bringing spiritual revival. Ezra's great concern was the ministry in the temple and the renewing of the covenant, and he brought with him priests, singers, Levites, and servants to maintain the temple services. He also carried with him a large amount of gold and silver donated by the king and some of the Jews, and, of course, he brought the scrolls of the Word of God, the most precious possession of all.

What makes a person a leader worth following? Do we imitate the leadership practices of the world and pray that they will work? Not according to Jesus (Matt. 20:25–28). We can learn a great deal about business from secular sources, but when it comes to leading and influencing people, the Lord has His own way of teaching us the principles and practices of Christian leadership. We see in Ezra the factors that were involved in making him a strong and successful leader.

THE WORD OF THE LORD

When we study the lives of the great leaders in the Bible, we discover that they were devoted to the Word of the Lord. Moses rehearsed the Word of God for the new generation entering the Promised Land—we call it Deuteronomy—and God reminded Joshua that his devotion to the Word would be the secret of his success (Josh. 1:8). David's love for the Word is very evident in his psalms. We aren't sure who wrote Psalm 119, but almost every verse magnifies the Word of God and points out the blessings that come when we obey it.

The apostle Paul told Timothy that knowing and obeying the Scriptures is God's way for us to discover and develop our leadership gifts. "All Scripture is God-breathed and is useful for teaching [what's right], rebuking [what's not right], correcting [how to get right] and training in righteousness [how to stay right], so that the man of God may be thoroughly equipped for every good work" (2 Tim. 3:16–17).

Other books may teach you how to make a living, but the Bible teaches you how to make a life that is worth living as you serve the Lord and His people.

Ezra "devoted himself" to studying God's Word. The verb "devoted" means to be steadfast and established. Studying God's Word was at the very heart of his life, not something he occasionally did when he felt like it. The believer who makes Bible study a priority will be used of the Lord to accomplish His will. But it isn't enough just to study; like Ezra, we must obey the truth that we learn. In fact, obedience is an essential for understanding spiritual truth. Jesus said, "Anyone who chooses to do the will of God will find out whether my teaching comes from God" (John 7:17 TNIV).

Along with studying and obeying the Word, we should also share it as the Lord gives opportunity. "Teaching" doesn't necessarily require a formal school setting; we can share the truth of the Word at almost any time and in almost any place. We are to be channels and not reservoirs. "Therefore every scribe [studying the Word] who has become a disciple of the kingdom of heaven [obeying the Word] is like a head of a household, who brings forth out of his treasure things new and old [sharing the Word]" (Matt. 13:52 NASB). Ezra was faithful in all three.

THE GLORY OF THE LORD

When Ezra approached the king about the Jews returning to their homeland, one thing was uppermost in his mind: that the Lord Almighty be glorified before this powerful pagan ruler. For that reason, Ezra didn't ask for an armed escort but trusted the Lord to protect His people and the treasures they carried (Ezra 8:21–23), and He did! Ezra's faith was strengthened by the Word of God (Rom. 10:17); he knew that God's faithfulness never failed. King Artaxerxes might be "king of kings" on earth (Ezra 7:12), but Jehovah God was "the God of heaven" who ruled heaven and earth (Ezra 7:12, 21, 23) and gave earthly kings their kingdoms (Ezra 1:2).

Each time we face a challenge, a problem, or an opportunity to serve, we should ask the Lord to help us bring Him all the glory in what we do, why we do it, and the way we do it. The presence of the glory of God with His people was one of the special blessings the Lord gave Israel (Rom. 9:4), and during their wanderings, the cloud of glory led them, and when they camped, the cloud rested over the tabernacle. God's glory was at the very heart of the camp! To have followed any other route or camped at any other site would have been rebellion against the Lord.

So with God's people today: "So whether you eat or drink or whatever you do, do it all for the glory of God" (1 Cor. 10:31).

THE HAND OF THE LORD

Like the apostles, Ezra balanced the Word of God and prayer (Acts 6:4), and when he prayed, the hand of the Lord worked for him. There are several significant references to the hand of the Lord in the book of Ezra.

7:6 Because of God's hand, the king gave Ezra everything he asked for.

7:9 Because of God's hand, the Jews made the long journey safely. See also 8:31.

7:28 Because of God's hand, Ezra gathered the leading men to assist him as the people journeyed.

8:18 Because of God's hand, He provided the skilled people needed for special tasks at the temple.

8:22 Because of God's hand, the Jews had faith that He would care for them and they wouldn't need military protection. This impressed the king. See also 8:31.

Ezra was a man of prayer, and because he prayed, God worked. Before the Jews started on their long journey to Judah, they paused to fast and pray and seek the face of the Lord (Ezra 8:21–23). When they arrived at their destination, Ezra soon discovered that many of the Jewish men had married pagan wives, and this had to be dealt with. Ezra fasted and prayed (see Ezra 9), and the Lord enabled him and the elders to solve the problem. Ezra's prayer in Ezra 9 should be compared with Daniel's prayer in Daniel 9 and Nehemiah's prayer in Nehemiah 9. Each of these prayers of humble confession was based on the promise given in 2 Chronicles 7:14.

Because he was a man of the Word, Ezra was a man of faith; and because of his faith and his desire to glorify God, he could cry out to God and expect God to answer.

THE FEAR OF THE LORD

It must have been a great disappointment to Ezra when he arrived in Jerusalem and found people in the Jewish remnant disobeying the Lord by marrying contrary to God's law. "We have been unfaithful," said Shecaniah, whose father had married a non-Jewish woman (Ezra 10:2), and the only answer was for the people to confess their sins and reaffirm their obedience to the covenant of the

Lord. "You are right!" said the assembly. "We must do as you say" (Ezra 10:12). The people feared the Lord and His commandments (Ezra 10:3), and therefore Ezra was able to deal with the problem.

Ezra not only devoted himself to the study of the Word, obeyed it, and taught it, but he applied the Word to his own life and the lives of the people. He had a healthy fear of the Lord and knew that obedience to the Word was the secret of blessing. When Paul listed the sins of both Jews and Gentiles in Romans 3:9–20, the climax of the list is, "There is no fear of God before their eyes." This is the sin that makes it easy for us to commit the other sins! When you fear God, you need not fear anyone or anything else, for God is on your side.

Because Ezra devoted himself to the Word of God, that Word equipped him for the good works God assigned to him. The Word made him a leader as well as a teacher and gave him the faith to trust God for the impossible. He served for the glory of God and not for personal gain, and he prayed that the hand of the Lord would be upon him and his people. The result? The Lord God was glorified in all that he did!

Ezra invites us to enroll in God's school of leadership. There is none better.

44

NEHEMIAH

"I am doing a great work and I cannot come down."
NEHEMIAH 6:3 NASB

Nehemiah wasn't a scholarly priest like Ezra or a gifted prophet like Ezekiel or Daniel. He was what we today would call a "layman." As cupbearer to King Artaxerxes Longimanus, he held a responsible office and enjoyed the intimate confidence of the king. It was Nehemiah's job to see that the king's food and wine were safe for him to eat and drink, but he also had responsibilities relating to the management of the palace. He had to be a person of integrity and dependability, and Nehemiah proved himself qualified. Being so close to the king, he could have used his influence for personal gain, but Nehemiah was a man of God who rejected the political intrigue that operated in most Near Eastern palaces and lived to serve God.

God called Nehemiah to leave the comfort of the palace for the dangers and difficulties of rebuilding the walls and restoring the gates of Jerusalem. The book of Nehemiah is a challenging training manual in godly leadership, for in fifty-two days, Nehemiah and his fellow workers overcame every obstacle and finished the work. Then Ezra joined them at Jerusalem and helped to celebrate by dedicating the walls and renewing the covenant of the Lord with the people.

One of the things that kept Nehemiah going was the realization that he was involved in a great work. Most people would have thought that his being cupbearer to the king was a much greater work than fitting stones into a wall, but Nehemiah had a different viewpoint, God's viewpoint.

If we don't accept our responsibilities as from the Lord and see them as great opportunities to glorify Him, we will eventually get discouraged and quit. Any work God gives us to do is a great work, whether keeping house, raising children, running a machine, managing a farm, driving a truck, or rebuilding a war-torn city. Knowing this will help to keep us going. As Paul wrote to the Christian slaves in Colosse, "It is the Lord Christ you are serving" (Col. 3:24).

The word "great" is used at least twenty times in the book of Nehemiah and is a key to the question we want to answer: How can we determine if we are truly serving the Lord and doing "a great work" for Him? One way is to take inventory by asking ourselves the following questions and answering them honestly.

DO WE HAVE A GREAT BURDEN?

Nehemiah wasn't drafted to go to the ruined city of Jerusalem; he volunteered for the task. His brother Hanani had just returned from a visit to the struggling Jewish remnant in Judah, and Nehemiah asked him how things were going there. Perhaps Nehemiah had been reading the book of the writings of the prophet Jeremiah: "Who will have pity on you, O Jerusalem? Who will mourn for you? Who will stop to ask how you are?" (Jer. 15:5). Hanani's reply was shocking: "Those who survived the exile and are back in the province are in great trouble and disgrace. The wall of Jerusalem is broken down, and its gates have been burned with fire" (Neh. 1:3).

God's people were in serious trouble. They were disgraced before the Gentiles. Their city wall was burned. The gates were broken down. Jehovah God was not being glorified in Zion, the city of the Great King. How did this recitation of bad news affect the cupbearer of the king? It broke his heart and he sat down and wept. Though he had a comfortable situation in the palace, Nehemiah identified with the plight of his people and wept over it. He could have said, "Well, it's their own fault!" Or, "They're a thousand miles from here, so what can I do about it?" Or, "Let me know the next time you're going back and I'll send some money and my worn-out clothes."

When God wants to bless us and make us a blessing to others, He usually starts by putting a burden on our hearts. I have no doubt that Nehemiah had thought and prayed about the Holy City many times before he met and questioned his brother. Though he was living comfortably in the Persian city of Susa, Nehemiah was one of those godly people "in whose heart are the highways to Zion" (Ps. 84:5 NASB). "If you could have bored a hole into his head," said evangelist D. L. Moody, "you would have found 'Jerusalem' stamped on his brain. If you could have looked into his heart, you would have found 'Jerusalem' there."[1] Nehemiah is an Old Testament example of a New Testament exhortation: "Set your minds on things above, not on earthly things" (Col. 3:2). He had moved into the company of the apostle Paul and had "great sorrow and unceasing anguish" in his heart (Rom. 9:1–3) because of the plight of Israel.

Are we working for the Lord because our hearts are burdened? Are we going to obey the Lord and see the burden transformed into a blessing?

DO WE SEE GREAT POSSIBILITIES?

Nehemiah sat down and wept, and then he knelt down and prayed (Neh. 1:4–11). It's through faith in prayer that God turns our burdens and battles into blessings. When Nehemiah considered the plight of the Jews in Judah, he didn't see calamity—he saw opportunity. Things in Judah might have been bad, but they didn't have to stay that way. After all, the Jews were God's covenant people, and the Lord would fulfill the covenant promises He made to them (Neh. 1:8–9;

---

1. John W. Reed, ed. *Moody's Bible Characters Come Alive* (Grand Rapids, Mich.: Baker, 1997), 192.

Deut. 30:1–5). By the great goodness of the Lord (Neh. 9:25, 35), the survivors would become builders and warriors, the walls would be rebuilt, and the gates would be restored.

The word for this experience is *vision*. Nehemiah wasn't an impractical dreamer whose flimsy dreams turned into nightmares. Nehemiah was a true man of faith—a godly visionary—who (to use the words of Vance Havner) "sees the invisible, chooses the imperishable, and does the impossible." He measured the problems by the greatness of God, not by his own weakness and inexperience. When you see possibilities instead of problems and opportunities instead of obstacles, then you are standing by faith with Nehemiah, Moses, Joshua, David, Paul and the apostles, and an army of heroes and heroines of faith in church history who believed God and changed the world.

DO I TRUST A GREAT GOD?

Nehemiah was a man of prayer[2] and he prayed to a great God. He began his first recorded prayer by addressing God as "O LORD, God of heaven, the great and awesome God, who keeps his covenant of love with those who love him and obey his commands" (Neh. 1:5). There are twelve instances of prayer recorded in the book, including a prayer of confession and contrition in chapter 9 that refers to the Lord's "great compassion" (vv. 19, 27) and "great goodness" (vv. 25, 35). As they prayed, Nehemiah and the other leaders called the Lord "our God, the great, mighty and awesome God" (9:32). It's worth noting that the ninth chapters of Ezra, Nehemiah, and Daniel are all prayers of confession and pleas for the mercy of God to save His people, and they are worth praying today.

In Nehemiah's first recorded prayer, he confessed his own sins and the sins of the people and reminded the Lord of His covenant promises to Israel. He knew he wasn't the only one praying for God's help (Neh. 1:11). He closed his prayer asking for God to give him success in dealing with the king, for he wanted to ask for a leave of absence so he could travel to Jerusalem. *Then he waited four months before addressing the king.* When your trust is in a great God, you can quietly wait for His leading and not be upset. Since the cupbearer saw the king at each meal, perhaps the king wasn't at Susa and Nehemiah had to wait for him to return. But Nehemiah didn't despair or give up trusting his great God. "My times are in your hands" (Ps. 31:15).

Nobody was supposed to manifest sadness or grief into the presence of the Persian ruler; it might have cost them their life. But Nehemiah's sadness of heart was reflected on his face, and the king asked him about it. Nehemiah sent a "telegraph prayer" to the Lord before stating his case (Neh. 2:1–5), and the Lord answered. God's people need to keep walking in the light so they can send these brief, silent, impassioned prayers to the Lord at any time. And keep in mind that Nehemiah's four months of private prayers prepared the way for this brief prayer that hit the mark like an arrow.

---

2. See Neh. 1:5–10; 2:4; 4:4, 9; 5:19; 6:9, 14; 9; 13:14, 22, 29, 31.

Being a wise leader, Nehemiah kept his workers armed and ready just in case their enemies decided to attack. "Nevertheless we made our prayer to our God, and because of them we set a watch against them day and night" (Neh. 4:9 NKJV). We must pray with our eyes open! (See Mark 13:33; 14:38; Eph. 6:18; Col. 4:2–4.)

DO I FACE GREAT PROBLEMS AND OBSTACLES?

Anybody who wants to accomplish something for the Lord will have to solve problems and overcome obstacles. Someone has defined "problems" as "those nasty things you see when you get your eyes off the goal." Nehemiah kept his eyes on the goal: rebuilding the walls and restoring the gates so that the Lord would be honored and the city would be secure. He knew how to face obstacles courageously and trust God to help him and the people overcome them.

His first challenge was overcoming the indifference of the people. Nebuchadnezzar had destroyed Jerusalem in 586 BC, and the first Jewish exiles returned in 538. They completed rebuilding the temple in 516 and probably made minor repairs to the city to make it a better place to live. Nehemiah arrived in Jerusalem in 444, which means that the inhabitants had been content to live without gates and walls for almost 150 years! They had gotten accustomed to the situation, and if anybody suggested a building program, they didn't respond enthusiastically. But God gave Nehemiah a band of burdened people who agreed to lead the way and get to work (Neh. 2:11–20).

Whenever God's people start to serve Him, the enemy fights back and tries to stop the work. Sanballat, Tobiah, and Geshem, who ran the local anti-Semitic organization, accused them of rebelling against the king (Neh. 2:19–20), and when that didn't stop the progress, they began to laugh at them and ridicule them (Neh. 4:1–3). The Jews prayed and kept on working, which is a good example for us to follow. But the three men weren't easily stopped, because they enlisted more help and threatened to attack Jerusalem. Nehemiah armed the men and posted guards. Everybody prayed, and the enemy backed off. "Fear may waken us," said Charles Spurgeon, "but it must never be allowed to weaken us."

If the enemy can't stop us by attacking from the outside, he will start working from the inside. First, some of the workers became discouraged and decided they just couldn't clean up the mess (Neh. 4:10). Then the poorer Jews cried out for help. The economic situation was tough, and some of the wealthier Jews were exploiting their fellow citizens by loaning money at very high interest rates. Crops had not been plentiful and a famine was in the offing. The poorer Jews cried out for relief and Nehemiah had to deal with the problem (Neh. 5).

If it isn't one thing, it's another! But that's why God gives good leaders to His people, and the enemy always attacks the leaders. Sanballat and his associates tried to get Nehemiah to compromise and stop the work, but he rejected their offer (Neh. 6:1–4). Then his enemies started a rumor that Nehemiah's life was in danger, and they suggested he meet them at the temple so they could protect him.

Nehemiah's response was, "Should a man like me run away?" (6:11). Nehemiah was a faithful shepherd and not a hireling (John 10:12–13).

The worst "inside" problem he faced was the sin of the Jewish men (including some priests and Levites) who married Gentile wives, contrary to the law of God (Neh. 13; Ezra 9–10). It took time and patience to untangle that situation, but that's what true leadership is all about. If there are no problems, then there's probably no progress. No friction, no motion. Satan never attacks a corpse.

DO I MAKE GREAT SACRIFICES?

Hirelings do their job for what they can get out of it, and then run away rather than face the enemy and guard the flock. But true leaders willingly and lovingly pay a price to make sure the people are cared for adequately. Nehemiah worked right with the people, day and night (4:21–23), and didn't take any "executive privileges." Instead of using the meal allotment given to the governor, he paid his own food bills and even fed over 150 guests at his own table (Neh. 5:14–19). There's no record that he sent Artaxerxes an expense account.

In a late-night prayer meeting back in the fifties, I heard attorney Jake Stam pray, "Lord, the only thing we know about sacrifice is how to spell the word." He was right. His own brother and sister-in-law, John and Betty Stam, were killed by Chinese Communists in 1934. If we make an occasional sacrifice, we let people know about it, but Nehemiah kept his personal accounts with the Lord and said nothing. True leaders don't demand that others pay a price. They set the example by making the first sacrifices and telling nobody about it.

Jesus made it clear that the chief was servant of all, and He proved it by dying on the cross. The spectators at Calvary taunted Him and cried, "Come down from the cross and we will believe!" Jesus could have replied in the words of Nehemiah, "I am doing a great work and I cannot come down" (Neh. 6:3 NASB).

Nehemiah's book opens with "great trouble" (1:3) but closes with "great joy" because their great God had enabled them to finish the work in fifty-two days. "The sound of rejoicing in Jerusalem could be heard far away" (12:43). And it all started with one man feeling a great burden on his heart to do something about the tragedy of Jerusalem.

What can one man do? Read Ezra and Nehemiah.

What can one woman do? Read about Deborah, Ruth, and Esther.

What can one child do? Read 2 Kings 5:1–6 and John 6:8–13.

The next time you feel a burden, talk to the Lord about it. He may have plans to turn it into a blessing in your life and in the lives of others.

Part
Two

LOOKING AT THE LIVES OF

NEW TESTAMENT
CHARACTERS

AND THEIR LIFE SENTENCES

INTERLUDE

The Old Testament is "the book of the generations of Adam" (Gen. 5:1 NASB) and ends on an ominous note: "I will come and strike the land with a curse" (Mal. 4:6). But the New Testament is the "record of the genealogy of Jesus Christ" (Matt. 1:1), and in the last chapter of the last New Testament book we find the promise, "No longer will there be any curse" (Rev. 22:3). Jesus Christ the last Adam is the exalted head of a new creation, and all who have trusted Him are a part of that miracle (2 Cor. 5:17) and will one day live in the new heavens and earth that He has promised (Rev. 21–22).

As we move into the New Testament to study the "life sentences" of some of its key people, we will begin with Jesus Christ our Savior, because without Him there would be no new covenant. If you are wrong about Jesus, you will be wrong about your own spiritual condition, the reality of sin, and the message of the gospel. If you are right about Jesus Christ and have trusted Him, then your sins have been forgiven, you belong to Him, and you can experience the abundant life that He came to give.

45

JESUS CHRIST

*"You are my Son, whom I love;
with you I am well pleased."*

LUKE 3:22

Large crowds of excited people gathered at the Jordan River to listen to a re-markable man who had suddenly come out of the wilderness. He did no miracles, but his messages were arresting, and even the Jewish religious leaders went to hear him. The heavens had been silent for four hundred years, but now John the Baptist appeared, the last and greatest of the Jewish prophets, and he was pro-claiming the arrival of the kingdom of God—not the kind of political kingdom that most of the Jewish people longed for, but a spiritual kingdom that brought eternal life and the forgiveness of sins. John was baptizing those who repented of their sins and believed his message, and his ministry marked "the beginning of the gospel about Jesus Christ, the Son of God" (Mark 1:1; see Acts 1:21–22; 10:37–38). The word "gospel" means "good news," and indeed it was good news, for the Messiah had come just as the prophets had promised. A new age was dawning!

Jesus came to the Jordan River from Nazareth where He had grown up and worked as a carpenter. He was thirty years old and as yet unknown to the nation at large, but He came to be baptized by John at the beginning of what would be a three-year ministry. When Jesus came up out of the water, the Father spoke to Him from heaven in the words quoted above. Mark says that heaven was "torn open" (Mark 1:10), and then God the Holy Spirit came down as a dove and rested upon Jesus. This dramatic scene is a revelation to us of who Jesus is and why we must trust Him and make Him Lord of our lives.

JESUS IS THE SON OF GOD

"You are my Son," said the Father, which means that Jesus Christ is God. When questioned by the religious leaders, John the Baptist said, "I have seen and I testify that this is the Son of God." This remarkable scene that inaugu-rated Christ's ministry reveals the divine Trinity, for God the Father spoke from heaven, God the Son was baptized in the Jordan River, and God the Holy Spirit descended from heaven as a dove and rested on Jesus. Near the end of Jesus' ministry, as He approached the cross, the Father identified Him again, this time on the Mount of Transfiguration: "This is my Son, whom I love; with him I am well pleased" (Matt. 17:5).

The prophet Isaiah foretold the coming of the Messiah: "Here is my servant, whom I uphold, my chosen one in whom I delight; I will put my Spirit on him and he will bring justice to the nations" (Isa. 42:1; Matt. 12:18–21). God the Father spoke of God the Son and promised Him the gift of the Spirit — the divine Trinity! Even Satan and his demons acknowledged the deity of Jesus Christ (Matt. 4:3; 8:29), and the newly converted Saul of Tarsus (who became Paul the apostle) boldly preached in the synagogues that Jesus is the Son of God (Acts 9:20).

When Jesus asked His apostles who He was, Peter replied, "You are the Christ, the Son of the living God" (Matt. 16:15–16), and Jesus didn't deny it. "If anyone acknowledges that Jesus is the Son of God," wrote the apostle John, "God lives in him and he in God" (1 John 4:15). John closed his first letter by reminding us, "He is the true God and eternal life. Dear children, keep yourselves from idols" (1 John 5:20–21). If you don't worship Jesus the Son of God, you don't worship God the Father, for Jesus said, "He who does not honor the Son does not honor the Father, who sent him" (John 5:23).

That is why John wrote his wonderful gospel — to present Jesus Christ as the Son of God and encourage people to trust Him and receive eternal life. "Jesus did many other miraculous signs in the presence of his disciples, which are not recorded in this book. But these are written that you may believe that Jesus is the Christ, the Son of God, and that by believing you may have life in his name" (John 20:30–31).

"What do you think about the Christ?" Jesus asked the Pharisees. "Whose son is he?" (Matt. 22:42). That is still life's most important question.

JESUS IS THE BELOVED SON

The first time we find the word *love* in the Bible is in Genesis 22:2 where God commands Abraham to "take your son, your only son, Isaac, whom you love" and offer him as a sacrifice. Immediately we think of Jesus. The first time we find the word *love* in Matthew, Mark, and Luke is in the baptism account where the Father calls Jesus "my Son whom I love." The emphasis in Genesis is on a father's love for his only son, and the statements in the Synoptic Gospels emphasize the heavenly Father's love for His only Son, a theme we are prone to neglect if not ignore. It is not until we get to the gospel of John and read John 3:16 that we discover God's love for a whole world.

It is important to understand that the relationship in the divine Trinity is that of love. "The Father loves the Son and has placed everything in his hands," said John the Baptist (John 3:35), and Jesus told the religious leaders of His day, "For the Father loves the Son and shows him all he does" (John 5:20). Later in His ministry Jesus said, "The reason my Father loves me is that I lay down my life — only to take it up again" (John 10:17). We usually think of Calvary as proof that God loves lost sinners, and this is true (Rom. 5:8), but Calvary is also evidence that the Son loves the Father. "The world must learn that I love the Father and that I do exactly what my Father has commanded me" (John 14:31), Jesus said.

But there is more remarkable truth to follow. Jesus loves His own just as the Father has loved Him, and the Father loves us as He loves the Son! "As the Father has loved me, so have I loved you" (John 15:9). Our Savior's prayer is that His people will "let the world know that you [the Father] sent me and have loved them even as you have loved me" (John 17:23). Jesus makes the Father known to us "that the love you [the Father] have for me may be in them and that I myself may be in them" (John 17:26).

The Father loves us as He loves the Son! The Son loves us as the Father has loved Him! The Father has freely given us His glorious grace in His beloved Son, Jesus. "We praise God for the wonderful kindness he has poured out on us because we belong to his dearly loved Son" (Eph. 1:6 NLT). We are "accepted in the beloved" as the King James Version states it.

JESUS IS THE OBEDIENT SON

The Father's love and pleasure are focused on His Son, and because we are in His Son, they are focused on us. "Here is my servant whom I have chosen, the one I love, in whom I delight," said the Father through Isaiah the prophet (Matt. 12:18; Isa. 42:1). The Father told Jesus, "With you I am well pleased," and He wants to say the same words to us. "I seek not to please myself but him who sent me," said Jesus (John 5:30). "The one who sent me is with me; he has not left me alone, for I always do what pleases him" (John 8:29). Our Lord said that His nourishment was "to do the will of him who sent me and to finish his work" (John 4:34).

Jesus at the age of thirty had not yet preached a sermon or done a miracle, yet the Father was well pleased with Him. Jesus had matured in a balanced way (Luke 2:52) and when old enough had gone to work in Joseph's carpenter shop (Matt. 13:55; Mark 6:3). It pleased the Father that Jesus was submissive to His parents (Luke 2:51) and that He learned how to work with His hands.

Ask the average Christian what pleases the Lord and the reply will be praying or tithing or studying the Bible; and these activities do please the Lord if they are done for His glory. But the Lord is also pleased when children respect their parents and when employees do their best work. "Live as children of light," Paul wrote to the Ephesians, "and find out what pleases the Lord" (Eph. 5:8–10). "Children, obey your parents in everything, for this pleases the Lord" (Col. 3:20).

The Father was pleased with the first thirty years of His Son's earthly life and ministry, but He was also pleased with what Jesus was doing that very day—being baptized by John. Why? Because that baptism pictured His future sacrifice on the cross for the sins of the world. "The reason my Father loves me," said Jesus, "is that I lay down my life—only to take it up again" (John 10:17).

As Jesus made His way to Jerusalem, He said to His disciples, "I have a baptism to undergo, and how distressed I am until it is accomplished!" (Luke 12:50 NASB).

The official *Catechism of the Catholic Church* states, "Baptism, the original and full sign of which is immersion, efficaciously signifies the descent into the tomb by the Christian who dies to sin with Christ in order to live a new life."[1] Martin Luther wrote that baptism was a symbol of death and resurrection and that those who are to be baptized should be completely immersed in the water.[2] John Calvin, theologian of the Reformed churches, wrote in his *Institutes of the Christian Religion*, "Yet the word 'baptize' means to immerse, and it is clear that the rite of immersion was observed in the ancient church."[3] In his *Notes on the Bible*, the founder of the Methodist Church, John Wesley, wrote on Romans 6:4, "*We are buried with him* allud[es] to the ancient manner of baptizing by immersion."[4] In fact, Wesley's practice was to immerse infants three times in water.

It seems evident that John buried Jesus in the waters of the Jordan River and brought Him up again as a picture of His death, burial, and resurrection. This act symbolized our Lord's baptism of suffering on the cross when the "waves and breakers" of God's wrath against sin swept over Him (Ps. 42:7). It is interesting to note that Jonah quoted Psalm 42:7 when he was under the sea in the great fish (Jonah 2:3), and Jesus called Jonah's "death, burial, and resurrection" experience "the sign of the prophet Jonah" (Matt. 12:39–41). Officially, the Jewish leaders taught that Jesus of Nazareth was dead. But in Peter's sermon at Pentecost, the emphasis was on the resurrection of Jesus Christ, for "the sign of Jonah" was the only sign Jesus would give to Israel.

But that isn't all. When John protested baptizing the Son of God, Jesus replied, "Let it be so now; it is proper for us to do this to fulfill all righteousness" (Matt. 3:15). Does the pronoun "us" refer to John and Jesus? I don't think so, for how could a sinful mortal like John cooperate with God in fulfilling all righteousness? I believe the pronoun "us" refers to the divine Trinity—the Father who spoke from heaven, the Son being baptized, and the Holy Spirit who descended like a dove. All three are involved in the great plan of redemption, and the Father was pleased that the Son would willingly endure suffering and death that He might be the Savior of the world. "The reason my Father loves me is that I lay down my life—only to take it up again" (John 10:17). Jesus "became obedient to death—even death on a cross" (Phil. 2:8).

Two more thoughts. The Holy Spirit descended as a dove, and the name "Jonah" means "dove." The dove also reminds us of Noah and the ark (Gen.

---

1. *Catechism of the Catholic Church* (New York: Image/Doubleday, 1995), 179.

2. Ewald M. Plass, *What Luther Says*, vol. 1 (St. Louis: Concordia, 1959), 57–58.

3. John Calvin, *Institutes of the Christian Religion*, vol. 2, bk. 4 (Philadelphia: Westminster, 1960), 1320.

4. John Wesley, *Wesley's Notes on the Bible* (Grand Rapids, Mich.: Zondervan, 1987), 500.

8:6–12), and Peter connects baptism with the flood and Christ's resurrection (1 Peter 3:13–22). Think on these things.

JESUS IS THE VICTORIOUS SON

The coming of the Spirit as a dove identified Jesus to John the Baptist (John 1:32–34), and since His coming into this world, the Spirit has been glorifying Jesus and revealing Him to seeking hearts. Jesus said of the Spirit, "He will bring glory to me by taking from what is mine and making it known to you" (John 16:14). "Whatever begins with the Holy Spirit," said J. Sidlow Baxter, "always leads to Christ." What a marvelous truth! The Spirit shows us Jesus in the Word and enables us to manifest Jesus to the world (John 15:26–27). "But you will receive power when the Holy Spirit comes on you; and you will be my witnesses" (Acts 1:8).

Jesus lived and ministered on earth in the power of the Spirit (Acts 10:37–38), and so must we. It is unfortunate that so many believers think that Jesus served as He did simply because He was God and exercised His divine powers. They argue that because they don't have the same divine nature as Jesus, God can't expect too much from them; but this kind of thinking is all wrong. When He served here on earth, Jesus depended on the Holy Spirit, prayer, and the Word of God, and these divine resources are available to us today. When Satan tempted our Lord in the wilderness, his first temptation was that Jesus use His divine powers to serve Himself and not live by faith in the Father's will (Matt. 4:1–4). When we seek to glorify Christ, the Spirit will joyfully minister in us and through us as we abide in Christ, in the Word, and in prayer.

Beginning with His miraculous conception by the Spirit (Luke 1:26–38), our Lord's entire life on earth was Spirit empowered, Spirit led, and Spirit controlled. After that glorious experience at the Jordan River, our Lord was led by the Holy Spirit into the wilderness to confront and defeat the Devil. (The ancient people of Israel had gone from the wilderness through the Jordan and into the Promised Land. Our Lord seems to typify the nation here.) Then the Spirit led Him back to Nazareth where He preached His first sermon in the synagogue and was rejected by the congregation (Luke 4:14–30). Whether He was healing damaged bodies, casting out demons, raising the dead, teaching the people, or instructing His disciples, Jesus was ministering in the power of the Spirit. The Son brought glory to the Father and the Father glorified the Son (John 12:28; 13:31–32; 17:1), and it was accomplished by the power of the Holy Spirit, who seeks no glory for Himself.

The conclusion is obvious: if the perfect Son of God needed the ministry of the Spirit to accomplish God's will, how much more do we today need the Spirit's power! We can do good works, but they won't glorify Jesus if the Spirit hasn't guided and empowered us. The church today has so much real estate, sophisticated technology, public relations savvy, and human talent that we can get along without the Holy Spirit.

The exalted Son of God at the Father's right hand longs to channel His triumphant power to His people on earth, but we prefer to live on substitutes. "You do not have, because you do not ask God" (James 4:2). How many prayer meetings have you attended lately in which the saints are crying out for the power of the Spirit to come upon the church? That was the secret of the power of the early church. "After they prayed, the place where they were meeting was shaken. And they were all filled with the Holy Spirit and spoke the word of God boldly" (Acts 4:31).

"There is one thing we cannot imitate," wrote Oswald Chambers; "we cannot imitate being full of the Holy Ghost."

But we will probably keep trying to fool others—and ourselves. Nevertheless, we can't fool the Lord.

46

ZECHARIAH AND ELIZABETH

Both of them were upright in the sight of God.

LUKE 1:6

I'm glad I'm growing old in England," said historian Arnold Toynbee on his eightieth birthday. "Americans are dedicated to the new and superefficient. It must be depressing to be old in the U.S."

Well, Professor Toynbee, we old folks in the United States aren't too depressed. We are glad for American efficiency, especially when it comes to medical technology, but we admit that we are occasionally grieved by a society that worships youth and tends to categorize seniors as out of step and in the way. When we read the Bible, we can't help but notice that the Jewish younger generation had a loving respect for their elders and even asked them for counsel. Many times we have wished it was like that in America.

Take Zechariah and Elizabeth, for example, people whom Dr. Luke describes as "well along in years" (Luke 1:7). The Levites served from age twenty-five to age fifty, but Jewish law doesn't specify the exact ages the priests began and ended their ministry. Furthermore, what was called "old age" in their day might not be considered old at all in our day. However, no matter what their ages, as a senior saint, I find a great deal of encouragement in what is recorded about Zechariah and Elizabeth. If you are not yet in the senior category, read on, because you will be there one day and may need these truths.

WE ARE NEVER TOO OLD FOR GOD TO USE US

The angel Gabriel bridged the "generation gap" when he visited elderly Zechariah in Jerusalem and then youthful Mary in Nazareth (Luke 1:26–38). God communicates with and calls both the old and the young. Like Abraham and Sarah, this priest and his wife were beyond the possibility of having a family, but God ignored their infirmities, performed a miracle, and gave them a son. And what a son! Jesus called John the greatest of "those born of women" (Matt. 11:11). John was a joy to his parents as he grew up (Luke 1:14), but they were probably dead before he began his public ministry.

Sarah was eighty-nine and Abraham ninety-nine when they conceived Isaac, a miracle if ever there was one. When the Lord is about to accomplish some wonderful thing, He often begins by doing the impossible. "Is anything too hard for the LORD?" the Lord asked Abraham (Gen. 18:14), and Gabriel told Mary that "nothing is impossible with God" (Luke 1:37). These are good reminders for all of us, regardless of our age.

God's people have a tendency to think that the Lord's senior saints have no important ministries to perform apart from leading in prayer, attending funerals, cooking for church feasts, and naming the church in their will. Some pastors even ignore the older folks ("They complain too much") and forget that Jesus commissioned His disciples to care for the sheep as well as the lambs (John 21:16–17). In most churches, the seniors are put into a Sunday school class that offers no escape but death. Though we are given parking places close to a church entrance, we don't always feel close to the church's heart. We long to sing some of the great hymns of the faith, and we yearn for the kind of preaching that makes Jesus and His grace very real. After all, for us seniors the time is running out, and we want to make the most of it.

But we are never too old for God to use us, whether the younger folks appreciate us or not. In the apostolic church, the older believers taught the younger believers how to act at home and in the assembly (Titus 2:1–8). The church leaders were called "elders" because that is what they were—older; and the younger people showed respect for their age, wisdom, and experience. Today, many younger believers think that nothing happened before 1980 and that gray hair or baldness is a mark of senility. If younger church leaders would start engaging the seniors instead of pitying them—or even worse, enduring them—the church would discover a great source of spiritual power.

One of our tasks as seniors is to teach the younger generation what the Lord has done in the past (Ps. 71:18), even though many young people think the past is unimportant. Well, they will either learn from their elders the easy way or learn by experience the hard way. We can still "bear fruit in old age" (Ps. 92:14), and we can be sure of the Lord's special care as we grow older (Isa. 46:4). Old age isn't for sissies, but it is for service, so let's not retire from life. We can still be used of the Lord.

WE ARE NEVER TOO OLD TO PRAY AND SEE GOD WORK

From the outset of their lives together, Zechariah and Elizabeth had prayed for the Lord to bless them with a family, but the answer hadn't come. Jewish couples longed for God to send them children, and this was especially true of the priestly couples who wanted sons to continue their ministry. God's plans are different from our plans (Isa. 55:8–9), but when He does answer, it is above and beyond anything we could ask or think.

Offering the incense at the golden altar in the Holy Place was a once-in-a-lifetime experience for a priest, and that day the lot pointed to Zechariah. God's hand was at work in a special way. The Lord sent Gabriel to tell Zechariah that his prayer had been heard and that his wife would bear him the son they had been asking God to give them. This son would be especially blessed of the Lord, for like Jeremiah, Ezekiel, and Zechariah, he would serve as a prophet and not as a priest. But the blessing gets better, for their son would be the herald of the Messiah! God was about to fulfill His promises and send the Redeemer into the world! The ministry of their son, John ("Jehovah has been gracious"), would "make ready a people prepared for the Lord" (Luke 1:17).

My wife and I have good reason to thank the Lord for senior saints who have included us in their prayers. My great-grandfather, whom I never knew, prayed that there would be a preacher of the gospel in every generation of our family, and there has been. I was supposed to die before my second birthday, but that prayer saved me. It also saved me when I was almost killed by a drunk driver who was traveling eighty miles an hour. Many older believers have interceded for us over these fifty plus years of our ministry, and now my wife and I are praying for the younger men and women now training to serve the Lord or already in active service. And they pray for us!

WE ARE NEVER TOO OLD TO FAIL

"Jews demand miraculous signs" (1 Cor. 1:22), and Zechariah was no exception, but he himself ended up being the sign! The Lord will patiently deal with doubt and eventually bring assurance — consider Gideon in Judges 6:36 – 40 — but unbelief is a sin that God abhors. When we don't believe God's Word, we make God a liar.

You would think that a priest steeped in God's Word would have great faith, but before we judge Zechariah, let's look at ourselves. How many times has God's Word told us His will and we have looked at ourselves instead of looking by faith to Him? Yes, Zechariah *was* an old man, and his wife was beyond the age of childbearing, and like Abraham and Sarah centuries before, having a baby was something they could laugh about (Gen. 18). But God said it would happen — and it did happen!

I have already pointed out that many of the leaders mentioned in Scripture failed in their one area of strength. Abraham's strength was his faith, but he faced a famine in Canaan and ran off to Egypt for help (Gen. 12:10 – 20). Humility was a distinguishing mark of Moses (Num. 12:3), but he lost his temper, struck the rock, and lost the privilege of entering the Promised Land with Israel (Num. 20). Integrity was David's greatest quality (Ps. 78:70 – 72), but he lied about his sins and tried to cover them up (2 Sam. 11 – 12). Peter was known for his courage, but he wilted in fear before some servant girls and denied his Lord (Matt. 26:69 – 75).

Zechariah had grown up surrounded by men and women who knew the Word of God and sought to obey it, and this steady diet of God's truth certainly produced faith in his heart (Rom. 10:17). But when confronted with an opportunity to be part of a miracle, he didn't believe the Lord and had to remain silent for the next nine months. Faith opens your mouth to praise the Lord (2 Cor. 4:13), but unbelief opens your mouth to question the Lord, and then it closes your mouth and you lose your song. While Elizabeth, Mary, and their relatives and friends were joyfully praising the Lord, Zechariah was silent, but he was writing a song of praise in his heart that one day he would sing.

One of the former presidents of the Moody Bible Institute in Chicago, Dr. William Culbertson, often closed his public prayers with a solemn, "And, Lord, help us to end well." As I have grown older, I have often thought of that prayer and prayed it for myself—"Lord, help me to end well." Youthful sins are sad, but the sins of experienced saints are tragic and can do a great deal of damage. The godly British preacher F. B. Meyer once told a friend, "I do hope my Father will let the river of my life go flowing fully till the finish. I don't want it to end in a swamp."

Lord, help us to end well!

WE ARE NEVER TOO OLD TO DO SOMETHING NEW

If any people are steeped in tradition, it is the orthodox Jews, and this applies even to the naming of children. A child's name is an important link with the past or with some special act or attribute of God, and this link is vitally important to a nation whose existence has often been in jeopardy. Sometimes an experience of the mother during the child's pregnancy or birth would determine the name, as in the case of Jacob's sons. It was traditional to name the firstborn son after his father, for if the father died, the son would keep his name and memory alive in the family.

All of Elizabeth and Zechariah's relatives and neighbors expected this miracle baby to be named after his father (Luke 1:59–66), but the couple shocked them by resisting tradition and giving their son the name John. It was the name commanded by Gabriel when he made the birth announcement to Zechariah: "Your wife Elizabeth will bear you a son, and you are to give him the name John" (Luke 1:13). The name means "the Lord is gracious."

The younger generation often criticize older people for glorifying what is old, rejecting what is new, and wanting to recapture "the good old days." They tell us that "the good old days" are only the combination of a bad memory and a good imagination, a statement that is clever but not always true. King Solomon solved that problem right up front in Ecclesiastes 1:9–11 by pointing out that it is the *younger* generation who has the bad memory! They say, "Look! This is something new," only because they don't know the past. What to them is new is actually only a recombination of what is old, which explains why Solomon said there is nothing new under the sun. The news coverage may be better and more interesting, but the news hasn't changed very much.

As old and orthodox as they were, Zechariah and Elizabeth obeyed the Lord and had the courage to bring a new name into the family. It is possible to be "geared to the times but anchored to the Rock," as the old Youth for Christ motto stated. Because the grace of God is one of His eternal attributes, the name John was really quite old but also very new. (In fact, babies are something old, but they are also something new.) To accept without question everything the younger generation says and does is dangerous, but to reject what is good and not encourage it is foolhardy. Blessed are the balanced — and the discerning!

WE ARE NEVER TOO OLD TO SING

If you had been mute for nine months and suddenly your speech returned, what would you say? Inspired by God's Spirit, Zechariah sang a song! Most people don't want to hear old men or old women sing solos, and some popular vocalists should retire from the stage earlier than they do. But I would like to have been in that home when the old priest Zechariah turned a Brit Milah (covenant of circumcision) into a concert! In his joy, he certainly had much to sing about, for God had done a miracle in his home, a miracle associated with the promised Messiah. And that is who he sang about — the Messiah!

Zechariah's song in Luke 1 was a song of redemption, for the Lord would redeem His people from the bondage of sin just as He had redeemed them from the bondage of Egypt (vv. 68–70). It was also a song of victory, for the Lord would enable His people to conquer their enemies and serve the Lord in peace (vv. 77–79). But going deeper, it was a song of forgiveness, for their debts would be canceled (vv. 76–77). It would be a Year of Jubilee (see Lev. 25:8–55; Luke 4:14–21)! Zechariah sang more about God's Son than about his own son! The old priest saw Israel at the dawning of a new day (vv. 78–79) in which darkness and death would flee away and forgiven sinners would walk with the Lord in peace.

Let's remember that Zechariah and Elizabeth enjoyed the favor and blessing of the Lord because of His grace and their faithfulness. "Both of them were upright in the sight of God." No wonder they rejoiced and Zechariah sang to the Lord. "Rejoice in the LORD and be glad, you righteous; sing, all you who are upright in heart!" (Ps. 32:11).

47

MARY,
THE MOTHER OF JESUS

"My soul glorifies the Lord."

LUKE 1:46

*W*hen the Lord chose Mary to be what Greek Orthodox theologians call *theotokos*, the "God-bearer," it was a high and holy honor that she accepted with humility and faith. However, too many Christian believers think that this honor so elevated Mary that her example is beyond anything we could ever hope to achieve, nor should we even try. With God's help, we might hope to follow Ruth's example of devotion or Hannah's example of prayer, but Mary's example of dedication is to many believers unattainable.

This attitude is wrong. Mary never glorified herself, but instead sang, "My soul glorifies the Lord." Elizabeth sang, "Blessed are you *among* women" not "*above* women" (Luke 1:42, emphasis added). Yes, Mary participated in a unique miracle, but in every other way, she was just like any believer today who wants to glorify God. Her last recorded words in Scripture are, "Do whatever [Jesus] tells you" (John 2:5), and her last appearance is in a prayer meeting with 119 other believers (Acts 1:12–15), awaiting the coming of the Holy Spirit. If in your life and service you want to magnify the Lord, then the example of Mary, recorded by Dr. Luke, certainly points the way.

WE MUST RECEIVE THE GRACE OF GOD (Luke 1:28, 30)

Grace is God's favor to people who don't deserve it, and that includes everybody on planet Earth. "Greetings, you who are highly favored!" Gabriel said to this young woman in Nazareth. "Do not be afraid, Mary, you have found favor with God." This doesn't mean that Mary's character or conduct had earned God's grace, because grace can't be earned. Grace is a gift that God bestows on the undeserving who confess their need and receive His gift by faith.

Gabriel's statement "you who are highly favored" is the translation of a Greek word used only twice in the New Testament, in Luke 1:28 and Ephesians 1:6. In Ephesians it is applied to all believers: "To the praise of his glorious grace, which he has freely given us in the one he loves." The *Linguistic Key to the Greek New*

Testament says it means "begracing with grace."[1] In other words, what Gabriel said to Mary, the Lord has said to every believer. We have all been "begraced by God's grace," or, as Weymouth translates it, "He has enriched us in the beloved One."

That being the case, we can't honestly excuse ourselves from following the example of Mary, whose great desire was to glorify the Lord in all that she did. The secret is not the ability of the creature but the grace of the Creator. Mary was a poor girl, but glorifying God doesn't depend on wealth. She belonged to a rejected race, but obedience doesn't require special citizenship. She came from Nazareth, a town that even the Jews despised (John 1:46), but God's blessing isn't the result of having a special address. All the things that the people of the world demand before we can have their approval and acceptance, grace laughs at and tosses aside.

Read Mary's wonderful "grace song" in Luke 1:46–55 and get the message it conveys: God's grace has turned everything in this world upside down! The humble servants are blessed and the proud are scattered. The weak are given amazing strength, but the powerful are toppled from their thrones and the "nobodies" take their place. The full go away hungry while the hungry are filled, and the rich go away poor while the poor are made rich. That's grace! According to Kathleen Norris, Mary's song is so subversive that during the 1980s, the government of Guatemala prohibited people from reading or reciting it publicly.[2] Is it "subversive" in our own lives?

Grace transformed scheming Jacob into the father of the twelve tribes of Israel. Grace made frightened Gideon into a victorious general and the Moabite widow Ruth into the great-grandmother of David the king and the ancestress of Jesus the Savior. Grace turned bigoted Saul of Tarsus into compassionate Paul the apostle, the greatest missionary and theologian in Christian church history. No wonder Robert Robinson wrote:

> O to grace how great a debtor
> Daily I'm constrained to be!
> Let Thy goodness, like a fetter,
> Bind my wandering heart to thee.

"I am the Lord's servant," Mary said to the angel. "May it be to me as you have said." With beautiful modesty and strong faith, she turned herself over to the Lord for whatever He wanted her to do. Unlike Zechariah the priest, she didn't ask, "How can I be sure of this?" — the equivalent of "How can this be?" — but "How will this be?" (Luke 1:18, 34). How will an unwed virgin give birth to a son? Gabriel explained that God's Spirit would accomplish the miracle because "nothing

1. Fritz Rienecker and Cleon Rogers Jr., *Linguistic Key to the Greek New Testament* (Grand Rapids, Mich.: Zondervan, 1982), 522.

2. Kathleen Norris, *Amazing Grace* (New York: Riverhead Books, 1999), 117.

is impossible with God" (Luke 1:35–37). Weymouth translates verse 37, "For no promise from God will be impossible of fulfillment," and he points out in a footnote that "impossible" can be translated "powerless." My favorite translation of verse 37 is from the 1901 American Standard Version: "For no word from God shall be void of power." God speaks the Word and releases transforming power!

God created all things and sustains all things "by his powerful word" (Heb. 1:3), the same Word that accomplished miracles in the lives of His servants from Moses to Paul. God spoke the Word, Mary believed the Word, and Jesus was conceived in her virgin womb. Jesus spoke the Word and water turned into wine, storms were stilled, the sick and the crippled were healed, and the dead were raised to life. Mary's body would be "overshadowed" by the Spirit of God, and her womb would be like the Most Holy Place in the tabernacle where the glory of God resided (see Ex. 25:20).

The song of Mary—the Magnificat—is a beautifully woven fabric of quotations and images from the Old Testament, particularly the song of Hannah in 1 Samuel 2:1–10. It's unlikely that Mary's family owned any scrolls of the Hebrew Scriptures, but she had heard these Scriptures read in the synagogue services and had committed many of them to memory. She must have especially loved the Psalms, because she alludes to 71:19; 89:10; 98:3; 111:9; 103:13, 17; and 107:9.

When we believe God's promises and act on them, the Holy Spirit works through that Word to release His power and achieve His purposes. The Spirit wrote the Word to reveal and glorify Jesus Christ, and the Spirit works in and through us as we obey the Word and trust God to work. As Elizabeth said to Mary, "Blessed is she who has believed that what the Lord has said to her will be accomplished!" (Luke 1:45). But God's blessing wasn't only for Mary, for it is received by all who trust His Word and act on it.

WE MUST YIELD TO THE WILL OF GOD (Luke 1:38)

She saw herself as "the Lord's servant" (Luke 1:38; and see v. 48), "the handmaid of the Lord," as the King James Version translates it. A handmaid was the lowest class of female slave. Perhaps Mary was recalling the words of Ruth when she spoke to Boaz (Ruth 3:9) or of Hannah when she prayed (1 Sam. 1:11). Mary may not have understood all the ramifications of her decision, but surely she realized what it would mean to her and to Joseph. She would be a virgin, engaged to be married yet obviously pregnant, and people would talk. But beyond that, she would suffer a sword in her soul as her Son was rejected and then crucified (Luke 2:35; John 19:25–27).

The will of God is the expression of the love of God for us personally, and His will comes from His heart (Ps. 33:11). Jesus saw God's will as nourishment, not punishment (John 4:31–34), that which builds us up and enables us to serve and glorify God. It isn't enough for us simply to know the will of God; we must also *do* the will of God from our hearts (Eph. 6:6). Faith leads to works, and works bring glory to God (Matt. 5:16).

Sometimes obeying the will of the Lord is difficult and even painful, but disobeying is even more painful. When we obey the Lord, difficulties work *for* us; when we disobey Him, they work *against* us. God's will either perfects us as we obey it or disciplines us as we resist it, but either way, God will see to it that His will is done. It wasn't easy for Mary to hear what people said about Jesus and then see what they did to Him, but it was all part of the plan of God.

One day while Jesus was teaching, a woman in the crowd cried out, "Blessed is the mother who gave you birth and nursed you." She was referring of course to Mary, who had said in her song, "From now on all generations will call me blessed" (Luke 1:48). Without denying the validity of the woman's statement, Jesus replied, "Blessed rather are those who hear the word of God and obey it" (Luke 11:27–28). Mary did that: she heard God's Word and obeyed it, and the Lord did the rest. That's how we magnify the Lord.

WE MUST DEPEND ON THE SPIRIT OF GOD (Luke 1:35)

We accept God's will and yield to the Lord by faith. Then we discover that the Spirit of God enables us to do what the Lord commands. "For nothing is impossible with God" (Luke 1:37). No wonder Mary rejoiced and sang, "The Mighty One has done great things for me" (Luke 1:49). Jesus instructed His disciples to wait in Jerusalem until they had been "clothed with power from on high" (Luke 24:49), and the book of Acts records what great things God did for and through the early church because the believers depended wholly on His Spirit.

Many churches today try to get along without the Spirit's power. The members are so accustomed to "business as usual" that they think what is going on is normal. So they continue pleading for money, using gimmicks to attract people, neglecting prayer, saying little or nothing about spiritual gifts, and doing very little to share the gospel at home and overseas. Revival comes when we admit our own inability to serve God in our own strength and wisdom and when we turn desperately to Him for the power only the Spirit can give.

"It may be said without qualification that every man is as holy and as full of the Spirit as he wants to be," wrote A. W. Tozer in *Born After Midnight*.[3] We could substitute "every church" for "every man." When was the last time you heard anybody in a public service pray fervently that the Spirit would fill the preacher, the worship leaders, yes, and the worshipers? With all our electronic equipment, we don't need as much help as the saints did in the apostolic era—or do we? Mary submitted to the Lord, was filled with the Spirit, and broke out in song, praising God. According to Ephesians 5:18–21, being joyful, thankful, and submissive is evidence that you are filled with the Spirit.

Following that admonition would take care of all the challenges local churches face today, from calling a godly pastor to sharing the gospel with the community and the world.

3. A. W. Tozer, *Born After Midnight* (Harrisburg, Penn.: Christian Publications, 1959), 8.

48

HEROD THE GREAT

The LORD's curse is on the house of the wicked.

PROVERBS 3:33

*I*n 1863 the American Quaker leader William Penn wrote, "If we will not be governed by God, we must be governed by tyrants." He was right, and no nation illustrates this better than the ancient people of Israel. Because of their repeated disobedience to the Lord, they frequently suffered under cruel despots who exploited and enslaved them until the Lord brought deliverance. Before Jesus was born and for decades afterward, "the house of Herod" ruled the Jewish people, and the founder of that house was Herod the Great (73–4 BC), the man who tried to kill Jesus. His enemies said that Herod "stole to the throne like a fox, ruled like a tiger, and died like a dog." Not a bad assessment. (Jesus called Herod Antipas a fox [Luke 13:32].) Caesar said he would rather be Herod's pig (*hus*) than Herod's son (*huios*), and his pun was right on target.

Born in 73 BC, Herod was made governor of Galilee at age twenty-five and ten years later was crowned king of Galilee, Judea, Ituria, and Traconitis. He was "king of the Jews," but he didn't know the God of Israel. He was a tyrant who stopped at nothing to protect himself and his throne and to guarantee the political success of his family. Historian Will Durant wrote, "His character was typical of an age that produced so many men of intellect without morals, ability without scruples, and courage without honor."[1] Another good assessment.

But the godless character of King Herod had long roots that go back many centuries. If we want to better understand Herod and his evil deeds, we must begin with the birth of twin boys into the household of Isaac and Rebekah. While we are doing this, we may learn something about ourselves.

TWO FEUDING BROTHERS (Gen. 25:19–34)

If God's covenant with Abraham was to be fulfilled, it was essential that Isaac and Rebekah have a family; but after twenty years of marriage, they were still without children. God answered their prayers in a way they never expected, for Rebekah conceived twin boys who began to "jostle each other" in the womb. The

---

1. Will Durant, *Caesar and Christ* (New York: Simon and Schuster, 1944), 531.

boys were feuding even before they were born, and this began what the prophet Ezekiel called "an ancient hostility" (Ezek. 35:5).

The boys were not alike. Jacob ("the heel-grabber") was a quiet person who preferred to stay at home among the tents, while Esau ("hairy") was an outdoorsman who became a skillful hunter. Jacob liked to cook and to think about the Lord and the covenant He had made with their grandfather Abraham and their father, Isaac. As for Esau, he had no interest in spiritual matters and one day sold his birthright to Jacob for a bowl of lentil soup and some bread and wine.

We learned in chapter 12 that Esau was a "profane" man who lived "outside the temple" (see Heb. 12:16) and had no interest in the things of God. Jacob was far from perfect, but he at least valued the family's spiritual heritage from Abraham. "The older [Esau] will serve the younger [Jacob]" (Gen. 25:23). The mistake Rebekah and Jacob made was in trying to bring this about in their own way instead of letting the Lord work it out (Gen. 27).

The two brothers illustrate to us the conflict that exists between the Spirit and the flesh in the life of the child of God. Esau, the firstborn, is rejected, and Jacob, the second-born, is given the inheritance. In New Testament terms, "You must be born again" (John 3:7). "For the sinful nature desires what is contrary to the Spirit, and the Spirit what is contrary to the sinful nature. They are in conflict with each other, so that you do not do what you want" (Gal. 5:17). If we yield to the flesh, we are in danger of committing the ugly sins named in Galatians 5:19–21, but if we yield to the Spirit, we produce the beautiful fruit of the Spirit named in Galatians 5:22–23. Because we are in Jesus Christ, we have been crucified with Him and are dead to the old life. As we "keep in step with the Spirit," we have Christ's life working in us and we bear fruit (Gal. 5:24–26).

The record shows that King Herod did not have the Spirit within, and therefore he manifested the works of the flesh. "For if you live according to the sinful nature, you will die; but if by the Spirit you put to death the misdeeds of the body, you will live" (Rom. 8:13). Herod's grandfather and father were Edomites, and his mother was an Arabian. Even though his parents "converted" to Judaism, that didn't put him into the covenant family of God. When King Herod declared war on the child Jesus, it was Jacob and Esau feuding again.

TWO WARRING NATIONS

The two boys grew up, married, and founded nations. Jacob became the father of the twelve tribes of Israel (Gen. 46), and Esau became the founder of the nation of Edom (Gen. 36). Edom means "red" and was a nickname that may have referred to the color of the lentil stew that Jacob sold his brother (Gen. 25:29–30).

Before they were born, Israel and Edom were at war with each other, and they continued their conflict for centuries to come. There were two brief truces: when Jacob and Esau met briefly at Mahanaim (Gen. 32–33) and when they buried their father, Isaac, at Mamre (Gen. 35:27–29). The nations of Israel and Edom

234 - Life Sentences

were enemies, and the Edomites did all they could to make life difficult for their cousins. They encouraged the Babylonians to destroy Jerusalem and its citizens (Ps. 137), and because they lived high in the hills of their country, the Edomites thought they were invincible (Obad. 8–10, 15). God's prophets announced that the Lord would one day judge Edom and the nation would be no more (Jer. 49:7–22; Lam. 4:21; Ezek. 25:12–14; Amos 1:11–12).

How tragic that an old family feud grew into a national crisis, but things will get worse. Just wait until Herod the Great arrives on the scene. He had ten wives and fourteen children who vied for attention and power. If anybody, including members of his family, got in the way of Herod's plans, he had them killed. When Jesus was born in Bethlehem of Judea, Esau attacked Jacob again and Edom declared war on Israel.

TWO OPPOSING KINGDOMS (Matt. 2)

The magi were a combination of priest, scientist, and astrologer. Herod's unexpected visitors were Gentiles and probably from Persia. From the number of gifts they brought, most people assume there were three of them, but Scripture doesn't tell us. When they arrived in Jerusalem, the whole city was upset, especially the man on the throne. The Greek word translated "disturbed" in Matthew 2:3 is translated "terrified" in Matthew 14:26 and "thrown into turmoil" in Acts 17:8. Things were really upset! Herod the Great was not about to be dethroned by some new king. Esau was once again defending his rights against Jacob, and Edom was attacking Israel. The kingdom of darkness was attacking the kingdom of light.

Herod lied when he said he wanted to worship the new king, for his intention was to kill the child. Herod didn't reveal his true character to the magi, for he was a servant of Satan, and Satan is a liar and a murderer (John 8:44). Jesus is the truth, but Herod was a liar; Jesus is the life, but Herod was an instrument of death. History repeats itself: Esau wanted to kill Jacob, and the Edomites wanted to wipe out the Jews in embattled Jerusalem.

The "house of Herod" was known for its murderers. Not only did Herod the Great attempt to kill Jesus, but he also had his favorite wife, Mariamne, killed. He also killed three sons, a mother-in-law, and a brother-in-law. Herod had the entire Jewish Sanhedrin killed except for two men, and he murdered forty-five descendants of the Maccabeans, the heroic Jewish family that had rescued Israel. Herod's son Herod Antipas killed John the Baptist (Matt. 14:1–12), and Herod Agrippa I killed the apostle James and would have killed Peter had the Lord not protected him (Acts 12). Satan is a liar and a murderer, and so are his servants, and the sons of the servants usually follow their father's wicked example.

When Herod discovered he had been outfoxed by the magi, he was furious and gave orders to kill every boy who was two years old or under in Bethlehem and its vicinity. (Jesus was probably a year old at this time.) Bethlehem was a small town and perhaps fifteen or twenty were slain, but even one is too many.

Esau attacked Jacob, but once again the God of Jacob outsmarted Esau and sent His Son to Egypt until it was safe for Joseph and Mary to return. Matthew quoted two Old Testament passages — Jeremiah 31:15 – 17 and Hosea 11:1 — to shed light on these events. Jeremiah saw Rachel as a mother in Israel, weeping over her children going into captivity, and Matthew applied that scene to the Bethlehem mothers whose little sons Herod killed. Hosea looked back and reminded the Jews of God's grace in calling them out of Egypt, and Matthew applied that to Jesus.

How sad that the king's counselors knew where the Messiah would be born and yet didn't go to see Him! The Gentile seekers followed the star, listened to the Word, believed the Scriptures, and met the Savior of the world! The king and the Jewish scholars knew the Scriptures but didn't obey them, and they missed the greatest opportunity of life.

Herod the Great was not only a liar and murderer, but he was also a great builder. He built the port of Caesarea as well as Masada and his luxurious "getaway," the Herodian. He rebuilt Samaria and added a pagan temple dedicated to Augustus Caesar. He also built a Greek amphitheater and promoted the Greek games. His crowning architectural achievement was the temple in Jerusalem. He infuriated the godly Jews when he put a golden Roman eagle at the entrance of the temple, but at least he showed where his heart really was. It wasn't Jehovah's temple; it was Herod's temple, and the Romans, whom Herod served, destroyed it when they captured Jerusalem.

Although Herod was a great builder, he was also a great destroyer of the things that mattered most. What good are ten wives if you live in lust but not love, or grand houses if you have no home, or great wealth if you don't have the things that money can't buy? Solomon said that "the wicked are brought down by their own wickedness" and "a cruel man brings trouble on himself" (Prov. 11:5, 17). God's curse was certainly on the "house of Herod" as it is on the house of those who defy the law of God and reject His grace. They may appear successful, but they are failures in the things that really count.

The kingdom of God and the kingdom of this world are still opposing one another, but God's kingdom shall succeed. "The world and its desires pass away, but whoever does the will of God lives forever" (1 John 2:17 TNIV).

49

SIMEON AND ANNA

They will still bear fruit in old age.

PSALM 92:14

Reviewing more than fifty years of ministry, my wife and I give thanks to the Lord for the senior saints who encouraged us along the way. Now we are the seniors encouraging the younger generation! We started our ministry very young, and if it hadn't been for those godly Simeons and Annas who helped us, we might have ended our ministry still very young. We find Simeon and Anna in Luke 2:25–38, when they met Joseph, Mary, and the baby Jesus in the temple. Their meeting was no accident; it was an appointment. Mary and Joseph were obeying God's Word (Luke 2:22–24, 27, 39), and God was guiding them (Prov. 6:20–23).

Dr. Luke says specifically that Anna was "very old" (Luke 2:36), but his statement about her exact age is somewhat ambiguous, and the translations don't agree. The New American Standard Bible text says she had "lived ... as a widow to the age of eighty-four." The New International Version text says she was a widow "until she was eighty-four," but the marginal note says she had been a widow for eighty-four years. If, like most Jewish girls, she had married at fifteen, and if she had seven years with her husband, then she was one hundred six years old, which is "very old" indeed.

As for Simeon, we are given no information about his age, although most people assume he too was up in years. A Jewish tradition says he was one hundred thirteen years old. His request, "Now dismiss your servant in peace," is hardly what a younger man would pray. I get the impression that Simeon was patiently waiting for the hour to arrive when he would go to be with the Lord, and that attitude suggests an older believer. He was a layman, not a priest, but his prayer to the Lord (the Nunc Dimittis—Latin for "now dismiss") sounds like the words of a very godly elderly saint.

Whatever their ages, Simeon and Anna are examples to all of us, but especially to older saints, because these two believers were flourishing in the courts of the Lord and bearing fruit in their old age (Ps. 92:13–14). If we follow their example, we can have the same happy experience no matter what our age might be.

LIVE IN THE FUTURE TENSE

The tendency of older people is to live in the past tense, in the so-called "good old days." I have a book in my library entitled *The Good Old Days Weren't That Good*, and as the author writes about medical matters, roads, caring for the needy, and communication, he proves his point. Some things were awful! True, there may be some things about the past that we miss, but there are more things that we don't miss. We can certainly learn from history and seek to imitate the best of the past, but it is obvious that we can't live in the past.

Simeon and Anna weren't looking back; they were looking ahead. Simeon was "waiting for the consolation of Israel" (Luke 2:25), and he and Anna belonged to that small group of devoted Jews who were "looking forward to the redemption of Jerusalem" (Luke 2:38). The spiritual life of the nation was very low at that time, but there was a godly remnant who believed God's Word and looked for the Messiah to come in their lifetime. God told Simeon that he would see the Lord's Christ before he died. What a promise!

Hope is one of the greatest forces in the human heart. The hope of a better life keeps the laborer working. The hope of peace keeps the diplomat negotiating. The hope of a cure for disease keeps the laboratory scientist experimenting and investigating. The lost world has a "hope so" philosophy of life and says "things will get better," but they have no basis for their so-called hope. As Christian believers, our hope is in Christ because He is our hope (1 Tim. 1:1). Simeon and Anna looked hopefully for the first coming of the Messiah, and their hope was rewarded. We look hopefully for His promised return, "the blessed hope—the glorious appearing of our great God and Savior, Jesus Christ" (Titus 2:13)—and His promises will not fail. Therefore, let's live in the future tense.

One of the best ways for us to live in the future tense is to invest in the younger generation and share what the Lord has taught us. As you read the book of Psalms, notice the phrase "the next generation" in Psalm 48:13; 71:18; 78:4, 6; 79:13; 102:18; and 145:4. And don't forget Paul's admonitions in his epistles to Timothy to guard the Word of truth and pass it on to the next generation. "And the things you have heard me say in the presence of many witnesses entrust to reliable people who will also be qualified to teach others" (2 Tim. 2:2 TNIV).

TRUST GOD'S PROMISES

The Lord promised Simeon that he wouldn't die until he saw the Messiah, and Simeon claimed that promise. The Lord had shown the widow Anna that the promised Redeemer was soon to come, and she worshiped, prayed, and waited in the temple until the promise was fulfilled.

The promises of God aren't lifesavers, to be used only in emergencies, but solid rocks on which we walk over the quicksand of this world day after day. The promises of God rest on His unchanging character, and they can never fail.

Evangelist D. L. Moody used to say, "God never made a promise that was too good to be true." If we believe that, then we should claim His promises and act by faith until promise becomes reality in our lives.

Many older believers have more faith in the predictions of the meteorologist than in the promises of the Lord, and they spend more time studying weather reports than reading God's Word. When Jesus is our Lord, the future is our friend, and the key to the future is believing the promises of God. "God's promises are checks to be cashed, not mottoes to hang on the wall," said Vance Havner. Do we believe that?

FOCUS ON JESUS CHRIST

Both Simeon and Anna devoted their waking hours to prayer and worship in the temple because they were waiting to meet the Lord's Christ. When Simeon saw Him, he took the baby in his arms and sang a wonderful hymn of praise. When Anna saw Him, she gave thanks to God and went out and told her friends, "The Messiah has come!"

How easy it would have been for these two aged saints to focus on their aches and pains, their disappointment with the reign of cruel Herod the Great, or their grief over the worldliness of the priesthood and the decay of the temple ministry. Instead, they kept their eyes and hearts focused on the promised Messiah, and the Lord didn't disappoint them. Churches and pastors aren't perfect (they never were), politics seem to grow worse by the day, and our bodies remind us that we are getting older, but God is still on the throne. "Let us fix our eyes on Jesus, the author and perfecter of our faith" (Heb. 12:2).

If the older saints don't get excited over some of today's sermons, it's probably because they want to hear about Jesus and the cross. In recent years, I have heard sermons that didn't mention Jesus even once, and yet they were delivered by preachers who would claim to be orthodox. I have also sung congregational praise songs (some of them four or five times) with lyrics that had no relationship to Jesus. "A sermon without Christ as its beginning, middle and end," said Spurgeon, "is a mistake in conception and a crime in execution."[1] I agree.

PRAISE THE LORD IN EVERY CIRCUMSTANCE

Simeon's hymn in Luke 2:28–32 is the fifth and last of the advent songs that Dr. Luke recorded for us. He began with Elizabeth's song in Luke 1:41–45, followed by Mary's glorious song in Luke 2:46–55. The old priest Zechariah regained his voice and sang, and his praise is found in Luke 1:67–79, and the angels appeared to the shepherds and praised God (Luke 2:13–14). The advent season ought to be filled with songs of praise and not shallow holiday ditties.

Simeon's hymn is an inspired pattern for us to follow in our own times of worship. To begin with, it's a hymn of praise to the Sovereign Lord (Luke

---

1. Spurgeon, *Metropolitan Tabernacle Pulpit*, vol. 27, 598.

2:28–29). The word translated "sovereign" gives us our English word *despot*. Simeon saw himself as the humble servant of an almighty Lord, and this brought joy and peace to his heart. On Sunday morning, May 4, 1856, Charles Spurgeon said to his London congregation, "There is no attribute of God more comforting to his children than the doctrine of Divine Sovereignty." Then he added, "Men will allow God to be everywhere except on his throne."[2]

The hymn was also what we would call a "gospel hymn," for Simeon had seen God's salvation. The name Jesus means "Savior." Simeon was now ready to die because he had seen the Savior. People are not prepared to die until they have seen Jesus in the Word and trusted Him! Simeon was also singing a missionary hymn, for this salvation is for all people, Gentiles and Jews (Luke 2:31–32). The Gentile nations were in darkness (Matt. 4:15–16), and Israel had lost the glory of God.

Simeon then turned to Mary and Joseph with a word of prophecy (Luke 2:33–35). The child was destined to be like a rock on which unbelievers would stumble but in which believers would find safety and security. As people's hearts were exposed to the truth, many would speak against Him but some would trust Him. There would come a day when He would be killed, and a sword would pierce Mary's soul. The salvation God had prepared was costly.

ALLOW THE HOLY SPIRIT TO GUIDE YOU

Simeon had the Holy Spirit upon him (Luke 2:25), and he was told by the Spirit that he would live to see the promised Messiah (Luke 2:26). The Spirit guided him to meet the Messiah in the temple (Luke 2:27). Anna was a prophetess (Luke 2:36), which means the Spirit was present and at work in her life. Led by the Spirit, she too arrived in the temple at just the right time and place to see Jesus. Then the Spirit enabled her to witness to others that the Messiah had arrived (Luke 2:38; Acts 1:8).

I once heard J. Sidlow Baxter say, "Whatever begins with the Holy Spirit always leads to Jesus Christ." Anna and Simeon were "keep[ing] in step with the Spirit" (see Gal. 5:25) and therefore came to Jesus in the crowded temple. If we are also "in step with the Spirit," we will see Jesus in the Bible, in the lives of God's people, and even in the seemingly disappointing experiences of life. The Spirit will also give us the power we need to bear witness of Christ, even to people who don't want to hear.

The aged apostle John was "in the Spirit" on the Lord's Day (Rev. 1:10) and saw awesome visions of Jesus! His physical eyesight may have been dim, but his spiritual vision was clear. Too many people read the book of Revelation looking for hidden clues concerning future events, when they ought to read it to see the glories of Jesus. The better we know Jesus, the more we will be like Him; and the more we are like Him, the better we can share Him with others.

---

2. Spurgeon, *Metropolitan Tabernacle Pulpit*, vol. 2, 185.

WITNESS ABOUT CHRIST TO THE VERY END

If God's gracious salvation is for all people (Luke 2:30–31), then let's imitate Simeon and Anna and tell as many people as possible about Jesus. When we meet together with some of our cronies, as we discuss pains and prescriptions and canes and restrictions, let's seek to speak a word for Jesus. When we assemble with the saints, let's "flourish in the courts of our God" and "bear fruit in old age" (Ps. 92:12–15). Not everybody in church who says, "Lord, Lord," is truly born again, and our witness might awaken some religious sinner just in time.

It is doubtful that Anna and Simeon possessed any wealth, but many of God's older stewards enjoy financial security and ought to share their wealth with evangelical ministries that are seeking to reach a lost world. We can't support everybody, so we should ask the Lord which ministries He wants us to encourage. Pray for wisdom and get all the facts, because it is too late in life to be wasting the resources the Lord has given you. Your "last will and testament" is also your "last will and testimony," so make sure Jesus is included. Let's be like King David who, when he was seventy, gave what he had to help build the temple for future generations.

No matter how old you are, take time to read Psalm 92:12–15, and ask yourself, "Is this a description of my Christian life?"

50

JOHN THE BAPTIST

"He must increase, but I must decrease."
JOHN 3:30 KJV

He was a miracle baby, born to aged parents, and he was a gifted prophet of the Lord, chosen by the Father to be the "advance man" for Jesus Christ. By preaching and baptizing, John prepared the way for Christ's ministry and announced "the beginning of the gospel" (Mark 1:1; Acts 1:21–22). He preached to great crowds of people who came from all over the nation to hear him, and even the Jewish religious leaders sent a committee to interrogate him. "What do you say about yourself?" they asked (John 1:22), but John preferred to talk about Jesus. When some of John's disciples got worried because the crowds following Jesus were larger than those following their master, John wasn't the least bit upset. "A person can receive only what is given from heaven," he replied (John 3:27 TNIV). Then John revealed the guiding principle of his life and ministry: "This my joy therefore is fulfilled. He must increase, but I must decrease" (John 3:29–30 KJV).

THE GOAL OF MINISTRY — "HE MUST INCREASE"

The Jewish Sanhedrin had every right to send priests and Levites to interview John the Baptist, because the Sanhedrin was the custodian and protector of the sacred law. It was their job to investigate every "prophet" who appeared in Israel and to determine if he was a false prophet or a prophet truly called of God (Deut. 13). John passed the test, because the Sanhedrin never questioned him again, although the leaders didn't obey his message. The common people believed he was sent by the Lord (Luke 20:1–8).

John knew that his public ministry would be brief, for his calling was to point people to Jesus and not to build a following for himself. Andrew and John were among John's disciples, and they left John and followed Jesus (John 1:35–42). It is likely that John baptized each of the twelve apostles (Acts 1:21–22). John the Baptist was careful to point out the superiority of Jesus Christ.

Jesus is the Word, John was only the voice (John 1:1, 14, 23). A voice without words can make noise and get attention, but it can't give instruction. Just as my words reveal my mind and heart to others, so Jesus the Word reveals the mind and heart of God to us. He is God's alphabet, the Alpha and Omega (Rev. 1:18; 21:6; 22:13), and He "spells out" to us what we need to know about God. "Anyone who has seen me has seen the Father" (John 14:9), said Jesus. John knew he was a voice, a witness sent from God, and that sharing his God-given message was the most important thing. He pointed to Jesus and called Him "the Lord," "the Lamb of God," and "the Son of God" (John 1:23, 29, 34).

Jesus is the Bridegroom, John was only the best man (John 3:26 – 30). In Judean weddings, the friend of the bridegroom arranged the details of the wedding and gave the bride to the bridegroom. The bridegroom came to the bride's home and took her to their new home, and when the best man heard the bridegroom's voice in the distance, he rejoiced that the marriage was about to take place. The focus of attention was on the bridegroom coming for his beloved; nobody paid much attention to the best man. John was gathering guests for the wedding and wanted his own disciples to follow Christ. He was helping to prepare the bride for the Bridegroom.

Jesus is the light, John was only the lamp (John 5:31 – 35). "He himself was not the light; he came only as a witness to the light" (John 1:8). John's light shone in the limited area of the Jordan Valley, but Jesus is "the light of the world" (John 8:12). When Jesus began His ministry, the people of Israel were living in darkness, afflicted with spiritual blindness (Matt. 4:13 – 16). "John was a lamp that burned and gave light," said Jesus, "and you chose for a time to enjoy his light" (John 5:35). The lamp merely carries the light, and all of God's children are light-bearers in this dark world (Matt. 5:14 – 16). When you are walking in a dark house at night, a tiny night-light can make a great difference; and one believer can make a big difference in today's dark world.

All three of these images preach the same message: Jesus Christ is the pre-eminent one and not the messenger who points to Him. This is the goal of all ministry: "He must increase." The servant's task is to make more and more of Jesus and less of himself or herself. As we grow in grace and in the knowledge of Christ, we will focus more and more on the Master and not on His servants.

THE PRICE OF MINISTRY — "I MUST DECREASE"

John not only knew what he was but he also knew *what he was not*. His honesty and humility are worthy of our imitation. If John 3:31 – 36 continues the words of John the Baptist, as many commentators believe, then John declares that he was from the earth and not from heaven. Jesus came to earth from heaven and therefore is above all things. "But we have this treasure in jars of clay to show that this all-surpassing power is from God and not from us" (2 Cor. 4:7). John was "a *man* who was sent from God" (John 1:6, italics mine), and he knew it.

John was not the Christ nor the great prophet God promised to send His people (John 1:19 – 21; Deut. 18:14 – 18). People want to treat spiritual leaders as gods — it happened to Peter (Acts 10:24 – 26) and to Paul and Barnabas (Acts 14:8 – 20) — but this kind of idolatry leads only to sin and judgment. Although he came "in the spirit and power of Elijah" (Luke 1:17), John made it clear that he was not the prophet Elijah who would come (John 1:21; Mal. 4:5; see Matt. 11:1–19; 17:10–13). Jesus called John "more than a prophet" because he had the privilege of introducing the Savior to the Jewish people.

John was from the earth and John was not the Christ, the Prophet, nor Elijah. Neither was he a reed bowing to the winds and trying to please everybody (Matt. 11:7). Today's culture is marked by "political correctness." We must not offend people by disagreeing with them or challenging their basic beliefs. John knew nothing of such compromise. He came with an ax to cut at the roots of the trees, a winnowing fork to separate the wheat from the chaff, and fire for burning up the dead trees and the useless chaff (Matt. 3:1–12). Our English word *radical* comes from the Latin *radix*, which means "root." With ax in hand, John was a radical who got to the root of the sin problem.

John was not a well-dressed prince in a king's palace (Matt. 11:8) but a prisoner in a king's dungeon (Matt. 14:1–12). He had the courage to warn Herod Antipas that his marriage to his brother Philip's wife was unlawful, so Herod put him in prison. John lost his freedom and ultimately lost his life, but that made no difference to him. He had done his job well, and the work would go on. John's life wasn't an easy one, nor is the life of any believer who seeks to magnify Jesus Christ.

Finally, John was not a miracle worker, for "John never performed a miraculous sign" (see John 10:40–42). This has always seemed strange to me, because John was himself a miracle baby and was filled with the Spirit in his mother's womb. He came in the "spirit and power of Elijah" (Luke 1:17), and Elijah worked many miracles. John's ministry was primarily to the people of Israel, and "Jews demand miraculous signs" (1 Cor. 1:22). If any servant of the Lord ought to have done miracles, it was John the Baptist, but John was not a miracle worker. However, what he said about Jesus brought salvation to lost souls *even after John was dead*! "And in that place many believed in Jesus" (John 10:42). What power there is in a Spirit-filled witness!

THE REWARD OF MINISTRY — "THIS JOY OF MINE IS NOW COMPLETE" (John 3:29 ESV)

John's life wasn't an easy one. It's likely that his aged parents died when he was a teenager, but they had faithfully taught him the Word of God and how to pray (Luke 11:1). He lived in the wilderness, communing with God and awaiting the hour when he would begin his brief ministry. He was a recluse (Luke 7:33), a courageous prophet who declared God's message of repentance and salvation. But in spite of the difficulties of his life, John is still associated with joy.

John brought joy to his parents and their relatives and friends (Luke 1:14, 58). Zechariah and Elizabeth delighted in his willingness to learn God's Word, and they rejoiced in his growth and spiritual maturity (Luke 1:80). In his mother's womb, John rejoiced at the sound of Mary's voice (Luke 1:39–45), and later he

244 - *Life Sentences*

rejoiced at the voice of the Savior (John 3:29). Certainly John was happy for the great privilege God had given him to present the Redeemer to the nation and point to the Lamb of God. John rejoiced to hear the voice of Jesus and to know that his God-given mission was completed.

As far as the record is concerned, the only time John lost his joy was when he was in Herod's prison and wondered whether Jesus was really the promised Messiah (Matt. 11:1–19). John was an outdoorsman, and confinement in a narrow prison surely irritated him, especially when he was there because he had obeyed God. John was born a priest but, like Jeremiah, Ezekiel, and Zechariah, he was called to be a prophet, a much more difficult and dangerous vocation. John had preached a message of judgment, but Jesus was going about doing deeds of mercy. "Are you the Coming One, or should we expect another?" was John's question to Jesus (literal translation), and the word translated "another" (*heteros*) means "another of a different kind." John was expecting a mighty judge, but Jesus was ministering as a tender shepherd. John had forgotten the voice from heaven and the descent of the dove when he baptized Jesus.

Neither John nor his disciples heard the words of praise that Jesus spoke about John (Matt. 11:7–19), but the words are recorded in the Bible for eternity. What Jesus thinks about us is far more important than the opinions of kings — or even our own opinions! Perhaps John thought he had failed in his ministry, but that wasn't the case at all. He had succeeded, and because he had, Jesus was able to carry on His work.

On dark and discouraging days, some of God's choicest servants have lost their joy and thought they had failed, including Moses, David, Elijah, and Jeremiah; but then they turned to the Lord by faith and recovered their joy. "The Lord rarely allows His servants to see how much good they are doing," said Scottish preacher George Morrison. It isn't good to be too introspective. Let's fix our eyes on Jesus and trust Him.

As far as we know, the Jewish leaders made no attempt to rescue John from Herod Antipas, and Herod murdered John because of a foolish oath (Matt. 14:1–12). A godly prophet is slain and a wicked king survives. "Truth forever on the scaffold / Wrong forever on the throne," wrote American poet James Russell Lowell in "The Present Crisis."

No, Mr. Lowell, not "forever," because there is coming an hour when Wrong will be dethroned and Truth will reign forever. The angel will announce "The kingdom of the world has become the kingdom of our Lord and of his Christ, and he will reign for ever and ever" (Rev. 11:15). Jesus Christ will return and defeat the Herods of this world and establish His glorious kingdom!

That's a future worth living for and worth dying for.

51

ANDREW

Nobody should seek his own good, but the good of others.

1 CORINTHIANS 10:24

If anybody had the word *others* written on his heart, it was Andrew, the first of our Lord's apostles to be saved when John the Baptist introduced Andrew and John to Jesus. Then Andrew found his brother, Simon, and introduced him to the Lord (John 1:29–42). The New Testament gives four lists of the apostles (Matt. 10:1–4; Mark 3:16–19; Luke 6:14–16; Acts 1:13), and Simon Peter is named first in all of them. Nobody questioned that he was the leader. Andrew is second in two lists (Matthew, Luke) and fourth in the other two, and Andrew is frequently identified in the Gospels as "Simon Peter's brother." But Andrew didn't care about rank or recognition; his great concern was for others, especially bringing others to Jesus.

The first three gospels don't say much about Andrew, but John's gospel gives us three fascinating scenes that have one thing in common: they all describe Andrew bringing people to Jesus. Andrew was interested in others and concerned about introducing them to his Master. That's why I chose 1 Corinthians 10:24 for his life sentence.

Let's meet these "others" and discover what Andrew did for them and what his ministry means to us today.

ANDREW BROUGHT HIS BROTHER, SIMON, TO JESUS
(John 1:40–42)

When John the Baptist pointed Jesus out to Andrew and John, they approached Him and asked for an interview, and Jesus graciously invited them to go with Him to His home. That private interview convinced them that Jesus of Nazareth was indeed the Messiah, and they wanted to share the good news with their own family. Andrew's brother, Simon, and John's brother, James, must have traveled with Andrew and John from Galilee to the Jordan, because the first thing Andrew did was to find his brother, Simon, and tell him about Jesus. "And he brought him to Jesus" (John 1:42) is a simple sentence with profound implications. We assume that John also found his brother, James, and introduced him to Jesus. All of the four fishermen were now in the family of God, and later Jesus would summon them to full-time ministry. They had no idea what Jesus had planned for them.

God's first question in Scripture is "Where are you?" (Gen. 3:9). Are you hiding from the Lord as were Adam and Eve? Are you in God's family or in the world? His second question is, "Where is your brother?" (Gen. 4:9). Cain tried to avoid facing up to his sin and said, "Am I my brother's keeper?" Answer a question with a question! Yes, we do have an obligation to our family to tell them about Jesus. The cemetery demoniac whom Jesus delivered wanted to travel with Jesus, but the Lord said to him, "Go home to your family and tell them how much the Lord has done for you." The man obeyed, and the people who heard his story were amazed, and some of them may have gone to hear Jesus and trusted Him (Mark 5:18–20).

Not everybody is saved in the same circumstances. John the Baptist was raised in a godly home and early opened his heart to the Lord. Andrew and John heard John the Baptist preach and were introduced to Jesus. Andrew found his brother, Simon, and brought him to Jesus. At Pentecost, Peter preached the Word and three thousand people trusted Christ. And so the cycle continues as faithful parents, preachers, and other personal witnesses share the good news of Christ. However, we must not limit our witness for Christ to our own family, because we have been commanded to take the message to the whole world. But as Oswald J. Smith said, "The light that shines the farthest will shine the brightest at home."

ANDREW BROUGHT A YOUNG BOY TO JESUS (John 6:1–13)

More than 5,000 people were in our Lord's congregation on the far shore of the Sea of Galilee, and He felt obligated to feed them. He also planned to preach a sermon to them about "the bread of life," so feeding the crowd was important. At the same time, He wanted to test His disciples to see if they truly understood what it meant to live by faith. It is in the daily challenges of life that we are given opportunities to glorify God, grow in faith, and meet the needs of people.

Our Lord's disciples had three different answers to Christ's question, "Where shall we buy bread for these people to eat?" Some of the apostles suggested sending the people away, which was their usual solution (Matt. 14:15; 15:23; 19:13–15). Get rid of the people and you will get rid of the problems! Philip immediately began to count the cost, as if a big budget would solve the problem. The church needs practical people like Philip, but they must be people of faith or they will hinder the miraculous work of the Lord. When you can explain what is going on in your ministry, the Lord didn't do it. When He does the impossible, He gets the glory.

When I was in the pastorate, I arrived early for services and walked around the sanctuary chatting with people before the prelude began. It was a great opportunity for doing pastoral work, meeting visitors, and building an invisible bridge between the pew and the pulpit. Andrew the home missionary must have been walking about in the crowd when he saw the boy with his little lunch. Jesus accepted Andrew's suggestion, the boy gave up his lunch, and Jesus did the rest. The boy went home with more bread and fish than he came with, but that's the way the Lord likes to work. "Give, and it will be given to you" (Luke 6:38).

We can understand that Andrew wanted to share Christ with his own brother, Simon, but why bother with a boy who was a stranger to him? Because the boy needed to know Jesus, and Jesus needed the boy's lunch to feed thousands of hungry people. If we don't reach the younger generation for Jesus, what future is there for the church? If we don't introduce them to Jesus, how can He take their gifts and multiply them to reach the world? The church's greatest asset isn't the money deposited in the bank but the children and youth who have something to give to Jesus, something He can bless and multiply and use to feed others.

ANDREW AND PHILIP BROUGHT THE GREEKS TO JESUS (John 12:20–33)

This event at the Feast of Passover was an illustration of what the Pharisees were saying to each other: "Look how the whole world has gone after him!" (John 12:19).

These Greek visitors to Jerusalem were probably seekers after truth rather than full proselytes to the Jewish religion. But whatever their religious experience, it wasn't satisfying the hunger in their hearts for spiritual reality. Greek philosophy didn't satisfy them, and apparently celebrating the Jewish Passover left something to be desired. They had heard about Jesus or perhaps had even listened to Him preach, and they wanted a personal meeting with Him. They sensed that He was what they needed, and they were right.

The Greek visitors approached Philip (he had a Greek name), and Philip took their request to Andrew, the man who knew how to bring people to Jesus. Introducing people to Jesus may seem like an individual enterprise ("personal evangelism"), but it is really a team operation (1 Cor. 3:5–9). John tells us what Jesus said but not what Jesus did, although we assume that He received these Greeks graciously and they heard the message He gave to the crowd around Him. It was a message about His death. He would be "lifted up," which in that day meant "crucified." Had these Greeks come such a long way to hear Him announce His shameful death?

But Jesus' death and resurrection broke down the wall between Jews and Gentiles and made it possible for those Greeks to be saved (Eph. 2:11–22). There could be no "harvest among [the Gentiles]" (Rom. 1:13) unless that seed—Jesus Christ—was planted in the ground. Out of His death comes life for the world. The next time you decide not to contribute to a missionary offering, remember what it cost Jesus to open the way for all nations to come. He said, "I, when I am lifted up from the earth, will draw all men to myself" (John 12:32)—not all people without exception but all people without distinction—Jew and Gentile, male and female, slave and free. All are welcome to come to the cross. All they need is an Andrew to show them the way.

ANDREW HELPED PETER BRING 3,000 PEOPLE TO JESUS
(Acts 1:12–15)

The last time we find Andrew named in the New Testament is at a meeting of the eleven apostles and a small group of believers in an upper room. They were spending ten days in prayer and anticipating the promised coming of the Holy Spirit (Luke 24:49; Acts 1:12–15). Andrew is listed fourth on the list of apostles. He never did become a part of the "inner circle" of Peter, James, and John, but that didn't worry him. Jesus had called him, he was still an apostle, and the best was yet to come! Nobody in that upper room was asking, "Who is the greatest?" (see Mark 9:34).

Andrew was praying for his brother, Simon Peter, who would preach the Word on the day of Pentecost, and because he prayed, Andrew had a part in the conversion of about 3,000 people! What a catch of fish!

Jesus was no longer on earth, so Andrew couldn't literally bring others to Him; but he could bring them to Jesus in prayer. Jesus had prayed for Andrew and the other apostles that their witness would bring sinners to salvation (John 17:20), and the band of believers claimed that blessing. The Holy Spirit did come at Pentecost, and the believers were filled with power as they praised and worshiped the Lord. Then Peter stood up and preached Jesus Christ to the crowd and invited them to believe and be saved, and about 3,000 accepted that invitation.

In one of the churches my wife and I served, there was a retired schoolteacher who taught in the primary department of Sunday school. Each year when the older pupils were promoted to the junior level, she kept a list of their names and prayed for every one of them until she knew they had professed faith in Jesus Christ. On many occasions during the years I ministered there, she came up after a service to tell me that somebody who had come forward to profess faith in Christ, or perhaps had been baptized, was on her list and she had prayed faithfully for his or her conversion. She didn't do the preaching, but she prayed for the preacher and for lost souls, and the Lord repeatedly answered. What G. Campbell Morgan said about Andrew, I could have said about her: "the strong, quiet soul who is content to remain largely out of sight."[1] But what prayer power there is in people who are concerned about others and want to bring them to Jesus!

Jesus gave nicknames to some of His apostles. Simon became Peter or Cephas, "a rock." James and John were called "the Sons of Thunder" (Mark 3:17). To Levi, Jesus gave the name Matthew, "the gift of God." But Andrew remained Andrew, which in Greek means "manly." The manliest (or womanliest) thing a person can do is to have a burden for the lost and seek to bring people to Jesus, first at the throne of grace, and then personally, if the Lord so directs.

Andrew is the "patron saint" of Scotland, Greece, and Russia. He ought to be the "patron saint"—the example—for every local church and every individual believer.

Is the word *others* written on your heart?

---

1. G. Campbell Morgan, *The Great Physician* (New York: Revell, 1937), 24.

52

SIMON PETER

The LORD will perfect that which concerns me.

PSALM 138:8 NKJV

*Y*ou will easily recognize Peter when you get to heaven," the speaker said with a smile. "He's the man with the foot-shaped mouth."

As the audience laughed, I groaned within. I didn't think the speaker was worthy to carry Simon Peter's sandals let alone joke about his sins. A foot-shaped mouth indeed!

Jesus commanded us to forgive our brothers and sisters even if they sinned against us seven times a day, but let a great Bible personality commit the same sin twice (like Abraham), or three times (like Peter), and we can't forgive them. Instead, we make that sin the key to their character, and this blinds us to the real person. To joke about sin is to minimize it, and sin is not a laughing matter. Sin put Jesus on the cross. Peter wept over his sins, but we who are more mature joke about them. As for our own sins, well, that's another matter.

The speaker had fallen into the same trap that has snared far too many Christians: they don't know the true Bible personality, so they accept a cheap caricature instead. They enjoy emphasizing the occasional bad things. Peter had a big mouth and often put his foot into it. Noah got drunk, and Abraham told the same lie twice. David was a voyeur, Thomas was a doubter, and John Mark was a quitter. Forget all the good things these people did and ignore what the Lord said about them. No matter what the truth is, keep the congregations laughing. Stick to the caricature.

The fact that Simon Peter had two names helps us get a better perspective on his character as well as our own. Simon was his given name—"the hearer"; Peter was his nickname—"a rock." Jesus had less than three years to transform this lump of clay into a rock—and He did it! All believers have two names: the old name, "child of Adam," and the new name, "child of God." Years ago, many Christians wore colorful pins with PBP/GINFWMY printed on them. If anybody asked what those letters stood for, the explanation was given: "Please be patient, God is not finished with me yet."

Peter could have worn one of those pins without embarrassment. That's why I selected Psalm 138:8 for Peter's "life sentence": "The LORD will perfect that which concerns me" (NKJV). It's the Old Testament equivalent of Philippians

1:6: "Being confident of this, that he who began a good work in you will carry it on to completion until the day of Christ Jesus." Both verses have encouraged me when I have messed up my assignment and disappointed my Lord. The victorious Christian life is a series of new beginnings. Each time Peter stumbled, Jesus forgave him and Peter got up and made a new beginning. In all these experiences, Jesus helped Peter grow in four specific areas of his spiritual life, areas in which we ought to be growing ourselves.

KNOWING JESUS

When Andrew brought his brother to Jesus, he said to him, "We have found the Messiah" (John 1:41). It wasn't a long introduction, but from our Lord's response, it is evident that Simon trusted Jesus. That started the process of transforming the clay into rock. The next day Jesus called Philip and Nathanael, so there were now six disciples following Jesus. They traveled with Him to a wedding in Cana and saw Him perform His first miracle (John 2). They made a trip to Samaria where He brought a sinful woman to salvation and then evangelized an entire town (John 4). Then they returned to Capernaum, where the fishermen made their homes, and there Jesus set up His headquarters.

The men continued their fishing business. They were washing their nets one morning when Jesus showed up, borrowed the boat for a pulpit, and preached to the people on the shore. Then He sent the men out in their boats and miraculously filled the nets and the boats with fish. Peter was so awestruck that he fell before Jesus in the boat and confessed his unworthiness. It was then that Jesus called them into full-time discipleship and they left everything to follow Him (Luke 5:1–11). In the days to come, by His teaching, His example, and His works, Jesus would reveal Himself to them and they would get to know Him better and better.

The disciples discovered that Jesus got up early in the morning and went to a secluded place to pray. They also discovered that He had amazing power over the wind and the waves, sickness, and even demons. He could feed thousands of people with only a few pieces of bread and fish. When He sat and taught the people, His words were remarkably nourishing, burning, convicting, and life changing.

When the crowd deserted Jesus because they didn't like His theology, He asked His disciples if they were leaving too, and Peter replied, "Lord, to whom shall we go? You have the words of eternal life. We believe and know that you are the Holy One of God" (John 6:68–69). That confession must have rejoiced the Master's heart. He took the twelve men on a retreat to Caesarea Philippi and asked, "Who do you say I am?" Peter replied, "You are the Christ, the Son of the living God" (Matt. 16:13–16). They had lived with Him, watched Him, and listened to Him, and had grown in their knowledge of this wonderful Jesus.

Peter found himself a member of a small inner circle of disciples along with James and John. Did Jesus choose them because they required more attention or because they needed special preparation for their future ministries? Probably the latter. Peter was the obvious leader of the disciple band; his name stands first in every list of the names of the apostles. James was the first apostle martyred (Acts 12:1–3), and John was the apostle who lived the longest and wrote the most New Testament books. Jesus took these three men to witness His glory on the Mount of Transfiguration (Matt. 17:1–8), to see His power in the house of Jairus, whose daughter He raised from the dead (Luke 8:40–56), and to share His agony in the Garden of Gethsemane (Matt. 26:36–56). Each of these experiences helped Peter and his friends to know Jesus better.

In getting to know Jesus, we also get to know ourselves better, and we soon discover we are not as strong as we think we are. In the upper room, Peter boasted that he would stand true to Jesus and even give his life for his Lord, only to discover that the words of three strangers so shattered him that he denied his Lord three times. When the temple guards came to arrest Jesus in the garden, instead of submitting to the will of God, Peter pulled out his sword and attacked them and almost killed a man.

Thirty years after the apostle Paul's conversion, he wrote, "I want to know Christ" (Phil. 3:10). Near the end of his life, Peter wrote, "His divine power has given us everything we need for life and godliness through our knowledge of him who called us by his own glory and goodness" (2 Peter 1:3). I can't know Sir Winston Churchill, because he's dead, but knowing about him won't automatically make me a great statesman. I can know Jesus Christ because He is alive, and the Holy Spirit reveals Him to us through the Word.

One of the last things Peter wrote was, "But grow in the grace and knowledge of our Lord and Savior Jesus Christ" (2 Peter 3:18). If God is to perfect us in our living and serving, we must learn more and more about Jesus and allow the Spirit to transform us to become like Him.

TRUSTING JESUS

If a complete stranger walked up to you in the shopping mall and asked you to lend him three hundred dollars, how would you respond? You would probably say what I would say: "Sorry, but it's out of the question." He might say, "Don't you trust me?" And you would no doubt reply, "How can I trust you? I don't even know you!"

The better you know people, the easier it is to relate to them. I recall a man who befriended me years ago and appeared to be a devoted believer. But the better I got to know him, the more I realized that he was trying to use me to open some doors that were important to him. Our brief friendship cooled quickly. This never happens in our friendship with Jesus Christ. The better we know Him, the more we can trust Him, and He permits us to experience trials and temptations so that He might increase our faith.

Consider how Jesus tested Peter and helped him grow in faith. To begin with, He tested him in matters that were familiar to him, such as boats and fishing. He commanded Peter to take his boat out to the deep water and cast in the nets. This seemed foolish to Peter, an experienced fisherman, because he and his partners knew that they caught fish in the shallow water at night, not in the deep water in the day. But that morning, the men caught so many fish they had to call for another boat (Luke 5). Peter learned that he could trust Jesus in the daytime when the sea was calm and Jesus was in the ship.

But in the next test, it was night and Jesus was in the boat asleep when a frightening storm came up (Matt. 8:23–27). The men woke Him crying, "Lord, save us! We are going to drown!" He stood up and commanded the wind and waves to be still, "and it was completely calm." Lesson number two about faith: Peter could trust Jesus at night in a storm when He was asleep in the boat. As the old song puts it, "With Christ in the vessel I can smile at the storm."

Lesson number three is perhaps the most famous of all: Peter learned he could trust Jesus at night in a storm *when neither of them was in the boat*! (See Matt. 14:22–32.) Jesus and Peter both walked on the water, and Jesus saved Peter from drowning when his faith began to waver. We can trust Jesus *even without a boat*! "Walking on water" is a great metaphor of the life of faith because it pictures the impossible. Yes, Peter started sinking, but he knew he was sinking and had sense enough to cry out for help. Some Christians are almost under the water and don't even know it!

Peter and the other apostles had to learn to trust Jesus more and more, especially after He told them He was going to Jerusalem to be crucified. Peter rebelled at that announcement and told Jesus He was making a mistake (Matt. 16:21–28). Jesus taught him on the Mount of Transfiguration that there can be no glory without suffering, and Peter developed that theme in his first epistle.

One of Peter's greatest tests of faith is recorded in Acts 12, when King Herod arrested him and planned to kill him. It is fascinating to see how Peter turned it all over to the Lord and went to sleep the night before the planned execution. Jesus had already told him that he would live until old age and die on a cross (John 21:18–19), so he knew that Herod's schemes would fail. Peter slept so soundly that the angel had to strike him on the side to wake him up!

Peter the "rock" depended on Jesus the precious Stone because "the one who trusts in him will never be put to shame" (1 Peter 2:6).

LOVING JESUS

We usually associate love with the quiet and poetic apostle John and not with impetuous and manly Peter, "the big fisherman," but Peter needed to grow in love as well as in knowledge and faith. In fact, Peter's love for Jesus was the theme of our Lord's breakfast meeting with seven of His disciples after the resurrection (John 21).

In the upper room, Peter had boasted of his love for Jesus. "Even if all fall away on account of you, I never will," he said, and, "Even if I have to die with you, I will never disown you" (Matt. 26:33, 35). In all fairness, we should note that the other men echoed Peter's words, but it seems that Peter was the most outspoken. So, after breakfast, Jesus asked Peter the most penetrating question

He had ever asked him: "Simon son of John, do you truly love me more than these?" (John 21:15).[1]

Peter told the truth: he did love Jesus, and he wasn't going to deny it. Yes, he had failed, but Jesus had forgiven him and was now about to restore him to his ministry. Peter was learning the lesson John wrote about years later: "Dear children, let us not love with words or tongue but with actions and in truth" (1 John 3:18). Making a passionate speech and wielding a sword were not valid evidences of his love, but staying awake and praying with and for Jesus would have qualified.

The better we know Jesus, the more we trust Him, and the more we trust Him, the more we learn to love Him. Peter wrote, "Though you have not seen him, you love him" (1 Peter 1:8). We don't need pictures or statues of Jesus in order to love Him, because we have the inspired portrait we need already written in Scripture. The old hymn expresses it perfectly:

> Break Thou the bread of life, Dear Lord, to me,
> As Thou didst break the loaves beside the sea;
> Beyond the sacred page I seek Thee, Lord;
> My spirit pants for Thee, O living Word.
>
> MARY A. LATHBURY

Those who spend time daily in the Word, meditating on what it says about Jesus Christ, will grow in their love for Him and prove it by the way they live and serve.

BECOMING LIKE JESUS

Becoming like Jesus, after all, is the goal of the Christian life and the purpose behind God's great plan of salvation, for we have been "predestined to be conformed to the likeness of his Son" (Rom. 8:29). It isn't enough for us to grow in the knowledge of Christ; we must also "grow in grace" (2 Peter 3:18) and become more like Christ. It is very easy to grow in "Bible knowledge" and yet never manifest the grace of Jesus Christ in our lives. It is easier to preach about humility than to practice it, or to study the Greek words for love than to love one another.

If you want to see Simon, the clay, living like Peter, the rock, follow Peter's ministry in the book of Acts. You will meet a man of prayer, a man obedient to the Word, a man who magnifies Christ in his preaching, and a man of compassion who cares for saints and lost sinners. He rejoices at the privilege of suffering for Jesus. He steps aside and allows James to lead the Jerusalem church. He makes sure the widows are cared for, and he opens doors of service for qualified believers in the church. He abandons his Jewish practices, goes to the home of Cornelius, and preaches the gospel to the Gentiles. He is called on the carpet by the legalists, but he doesn't retreat. When the church leaders meet in Jerusalem to discuss the place of the Gentiles in the plan of God, Peter stands with Paul

---

1. The two Greek words for love—*agape*, God's sacrificial love, and *phileo*, friendship love—are used interchangeably in the Gospels, and it is difficult to build a case for making a distinction in this passage.

and Barnabas defending the freedom of the gospel (Acts 15:1–11). Praise God! A Gentile doesn't have to become a Jew in order to become a Christian!

The better we know Jesus, the more we trust and love Him. This combination of spiritual knowledge, faith, and love, combined with God's grace, enables us to become more and more like Jesus! Peter called it growing in the grace and knowledge of Jesus (2 Peter 3:18), and Paul called it "perfecting holiness out of reverence for God" (2 Cor. 7:1).

How did the Simon of the Gospels become the "rock" of the book of Acts? Of course, the Lord had prayed for Peter, taught him, and given him many opportunities to learn and grow, but there were three events in Jerusalem that opened the door to Peter's life of fullness and fruitfulness.

Let's begin with *the crowing of the cock* and remember that when it happened, Jesus "turned and looked straight at Peter" (Luke 22:61). It wasn't the angry scowl of a judge but the pained look of a friend whose heart had been broken. At that moment, Peter saw himself and realized what he had done to Jesus, and then he went out and wept bitterly. For each of us, there must come an hour of honest confrontation with our true self and humble confession of our sins to the Lord.

The second event was *the crucifixion of the Savior.* Peter saw a part of the official trial of Jesus, but he didn't see it all, nor did he go to the cross as John and the women did. However, Peter knew what crucifixion was and the shame and suffering his Master would endure. Peter's words must have seared his heart: "I am ready to go with you to prison and to death" (Luke 22:33). But it was Simon of Cyrene who carried the cross for Jesus, not Simon Peter. Christ died our death for us that we might live His life for Him. "And he died for all, that those who live should no longer live for themselves but for him who died for them and was raised again" (2 Cor. 5:15).

Event number three was *the coming of the Holy Spirit.* Jesus told the apostles to stay in Jerusalem until they had been "clothed with power from on high" (Luke 24:49), and on the day of Pentecost, that promise was fulfilled. In the power of the Spirit, Peter boldly preached the gospel and 3,000 people were saved. He performed miracles of healing, he exposed the works of the Devil, he confronted his opponents and shut their mouths, and he brought great glory to the name of Jesus. He gave direction to the church and strengthened the saints when persecution began. He was a different man.

We, too, can become different people. God never gives up on us even though we may decide to give up on ourselves. The moment you were born again, Jesus said, "You are — you shall be!" We are nothing but lumps of clay, but Jesus can turn us into rocks.

The eminent Greek scholar A. T. Robertson wrote about Peter: "It was slow in coming, but when the fruit was ripe, it was rich and gracious. He was a man worth the making and Jesus knew it. He loved Peter from the start, and to the end."[2]

Don't wait for the crowing of the cock, but start right now to claim Peter's "life sentence": "The LORD will perfect that which concerns me."

---

2. A. T. Robertson, *Epochs in the Life of Peter* (Grand Rapids, Mich.: Baker, 1974), 3.

53

THE APOSTLE JOHN

The disciple whom Jesus loved.

JOHN 13:23

John wrote his gospel to demonstrate that Jesus Christ is the Son of God. He wanted people to read the facts, put their faith in Jesus, and receive the free gift of eternal life (20:30–31). John's name never appears in the book, but we know that he was a dependable eyewitness of what he recorded (John 21:24).

John was one of the two unnamed disciples who left John the Baptist to follow Jesus. The other one, Andrew, brought Simon to Jesus, and John brought his brother, James (John 1:35–42). Usually in his gospel, when John referred to himself, he used the phrase "the disciple whom Jesus loved" (John 13:23; 19:26; 20:2; 21:7, 20). The word *love* is used only six times in the first twelve chapters of John, but in the Lord's upper room discourse and prayer, recorded only by John (John 13–17), it is used thirty-one times.

John teaches us four important truths about Christian love.

JESUS LOVES US

John 3:16 informs us that God loves the world, but John's special name tells us that He also loves individuals. His love is personal (John 11:5). Jesus had many followers but only twelve disciples whom He called apostles ("sent ones"). Within this band of apostles He had an inner circle made up of Peter, James, and John, and within that "inner circle," John was "the disciple whom Jesus loved."

John didn't write, "the *only* disciple whom Jesus loved," because that would have been untrue. "Having loved his own who were in the world, he loved them to the end" (John 13:1 TNIV). Jesus loved all of His apostles even as the Father loved Him (John 17:23), so John wasn't enjoying an exclusive privilege. Nor did John write, "the disciple who loved Jesus," as though nobody else in the group loved Jesus. That would have been sheer arrogance. John did love Jesus, but so did Peter (John 21:15–19) and all the other apostles except Judas.

The Lord has every right to express His love to His children in whatever ways will please and glorify Him the most. Only two of the apostles—Matthew and John—were chosen to write accounts of the Lord's life and ministry, and only Peter and John wrote epistles to be included in the New Testament. Does this mean the other men had nothing to say or were unworthy of the privilege? Of course not! God is sovereign and has every right to distribute His gifts and blessings as He pleases. He manifests His love personally and individually, and no believer should be envious of what God gives to others (Matt. 20:1–16).

It is possible that John was the youngest of the apostles and that Jesus felt a special love and concern for him. John was the poet and mystic of the group, the one whose writings would especially probe the intimate mysteries of the Christian life, and Jesus was preparing him for this ministry. If Paul is the apostle of faith and Peter is the apostle of hope, then John stands as the apostle of love, a love he learned from his Master. Jesus gave John a special place at the table at the Last Supper, and there John leaned on the bosom of his Lord. At the cross, Jesus gave him the precious gift of His mother, Mary.

Jesus doesn't have "favorites," but He does have intimates. There are some people whom He has drawn close to His own heart and with whom He has shared a special love. God cared for all His prophets, but Daniel was "greatly beloved" (Dan. 9:23; 10:11, 19 KJV), or as the New International Version translates it, "highly esteemed." (The official Jewish translation is "precious man.") But this intimate love was balanced by difficulties and trials, and both Daniel and John knew what it meant to suffer for their Lord. The closer we come to His heart, the more the world will treat us as it treated Him.

No matter what privileges Jesus gives to others, we who trust Him can all say with Paul, "I live by faith in the Son of God, who loved me and gave himself for me" (Gal. 2:20).

WE SHOULD LOVE JESUS

"We love because he first loved us," wrote the apostle John (1 John 4:19). Jesus shared His love with John, and John received it and grew in his love for Christ. The impulse to love must come from the Lord, and we must be careful to recognize it and yield to it. We don't manufacture love by trying to work up holy feelings. "God has poured out his love into our hearts by the Holy Spirit whom he has given us" (Rom. 5:5). The Holy Spirit loves Jesus and wants to glorify Him in and through our lives. But how do we go about growing in our love for Jesus? Here is what John heard Jesus say in the upper room, and he recorded it for our learning: "If you love me, keep my commands.... Anyone who loves me will obey my teaching. My Father will love them, and we will come to them and make our home with them" (John 14:15, 23 TNIV).

To keep His commands, we must know what they are, and this means taking time daily to hear His voice in the Word. "Oh, how I love your law! I meditate on it all day long" (Ps. 119:97). The way we treat the Bible is the way we treat Jesus. To know Him in His Word is to love Him, and to love Him is to obey Him. To obey Him prepares us to receive even more of His truth and love and to go deeper into that love. This quiet intimacy with Jesus can accomplish much more in our hearts than the noisy "religious gymnastics" that take place in some so-called praise services.

But how can we tell if we truly love Jesus? John's own example helps us answer that question. When we love Jesus, *we want to be with Him and near Him* (John 13:22–23). Of course, we today can't have physical contact with the Lord as John did, but James 4:8 admonishes us, "Come near to God and he will come near to you." A. W. Tozer reminds us that, in the spiritual realm, "nearness is likeness." Godliness is God-likeness, and people become like the god they worship (Ps. 115:1–8). If we sincerely worship the true and living God, we will become like Him.

We will also, like John, *learn His secrets* (see, e.g., John 13:21–27). "The LORD confides in those who fear him; he makes his covenant known to them" (Ps. 25:14). John knew what was happening because he was close enough to Jesus to hear His voice. "He who has ears to hear, let him hear" (Mark 4:9).

Loving Jesus will mean *identifying with Him in His suffering and shame*, for John was the only apostle who stood by the cross (John 19:26). He was also the first apostle to visit the empty tomb (John 20:1–9), because *love longs to see the living Christ*. Love isn't afraid to run when the goal is Jesus. And real love *recognizes Jesus*, no matter what the circumstances (John 21:7). When Jesus calls, *love will always follow Him* (John 21:20), and the person who truly loves Christ will *bear witness of Him to others* (John 21:24).

Loving Christ makes a difference in our lives!

WE SHOULD LOVE OTHER BELIEVERS

James and John received the nickname Boanerges from Jesus; it means "Sons of Thunder" (Mark 3:17). The nickname suggests that the two brothers knew how to get angry and stir up a storm. One day they saw a man whom they didn't know casting out demons in the name of Jesus, and they told him to stop. "He is not one of us," John explained to Jesus (Luke 9:49–50). Of course, Jesus rebuked them for their arrogant and exclusive attitude, which meant they should stop playing God in other people's lives. The two brothers needed to learn to love other followers of Jesus, regardless of their association. God has His loyal servants in many places, and we should encourage them.

Using their mother, Salome, as their spokesperson, James and John caused a storm among the disciples when they asked for two special thrones in the promised kingdom (Matt. 20:20–28). Whether the other ten apostles were angry at the selfish nature of the request or the fact that they hadn't thought of it first, we aren't sure; but they certainly were indignant. James and John wanted thrones, but they had forgotten to obey the royal law found in Scripture, "Love your neighbor as yourself" (James 2:8). Living in love is greater than reigning from a throne.

"What causes fights and quarrels among you? Don't they come from your desires that battle within you?" asks James 4:1. We are at war with each other because we are at war with ourselves, flesh warring against the Spirit; and we are at war with ourselves because we are at war with God. God loves us, and if we love Him, we will love one another.

John did learn this important lesson of love, because ten times in his writings he reminds us that Jesus commanded us to "love one another" (John 13:34–35; 15:12, 17; 1 John 3:11, 23; 4:7, 11, 12; 2 John 5). Tradition tells us that when John was a very old man, he would be carried to the church meetings in Ephesus and say to the congregation, "Little children, love one another."

I am impressed with the number of ministries John and Peter had together in spite of the differences in their personalities, Peter the impetuous and John the insignificant. But they loved Jesus, loved each other, and loved the lost, and this united them.

They were probably the two disciples Jesus appointed to secure the animals for Jesus' triumphal entry into Jerusalem (Mark 11:1), and they were appointed to prepare the Passover feast for the Lord (Luke 22:8). Together they witnessed the first part of Jesus' trial (John 18:15–16), and together they ran to the tomb on Easter morning (John 20:1–9). They ate together with Jesus after His resurrection, and when Jesus restored Peter to apostleship, John followed them (John 21). John and Peter went together to the temple to pray, healed a crippled beggar on the way, and ended up in jail together. They were tried together, and together they gave witness of the resurrection of Christ (Acts 3–4). After Philip the evangelist took the gospel to the Samaritans, the church in Jerusalem sent Peter and John to minister to the new converts, and Peter and John preached in the Samaritan villages on their way back to Jerusalem (Acts 8:1–25). No fire from heaven this time!

WE SHOULD LOVE THE LOST

Jesus was journeying to Jerusalem and wanted to spend the night in a Samaritan village, but the Samaritans refused to welcome Him. Going to Jerusalem indeed! To a Samaritan, the only acceptable place of worship was on Mount Gerizim in Samaria (John 4:19–24). James and John became very angry and asked Jesus for permission to call down fire from heaven to burn up the village. The brothers had recently been with the prophet Elijah on the Mount of Transfiguration and felt capable of performing such a feat (Luke 9:28–36, 51–55). Jesus rebuked them, and rightly so; for what does our Lord's message of love have to do with burning up the people who disagree with us?

There are times when the unsaved irritate us and even make us angry, and we would like to call down fire from heaven, but that is not the way Jesus runs His kingdom. Years ago in Omaha, Nebraska, the Omaha Gospel Tabernacle was a vibrant center for evangelism and missions. The pastor, R. R. Brown, when he was a student, had asked A. B. Simpson, founder of the Christian and Missionary Alliance, "What are the qualifications of a soul winner?" Simpson replied, "To be a great soul winner, you must first be a great lover." Brown took that lesson to heart and built a church with compassion for the lost at home and around the world.

When lost sinners act like sinners and we get upset, let's respond by acting like Christians and showing them love. When believers in the church family irritate us, let's imagine the apostle John at the pulpit saying, "Little children, love one another." Most of all, let's focus on our wonderful Lord and let the Spirit fill us with His love. "By this all men will know that you are my disciples, if you love one another" (John 13:35).

54

JUDAS ISCARIOT

"Why this waste?"

MATTHEW 26:8

In the four Gospels, more is written about Simon Peter than about any of the rest of the twelve apostles, but the runner-up is Judas. Peter's name is always at the top of the list, but the name of Judas is always at the end.

Jesus called Judas "the one doomed to destruction" (John 17:12), which is translated "the son of perdition" in the King James Version and New King James Version. The word translated "perdition" or "destruction" is translated "waste" in John 6:12. Judas was the "son of waste." When Mary of Bethany anointed Jesus, Judas was likely the first to ask, "Why this waste?" Then the rest of the apostles took up the attack.

After you review the life and death of Judas, you may want to ask, "Why this waste?" He cheapened and destroyed just about everything the Lord gave him.

CHEAPENING A GOOD NAME

Millions of baby boys have been named Simon, Peter, Thomas, Andrew, James, John, Matthew, or Philip, but it is doubtful that any parent would name a son Judas. In the New Testament there are six men named Judas, including another apostle (Matt. 10:3) and a brother of Jesus (Matt. 13:55). The name comes from "Judah," the fourth son of Jacob by Leah, and it means "praise" (Gen. 29:35). It is a fine name with a significant meaning, but one of our Lord's apostles came along and cheapened it. "The raw material of a devil is an angel bereft of holiness," said Charles Spurgeon. "You cannot make a Judas except out of an apostle."

Some people are "toxic." No matter where they go, they incite disagreement and division, and no matter what they do, they cause trouble. Judas belonged to that group. Every precious thing that Judas received from the Lord, he cheapened and wasted, including his own life. "The memory of the righteous will be a blessing, but the name of the wicked will rot" (Prov. 10:7). Judas's name has rotted.

CHEAPENING AN OFFICE AND MINISTRY

When Jesus called twelve of His disciples to become His apostles and serve with Him (Mark 3:13–19), He included Judas. This means that Judas had been

+ WASTED HIS LIFE

baptized by John the Baptist (Acts 1:15–26) and had made some kind of profession of faith. However, his baptism and call are no guarantee that he was a believer. Jesus chose Judas to be an apostle, but Judas was never "chosen" in the evangelical sense and given by the Father to the Son (John 13:18; 6:66–71; 17:6–12). He had not been washed (John 13:10–11), and Jesus knew from the beginning that Judas would betray Him (John 6:64).

Eleven of the apostles were from Galilee; Judas was the only apostle to come from Judea. "Iscariot" means "man of Kerioth," a town in the south of Judea (Josh. 15:25). Is this geographical data significant? Perhaps. Most of the people in Judea looked down on the citizens of Galilee and considered them rude "peasants." Their accent gave them away (Matt. 26:73; Acts 2:7) and they lacked the refinement claimed by the Judeans. When Philip told Nathanael that the Messiah was Jesus of Nazareth, Nathanael replied, "Nazareth! Can anything good come from there?" (John 1:46). When the apostles argued about who was the greatest among them, it is possible that Judas used his citizenship to bolster his own case.

Another consideration is that the Romans weren't as strict on the people of Galilee as they were on those in Judea. Herod Antipas gave the Galileans privileges that the Judeans never enjoyed. The people of Judea may have been somewhat envious of the Galileans and desirous of seeing some of the harsh Roman policies changed. Even Pilate in Jerusalem had slain some Galileans who were worshiping at the temple (Luke 13:1–5). A fervent Jewish nationalism was thriving in Judea, and Judas may have been sympathetic with it. Perhaps he thought that Jesus would overthrow Rome and establish the Jewish kingdom. Even after the resurrection, the disciples had the same dream (Acts 1:6–9). In short, Judas may have followed Jesus from motives that were political and national rather than spiritual, and when Jesus rejected the crown (John 6:14–15), Judas began to change his ideas.

Being from Judea and serving as the treasurer of the disciple band, Judas may have expected special treatment from Jesus. How did Judas respond when Jesus went off with Peter, James, and John and left the others behind, or when He did a special miracle just for Peter? Perhaps it was Judas who ignited the arguments about who among them was the greatest.

But we must keep in mind that Judas did minister in the name and power of Jesus Christ just like the other apostles (Matt. 10; Mark 3:13–19). Had he not preached and performed miracles, the other men would have suspected he was a fraud. As it was, they were shocked when they learned he was a counterfeit. The fact that Jesus made him the treasurer of the group indicated that He had confidence in him. We wonder how Judas responded to some of the statements Jesus made about money and honesty, such as Matthew 7:15–23 and Luke 16:19–31. Judas cheapened the significance of what it meant to be an apostle of Jesus Christ.

Judas's suicide was no secret, and the word surely got out that he had cooperated with the Jewish leaders in the arrest of Jesus. This kind of news didn't make it easier for the apostles to minister the truth in the days that followed. How did the public know that the apostles could be trusted if one of their own number was a fraud? False ministers are still with us (2 Cor. 11:13, 26), and Satan is still at work.

CHEAPENING A PRECIOUS GIFT

Mary of Bethany had sat at Jesus' feet, listened to His Word, and understood that her Lord would be arrested and crucified. Therefore, she purchased some expensive perfume and anointed His body for burial (John 12:1–8). It was a beautiful act of worship that Jesus accepted, and when Judas started criticizing her and the other men joined in, Jesus came to her defense. His rebuke of Judas and the other disciples must have cut them deeply. How often those who criticize others the most are themselves guilty of hidden sins that are far worse. They think they can make themselves look better by making others look worse. Judas wanted the money, but he didn't get it.

Had Judas taken this rebuke seriously, it could have saved his life. Instead, he sought revenge and went to the Jewish leaders to negotiate a price for turning Jesus over to them (Matt. 26:1–16). "What will you give me?" suggests that the love of money was also a factor in Judas's betrayal of Jesus. The leaders wanted to arrest Jesus but were afraid it would cause a riot during Passover, so Judas solved their problem for only thirty pieces of silver. The fact that Judas went from the feast in Bethany straight to the chief priests indicates that he was smarting from the rebuke Jesus gave him.

Hardly a man or woman has ever given his or her best to Jesus without being criticized by somebody. This includes Moses, Samuel, David, the prophets and apostles, and believers in every century. Secret sinners like Judas turn a beautiful worship service into an ugly argument, but the Lord always defends His own, if not on earth, certainly at the judgment seat of Christ.

CHEAPENING A HOLY OCCASION

Passover was a high and holy season for the Jews, and this particular Passover was especially important to Jesus. As the men entered the upper room, Jesus gave each one a kiss of peace, and this included Judas. He told them, "I have eagerly desired to eat this Passover with you before I suffer" (Luke 22:14). They reclined at the table, with Judas in the place of honor at His left, and John at His right. The disciples had been arguing over who was the greatest, so Jesus got up and washed their feet and ended the argument.

While they were eating, Jesus announced that there was a traitor in their midst, but He didn't identify him. He honored Judas by giving him the bread dipped into the dish, so surely Judas now realized that the Master knew his heart. Jesus sent him on his way with, "What you are about to do, do quickly" (John 13:27). The authorities must arrest Him in time for His death on the cross as the Lamb of God. Once Judas was gone, Jesus instituted the Lord's Supper and then taught His disciples.

Judas brought Satan into the upper room (John 13:2, 27). Judas participated in the Passover and defiled it. His heart didn't respond to the Lord's kiss, to the place of honor at the table, or to the washing of his feet. "You are clean," said Jesus to the men, "though not every one of you" (John 13:10). Did Judas get the message? When Jesus announced there was a traitor at the table and handed Judas the bread, Judas wasn't moved. This was the climax of his deceit and treachery. Judas was disappointed when Jesus refused the crown (John 6:14–15), and he was openly critical when Mary anointed the Lord (John 12:1–8). But now Judas had reached his hour of decision, and he chose the wrong road.

CHEAPENING A TOKEN OF LOVE

When Judas betrayed the Lord, he identified Him to the soldiers by kissing Him fervently (Matt. 26:48–49; Mark 14:44–45; Luke 22:47–48). A kiss should be an expression of true affection and loyalty, but Judas turned it into a tool of deception and treachery. Jesus had kissed Judas and the other disciples when they arrived in the upper room for the Passover feast, and His kiss was sincere. In a few hours, He would back up that kiss by dying for them on the cross. "Wounds from a friend can be trusted, but an enemy multiplies kisses" (Prov. 27:6).

At least five times in the New Testament epistles we find the admonition, "Greet one another with a holy kiss" (Rom. 16:16; 1 Cor. 16:20; 2 Cor. 13:12; 1 Thess. 5:26; 1 Peter 5:14). Of course, the men kissed the men and the women kissed the women. J. B. Phillips in his paraphrase of the New Testament renders it, "Shake hands all around," and Eugene Peterson in *The Message* uses "holy embraces all around." Whether kissing, shaking hands, or embracing, the meaning is clear: express to one another a love that is sincere and devoted. A *holy* kiss (or handshake or hug) cannot be hypocritical.

CHEAPENING LIFE ITSELF

When in the upper room Jesus announced that a traitor was present, He quoted Psalm 41:9: "He who shares my bread has lifted up his heel against me" (John 13:18). When David wrote those words, he may have been referring to his friend and trusted counselor Ahithophel, who gave his support to Absalom in the great rebellion (2 Sam. 15–17). Judas, like Ahithophel, pretended to be loyal to Jesus but then went to work for the officials who wanted to kill Jesus. When Ahithophel learned that Absalom wasn't following his advice, he went home and hanged himself.

When Judas realized that he had betrayed the Son of God, he returned to the chief priests, threw the silver coins into the temple, and confessed that he was guilty of betraying innocent blood. His attitude was that of regret and remorse, not repentance (Matt. 27:3–10). Then, like Ahithophel, he went out and hanged himself on the piece of property he had purchased with money stolen from the treasury Jesus entrusted to him. Jesus left behind an empty tomb; Judas left behind a cemetery. "But woe to that man who betrays the Son of Man!" said Jesus. "It would be better for him if he had not been born" (Matt. 26:24).

Satan is a liar and a murderer (John 8:44) as well as a thief (John 10:10). Satan controlled Judas's life, so Judas ended up a liar, a thief, and a murderer—only he murdered himself. To use Paul's term, Judas "[gave] the devil a foothold" (Eph. 4:27). Read Ephesians 4:25–32 and note the sins Paul warns us about. You will see that Judas committed many of them—lying, stealing, and bitterness, for example. Satan the murderer influenced Judas to kill himself. For both of them, life was cheap, so why go on living? "What good is it for a man to gain the whole world, yet forfeit his soul?" (Mark 8:36).

Judas had many opportunities to hear Jesus teach and preach, see Him perform miracles, and witness Him pleading with sinners to trust Him, yet he hardened his heart and rejected the Savior. Judas even preached sermons and performed miracles, yet he never opened his heart to Jesus Christ. How many people today are religious but lost, even serving other people, yet totally without faith in Jesus Christ. I wonder how Judas responded when he heard Jesus say, "Walk while you have the light, before darkness overtakes you" (John 12:35).

"As soon as Judas had taken the bread, he went out. And it was night" (John 13:30). In spite of the brightness of the Passover moon, the darkness had overtaken him—forever.

John Bunyan may have had Judas in mind when he wrote at the conclusion of *The Pilgrim's Progress*, "Then I saw that there was a way to hell, even from the gates of heaven ..."

55

SALOME,
THE WIFE OF ZEBEDEE

"It is more blessed to give than to receive."

ACTS 20:35

*T*he only thing many people remember about Salome is that she asked Jesus to give her two sons the thrones on either side of His throne when He established His kingdom (Matt. 20:20–28). If that's all you know about her, then you have been deprived of a blessing, because Salome is one of the truly great women in the gospel records. Her name is derived from the familiar Hebrew word *shalom*, which means "peace, well-being." Let's open the family album and study three snapshots that, if we understand them, will help us pray better and serve Jesus better.

SACRIFICE AND SERVICE

Zebedee, the fisherman, his wife, Salome, and their two sons, James and John, all served Jesus faithfully. The two boys were apostles, and Salome was one of the women who ministered to Jesus and the Twelve as they ministered from place to place (Mark 15:40–41; Luke 8:1–3). Zebedee stayed home and sold fish to provide for the needs of his wife, the apostles, and Jesus. I have heard people criticize Zebedee for staying home and not following Jesus, but his work at home helped sustain the work in other places. Matthew calls Salome "the mother of Zebedee's sons" (Matt. 20:20; 27:56), and only Mark uses her given name (Mark 15:40; 16:1).

"If you want something said, ask a man," wrote British prime minister Margaret Thatcher. "If you want something done, ask a woman." As they moved from place to place, Jesus and His apostles needed things done that could best be done by the women. Jesus didn't supply His physical needs by performing miracles, as Satan urged Him to do (Matt. 4:1–4), but trusted the Father to provide through His people. Salome and her friends were faithful to serve Jesus and to meet His needs.

Salome was sister to Mary, the mother of Jesus, which means that, from the human standpoint, James and John were cousins to Jesus. Perhaps Salome was taking advantage of this special relationship when she asked Jesus to give thrones to her two sons when His kingdom was established. After all, He had promised to give thrones to all His apostles (Matt. 19:28), so why not give the best thrones — those nearest to His — to His own cousins?

Zebedee, Salome, James, and John were all involved in serving Jesus, and that is the way every Christian family ought to be. Zebedee made a sacrifice when he permitted his wife to minister to Jesus and the apostles, and Salome paid a price as she occasionally left her home to travel with the Master. John Henry Jowett said that ministry that costs nothing accomplishes nothing, and their ministry was costly. Paul had the same conviction when he wrote about "the sacrifice and service coming from your faith" (Phil. 2:17).

God bless those parents who sacrifice for the Lord and serve Him and who teach their children to follow their example!

REQUEST AND REBUKE

As they planned this event, James and John and their mother seem to have forgotten the words of Jesus from the "ordination address" He gave after He selected His apostles. We call it the Sermon on the Mount (Luke 6:12–49). They forgot that Christians receive by giving and reign by submitting. Our true wealth is spiritual and eternal. If we put God's rule and God's righteousness first, He will provide everything we need (Matt. 6:33). "It is more blessed to give than to receive" (Acts 20:35). To ask for special thrones was to move from servants to rulers, and Jesus had come as a servant. The "things" of this world that attract people so much are but "fringe benefits" to the sacrificing servants of the Lord. "The first duty of every soul is to find not its freedom but its Master," said P. T. Forsythe, and that means bowing at His throne, not asking for a throne.[1]

Some things about the prayer of Salome and her sons are commendable. To begin with, let's give them credit for believing the Lord's promise that each disciple would have a throne in the coming kingdom (Matt. 19:28). Jesus had told them He was going to die, so it took great faith to envision a kingdom in His future. Let's also commend them for bowing in humility before Jesus — at least outwardly — and in agreeing in their request (Matt. 18:19). God's people are supposed to humble themselves and pray (2 Chron. 7:14).

But their timing was off and their motive was selfish. According to the scholars who have harmonized the four Gospels, this event took place on the Monday of our Lord's final week of servant ministry. In four more days, He would be crucified. It wasn't really the best time to be asking for glory and power when Jesus was about to die in shame and weakness. When we pray, let's remember that our High Priest in heaven still has the Calvary wounds in His body. Do we want to bring Him cheap selfish prayers when He gave His all for us?

As well as being selfish, the mother and sons' motive was wrong. Salome

---

1. P. T. Forsythe, *Positive Preaching and the Modern Mind* (London: Independent Press, 1953), 28.

wanted to exalt herself and her two sons; she wasn't too concerned about exalting Jesus. She forgot the prayer Jesus taught the disciples to pray, recorded in Matthew 6:9–13. It opens with "hallowed be your name" and includes "your will be done on earth as it is in heaven." Lucifer tried to capture God's throne, was judged, and became Satan, the adversary of God (Isa. 14:12–15). Do we want to follow his example or the example of Jesus (Phil. 2:5–11)?

Jesus' cousins were praying in ignorance instead of according to the Word of God. "You don't know what you are asking," said Jesus (Matt. 20:22). It has well been said that prayer is not a device for getting man's will done in heaven, but God's will done on earth. No wonder the other disciples became indignant (Matt. 20:24). Selfish prayer always creates division and dissension (James 4:1–10). James points out that wrong praying is the result of yielding to the flesh (v. 4), imitating the world (v. 4), and obeying the Devil (v. 7)—the three great enemies of the believer. This explains why Jesus gave that short lesson about "the rulers of the Gentiles" (Matt. 20:24–28). The Romans were masters of exalting leaders and treating them like gods, but the Romans are not our examples.

The church today has too many celebrities and not enough servants. We pattern our leadership after that of the great corporations and our activities after those of Hollywood. Instead of opposing the world, the church tries to appease the world. No wonder Jesus rebuked Salome and her sons. He didn't want that kind of philosophy to infiltrate His church. He was successful with them, but the contemporary church doesn't seem to agree with Jesus. "Love not the world" (1 John 2:15 KJV) has been revised to read, "Look and live like the world."

CROSSES AND CROWNS

This fine mother and her two sons didn't know what they were asking for. They forgot that Jesus had told them several times that His earthly ministry would end on a Roman cross, for there are no crowns without crosses! Jesus was about to drink the bitter cup of sorrow and be baptized in the waters of suffering. "All your waves and breakers have swept over me" (Ps. 42:7). He would be made sin for us and bear the curse of the law. Then He would rise from the dead and return to His glorious throne in heaven. Matthew Henry said it well: "They know not what they ask, who ask for the end but overlook the means, and so put asunder what God has joined together."[2] First the suffering, then the glory; first the cross, then the throne.

James and John said they were able to drink the cup and endure the baptism, and their answer has always amazed me. They didn't realize what they were saying. James was the first of the apostles to give his life for Jesus (Acts 12:1–3), and John lived the longest of the apostles and was exiled on Patmos because of his faith. James got his crown at the cost of his life (Rev. 2:10), and John wrote the book of the Revelation, which contains the word *throne* forty-seven times.

---

2. Matthew Henry, Commentary on Matthew 20:22.

"It is more blessed to give than to receive." "Give and it will be given to you" (Luke 6:38). "Seek first his kingdom and his righteousness, and all these things will be given to you" (Matt. 6:33). This is the mathematics of spiritual ministry.

DEDICATION AND DEVOTION

Let's not leave Salome in this embarrassing situation, because things didn't stay that way. When Jesus was on the cross, Salome was there with several other women, including her sister, Mary, the mother of Jesus (Luke 23:49; John 19:25–27). John was also there, but not one of the other apostles. What were Salome and John thinking about as they saw Jesus hanging there? No doubt they were ashamed that they had asked Him for thrones, for nothing purifies one's motives and clarifies one's prayers like a vision of the cross of Jesus Christ.

> When I survey the wondrous cross,
> On which the Prince of glory died,
> My richest gain I count but loss,
> And pour contempt on all my pride.
> Forbid it, Lord, that I should boast
> Save in the death of Christ my God;
> All the vain things that charm me most,
> I sacrifice them to His blood.
>
> ISAAC WATTS

I have often wondered how Salome felt when Jesus gave His mother, Mary—her sister—into John's loving care. Standing there at the cross certainly helped Salome get a clearer perspective on prayer and the Christian life.

When we turn to the book of Acts, we don't find either Zebedee or Salome mentioned. But we are told that in that upper room meeting, 120 people were gathered for prayer, among them "the women and Mary the mother of Jesus, and ... his brothers" (Acts 1:14–15). It seems to me that if Mary was there as well as "the women" who traveled with Jesus (Luke 8:1–3), then Salome was also there. She was a woman of prayer, and she was praying with the believers in Jerusalem. The throne of grace was the only throne that interested her.

I further suggest that she was present on Pentecost, praising the Lord and praying for Peter as he delivered the Word (Acts 2). This means she was a part of that first church fellowship described in Acts 2:42–47, assisting the new believers and encouraging them in the faith.

When Salome's son James was martyred (Acts 12), nothing was said about Salome. Perhaps by then she and Zebedee had both died and therefore had the joy of welcoming their son to glory. If she was still living at his death, she probably prayed, "Thank You, Lord, for giving him his crown! Praise the Lord!"

Don't ask for a throne. Instead, live your life in the will of God so that you will deserve one.

56

THE SAMARITAN WOMAN

Above all else, guard your heart,
for it is the wellspring of life.

PROVERBS 4:23

This is the story of "the bad Samaritan," the woman who let one man after another stomp on her heart and harden the soil, leaving her miserable (John 4:1–42). She had been married five times and divorced five times and now had a live-in lover who was not her husband. She had not guarded her heart, and the consequences were difficult and painful. Then Jesus came on the scene and her life was changed. Let's consider the four different hearts involved in this scenario.

THE HEART OF JESUS

"Now [Jesus] had to go through Samaria" (John 4:4). The verb speaks of obligation and compulsion. There were two other routes between Judea and Galilee, either of which would have enabled Him to bypass Samaria. "For Jews do not associate with Samaritans" (John 4:9). But our Lord's choice of routes had nothing to do with geography or national prejudice. The route was chosen by the Father so that Jesus would meet a woman who needed to be saved. "I seek not to please myself," said Jesus, "but him who sent me" (John 5:30). That's the only way to travel.

An evangelist friend of mine was driving from the airport with the pastor of the church where he was to speak, and he noticed that the gas gauge was very close to "empty." As they drove along, he called this to the pastor's attention, but the man said, "Not yet." They left the city and were in the rural area and the gauge moved closer and closer to "empty." Then the pastor said, "We'll get gas here," and pulled into the most antiquated rundown gas station my friend had ever seen. The man who came out to pump the gas had a large cancerous growth on his face and was piteous to behold. But by the time the man had filled the tank, the pastor had witnessed to him and led him to faith in Christ. Then my friend knew why the pastor had waited so long: the Father was telling him where to buy the gas so he could win a soul who was very close to eternity.

The heart of Jesus is filled with love for people who are rejected by others. The people in that Samaritan town knew this woman and probably avoided her, but Jesus arrived just in time to meet her and chat with her about her greatest need. Jewish rabbis didn't talk with women in public, and no self-respecting man who knew her reputation would have spoken to this woman. But Jesus came "to seek and to save what was lost" (Luke 19:10), and that should be the burden of my heart and yours.

THE HEART OF THE SINNER

John wrote his gospel so that his readers would "believe that Jesus is the Christ, the Son of God, and ... by believing ... have life in his name" (John 20:31). As we read John 4, we see the woman gradually learning who Jesus is and then trusting Him for salvation. Water and the harvest are the two major metaphors in this passage, and the background for the harvest metaphor is our Lord's parable of the sower (Matt. 13:1–9, 18–23).

As Jesus opened the conversation, the woman had a *hard heart*. She saw Him only as "a Jew" and wondered that He would speak to her, a Samaritan (John 4:7–9). But Jesus kept speaking to her and offered her the living water that would satisfy her thirsty heart. Then she said He was "greater than Jacob" and asked for the water. Now she had the *shallow heart* that eagerly responds but is unprepared to receive the seed (John 4:10–15).

There is no conversion without conviction, so Jesus began to plow up the soil by telling her to call her husband. He revealed that He knew all about her and her sins, and she then considered Him a prophet (John 4:16–20). Now she had a *crowded heart*, evidenced by her trying to change the subject by discussing religion. Jesus answered her question with clarity and power, and she said she knew the Christ was coming. Jesus announced that He was the Christ, and she believed Him and was saved. Immediately she went to spread the good news in the town (John 4:21–30). Now she had the *fruitful heart* that gave evidence of her new birth. She began by calling Jesus "a Jew" and ended by confessing Him as "the Christ" and sharing this great truth with others.

No matter how hard the sinner's heart may be, if we are patient, the Lord can use our loving witness to change that heart and bring saving faith. We must trust the Spirit to plow up the soil, pull out the weeds, and prepare the heart to receive the life-giving seed of the Word of God. Once planted and nurtured, that seed imparts life and produces fruit to the glory of God.

THE HEARTS OF THE WORKERS

When the apostles returned with the food they had purchased, they were surprised that Jesus was conversing with the woman but were wise enough not to interfere (John 4:27, 31–38). After she left, the men urged Jesus to eat, and He responded with a brief lesson on what it means to do the Lord's work in the Lord's way.

Doing God's will is not punishment; it is nourishment. Witnessing and winning others to Christ nourishes the inner person. Jesus picked up the metaphor of the seed and the harvest and reminded the Twelve that there are many workers in the harvest field and each has his or her own appointed task. Some people plow up the soil, others sow the seed, others help to pull up the weeds, and still others reap the harvest. But each worker is a part of the "team" and will receive a reward. There is no competition in the harvest fields, and all the faithful laborers will rejoice together. It is possible that John the Baptist was one of the "others" who had ministered to this woman (see John 3:23 and 4:38).

The apostle Paul used this same metaphor to teach the same lesson in 1 Corinthians 3:6–9. No matter how gifted or famous the laborers are in the local church, they are all servants of God and it is God who gives the increase. One plants, another waters, another harvests, but it is "God, who makes things grow" (v. 7). He alone must receive the glory. "For we are God's fellow workers" (v. 9).

THE HEARTS OF THE SEEKERS

Boldly the woman returned to the town and bore witness of who Jesus was and what He had done for her (John 4:28–29), and the people went out to the well to meet this wonderful visitor. Many of the Samaritans put their faith in Jesus Christ, some because of the woman's testimony and many more because of what they heard Jesus Himself say. God gave a great harvest in a difficult place. Just about the time we expect nothing to happen, the Lord works in remarkable ways to open the hearts of the lost.

These Samaritans knew who Jesus was, and they trusted Him. They had the assurance of salvation because they heard the gospel for themselves. But one of the wonderful things about their conversion experience is that they saw the whole world as needing what they now possessed. They said that Jesus was "the Savior of the world" (John 4:42). Both the Jews and the Samaritans were quite clannish when it came to their religious faith, but they realized that they couldn't keep Jesus to themselves. He loves the world, He died for the sins of the world, and He commands us to make disciples in all the world.

The mathematics of ministry is interesting. One woman came to faith in Christ, and her witness helped to win a town. Peter led a beggar to faith in Christ, and because of the change in the man's life, many heard the gospel and two thousand were saved (Acts 3:1–4:4). Plant the seed by faith. It has a way of multiplying.

Before we leave this text, let's notice the lesson in geography. In John 2:23, Jesus was in Jerusalem but left for Judea (John 3:22). From Judea, He went to Samaria (John 4:4), and the chapter ends by declaring Jesus "the Savior of the world" (John 4:42). Jerusalem — Judea — Samaria — the world. It's the same geographical pattern that is found in Acts 1:8!

Jesus set the example and gave the commission. Now let's obey.

57

THE WOMAN TAKEN
IN ADULTERY

The Lord is my light and my salvation.

PSALM 27:1

How we respond to the account of the woman caught in adultery helps us better understand our own character. The secret sinner who dwells on such things longs for more details or supplies them from his or her own imagination. The legalist is disappointed that Jesus didn't recommend capital punishment. But the believer who has experienced the grace of God gives thanks that there is forgiveness with the Lord. We don't have to commit this particular sin to know how gracious and merciful the Lord is. "Then neither do I condemn you.... Go now and leave your life of sin" (John 8:11). If you have ever heard those words spoken to your own heart, then you will want others to hear them too. You want them to be able to say from their hearts, "The Lord is my light and my salvation."

The scribes and Pharisees had plotted the bringing of the woman to Jesus, hoping to trap Him. If He forgave the woman, then He broke the law of Moses and was in trouble with the Jews. If He condemned her to be stoned, then He was in trouble with the Romans who alone could execute condemned offenders. They must have planned the trap carefully; how could they have caught her "in the very act" unless they had been waiting for it to happen? But where was the man with whom she had sinned? The law required both parties to be judged (Lev. 20:10; Deut. 22:22).

Four different lights are shining in this passage, the most important one being Jesus Himself, the Light of the World.

THE LIGHT OF CREATION

It was daybreak, and Jesus was in the temple teaching the people. The scribes and Pharisees interrupted His ministry by thrusting the woman before Him and demanding an immediate answer. How rude can hypocritical religious leaders get?

Creation reveals that there is a God who is powerful enough to make the earth, wise enough to plan and sustain it, and good enough to use it for the benefit

THE WOMAN TAKEN IN ADULTERY — 273

of all who live. "For since the creation of the world God's invisible qualities—his eternal power and divine nature—have been clearly seen, being understood from what has been made, so that people are without excuse" (Rom. 1:20 TNIV).

But the God of creation, with all His wisdom, glory, and power, can never forgive people or rescue them from judgment unless He deals with sin. When Paul addressed the Greek intellectuals on Mars Hill, he began with creation but ended with the death and resurrection of Jesus Christ (Acts 17:27–32). The scientist can study creation and never meet the true and living God. The artist can admire it and the pantheist worship it, but creation itself offers no remedy for the guilty sinner.

THE LIGHT OF THE COMMANDMENTS

The accusers knew the law of God; they had spent their lives reading it, studying it, and discussing it. They could say, "Your word is a lamp to my feet and a light for my path" and "The unfolding of your words gives light" (Ps. 119:105, 130). They agreed with Solomon: "For these commands are a lamp, this teaching is a light" (Prov. 6:23). What nation had a greater law than Israel? And what nation had such wise teachers to interpret that law? The woman didn't stand a chance. "Moses commanded us ..."

If you ask the average person today, "What must we do to go to heaven?" the reply will probably be, "Why, keep the Ten Commandments." People who give that answer are ignorant of two important truths: (1) the Ten Commandments weren't given to save us, and (2) even if they were, nobody can keep the Ten Commandments. The only person ever to walk on this earth and perfectly obey the law of God was Jesus Christ, and of ourselves, we can't imitate Him.

The law of God is like a mirror that reveals our blemishes but can't remove them (James 1:23–25). (Did you ever use a mirror to wash your face?) "Therefore by the deeds of the law no flesh will be justified in His sight, for by the law is the knowledge of sin" (Rom. 3:20 NKJV).

Twice during this confrontation, Jesus stooped down and wrote on the ground with His finger. This should have reminded the accusers that the law was written "by the finger of God" (Ex. 31:18) and that they too would one day be judged. Perhaps some of them remembered Jeremiah 17:13, "Those who turn away from you will be written in the dust because they have forsaken the LORD." If your name isn't written in the Lamb's Book of Life, it is written in the dust and will disappear.

THE LIGHT OF CONSCIENCE

The fact that Jesus said nothing encouraged the religious leaders to press Him even further, because they were sure they had Him cornered. Then He stood up and said, "If any one of you is without sin, let him be the first to throw a stone at her" (John 8:7; see Deut. 22:22–24). He wasn't accusing them of being adulterers; He was simply reminding them that they were sinners and perhaps had occasionally committed this same sin in their hearts (Matt. 5:27–30).

Both the New International Version and the New American Standard Bible omit from verse 9 the phrase "being convicted by their own conscience," but it is found in many Greek manuscripts. Let's give these men credit for being honest with themselves and, we hope, with the Lord. Our Lord's words don't imply that every judge or juror must be perfect in order to try another person, but only that our motives for judging and condemning are right. Their motives were sinful; therefore they had no right to condemn her.

Conscience is not the law of God. Conscience is the window that lets in the light of God's law and helps us to know right from wrong. The word *conscience* is used more than thirty times in the New Testament and plays an important part in Paul's theology. If the "conscience window" gets dirty because of our deliberate disobedience, then the light within gets dimmer, and conscience no longer accuses us. Titus 1:15 calls this a "corrupted conscience." If we continue in sin, we end up with a "guilty conscience" (Heb.10:22) and the light within becomes darkness (Matt. 6:22–24). Cultivating "a good conscience" is a great blessing and a serious responsibility (Acts 23:1; 24:16).

Conscience could not help this woman. It could accuse but never forgive or wash away sin.

THE LIGHT OF JESUS CHRIST

Ultimately, sinners must be left alone with Jesus Christ, the Light of the World, for He is their only hope. The sun, the light of our visible world, was just coming up as these events took place. Jesus is to believers what the sun is to our universe — the center of our universe and the source of life and light for all that lives. God gave a pillar of fire to give light to Israel, but He gave Jesus Christ to bring life to all who believe. He is the light of the world, and His gift of salvation is available for all. He came to save the world, not to condemn it (John 3:16–21). To reject Him is to walk in darkness; to follow Him is to enjoy the light of life.

It must have thrilled the woman's heart to hear Jesus say, "Then neither do I condemn you" (John 8:11). Our assurance of forgiveness isn't in our feelings or the words of some religious leader, but in the Word of the Lord. But God's forgiveness brings with it the obligation to seek to obey the Lord and follow Him. We aren't saved by our obedience, but our obedience proves that we have been saved. The New International Version gives the impression in verse 11 that the woman had lived "a life of sin," but the Greek text simply reads, "Go, from now no longer sin." Whatever her past life had been, she was now forgiven. God said, "Their sins and lawless acts I will remember no more" (Heb. 10:17).

Blessed are those whose transgressions are forgiven,
whose sins are covered.
Psalm 32:1 TNIV

58

MARY AND MARTHA
OF BETHANY

And now these three remain: faith, hope and love.

1 CORINTHIANS 13:13

ethany is a tiny village less than two miles from Jerusalem. Few people would pay much attention to it except that Jesus visited Bethany as the guest of Mary and Martha and their brother, Lazarus, whom Jesus had raised from the dead (John 11). Jesus had a special relationship with these believers, for John 11:5 informs us that "Jesus loved Martha and her sister and Lazarus." When you read through the four Gospels, you will make three visits to Bethany. You will hear nothing from Lazarus, but the action and interaction of the two sisters will prove to be interesting and instructive. In spite of their differences and weaknesses, Martha and Mary illustrate the three great Christian virtues of faith, hope, and love, virtues that ought to be present in every Christian life, ministry, and home.

FAITH—LISTENING TO HIS WORD (Luke 10:38–42)

Imagine preparing dinner for Jesus and His disciples—thirteen men! Apparently they had arrived early in Bethany, because Martha wasn't quite ready for them, and this helped to create tension between the two sisters. Mary had been helping her sister[1] before Jesus arrived, but then she went to sit at the feet of Jesus to listen to Him teach. As Martha continued to prepare the meal, she became more and more irritated until finally she burst into the room, interrupted the lesson, and criticized both Jesus and Mary.

This embarrassing scene certainly reveals the personality differences of the two sisters. Martha was the active one who spoke up readily, while Mary was the quiet, meditative listener. They were female versions of Peter and John. The Lord loves and uses all kinds of people, so there is no reason why the vocal activists

---

1. The word "also" is in the Greek text of Luke 10:39 but is omitted from most English translations. One will find it in the New King James Version and the American Standard Version of 1901. "Mary had already rendered service and taken her part in the work, then sat at His feet," wrote G. Campbell Morgan. "She left the work too soon to please Martha." [Morgan, *Great Physician*, 234].

and the quiet contemplatives can't accept each other and work together. Moreover, they need each other. God's family is composed of a variety of people with different gifts and personalities, but there is one Lord who empowers and blesses them all.

Martha's problem wasn't that Mary had deserted her or that Jesus had taken Mary from her proper work. Martha's problem was that she was being pulled apart by her many tasks because she wasn't functioning by faith. She didn't believe that Jesus really cared. The wording of Martha's question in Luke 10:40 indicates that she expected a negative answer — "You don't care, do you?" Martha was distracted and divided as a result of unbelief. It wasn't a personality problem ("Well, that's just the way I am!"); it was a spiritual problem. She didn't believe that Jesus really cared, and this made her anxious and troubled. The disciples had committed a similar sin when they were on the stormy sea, and Jesus asked them, "Where is your faith?" (Luke 8:22–25). As we grow in the Word, we grow in faith (Rom. 10:17).

Life is molded by the choices we make. Martha had made a good choice in deciding to prepare a meal. Jesus said that Mary had made a better choice by sitting at His feet and listening to His words. The spiritual food would last much longer! But the best choice of all would be to combine the two, to be both a worshiper and a worker, and to do our work empowered by the strength found in the Word of God. Had Martha taken time to fellowship with the Lord, she would have stopped feeling sorry for herself and being critical of Mary and Jesus, and she would have been at peace (Matt. 11:20–28). Like King David, all of us need devoted hearts and skillful hands (Ps. 78:72).

There is always time for the will of God and strength for the work of God. The late Alan Redpath used to remind us, "Beware of the barrenness of a busy life."

HOPE — RESTING ON HIS PROMISES (John 11)

When their brother, Lazarus, became ill, Martha and Mary sent word to Jesus, "Lord, the one you love is sick" (John 11:3). They didn't tell Him what to do; they simply shared their burden with Him. Whatever differences they may have had in the past, the sisters were now united in their concern for their brother and their confidence in Christ. Jesus sent them a message that the sickness would not end in death but in the glorification of the Son of God.

It would have taken the messenger one day to travel from Bethany to where Jesus was, and another day for him to return to Bethany with Jesus's message. After the messenger left, Jesus waited two more days and then spent one day traveling to Bethany. When He arrived, He learned that Lazarus had been in the tomb four days. This means that Lazarus had died the very day the messenger arrived back in Bethany with Christ's message of hope: "This sickness will not end in death." But Lazarus died! "This will bring glory to God." But Lazarus is dead! Jesus reminded the sisters that He had sent this message and that it would prove true (John 11:40).

Martha and Mary had almost lost their hope. Why didn't Jesus come immediately? Why did He allow their brother to die? Why didn't He speak the word of power right where He was and heal their brother? Both of them said to Jesus, "Lord, if—" (John 11:21, 32), and that kind of speech only makes matters worse. We can say "Lord" and trust Him, or we can say "if" and doubt Him and second-guess Him, but we shouldn't put the two together.

Our hope is in the Lord, not in circumstances ("Things are looking better") or feelings. His purpose is always God's glory, and His schedule is never wrong. When Jesus came for dinner in Luke 10:38–41, He arrived early; but this time He deliberately delayed. In that first experience, there was the delicious odor of food, but now there was the noxious odor of death. Our circumstances change. We are comfortable with uniformity, but no two experiences with Jesus are the same. Nevertheless, "Jesus Christ is the same yesterday and today and forever" (Heb. 13:8). Martha's theology was correct, that her brother would be raised from the dead in the last day (John 11:24), but why postpone the blessing? Jesus *is* the resurrection and the life (John 11:25)! The presence of Jesus is the presence of power and victory over every enemy, including death. Jesus raised Lazarus from the dead, and as a result, many of the friends of Mary and Martha put their faith in Him (John 11:45). This was our Lord's last and greatest public miracle.

Because Mary sat at Jesus' feet and listened to His Word, she and her sister could come to His feet and lay their burdens before Him (John 11:32). Nothing is hopeless to the Christian who knows how to come to the feet of Jesus and rest on His promises. Jesus may delay His answer, but His delays are not denials. The situation may look hopeless, but Jesus Christ *is* our hope (1 Tim. 1:1)! All Martha and Mary had to do was rest in the promise that Jesus sent them by the messenger and all would be well.

LOVE—GIVE HIM YOUR VERY BEST (John 12:1–8)

Mark 14:3 tells us that this event took place in the house of Simon the leper, and this raises some puzzling questions. Who was Simon the leper, and was he still alive? He must have been delivered from his leprosy and the house cleansed or no orthodox Jew would have entered the house. Did Jesus heal him, and is that why the house bore that name? Why would Martha cook a meal in somebody else's house when her own house wasn't far away? Perhaps Martha, Mary, and Lazarus had purchased this house after Simon died and the name stayed with it. Well, we can make conjectures and get nowhere, so let's just accept the biblical account and learn from it.

Mary had sat at our Lord's feet and learned from Him, so she knew that Jesus would die, be buried, and then rise again. She decided to anoint Him in preparation for the event. The other women would come early to the tomb to prepare the body, but they would find the tomb empty. Mary knew better and didn't make the trip. It would have cost the annual wage of a laborer to purchase this ointment, but love doesn't count the cost. She could have used the precious ointment on her brother's body, but she saved her best for Jesus.

In Luke 10 we had the odor of food, and in John 11 we had the odor of death, but here we have the glorious fragrance of precious ointment filling the house. Every home has a fragrance, depending on how the people treat Jesus. When I was in pastoral ministry, I often visited homes where it was obvious that "something smelled," and sure enough, later the truth came out. But I also visited many homes where the fragrance of Jesus permeated the place (2 Cor. 2:14–17). That's what we want for our homes.

In Luke 10, we heard Martha criticizing Jesus and Mary as she bustled about fixing the meal. But here in John 12, Martha is serving as large a crowd and making no complaint at all. Her experience with her sister in John 11 strengthened their love for each other and deepened their love for Jesus. Martha learned to go to the feet of Jesus and let Him help her. Her brother was alive, and Jesus did it!

Martha had criticized Mary in Luke 10, but here in John 12, it is Judas and the other disciples who criticize her. In every fellowship, there is usually at least one counterfeit like Judas who attacks dedicated people for selfish reasons. I have learned that malicious critics in churches are usually covering something up, and if you wait long enough, the truth will come out. The Lord defended Mary (Rom. 8:33–34) and announced that the report of what she had done to Jesus would be taken around the world (Mark 14:9). See how the blessing spreads: in Luke 10, Mary was a blessing to Jesus, in John 11 to her friends, and now to the whole world!

Mary expressed her love for Jesus openly and generously. The Judases of this world criticize those who love Christ and give their best at His feet, but that shouldn't stop us from doing it. Mary and Martha were both serving Jesus and giving their best, and they were at peace with one another and were blessing the world. Where is Judas?

Are we showing hospitality to Jesus, listening to His Word, and sharing our burdens and our best gifts with Him? "And I pray that Christ will be more and more at home in your hearts as you trust in him" (Eph. 3:17 NLT). Another translation is "that Christ may settle down and feel at home in your hearts." How the Lord must rejoice when we love one another, meditate on the Word, serve Him, share our burdens with Him, and give Him the best that we have!

The way we treat others, especially those in need, is the way we treat Jesus. "Lord, when did we see you hungry and feed you, or thirsty and give you something to drink?" the righteous will ask at the judgment. Jesus will reply, "I tell you the truth, whatever you did for one of the least of these brothers of mine, you did for me" (Matt. 25:37, 40). Hospitality to the needy is hospitality to Jesus, and He won't forget it.

59

JOSEPH,
CALLED BARNABAS

He was a good man, full of the Holy Spirit and faith.

ACTS 11:24

*B*ehind many outstanding men and women in history are individuals I call "hinge people." These are persons who help open doors for others and get them moving on the road of achievement. Sometimes the achievers end up surpassing those who gave them that extra "push," and that's what "hinge people" like to see. I suppose the technical term would be *mentors*. Joseph from Cyprus was such a man. He was so effective in the ministry of helping others that he was given the nickname Barnabas, which means "son of encouragement" (Acts 4:36; 11:23; 13:43).

Barnabas was born of Jewish parents in Cyprus and was a Levite. His aunt was Mary, the mother of John Mark (Acts 12), so Mark was his cousin (Col. 4:10). We aren't told about his conversion experience, but he came to Jerusalem and got involved with the church there. I suppose he lived with his aunt Mary. Wherever you find a good man or woman filled with the Spirit and with faith, you will see the Lord work in remarkable ways. Barnabas could open the ways for others because he himself was an "open man" before the Lord.

OPEN HANDS (Acts 4:36–5:11)

According to the law of Moses, the priests and Levites were not permitted to own land in Palestine (Num. 18:20; 26:62), so it is probable that the land Barnabas sold was in Cyprus and that he brought the money with him to Jerusalem. There was a "stewardship revival" going on in the Jerusalem church at that time as believers generously gave of their wealth to help the needy, and Barnabas gave the Lord all the money he received from the sale of the land.

But whenever the Holy Spirit is at work, the Devil starts to manufacture counterfeits, in this case, Ananias and Sapphira. The fact that Dr. Luke put Barnabas's gift and their gift next to each other in his record suggests that this husband and wife saw what Barnabas did and decided to imitate it. Anything he could do, they could do better, or at least pretend that they could do better. When they sold their property, they could have kept all the money or brought whatever portion they wanted to bring, but they gave the impression that, like Barnabas, they had brought the full price. Ananias and Sapphira both lied to the Spirit about their contribution, and both of them died for their sin.

The believers soon learned that Barnabas was a good man to send with relief offerings to the poor in response to God's command (Acts 11:27–30). "Therefore I command you to be openhanded toward your brothers and toward the poor and needy in your land" (Deut. 15:11). "'It is more blessed to give than to receive'" (Acts 20:35).

OPEN DOORS (Acts 9:26–30; 11:19–26)

The first time Saul tried to meet with the apostles and church leaders in Jerusalem, they closed the door on him. They questioned the reality of his conversion and were afraid that his wanting to see them was only a scheme to arrest them. The verb in Acts 9:26 means "he repeatedly tried to join with them," which means that Saul was rebuffed and rejected many times, but he kept trying. The church today honors Saul, so this situation seems strange to us; but had we been there, we might have acted the same way. After all, at the beginning of this chapter, the unconverted Saul was "breathing out murderous threats against the Lord's disciples," so it seemed safe to keep the doors closed and locked. The apostles had even done this to Jesus, but He was able to walk right in (John 20:19–22).

Barnabas practiced an "open door" policy when it came to fellowship with the brethren. The apostles' attitude was, "We'll keep our distance until you prove yourself safe," but Barnabas said, "No, let's receive him until the Lord shows us otherwise." He took Saul (the verb literally means "took him by the hand"), brought him to the apostles, and explained what the Lord had done in his life. Barnabas was a "hinge person" who opened the doors for Saul in Jerusalem.

But the blessing doesn't stop there. God in His grace had sent the gospel to the Gentiles in Antioch, and the apostles sent Barnabas to investigate this new "open door" (Acts 11:19–24). After all, lay Christians and not apostles had started the church, and it was made up primarily of Gentiles. But Barnabas saw the grace of God in what was going on, and he heartily entered into the ministry. But the story continues. The Lord reminded Barnabas that Saul's calling was primarily to the Gentiles (Acts 9:15), so he went to Tarsus and enlisted Saul for the work in Antioch (Acts 9:29–30; 11:25–26). Barnabas kept the hinges "oiled" and encouraged Saul in his ministry. In the years that followed, Saul learned to pray for open doors (Col. 4:3).

OPEN EARS AND EYES (Acts 13:1–14:28)

After a year of service in Antioch, Barnabas and Saul were presented with a new challenge. They were worshiping together with the other believers when the Lord called them to leave Antioch and take the gospel to the other nations. God selected the first and last names on the list, Barnabas and Saul, and very soon Saul's name would be changed to Paul. "I tell you," said Jesus, "open your eyes and look at the fields! They are ripe for harvest" (John 4:35). Barnabas and Saul had open ears to the call and open eyes to the challenge. Like Isaiah the prophet, as they worshiped the Lord, His special call came to them (Isa. 6). They heard God's call and responded with obedience.

The gospel had begun in Jerusalem, moved into all Judea and Samaria, and was now going to the ends of the earth (Acts 1:8). The church commissioned them and no doubt gave them money to assist them in their travels, although 1 Corinthians 9:6 indicates that both Saul and Barnabas worked to earn their bread. Travel wasn't easy in those days, but they set out by faith, knowing that the Lord was with them.

Barnabas took his cousin John Mark along as their aide. Mark was supposed to free up Barnabas and Saul to devote themselves to ministry, but unfortunately he left them and returned to Jerusalem (Acts 13:13). Why did he leave? Some think he was just plain homesick, while others think he didn't like to see Paul (his new name, Acts 13:9) taking over the leadership of the mission. What began as "Barnabas and Saul" now became "Paul and his companions" and then "Paul and Barnabas" (Acts 13:13, 42–43, 46). John Mark felt better when his cousin was in command, although Barnabas didn't seem to mind the change. But perhaps John Mark couldn't get accustomed to Paul's emphasis on the grace of God and his refusal to make the believing Gentiles conform to the Jewish law. After all, Peter was John Mark's "spiritual father," and even Peter and Barnabas would compromise and lapse into legalism (Gal. 2:11–14).

The first missionary journey was a great success, and at the church in Antioch, Paul and Barnabas gave a report that glorified the Lord who had "opened the door of faith to the Gentiles" (Acts 14:27). When we have open eyes and ears, we see the open doors and hear the Lord telling us what to do.

OPEN RECORDS (Acts 15:1–35)

Paul and Barnabas remained in Antioch administering the Word and taking advantage of the open doors the Lord had given them. But the enemy had his plan: he sent some legalists from Jerusalem to Antioch to try to close the doors to the Gentiles. These freelance preachers taught that the Gentiles had to become Jews in order to become Christians, and Paul and Barnabas had "sharp debates" with them over this issue (Acts 15:1–5, 24). At stake was the truth of the gospel, and that involved the freedom of the child of God in Christ (see Gal. 1–2). The church at Antioch sent Paul and Barnabas and some other believers to Jerusalem to discuss the issue with the apostles.

The interesting thing about this conference—it wasn't a formal "church council" in the denominational sense—is that the attendees were free to speak and disagree, and then the leaders summarized the issue and called for a decision. Since Peter was the first apostle to go to the Gentiles (Acts 10), he spoke up for the gospel of the grace of God, and then Barnabas and Paul gave witness of what the Lord had done in Antioch and on their first missionary journey (Acts 15:12).

282 — Life Sentences

They opened the records for all to see, because they had nothing to hide. Their consciences were clear before God and men. The Gentiles were saved without first adopting the Jewish way of life, and they didn't adopt it after they were saved!

One of the problems in churches today is that God's people have "historical amnesia" and have forgotten God's work in the past. They are so infatuated with finding new and exciting ways to live for Christ and serve Him that they have turned away from the clear and simple principles and methods that have worked since the days of the apostles. Yes, we must make good use of modern means of transportation and communication, but we must not alter the gospel of the grace of God or ignore the necessity for prayer and the ministry of the Word (Acts 6:4; Gal. 1:6–12). All our gimmicks, gadgets, clever slogans, and slick promotions can never take the place of the Spirit of God.

The gathering listened to the report of the past from Peter, Paul, and Barnabas, and then heard the God-given counsel for the present given by James. He summarized the facts about the Spirit's working, tied these events to the Word of God (Amos 9:11–12), and then gave some practical conclusions for the churches to consider and apply. This was accepted by the conferees and summarized in a letter sent to the churches in Antioch, Syria, and Cilicia. It was taken to Antioch by Paul and Barnabas, who remained there to teach the Word and protect the truth of the gospel. Their friendship was no doubt deepened from the Jerusalem experience, but they would find it tested again.

OPEN HEARTS (Acts 15:36–41)

It was only right that Paul and Barnabas visit again the churches they had helped to found. Not only must they silence the legalists (Judaizers) who wanted to shackle the Gentiles with the law of Moses, but they needed to encourage the young believers to grow in the Lord and continue to reach out to the lost.

The suggestion by Barnabas that they take John Mark along was perfectly in order. Any problems Mark had with Paul's emphasis on grace were certainly answered at the Jerusalem conference, and there was no question that Paul was now the leader of the team. The conferences proved that Peter, Paul, and Barnabas were in agreement, and John Mark deserved another chance to prove himself. But Paul disagreed with Barnabas and felt that John Mark was not trustworthy and able to cope with the rigors of travel.

There had been a "sharp disagreement" with the Judaizers (Acts 15:2), and now there was a sharp disagreement between Paul and Barnabas (Acts 15:39). Paul and Barnabas could agree on doctrinal matters and help bring peace to the churches, but they couldn't patch up their personal disagreements on the management of the missionary team. Both the Bible and church history record the unfortunate quarrels of godly people who seemed unable to get along with one another, and that reminds us that "the best people are but people at their best."

Perhaps the heart of the problem was the problem of the heart and both men were at fault. Paul's major question was, "What can John Mark do for the work?"

while Barnabas was asking, "What can the work do for John Mark?" Certainly the Lord is as concerned for the workers as He is for the work, for He wants us all to become more like Jesus Christ. He spent thirteen years preparing Joseph in Egypt and eighty years preparing Moses in Egypt and in Midian. Even Paul spent time in Arabia receiving special training from the Lord.

Both men were adamant, so the only solution was to separate. Paul chose Silas as his associate, and Barnabas took his cousin Mark and headed for his home territory in Cyprus. Since in the book of Acts, Dr. Luke is telling Paul's story, he doesn't follow Mark and Barnabas, but near the close of his life, Paul himself tells us that he and Barnabas and John Mark were finally reconciled. When writing to the church at Colosse, Paul sent greetings from Mark and indicated that he intended to send Mark to Colosse to help the believers work out their problems. Since Paul was in prison, he wasn't able to go himself. In his second letter to Timothy, Paul told Timothy, "Get Mark and bring him with you, because he is helpful to me in my ministry" (2 Tim. 4:11).

I have been privileged to teach preaching and pastoral work in several schools. I have often wondered what happened to the students who dropped out or left school because somebody told them they weren't called to the ministry. In my travels, I have occasionally met some of these former students and discovered that the Lord was using them in remarkable ways. Like John Mark, they teamed up with a mentor, went out by faith, and made a success of their lives. We should never give up on anybody. God gave second chances to Moses, David, Jonah, and Peter, and His is a good example for us to follow.

Anybody can tear things down, but it takes faith and patience to build things up. Barnabas was a good man, filled with the Holy Spirit and faith, and he was a "son of encouragement" to the very end.

60

STEPHEN

"Be faithful, even to the point of death,
and I will give you the crown of life."

REVELATION 2:10

The name "Stephen" comes from the Greek word *stephanos*, which means "a victor's crown," the crown the winning athletes received at the Greek Olympics. Stephen lived up to his name, for he won his crown by being the first martyr of the Christian church. Our Lord promises to bless all His children who are faithful to Him. Stephen received a crown in heaven, but he also earned a crown on earth. How? By being faithful to use his gifts and opportunities so that the Lord could "promote" him to new ministries. All we know about Stephen is recorded in two chapters in Acts, yet what an encouragement he is to God's servants! He was a person of godly character, and that character revealed itself in his life and ministry.

HUMILITY—THE SERVANT (Acts 6:1–7)

Unity is important to the church, for without it we have difficulty witnessing to a lost world (John 17:20–23). How can outsiders believe in a God of love if His people don't love one another? The first threat to the unity of the Jerusalem church wasn't doctrinal; it was practical and had to do with leadership and administration. The apostles were so busy in their various ministries that they occasionally overlooked some of the widows who depended on the church for their daily needs. These were Hellenistic Jews who had come from other countries to Jerusalem to celebrate the Jewish feasts. They had been converted and had remained to learn more about Christ. These Greek-speaking Jews were overlooked while the Hebrew-speaking Jews were fed, so this led to division and criticism. In most churches, if somebody feels ignored and left out, there is bound to be trouble. It might easily have turned into a racial or cultural conflict.

The solution to the problem was not to preach a sermon on unity or to send these people back home. The simple solution was to relieve the apostles of the responsibility of serving tables and to appoint others to handle that ministry. Many students call these seven men the first "deacons," for the word *deacon* simply means "servant." Stephen is named first, and he turned out to be the church's first martyr. He was a remarkably gifted man—he even did miracles—and yet he was happy to serve tables. His humility and faithfulness helped build his character and prepare him for greater things.

God's leaders always begin as God's servants and then grow into the place of leadership God is preparing for them. This was true of Joseph, Moses, Joshua, Samuel, David, Nehemiah, and a host of people who worked with Paul. Faithfulness in a few things opens the way to opportunities to work with more things (Matt. 25:21). Humility isn't thinking poorly of ourselves ("Oh, I'm not worth much!") but just not thinking of ourselves at all. Stephen thought of others and of maintaining the unity of the church.

COURAGE—THE DEFENDER (Acts 6:8–15)

Many church constitutions state that the pastors are responsible for the "spiritual ministry" and the deacons the "financial and material" ministry. This concept isn't biblical, and it is very difficult to separate the two. What we do with "material things" should be as Spirit-led as how we plan a prayer meeting or an evangelistic outreach. When Stephen finished serving the tables each day, he would often go to the Synagogue of the Freedmen where he knew there were men with whom he could discuss the Scriptures. He wasn't changing from spiritual to material; he was only changing people and locations. It is gratifying when church officers can also teach and preach the Word, for both Stephen and Philip became preachers (Acts 6:5; 8:4–40). Stephen used the Old Testament to prove that Jesus of Nazareth is indeed the Messiah and the Son of God, and his listeners couldn't refute him. The Spirit of God used the Word in such a way that Stephen's listeners either had to accept what he said or silence him, and they chose the latter. They treated Stephen exactly the way Jesus was treated, paying false witnesses and making false accusations (Matt. 26:59–66; Acts 6:11–14). What a joy it is when God's servants are treated like Jesus and share in the fellowship of His sufferings (Phil. 3:10)!

Jesus had said that there would be a new temple (John 2:19) and that worship would not be limited to Jerusalem (John 4:20–24). He had also set aside the Jewish dietary laws and the Pharisees' strict observance of the Sabbath. He came to fulfill the Old Testament types and symbols, not to perpetuate them; but many of the Jewish people couldn't easily set aside these traditions. Stephen didn't "argue religion." He opened the Scriptures and explained how they pointed to Jesus and His work of redemption on the cross. His listeners hardened their hearts against him and against the truth he presented, and this led to his arrest and a trial before the religious leaders.

Perhaps the greatest obstacle today to evangelism isn't anger and opposition but ignorance, apathy, and unconcern. The Bible isn't important to most people, and it isn't politically correct to discuss religion or to claim that only one faith is true. If Stephen were alive and witnessing today, he wouldn't adopt a new approach. Filled with the Spirit and the love the Spirit imparts, he would patiently present Jesus and back up his claims with the Scriptures. The gospel is still "the power of God for the salvation of everyone who believes" (Rom. 1:16).

The American Methodist preacher Clovis Chappell wrote:

> Oh, for a church the world cannot treat with indifference! Oh, for a band of saints that it is absolutely impossible to ignore! Oh, for a ministry that will divide audiences and communities and cities and continents into those who are either out and out for Christ or out and out against Him.... But the direst of all dire calamities is for it to become so effete, so powerless, so dead that it is not worth fighting.[1]

WISDOM — THE INTERPRETER (Acts 7:1 – 53)

Stephen understood the Scriptures. He knew not only the people and events of Jewish history but also God's plan for His chosen people. He had insight as well as information. Like Moses, he knew both God's acts and God's ways (Ps. 103:7), and this is why he was able to interpret and apply Israel's history with such power.

One of God's great gifts to Israel was the presence of His glory in their midst (Ex. 40:34–38; 1 Kings 8:1–11; Rom. 9:1–5), so Stephen started his message with "the God of glory." Abraham was an idolater when God called him, and the revelation of the glory of the true and living God turned the idols in Ur of the Chaldees into nothing. The Jewish people in Stephen's day had turned their traditions into an idol, and they could no longer see the glory of God. Stephen made it clear that from very early in their history, even when they were in Egypt and then in the wilderness, Israel had worshiped idols. This was something nobody could deny.

The main thrust of Stephen's message was this: Israel rejected their God-sent redeemers the first time but accepted them the second time. Jacob's sons rejected Joseph and sold him into Egypt. They didn't recognize him the first time they went down to Egypt, but he made himself known the second visit (Acts 7:13). They rejected Moses when he first attempted to deliver them from Egypt but accepted him forty years later when he came the second time (Acts 7:35–36). Now God had sent His Son Jesus, just as Moses had promised (Acts 7:37–38), and the people rejected Him. Their opposition to Stephen and to the witness of the church was only further evidence of their spiritual blindness and hardness of heart (Acts 7:51–53). Stephen wasn't only a witness, he was also a prosecuting attorney and a judge! They were guilty!

GRACE — THE INTERCESSOR (Acts 7:54 – 60)

Then why didn't the Lord punish His rebellious people immediately? Because on the cross, Jesus had prayed, "Father, forgive them, for they do not know what

---

1. Chappell, *More Sermons*, 32.

they are doing" (Luke 23:34). Their punishment was postponed. Stephen prayed a similar prayer, and how gracious the Lord was to answer! When Jesus comes the second time, the nation will repent and receive Him (Zech. 12:10–14:21).

Before Stephen had given his defense, his accusers saw his face become radiant with the glory of God, the glory that Abraham, Moses, and Solomon had seen in their day (Acts 6:15). At the end of his defense, Stephen looked up and saw Jesus in His heavenly glory, standing to welcome His faithful servant. "Blessed are the pure in heart, for they will see God" (Matt. 5:8). The God of all grace was welcoming His servant to eternal glory (1 Peter 5:10).

Stephen had so much to live for, and we wonder why God permitted him to be killed. But his prayer and the witness of his death accomplished more than most people's lives. For Stephen, his death meant coronation, and he received his crown. Stephen gave an unforgettable demonstration of Christlike love for his accusers and his murderers, and this must have deeply affected Saul the persecutor who was standing there. Years later he mentioned Stephen's death to the Lord (Acts 22:20). It was one of the goads that God used to convict Saul of his need for a Savior (Acts 26:14).

What did his death do for the church in Jerusalem? It led to greater persecution so that the saints were scattered like seeds, and wherever they landed, they produced fruit. (See Acts 8:1–4; 11:19–21.) Like Israel in Egypt, the more the church suffers, the more it multiplies.

What did Stephen's death mean to Israel? This was the third significant murder in the New Testament, and it meant that the longsuffering of God would soon end. Their sins had only grown worse. Israel had *allowed* John the Baptist to be killed, they had *asked* for Jesus to be killed, and now *they themselves killed Stephen*. They had sinned against God the Father, God the Son, and God the Holy Spirit (Acts 7:51). They had rebelled against the entire Godhead, and there was nothing else the Lord could do to change them.

When the well-known British preacher Joseph Parker was a young man, he used to go to the town green, listen to the atheists and agnostics speak, and then debate with them. One day a man shouted to him, "What did Christ do for Stephen when he was stoned?" Parker's reply silenced him: "Christ gave him grace to pray for those who stoned him."

What a prelude for going to heaven!

61

PAUL THE APOSTLE

But by the grace of God I am what I am.

1 Corinthians 15:10

*D*ealing with both the grace of God and the apostle Paul in one brief essay is like trying to climb two mountains at one time. But it would be foolish to try to write about Paul while ignoring the grace of God, because the only way Paul can be understood is in the light of God's grace as revealed in Jesus Christ.

Saul of Tarsus was quite satisfied with his self-righteous religious career until on the way to Damascus he made two devastating discoveries: Jesus Christ was alive and Saul of Tarsus was dead in sin and a total failure in himself. It was then that Paul believed in Jesus, submitted to His lordship, and experienced personally the grace of God. From that moment on, it was the grace of God that made possible what Paul was and what Paul did, and he wasn't ashamed to admit it. He gloried in God's grace. He mentioned grace at least one hundred times in his thirteen epistles, and grace is both the greeting and the benediction in all of them.

Paul was not only saved by grace (Eph. 2:8–9) but he also *lived* by grace. For him, the Christian life was grace from start to finish. His testimony was "not I, but Christ" (Gal. 2:20 KJV) and "not I, but the grace of God that was with me" (1 Cor. 15:10). As a rabbinical student and then as a Pharisee, he knew the law and tried to obey it, but when he became a Christian, he agreed with John 1:17, "For the law was given through Moses; grace and truth came through Jesus Christ." Paul learned early that trying to keep the law would bring out the worst in him (Rom. 7), but depending on God's grace would bring out the best in him. He opted for grace.

Let's listen to Paul and learn from him about some of the blessings we have because we depend on the wonderful grace of God.

WE ARE SPIRITUALLY WEALTHY

In spite of our feelings or our circumstances, as God's children we have access to "the riches of God's grace ... lavished on us" in and through Christ Jesus (Eph. 1:7–8). When he was an unbelieving student of the Jewish law, Paul prided himself in his wealth of knowledge and religious achievement. But after meeting the Lord and trusting in Him, Paul saw all of his past as "loss" in contrast to all the spiritual wealth he gained in Christ (Phil. 3:1–11). He was "poor, yet making many rich; having nothing, and yet possessing everything" (2 Cor. 6:10). He told Timothy, "The grace of our Lord was poured out on me abundantly" (1 Tim. 1:14). When we are rich in God's grace, we are rich in everything good and godly, everything we need for life and ministry.

One aspect of this wealth is the calling and gifting involved in our service for the Lord. Paul was grateful to God that He had enriched the Corinthian believers so that they lacked no spiritual gift (1 Cor. 1:4–9). What they lacked were the spiritual graces needed to serve together in love. Paul identified himself as "an apostle of Christ Jesus by the will of God" (Eph. 1:1), and that calling was a part of the grace of God. When God saves us, He enriches us with one or more spiritual gifts, and through the Word He equips us to use those gifts for His glory (1 Cor. 12:7–11; 2 Tim. 3:16–17). The more we become like Christ in character and conduct, the more His grace can make us a blessing to others. There are many people more talented than we are, but talent isn't the secret of ministry success. Godly Robert Murray M'Cheyne wrote to a missionary friend, "It is not great talents God blesses so much as great likeness to Jesus. A holy minister is an awful weapon in the hand of God."[1]

We are rich in Jesus. Why look elsewhere for the spiritual resources we need? "For you know the grace of our Lord Jesus Christ, that though he was rich, yet for your sakes he became poor, so that you through his poverty might become rich" (2 Cor. 8:9).

WE ARE ADEQUATE IN CHRIST

"I worked harder than all of them—yet not I, but the grace of God that was with me" (1 Cor. 15:10). Keep in mind that Paul had physical handicaps that most of us would have used as excuses for staying home, yet he evangelized the regions beyond. He endured "troubles, hardships and distresses ... beatings, imprisonments and riots ... hard work, sleepless nights and hunger" but didn't complain about it. He had a thorn in his flesh, a "messenger of Satan" that tormented him, yet he kept on going. "My grace is sufficient for you," the Lord told him. Paul believed it, and God's grace transformed the thorn into a throne. "For when I am weak, then I am strong" (2 Cor. 12:7–10).

When you read your Bible and church history, you will discover that God's greatest works have been done by men and women who were weak in themselves but strong in the grace of Christ. When Paul looked at himself in the mirror, he didn't see a hero; he saw a broken and needy man who was nothing apart from God's grace. The reason for Paul's endurance and accomplishments is an open secret: "I can do everything through him who gives me strength" (Phil. 4:13). Grace provides, faith appropriates, and God is glorified.

---

1. Robert Murray M'Cheyne, *Memoir and Remains of Robert Murray M'Cheyne*, ed. Andrew Bonar (London: Banner of Truth, 1966), 282.

God's calling always includes God's enablement. He never leads us into any situation that is beyond us if we trust Him and obey His will. "God is able to make all grace abound to you, so that in all things at all times, having all that you need, you will abound in every good work" (2 Cor. 9:8).

WE HAVE THE WISDOM WE NEED

Living by God's grace includes learning from God's grace. "[Grace] teaches us to say 'No' to ungodliness and worldly passions, and to live self-controlled, upright and godly lives in this present age" (Titus 2:12). Paul didn't live "according to worldly wisdom but according to God's grace" (2 Cor. 1:12). Some of the leaders in the Corinthian church were trying to do the work of God according to the wisdom of this world, a mistake that is with us today (1 Cor. 1:18–31). While the church should follow good business practices and principles, the church is not a business and must operate according to the principles clearly stated in the Scriptures.

Paul prayed that the saints in Colosse would be "fill[ed] with the knowledge of [God's] will through all spiritual wisdom and understanding" (Col. 1:9). That should be our prayer before every pastoral staff meeting, every church board meeting, every congregational business meeting, and every committee meeting. Joshua was a great general, but he committed two costly blunders because he didn't seek God's wisdom (Josh. 7; 9). Confident of his own wisdom, he ran ahead of the Lord and led the nation into defeat.

The church of Jesus Christ has a great deal of knowledge these days, and many of our evangelical schools are known for academic excellence. But much knowledge without wisdom—knowing how to use knowledge—is a dangerous thing. Paul's admonition "Continue to work out your salvation with fear and trembling" was written to *a church* (Phil. 2:12), and it was a reminder that the churches must not imitate other churches but seek God's specific will for their own congregation. Instead of running from one conference or seminar to another and borrowing ideas and programs that might not be biblical, church leaders today would do well to get alone with God, search the Word and pray, and seek to determine His will.

Paul had this in mind when he said to the elders of the Ephesian church, "Now I commit you to God and to the word of his grace, which can build you up and give you an inheritance among all those who are sanctified" (Acts 20:32). When we live by grace, our guidebook isn't the latest religious bestseller; it is the Word of God's grace. Spiritual leaders in whom the Word of grace dwells richly don't have to borrow clever ideas from the world or sermon outlines from other preachers, because God's grace gives them the wisdom they need to care for the family of God (Col. 3:16).

WE HAVE SPIRITUAL AUTHORITY

In an earlier study, we learned that we live in a world in which death is reigning because sin is reigning (Rom. 5:14, 17, 21). However, "through Christ Jesus the law of the Spirit of life" has set us "free from the law of sin and death" (Rom. 8:2). Yes, we still have a sinful nature, and yes, this mortal body will die one day if Jesus doesn't return first. We can overcome every spiritual enemy because grace is reigning (Rom. 5:21)! As we walk in the Spirit, we can reign in life through Christ Jesus. The Father has given all authority to His Son (Matt. 28:18) who is now seated at the Father's right hand (Eph. 1:20), and by faith we can allow Jesus to exercise His authority through us.

WE ARE "MORE THAN CONQUERORS THROUGH HIM WHO LOVED US" (Rom. 8:37)

How did the people of Israel conquer their enemies in the Promised Land? By trusting the Lord, obeying His orders, and making themselves available to follow Him. How did the early church spread the gospel throughout the Roman Empire? By trusting the Lord, making themselves available to the Spirit, and following God's leading for His glory. To paraphrase what British evangelist Henry Varley said to D. L. Moody, "There is no limit to what God can do in, for, and through the Christians who will yield themselves to God and seek to glorify Him."

Exercising spiritual authority—allowing grace to reign in our lives—doesn't make God's servants arrogant; instead, it humbles them. It isn't a guarantee of health, wealth, and prosperity, because it might lead to persecution, suffering, and death. But when grace reigns in us and we reign in Christ, what happens to us doesn't really matter as long as God's work is done and His name is glorified (Rom. 8:31–39). We share the throne with Jesus (Eph. 2:4–10) and "reign in life through the one man, Jesus Christ" (Rom. 5:17).

WE HAVE THE DESIRE TO PRAISE AND WORSHIP THE LORD

The most important ministry of the local church is the worship of God. Everything the church is and does flows out of the worship of Jesus Christ, for He said, "Apart from me you can do nothing" (John 15:5). In too many churches today the sanctuary is a theater and worship is only religious entertainment. Rarely do we hear an invocation that asks God to give grace by His Spirit so that His people might worship Him acceptably and in godly fear.

Too many believers today don't think they need grace to worship "in spirit and in truth" (John 4:23), because they have learned to imitate true worship by their own clever human abilities and techniques. They forget the admonition, "Let the word of Christ dwell in you richly in all wisdom, teaching and admonishing one another in psalms and hymns and spiritual songs, singing with grace in your hearts to the Lord" (Col. 3:16 NKJV). The grace must be in the heart before the praise can be on the lips.

It takes grace to sing to the Lord from the heart. It took grace for David to sing to the Lord in those psalms that so bless us today. It took grace for Jesus to sing a hymn and then go out to die on the cross. It took grace for Paul and Silas to sing hymns in that Philippian prison. Just as our speech must "always [be] full of grace" (Col. 4:6), so our worship must "always be of grace" or it will not please and glorify the Lord. Aaron's two sons brought "unauthorized fire" before the Lord and died because of it (Lev. 10:1–3). If God killed believers today for presenting unauthorized worship, how large would our congregations be?

"But by the grace of God I am what I am," wrote Paul. He didn't depend on his excellent education, his personal talents, or his fine heredity. God can use those things if we dedicate them to Him, but the secret of Christian life and ministry is *depending completely on the grace of God*. I could go on and list many more blessings we have because of the grace of God, but discovering them in your own Bible would be a good spiritual exercise for you.

Evangelist D. L. Moody once spent several days studying what the Bible said about the grace of God. He became so excited that he went out of the house and said to the first man he met, "What do you know about grace?" The startled man replied, "Grace who?" "The grace of God!" said Moody, and he proceeded to tell him about Jesus.

> Through many dangers, toils and snares,
> I have already come;
> 'Tis grace hath brought me safe thus far,
> And grace will lead me home.
>
> JOHN NEWTON

"As God's fellow workers we urge you not to receive God's grace in vain" (2 Cor. 6:1).

62

LYDIA

He rewards those who earnestly seek him.

HEBREWS 11:6

When Jesus was serving on earth, a company of women ministered to Him and His disciples (Luke 8:1–3). Believing women also assisted the apostle Paul from time to time. Thirty-three of Paul's co-laborers are named in his letters and the book of Acts, and at least a third of them are women. Lydia was the first convert to Christ in Europe, and her conversion took place in Philippi (Acts 16:6–15). From this event, we are reminded of the factors that are involved in the responsibility we have of spreading the gospel.

GOD'S MESSENGERS

Paul was on his second missionary journey, and with him were Silas, who had replaced Barnabas, and Timothy, who had replaced John Mark. God's servants had parted, but God's work went right on. Not only were they seeking to evangelize the cities, but they were also encouraging the young churches and sharing the letter from the Jerusalem conference. This greatly encouraged the Gentile believers (Acts 15:30–41).

" 'Everyone who calls on the name of the Lord will be saved.' How, then, can they call on the one they have not believed in? And how can they believe in the one of whom they have not heard? And how can they hear without someone preaching to them? And how can they preach unless they are sent?" (Rom. 10:13–15). Those words summarize the church's theology of missions. They explain why Paul and his friends were so far from home. They weren't traveling because of pity for "pagan people" or because of sentimental philanthropic motives, as noble as these may be. "For Christ's love compels us" (2 Cor. 5:14) is the motive that kept Paul going. They were Christ's ambassadors.

No matter who we are and where we live, because we know Jesus Christ as our Savior and Lord, we are obligated to share the good news. Paul and Silas were an official team from the church at Antioch, and then Paul added Timothy. You and I don't need any official papers to witness for Christ right where we are. In fact, we are already witnesses—either good ones or bad ones! God wants us to witness wherever we are *and wherever we are not*! When we can't go, we can help others to go.

GOD'S PROVIDENCE

When the three men attempted to go into Asia, the Lord closed the doors. The same thing happened when they headed for Bithynia. Then one night at Troas, God gave Paul the directions he needed and they headed for Europe. (The word "we" in Acts 16:10 shows that Dr. Luke had now joined the team.) But even after they arrived in Philippi, the men didn't immediately plunge into a program of evangelism. Luke reports that they "stayed there several days" before looking for opportunities to witness (Acts 16:12).

My wife and I were privileged to minister in Kenya, East Africa, for three weeks, both to the national church and to the missionary staff of the Africa Inland Mission. After welcoming me to Africa, the first thing the bishop of the AIM national church said to me was, "You are in Africa now, so take off your watch." He had worked with Americans for many years and knew our tendency (compulsion?) to live by the clock and be enslaved to schedules. We learned to be patient. If the meeting was scheduled for seven o'clock in the evening and didn't start until eight o'clock, nobody was upset and the conference went right on. They knew that the Lord wasn't in a hurry and that there was always time for the will of God.

This doesn't mean that these believers weren't urgent about the Lord's work, because they were; but they weren't frantic and overwrought about deadlines. Referring to the well-known book *Your God Is Too Small*, Dr. Richard J. Mouw wrote, "But if I had to choose the variation on Phillips's title that best captures my recent exercises in corrective theology, it would be *your God is too fast*."[1] We have all heard slogans admonishing us to "win the world in your generation," and perhaps you have participated in meetings planned to convert an entire city in two weeks. It's the American way. "The king's business required haste" (1 Sam. 21:8 KJV) may be a good verse for motivating people, but you have to take it out of context.

I'm not recommending indolence and delay. Far from it. Like the bridesmaids in our Lord's parable (Matt. 25:1–13), we have a tendency to fall asleep and occasionally need to be aroused; but even when we are asleep, God's providence goes right on. We can lose the guidance of God faster by rushing ahead than by lagging behind, and the consequences of haste are harder to repair. "Do not be like the horse or the mule" (Ps. 32:9). After Paul and his associates arrived in Philippi, they rested from their journey, prayed, and planned to look for a Jewish prayer meeting on the Sabbath.

GOD'S GRACE

By the river outside the city gate, Paul and his friends found a prayer meeting assembled, composed entirely of women. A man had spoken to Paul in the night vision, but now God led them to a small group of women. When he was an

---

1. Richard J. Mouw, *How My Mind Has Changed*, ed. James M. Wall and David Heim (Grand Rapids, Mich.: Eerdmans, 1991), 24.

unconverted Pharisee, Paul would pray each morning: "I give thanks that I am a Jew and not a Gentile, a freeman and not a slave, and a man, not a woman." Of course, the gospel changed all that for Paul (Gal. 3:28). It required ten men to form a synagogue, so the Jewish population in Philippi was very small; or perhaps the Roman authorities had ordered the Jews to leave the city and only Gentile seekers had remained (Acts 18:1–4).

The most prominent of the women, and probably the wealthiest, was Lydia, a cloth merchant from Thyatira. Her home city was famous for its purple cloth, which was made into togas for the Roman officials. She was probably a widow who was managing the family business. She had abandoned the pagan religion of Thyatira and become a "God-fearer," seeking the truth. The Lord was present in this small gathering of women, and as Paul and his friends prayed and quietly conversed with the women, God opened Lydia's heart and she was saved. She was a successful woman, wealthy and religious, but she still needed Jesus. The members of her household were also converted, and all of them were baptized.

Lydia's conversion in that small gathering was the beginning of a great ministry that became known as "the church in Philippi." Likewise, it was in a small meeting on Aldersgate Street in London where John Wesley felt his heart "strangely warmed" and the Methodist Church was born. "Who despises the day of small things?" (Zech. 4:10). Later the Roman jailer in Philippi would be saved along with his family, and they would become part of the church. Lydia opened her home to Paul and his associates and saw to it that their needs were met. Her generosity was an example that helped to motivate the church to help support Paul's missionary ministry (Phil. 4:14–16).

GOD'S WISDOM

The story of the arrest and imprisonment of Paul and Silas and their miraculous deliverance is well known (Acts 16:16–40). The issue was money, not truth or the law. Paul would face a similar battle in Ephesus (Acts 19:23–41). Paul was a Roman citizen and could have used that fact to prevent his being beaten by the officials, but he submitted to the humiliation and shame for the sake of the infant church. Even more, the Lord used their witness to reach the jailer and his household.

When the officials realized they had broken the Roman law, they sent a messenger to tell Paul and Silas that they were free to leave the prison, but Paul refused to accept such treatment. Why? Because he wanted everybody to know that what the officials had done was wrong, that the officials had apologized, and that the church wasn't an illegal group. Paul and Silas left the jail and publicly went to the home of Lydia and identified themselves with the new believers. Thanks to Paul, we can be sure that the Roman officials were very careful how they treated the Christians.

God gave Paul the wisdom to turn a difficult experience into a great victory, and the Lord turned the curse into a blessing (Deut. 23:5). Furthermore, he and

Silas set a great example before these new Christians. The men accepted their suffering graciously and used it to the glory of God and the good of the church (Phil. 1:20–2:18).

Lydia was a seeker. She was worshiping the God of Abraham, Isaac, and Jacob, but she didn't know about Jesus. God "rewards those who earnestly seek him." He may not do it immediately, and His way of doing it may surprise us, but He will never fail. The Lord sent Paul to share the gospel with Lydia, and she became a devoted Christian believer. She opened her heart, her home, and her hands to the Lord Jesus Christ, and He did the rest! The gospel is still "the power of God for the salvation of everyone who believes" (Rom. 1:16).

63

PHOEBE

*She has been a great help
to many people, including me.*

ROMANS 16:2

Phoebe's name comes from Phoibos, one of the names for the Greek god Apollo, and it means "radiant, the shining one." She was a Gentile, but unlike many Gentile Christians in the early church, she didn't abandon her "pagan" name when she confessed Christ and was baptized. Why should she change her name when her faithful service was like a light that kept shining and glorifying God (Matt. 5:16)? The Lord did change her life, and she became a "great help" to many of God's people.

Let's meet some of these people.

HELPING BELIEVERS IN THE LOCAL CHURCH

Cenchrea was a small seaport town about seven miles from Corinth, and it was there that Phoebe lived and served in the local assembly. Paul called her "a servant of the church," which implies she was officially appointed to ministry by the church. This is the first place in Romans where Paul uses the word *church*. We find it five times in this chapter.

"Servant" is the Greek word *diakonos*, which becomes "deacon" in some English translations. Some students think Phoebe was a deaconess of the church and ministered primarily to the women (1 Tim. 3:11 NIV marginal note). This would include preparing female converts for baptism, visiting the sick and needy in their homes, and teaching the women how to be good Christian wives and mothers. When we remember how the women in the East were secluded in that day, we can see how important her work was.

The word for "helper" in the Greek could also mean a patroness or guardian. Perhaps Phoebe had some legal position at the port of Cenchrea and assisted foreigners with legal issues before the Roman officials. This would have given her opportunities to witness for Christ and demonstrate the love of Christ to strangers.

In spite of their faults and weaknesses, Paul believed in the local church—and nobody knew those weaknesses better than he did! No family is perfect and no church family is perfect, but this lack of perfection isn't an excuse for us to drop out and do nothing. Let's follow Phoebe's example and let our lights shine in a local church.

HELPING GOD'S CHOSEN LEADERS

Paul says that Phoebe had been "a great help" to him, although he doesn't say how. In fact, as we read Romans 16, we discover that Paul was a "friend maker" as well as a soul winner. In this chapter he mentions twenty-six people who in one way or another were involved in his ministry. Paul could do miracles and was a gifted minister of the Word, but he still needed the companionship and assistance of God's people, and this included the women. Paul was not a "loner," nor was he a misogynist, treating the women like second-class saints. Throughout this chapter he gives recognition and appreciation to all kinds of people, men and women, and confesses that he couldn't have done the job without them.

We aren't told what special contributions Phoebe had made to Paul's ministry, but it is likely that she was the one who carried the Roman epistle to the churches in Rome. Like Lydia in Philippi, she was well-to-do; otherwise she couldn't have made that dangerous trip. No woman would dare to travel that distance alone, so she must have had servants with her to guard her. The greatest treasure she had with her was Paul's letter to the Romans, and she delivered it safely to the leaders in Rome. The Roman government had an effective postal system, but only government officials and military personnel could use it. The next time you read Romans, pause to give thanks for Phoebe.

Paul wrote the Roman epistle for several reasons. He had never visited the churches there but planned to do so as soon as he delivered the "love offering" to the poor saints in Jerusalem (Rom. 1:13–15; 15:25–29). But his enemies had spread lies about him (Rom. 3:8), so he sent the letter to explain what he believed and taught. The letter is the greatest single summary of Christian doctrine in Scripture. He explains the doctrines of sin and judgment, justification and sanctification, and the place of Israel in the plan of God; but he also explains how Christians ought to live to the glory of God. If the believers in Paul's day needed this compendium of theology, how much more do we need it today!

Over the centuries, the Roman letter that Phoebe delivered has been used of God to change lives and even influence world events. Augustine was brought to Christ by reading Romans 13:13; and Romans 1:17 — "The just shall live by faith" (KJV) — was the verse that changed Martin Luther's life. It was while someone was reading aloud the preface to Luther's commentary on Romans that John Wesley felt "his heart strangely warmed" and he received the assurance of salvation. John Bunyan found peace through trusting Romans 3:24–25, and that same passage brought peace to hymn writer William Cowper. Believers today find enlightenment and encouragement from the letter that Phoebe carried to Rome.

Phoebe was a helper to Paul, and Christian leaders today need our love, support, and prayers. The Christian leaders my wife and I have met during these more than fifty years of ministry have all given the glory to the Lord and have expressed their appreciation for the people who helped them along the way. No leader can do it alone. Where would Paul have been without Barnabas, Silas, Priscilla and Aquila, Timothy, Titus, a host of other friends—and Phoebe?

HELPING GOD'S PEOPLE TODAY

Paul's words about Phoebe in Romans 16:1–2 were actually her "letter of recommendation" to the believers in Rome from him and the churches at Cenchrea and Corinth. Letters of recommendation were very important to Christians in that day because they identified the true and loyal believers and kept out the troublemakers and heretics (Acts 18:27; 2 Cor. 8:16–24; 3 John 9–12). They also opened doors for believers who were traveling and needed hospitality (2 John 7–11). Phoebe was the kind of Christian Paul had no hesitation to recommend to the brothers and sisters in Rome. I hope I am the kind of Christian others can recommend to their friends.

The key word here is "receive" (Rom. 16:2). The Roman epistle Phoebe was carrying dealt with the matter of believers receiving one another and not fighting over their personal differences (Rom. 14:1–15:13). The Gentile believers in the church enjoyed the freedom given by the gospel, but some of the Jewish believers, whose faith was weak, were still in bondage to laws and traditions. The stronger believers were judging the weaker ones, and the weaker believers were stumbling over the conduct of the stronger believers. Paul gave them the solution to their problem: accept one another in Christ (Rom. 14:1, 3; 15:7). Anybody who has been received by the Lord, we should receive. Christ died for us that we might be one in Him, so let's not make our personal differences into barriers; let's build bridges.

We receive other believers "in the Lord," not because of their race, social status, education, political affiliations, or personalities. We receive them (and they receive us) as "saints," set-apart ones who belong to the Lord. We receive them in a manner worthy of the way Jesus has received us. Paul often used the word *worthy* when writing about Christian conduct. Our conduct should be worthy of our calling (Eph. 4:1), worthy of the gospel (Phil. 1:27), and worthy of the Lord (Col. 1:10; 1 Thess. 2:12; 3 John 6). I would like to know how the Roman believers received Phoebe. After all, she was a Gentile, a woman, an apostolic messenger, and a wealthy person. But more important, how am I treating God's people who may not agree with me about some minor matters in the Christian life?

No matter what our name or gender, we all need to be like Phoebe and carry the "radiant light" into this dark world; for if there were more light, there would be less darkness.

We must carry God's Word in our hearts and share it with those who need it.

We must be servants of the Lord and His church.

We must be "great helpers" to as many people as possible.

We must receive one another—serve one another—commend one another.

64

MY OWN LIFE SENTENCE

"... who brings forth out of
his treasure things new and old."
MATTHEW 13:52 NASB

About halfway through the writing of this book, it struck me that some of my readers might ask, "Well, what is *your* life sentence?" I am not worthy to be classed with the Bible greats I have mentioned in this book, but as I thought and prayed about it, I finally decided on Matthew 13:52: "... who brings forth out of his treasure things new and old" (NASB). Let me explain why.

First, I have devoted my life to the study and teaching of the Bible, the Word of God. I have pastored three churches, taught Sunday school classes, spoken at Bible conferences in many countries, expounded the Bible over the radio and in books, and taught preaching in seminaries. Nobody would ask me to referee a baseball game or direct a presentation of *The Messiah*, but they might ask me to preach or teach from the Bible.

Second, I have tried to be appreciative of both the new and the old in the Christian life and in the church, and I have attempted to encourage God's people—especially ministers—to keep them in balance. I have lived through translation wars, worship wars, music wars, and generational wars of various kinds and have the scars to prove it. I have tried to help the younger generation catch up on the past and the older generation catch up on the present, but I haven't always been successful.

Finally, as I have gotten older and (I hope) have matured somewhat, I have seen the folly of all this fussing about "generation gaps" and "contemporary" versus "traditional." About all these battles accomplished was to bring more income to the people who publish books and music and the people who make and distribute recordings, guitars, drum sets, and sound systems. In their attempt to bring forth only the new, they have ignored the old and given the church a bad case of amnesia. When God's people forget the past, they have lost their foundation.

Before I share some thoughts about my life sentence, I want to quote the entire statement our Lord made in Matthew 13:52: "Therefore every scribe who has become a disciple of the kingdom of heaven is like a head of a household, who brings forth out of his treasure things new and old" (NASB). My life sentence reminds me that I have three wonderful privileges, and so do you, regardless of your age or calling.

LEARNING GOD'S WORD—THE SCRIBE

At one time, the scribes were a noble group of godly men who gave a living witness to the Word of God. Founded by Ezra, they were dedicated to preserving and proclaiming God's truth (Ezra 7:10). But most of the scribes in Jesus' day were lost in the minutia of the Scriptures and therefore completely missed the message. They knew how many Hebrew letters were in each book, paragraph, and line, and they could quote what the famous rabbis had said about each verse, but these studies never did the scribes or their pupils much good. It was like hungry people today reading the nutritional information on the cereal box but never eating the cereal.

The scribes thought that a detailed examination of the Scriptures was the secret of salvation, but they were wrong. "You diligently study the Scriptures," Jesus told them, "because you think that by them you possess eternal life. These are the Scriptures that testify about me, yet you refuse to come to me to have life" (John 5:39–40). It is possible to be acquainted with the Word of God but not know the God of the Word.

I want to be a diligent student of the Word, but not like the scribes; because *I want to see Jesus Christ* in the Word. "Woe to you experts in the law," said Jesus, "because you have taken away the key to knowledge" (Luke 11:52). The key to the Word is Jesus. "And beginning with Moses and all the Prophets, he explained to them what was said in all the Scriptures concerning himself" (Luke 24:27). It is a great privilege to study the Bible and get better acquainted with Jesus and learn to love Him more. But if my studies don't make me more like Jesus, then I am wasting my time.

OBEYING GOD'S WORD—THE DISCIPLE

According to Jesus, scribes are supposed to become disciples. The truth that we learn must be truth that we live. Disciples learn, not just by listening to a teacher, reading a book, or filling in the blanks on a lesson sheet. They also learn by obeying what the teacher and the books say. Perhaps the best modern equivalent of *disciple* is *apprentice*, for an apprentice must practice what he or she has been taught. That is what James meant when he wrote, "Do not merely listen to the word, and so deceive yourselves. Do what it says" (James 1:22). You don't learn to swim by watching a video or listening to a lecture. You dive into the water and start imitating a master swimmer.

The missing ingredient in Bible study today is *obedience*. A church member said to her pastor, "I have completed six different study courses on evangelism and I have never yet led one person to Jesus Christ." She studied the lessons, filled in the blanks, and passed the tests, but she didn't obey what Jesus taught her. Jesus said, "Anyone who chooses to do the will of God will find out whether my teaching comes from God or whether I speak on my own" (John 7:17 TNIV). To quote the British preacher of the Victorian era, F. W. Robertson, "Obedience is the organ of spiritual knowledge." We don't really "know" a subject or a truth until we have put it into practice.

This is why the Lord permits us to go through trials. Our trials give us opportunities to obey the Lord, trust His Word, and put into practice what we think we have learned. Sometimes we don't know what the test was until we have failed it, but that's okay—we go right back and try again. Even our failures can help us develop some "spiritual muscles" and greater discernment.

SHARING GOD'S WORD—THE HOUSEHOLDER

Our Lord's image of the householder isn't too difficult to understand. The disciples told Jesus they understood what He had been teaching them, so He said, "Therefore you have the responsibility to share what you know with others." We can't give to others what we don't have ourselves, but if we don't share it, we won't have it very long. We keep the truth by obeying it and giving it away. "Give, and it will be given to you" (Luke 6:38).

Each of us has a treasure of truth in our minds and hearts, a treasure kept full as we study and obey the Scriptures. From that treasure we share with others "things new and old," according to their needs. We have many "Athenians" in the church today, people who "spend their time in nothing other than telling or hearing something new" (Acts 17:21 NASB). I have been privileged to minister to many young pastors, and I fear some of them think that nothing really important happened before 1975. However, some of my peers think nothing good has happened since 1945! We need to dispense both the old and the new if we are to be faithful householders. The younger generation needs to catch up on the past just as the older generation needs to catch up on the present.

The new grows out of the old. We don't "replace" the old with the new; we allow the new to grow out of the old, the way a tulip grows out of a bulb. Every baby is new and exciting, but in time, he or she becomes pretty much like every other child. Jesus didn't come to destroy the old but to fulfill it. You can destroy an acorn by beating it with a hammer or by planting it and allowing it to become an oak tree. In the kingdom of God, the new comes, not by substitution but by transformation.

The scribe was concerned primarily with preserving the old, and that is very important. But the disciple is interested in discovering the new, and that, too, is important. It is our obedience as disciples that makes the old truths new to us as we go through new experiences and face new challenges. We discover new insights in old promises and new applications for old principles. The roots may be old, but the flowers and fruits are new, and this makes life exciting.

Early in my ministry I learned that I couldn't preach or pastor effectively unless, like Isaac, I dug again the old wells and drank from them (Gen. 26:18) or, like Jeremiah, walked in the "ancient paths" (Jer. 6:16; 18:15). So I began to get acquainted with the preachers of the past—Charles Spurgeon, G. Campbell Morgan, George Matheson, George Morrison, Joseph Parker, Robert Murray M'Cheyne, and Jonathan Edwards, to name only a few—and much to my surprise, I found they weren't "old" at all, because they preached the timeless Word of God. What they said was very relevant to life today. Over the years, I have taken a lot of kidding because of my fascination with the preachers of the past, but it hasn't mattered to me. I know how exciting it is to have a growing treasury of the new and the old and to see how the Lord puts them together to enrich my life and ministry.

I have spent much of my life trying to get people to understand that the church needs both the old and the new. The new grows out of the old and for that reason really isn't "new" at all. The most recent piece of sophisticated electronic equipment is only a fresh combination of elements that have been around for a long time. Dr. H. A. Ironside used to say, "If it's new, it's not true, and if it's true, it's not new." He agreed with King Solomon: "Whatever is has already been, and what will be has been before" (Eccl. 3:15).

So, if you have ever heard me preach or teach, or if you have read something I have written, you have probably discovered that what I have to say is a combination of the old and the new, with the new coming out of the old. Few experiences thrill me as much as finding new combinations of spiritual truths in the old pages of the Bible and then seeing what happens when I seek to practice them and share them.

That is why I have chosen Matthew 13:52 as my life sentence. As I minister the Word, I want to be a bridge builder between the past and the present, because that is what prepares people for the future. I want to be like Ezra who "devoted himself to the study [the scribe] and observance [the disciple] of the Law of the LORD, and to teaching its decrees and laws in Israel [the householder]" (Ezra 7:10).

That's what I'd call a balanced ministry.

CONCLUSION:
YOUR LIFE SENTENCE

*I*f by faith you know Jesus Christ as your Savior and Lord, then you ought to ask your Father for a life sentence that sums up who you are and what you do for Him in this world. That verse might leap out at you one day while you are reading your Bible, or it may show up in a Sunday school lesson or a sermon. Seek and you will find.

If you don't know Jesus personally, then you won't find a *life* sentence. You'll find a *death* sentence. "For the wages of sin is death, but the gift of God is eternal life in Christ Jesus our Lord" (Rom. 6:23). Only a comma separates the death sentence from the life sentence. That is how close you are to salvation — or judgment; so please find your life in Christ today and trust the Savior.

Sometimes the discovery of a life sentence changes people's lives completely. Romans 1:17 shattered the theology of Martin Luther and transformed him into a reformer. Isaiah 54:2–3 turned William Carey into the father of the modern missionary movement, and Matthew 28:20 had a similar impact on David Livingstone. First Corinthians 3:11 made Selina, the Countess of Huntingdon, a force for God during the evangelical awakening in eighteenth-century England, and 2 Corinthians 12:9 empowered Catherine Booth to be "the mother of the Salvation Army."

Yes, the whole Bible is yours, but somewhere in its pages is a sentence that is especially yours — your life sentence. Find it, believe it, and act upon it, and the Lord will help you live it out to enrich yourself, bless others, and bring glory to God.

APPENDIX 1:

CHART OF SUGGESTED
DAILY READING PATTERNS

Day	Chapter	Biblical Reading
☑ 1 **Week One** . . . . The Lord God		Psalm 104
☑ 2 . . . . Lucifer		Isaiah 14:12−17
☑ 3 . . . . Adam		Genesis 2:15−25
❏ 4 . . . . Eve		Genesis 3:1−20
❏ 5 . . . . Cain		Genesis 4:1−16
❏ 6 . . . . Abel		Hebrews 11:1−4
❏ 7 . . . . Noah		Genesis 6:9−22
❏ 8 **Week Two** . . . . Abraham		Hebrews 11:8−19
❏ 9 . . . . Sarah		Genesis 21:2−21
❏ 10 . . . . Isaac		Genesis 22:1−19
❏ 11 . . . . Rebekah		Genesis 27:1−40
❏ 12 . . . . Esau		Hebrews 12:14−17
❏ 13 . . . . Jacob		Genesis 32:22−32
❏ 14 . . . . Rachel		Genesis 30:1−24
❏ 15 **Week Three** . . Joseph		Genesis 50:15−26
❏ 16 . . . . Job		Job 1:1−22
❏ 17 . . . . Moses		Exodus 33:12−23
❏ 18 . . . . Aaron		Exodus 32:1−35
❏ 19 . . . . Miriam		Exodus 15:1−21
❏ 20 . . . . Joshua		Joshua 1:1−18
❏ 21 . . . . Rahab		Joshua 2:1−24
❏ 22 **Week Four** . . . Deborah		Judges 5:1−31
❏ 23 . . . . Gideon		Judges 6:1−40
❏ 24 . . . . Samson		Judges 16:23−31
❏ 25 . . . . Ruth		Ruth 1:1−22
❏ 26 . . . . Eli		1 Samuel 4:12−22
❏ 27 . . . . Hannah		1 Samuel 2:1−11
❏ 28 . . . . Samuel		1 Samuel 12:1−25

APPENDIX 2:

LIST OF RECOMMENDED RESOURCES ON BIBLE CHARACTERS

Barclay, William. *The Master's Men*. New York: Abingdon, 1959.

Blaiklock, E. M. *Professor Blaiklock's Handbook of Bible People*. London: Scripture Union, 1979.

Buechner, Frederick. *Peculiar Treasures: A Biblical Who's Who*. San Francisco: Harper & Row, 1979.

Chappell, Clovis. *Meet These Men*. Grand Rapids, Mich.: Baker, 1974.

———. *Sermons on New Testament Characters*. New York: George H. Doran, 1924.

———. *Sermons on Old Testament Characters*. New York: George H. Doran, 1925.

Havner, Vance. *Moments of Decision*. Old Tappan, N.J.: Revell, 1979.

Hiebert, D. Edmund. *Personalities around Paul*. Chicago: Moody, 1973.

LaSor, William S. *Great Personalities of the New Testament*. Westwood, N.J.: Revell, 1961.

———. *Great Personalities of the Old Testament*. Westwood, N.J.: Revell, 1959.

Matheson, George. *The Representative Men of the Bible*. 2 vols. London: Hodder & Stoughton, 1902–1903.

———. *The Representative Men of the New Testament*. London: Hodder & Stoughton, 1910.

———. *The Representative Women of the Bible*. London: Hodder & Stoughton, 1907.

McCartney, Clarence E. *Peter and His Lord*. New York: Abingdon, 1937.

———. *The Wisest Fool and Other Men of the Bible*. New York: Abingdon-Cokesbury, 1949.

Meyer, F. B. *David: Shepherd, Psalmist, King*. New York: Revell, 1895.

———. *Israel: A Prince with God*. New York: Revell, n.d.

———. *Joseph: Beloved, Hated, Exalted*. New York: Revell, n.d.

———. *Joshua and the Land of Promise*. London: Morgan & Scott, n.d.

———. *Moses: The Servant of God*. New York: Revell, n.d.

———. *Samuel the Prophet*. London: Morgan & Scott, n.d.

Morgan, G. Campbell. *The Great Physician*. New York: Revell, 1937.

Pink, Arthur W. *The Life of David*. 2 vols. Grand Rapids, Mich.: Zondervan, 1958.

Redpath, Alan. *The Making of a Man of God*. Westwood, N.J.: Revell, 1962.

Sanders, J. Oswald. *The Cultivation of Christian Character*. Chicago: Moody, 1965.

Whyte, Alexander. *Bible Characters from the Old and New Testaments*. Grand Rapids, Mich.: Kregel, 1990.

Wiersbe, Warren W., ed. *Bible Personalities: A Treasury of Insights for Personal Growth and Ministry*. Grand Rapids, Mich.: Baker, 2005.

CHARACTER INDEX

Aaron, 89–92, 93, 95–96, 97, 120, 129, 132

Abel, 33–34, 36–38, 56, 139. *See also* Cain

Abiathar, 122

Abiram, 91

Abraham, 16, 38, 42, 43–48, 49, 50, 51, 52, 54, 55, 58, 59, 66, 68, 70, 93, 120, 126, 132, 133, 139, 141, 164, 166, 174, 178, 179, 189, 200, 218, 223, 224, 233, 249, 287

Abram, 36

Absalom, 19, 140, 149, 263

Achan, 174

Adam, 21, 22–26, 27, 31, 32, 33, 36, 52, 83. *See also* Eve

Adonijah, 122, 140, 149

Adoniram, 158

Adullam, 142

Adulterous woman, 272–74

Agag, King, 135

Ahab, King, 159, 160, 162, 169, 170, 171

Ahasuerus, 201

Ahijah, 156, 158

Ahithophel, 263

Amnon, 140, 149

Amoz, 178

Amram, 93

Ananias, 279–80

Andrew, 118, 245–48, 255

Anna, 93, 236–40

Artaxerxes, King, 204, 207, 211

Asaph, 105, 138, 140

Asherah, 169

Ashtoreth, 159

Baal, 159, 160, 161, 169, 170, 171

Balaam, 132

Barak, 106, 107

Barnabas, 242, 254, 293. *See also* Joseph, called Barnabas

Bathsheba, 42, 104, 119, 137, 141, 149, 174

Belshazzar, King, 198

Benjamin, 72, 73, 74, 75, 76, 77, 106, 133, 134

Bethuel, 59

Bilhah, 66, 72

Boaz, 103, 116, 117, 118, 119, 230

Cain, 32–35, 36, 56, 63, 246. *See also* Abel

Canaan, 42

Cephas. *See* Simon Peter

Cyrus, 196, 197, 198

Daniel, 43, 130, 157, 192–96, 199, 256

Darius, 195, 198

Dathan, 91

David, 15, 19, 30, 36, 42, 43, 103, 104, 105, 107, 108, 118, 121, 129, 133, 134, 135, 136, 137–43, 144–48, 149, 153, 155, 156, 157, 158, 174, 194, 200, 201, 204, 225, 249, 262, 263, 285

David, King, 116, 119, 170, 229, 276

Deborah, 93, 105–7

Delilah, 114

Diana, 30

Dinah, 73

Diotrephes, 201

Edom. *See* Esau

Ehud, 105

Eli, 120–23, 124, 134

Eliab, 145

Elihu, 78, 80

Elijah, 159–63, 164, 165, 166–67, 168, 171, 258

Elisha, 160, 161, 162, 163, 164–68

Elizabeth, 223–27, 228, 230, 243

Elkanah, 125, 126

Enoch, 34, 39

Ephraim, 38, 73, 106

Esau, 32, 38, 55, 56–57, 60, 61, 62–64, 65, 66, 67, 68, 71, 73, 89, 200, 233, 235

Eshtaol, 115

Esther, 43, 197–202

Ethbaal, 169, 170

Eve, 19, 21, 25, 27–31, 32, 33, 36, 52. *See also* Adam

Ezekiel, 131, 139, 181, 184, 187–91, 192, 196, 197, 198, 199, 244

Ezra, 197, 203–6

Gabriel (angel), 31, 195, 223, 224, 226, 228–29

Gehazi, 168

Geshem, 210

Gideon, 105, 107, 108–11, 118, 142, 225, 229

Goliath, 25, 118, 137, 142, 144

SCRIPTURE INDEX

ABOUT THE AUTHOR

Warren W. Wiersbe, former pastor of the Moody Church and general director of Back to the Bible, has traveled widely as a Bible teacher and conference speaker. Because of his encouragement to those in ministry, Dr. Wiersbe is referred to as "the pastor's pastor." He has ministered in churches and conferences throughout the United States as well as in Canada, Central and South America, and Europe.

Dr. Wiersbe has written more than 150 books, including the popular BE series of commentaries on every book of the Bible, which has sold more than four million copies. At the 2002 Christian Booksellers Convention, he was awarded the Gold Medallion Lifetime Achievement Award by the Evangelical Christian Publishers Association.

Dr. Wiersbe and his wife, Betty, live in Lincoln, Nebraska.